MYSPACE DARK HORSE PRESENTS 2

DARK

FEATURING WORK BY

Jon Adams	Jason Graham	Arvid Nelson
Scott Allie	Mario Guevara	Steve Niles
John Arcudi	Gilbert Hernandez	Nate Piekos
Gabriel Bá	Kyle Hotz	Ann Romano
Eric Canete	Jim and Ruth Keegan	Francisco Ruiz Velasco
Joe Casey	Ilias Kyriazis	Ben Truman
Marian Churchland	Paul Lee	Tim Truman
I. N. J. Culbard	David Malki!	Jeff Wamester
Guy Davis	Brothers Mattkinson	Gerard Way
Evan Dorkin	Tara McPherson	Zack Whedon
Ian Edginton	Pop Mhan	Steven Young
Juan Ferreyra	Fábio Moon	

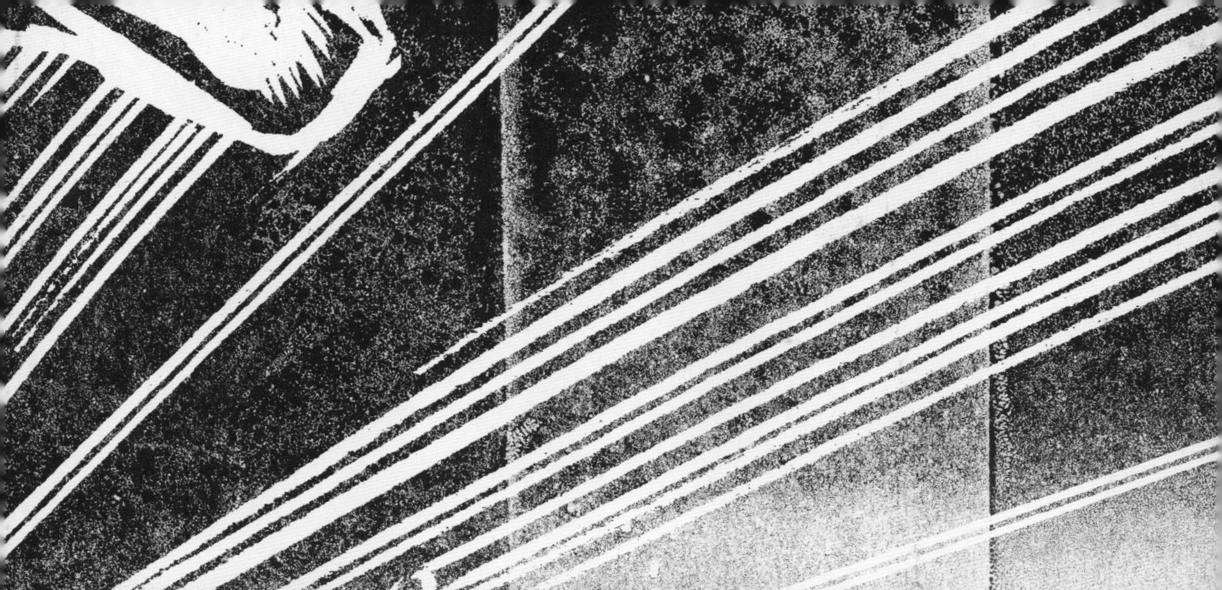

MYSPACE HORSE PRESENTS™ 2

Dark Horse Books®

PUBLISHER
Mike Richardson

EDITORS
Scott Allie & Sierra Hahn

ASSISTANT EDITOR
Ryan Jorgenson

COLLECTION DESIGNER
Scott Cook

COVER ARTIST
Eric Canete

"Retro Rockets Go!"; *Wondermark*: "Ransom!"; "Manga"; and *Legion of Blood*: "The Messenger" edited by Dave Land.

"Hobo Fet" edited by Randy Stradley with Freddye Lins.

B.P.R.D.: "Revival" edited by Scott Allie with Rachel Edidin.

"How to Heal a Broken Heart: Method 37" edited by Chris Warner with Samantha Robertson.

Criminal Macabre: "The Creepy Tree" and "The Trouble with Brains" edited by Shawna Gore with Jemiah Jefferson.

The Adventures of Two-Gun Bob; "Sailor Steve Costigan: A New Game for Costigan"; *Solomon Kane*: "The Nightcomers"; and *Conan*: "Trophy" edited by Philip Simon with Patrick Thorpe.

Special thanks to Joss Whedon, Natalie Farrell, Michael Boretz, Mike Mignola, Ryan Jorgensen, Rachel Edidin, Freddye Lins, Brendan Wright, Dan Jackson, and Jeremy Atkins. Special thanks also to Sam Humphries and Jessica Chanen at MySpace, and Erik Henriksen and Wm. Steven Humphrey at *The Portland Mercury*.

MYSPACE DARK HORSE PRESENTS™ VOLUME TWO

This volume reprints the online comic-book anthology *MySpace Dark Horse Presents* #7–12.

Published by
Dark Horse Books
A division of
Dark Horse Comics, Inc.
10956 SE Main Street
Milwaukie OR 97222

darkhorse.com

To find a comics shop in your area, call the Comic Shop Locator Service toll-free at (888) 266-4226.

First edition: February 2009
ISBN 978-1-59582-248-2

10 9 8 7 6 5 4 3 2 1

Printed in China

ONE DAY AT A TIME

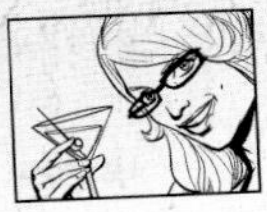

by Ann Romano

COLLECTIBLE NERD EDITION

ITEM! We're going to be honest with you, dears. (After all, we didn't get to be the revered, beloved, and desired writer of **Hollyweird's finest gossip column** by playing loosey-goosey with the truth. Well, okay, so maybe we did. But still.) It started like this: **Hubby Kip** dragged us off of Rodeo Drive (where there was a *fantastic* price on a Stella McCartney bag you'd have *died* for) to drive all the way to San Diego for some sort of **funnybook convention**. Needless to say, after four and a half hours of following Kip around, getting leered at by midgets dressed as Yoda, and seeing blockbuster megastars like **Lori Petty** desperately selling their autographs for a quarter, we needed a martini, a cosmo, or both. So there we were at the bar at the San Diego Hyatt when Dark Horse Associate Editor **Sierra Hahn** recognized us and asked us about some sort of **MySpace funnybook business**. Frankly, we weren't paying that much attention (cosmos do not drink themselves, people!), and our first response wasn't suitable for publication in this PG-13 collection.

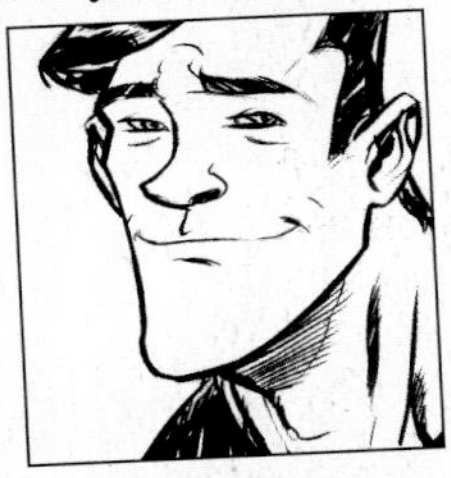

GETTING HAMMERED

But then another member of Dark Horse's goon squad, **Scott Allie**, flashed the company MasterCard and offered to buy us three or four martinis—and before we knew it, Scott's twin had shown up, and both of them were quite blurry and very convincing . . . and it didn't hurt that they promised they'd introduce us to **Nathan Fillion**. And while we might not have gotten a good Captain Hammering from the magnificent Mr. Fillion (as we, like any sane woman, had demurely and patiently hoped for for so, so long) we were nonetheless grateful enough for the drinks to tipsily crank out the fine work you'll read on page 41. (Let's call it a **"graphic novelette,"** shall we?)

Obvs, we're *très* delighted about our work now being available for purchase in geekery supply stores across the nation, where, hopefully, our gossipy genius will fit right in amongst those **creepy William Shatner dolls** and ***Battleship Galactistar* model kits**. We already feel totes at home in this collection, with our graphic novelette sandwiched betwixt a story about **sociopathic dairy products** and something or other that looks like it was drawn when **John McCain** was toddling about in Pampers. (Or, you know, toddling around in whatever the most popular brand of diapers was in the early 1700s. As you well know, we're entirely too busy to be bothered with "historical research.")

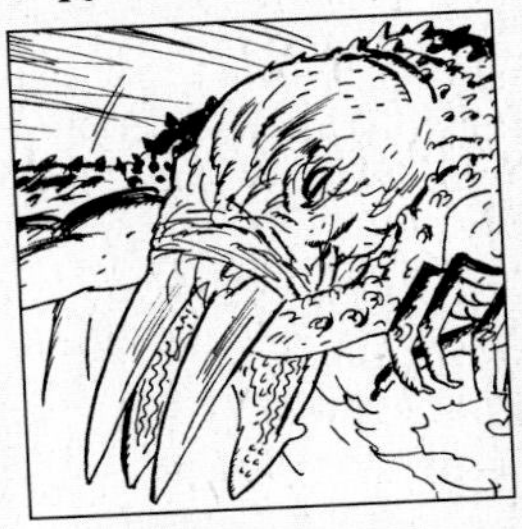

MODEL BEHAVIOR

And that's not even to mention the other A-list company we find our august work alongside, such as a rip-roaring superhero tale that, for some inexplicable reason, makes us think Kip might not look so bad in **guyliner**; a story about some soldiers (we're assuming they're contracted with **Blackwater**) fighting a hideous frog monster that bears a striking resemblance to moody supermodel **Naomi Campbell**; and a story about some desert-wandering doofus who eerily reminds us of California's favorite **neanderthalic governor**. It's not our usual crowd, mind you, but they seem like a fun-enough bunch (and we'll wager our fav pair of **Jimmy Choos** that this **Cal McDonald** can put away Jack 'n' Cokes with the best of 'em, which is all we're really looking for in people we want to hang out with, anyway). In other words, we're happy to be here, even if we have yet to receive that Captain Hammering we're still ever-so-patiently waiting for. (Confidential to **N.F.**: Scott has our number!)

LEAVE BRENDAN FRASER

A Plea t

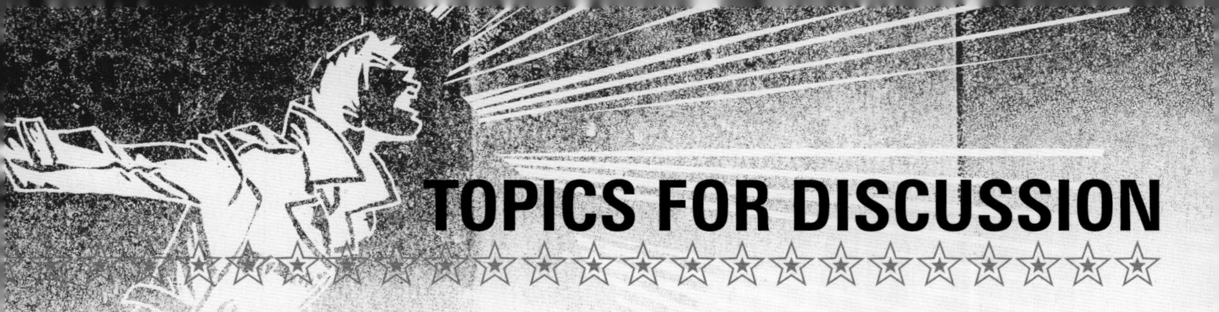

TOPICS FOR DISCUSSION

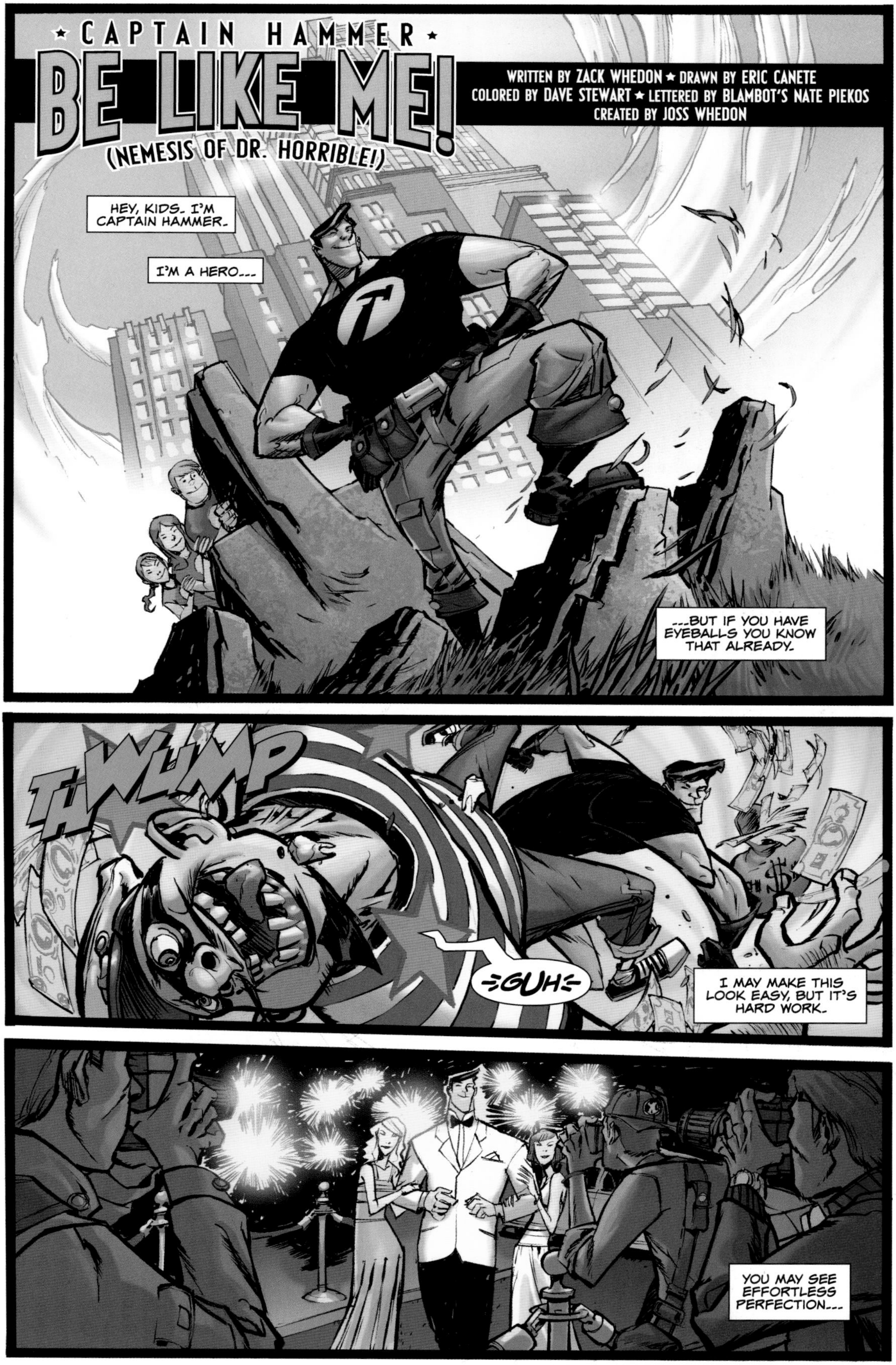
★ CAPTAIN HAMMER ★
BE LIKE ME!
(NEMESIS OF DR. HORRIBLE!)
WRITTEN BY ZACK WHEDON ★ DRAWN BY ERIC CANETE
COLORED BY DAVE STEWART ★ LETTERED BY BLAMBOT'S NATE PIEKOS
CREATED BY JOSS WHEDON
HEY, KIDS. I'M CAPTAIN HAMMER.
I'M A HERO...
...BUT IF YOU HAVE EYEBALLS YOU KNOW THAT ALREADY.
THWUMP
GUH
I MAY MAKE THIS LOOK EASY, BUT IT'S HARD WORK.
YOU MAY SEE EFFORTLESS PERFECTION...

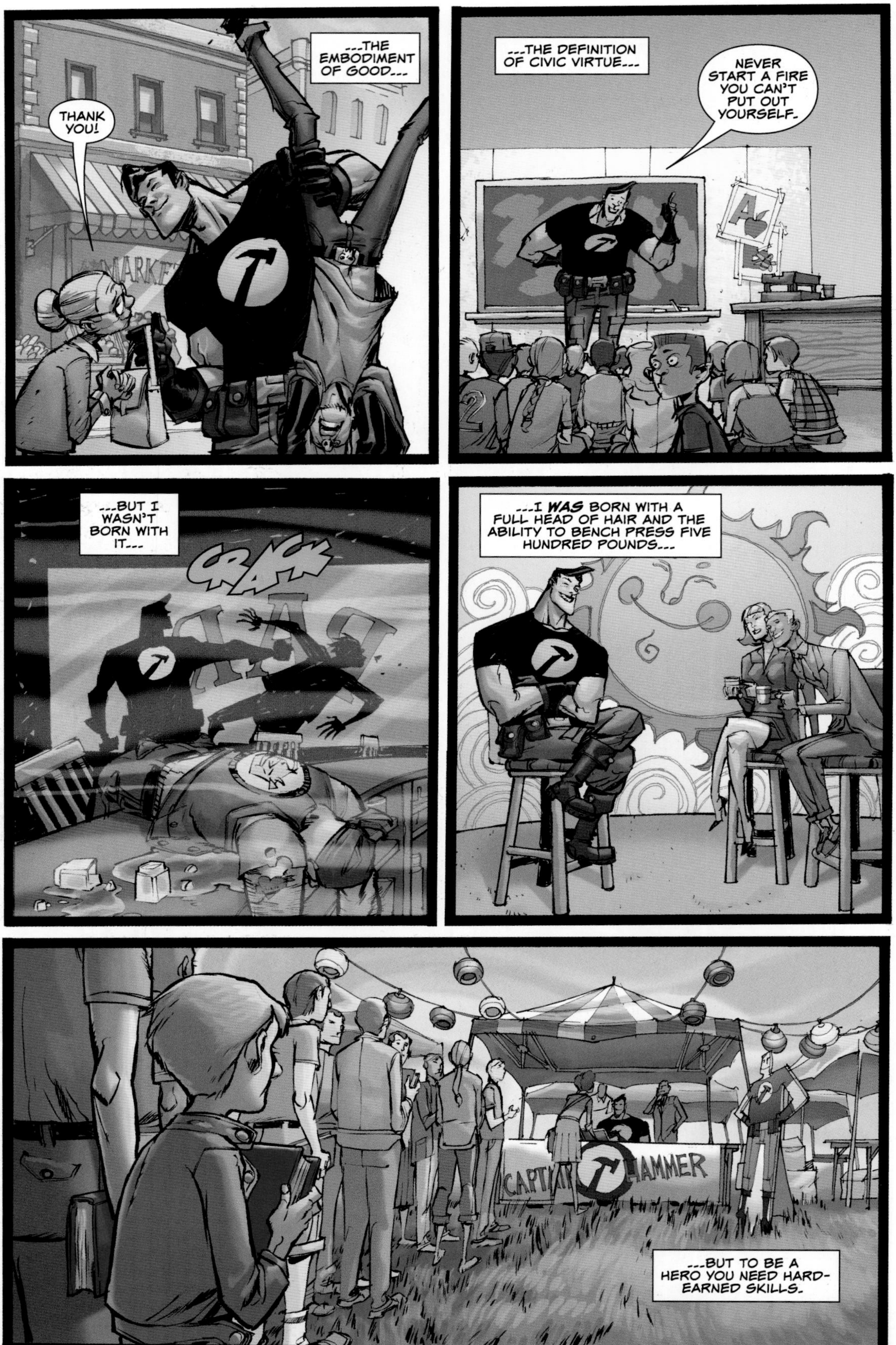

...THE EMBODIMENT OF GOOD...
THANK YOU!
MARKET
...THE DEFINITION OF CIVIC VIRTUE...
NEVER START A FIRE YOU CAN'T PUT OUT YOURSELF.
...BUT I WASN'T BORN WITH IT...
CRACK
...I WAS BORN WITH A FULL HEAD OF HAIR AND THE ABILITY TO BENCH PRESS FIVE HUNDRED POUNDS...
CAPTAIN HAMMER
...BUT TO BE A HERO YOU NEED HARD-EARNED SKILLS.

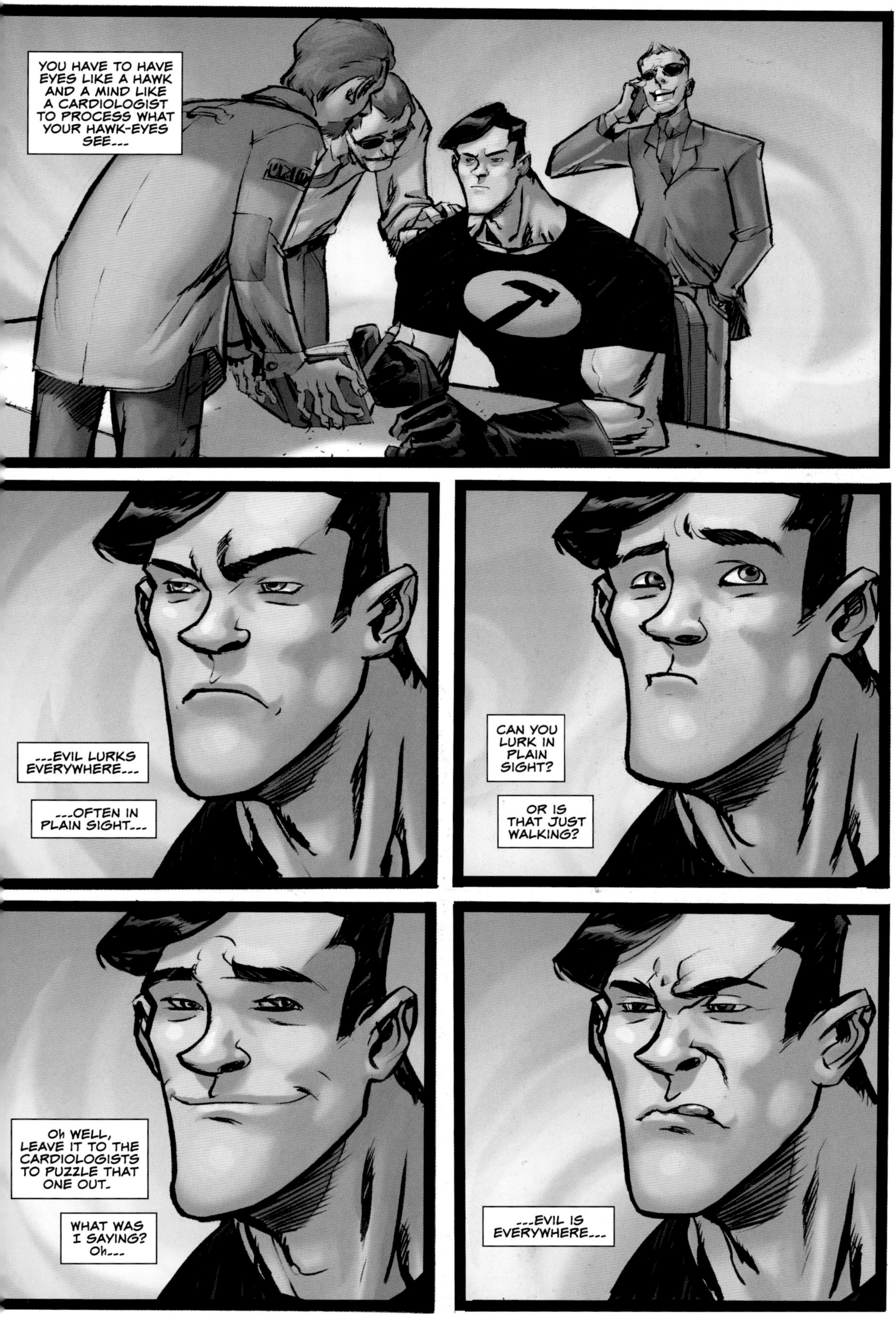
YOU HAVE TO HAVE EYES LIKE A HAWK AND A MIND LIKE A CARDIOLOGIST TO PROCESS WHAT YOUR HAWK-EYES SEE---
---EVIL LURKS EVERYWHERE---
---OFTEN IN PLAIN SIGHT---
CAN YOU LURK IN PLAIN SIGHT?
OR IS THAT JUST WALKING?
Oh WELL, LEAVE IT TO THE CARDIOLOGISTS TO PUZZLE THAT ONE OUT.
WHAT WAS I SAYING? Oh---
---EVIL IS EVERYWHERE---

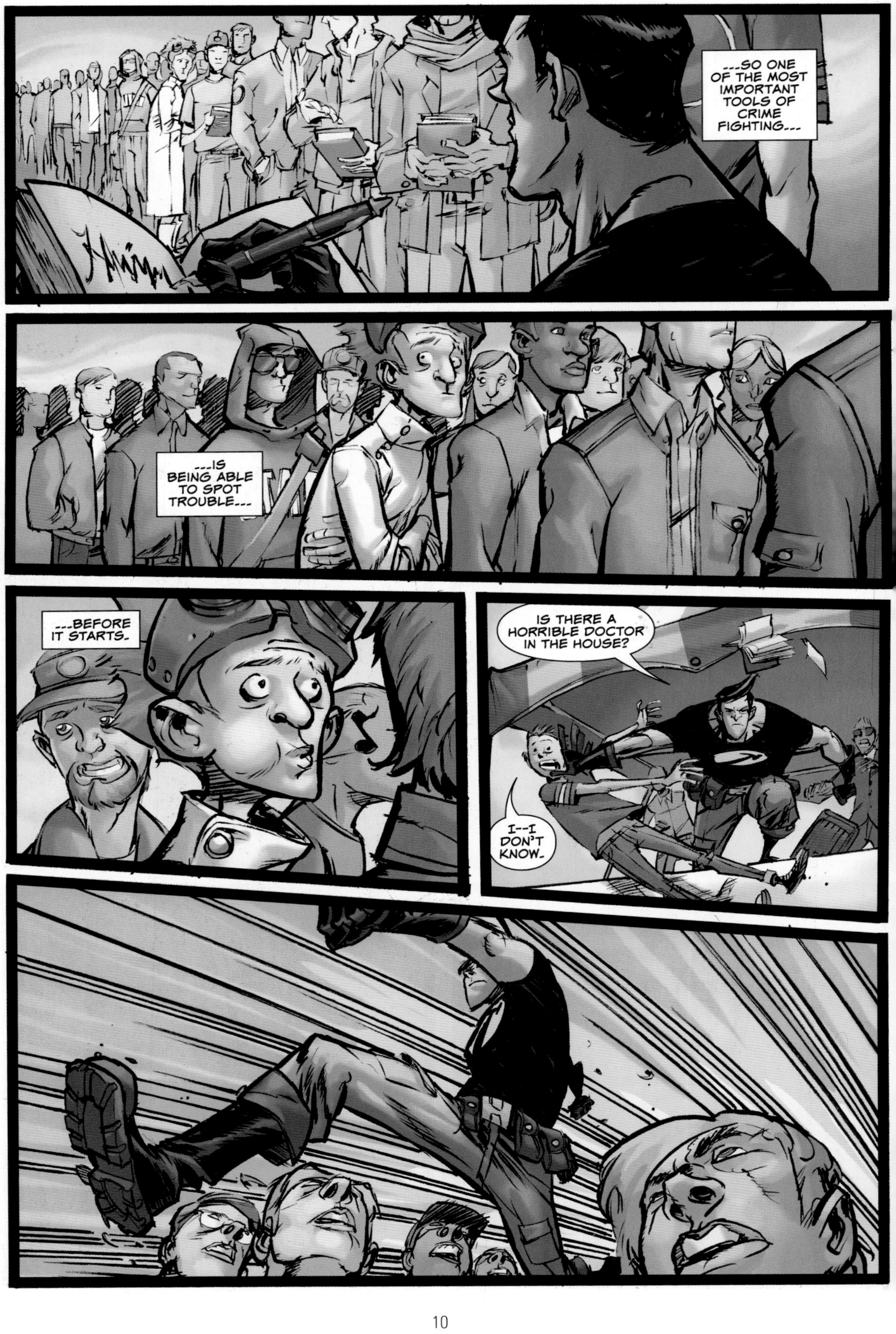

---SO ONE OF THE MOST IMPORTANT TOOLS OF CRIME FIGHTING---
---IS BEING ABLE TO SPOT TROUBLE---
---BEFORE IT STARTS.
IS THERE A HORRIBLE DOCTOR IN THE HOUSE?
I--I DON'T KNOW.

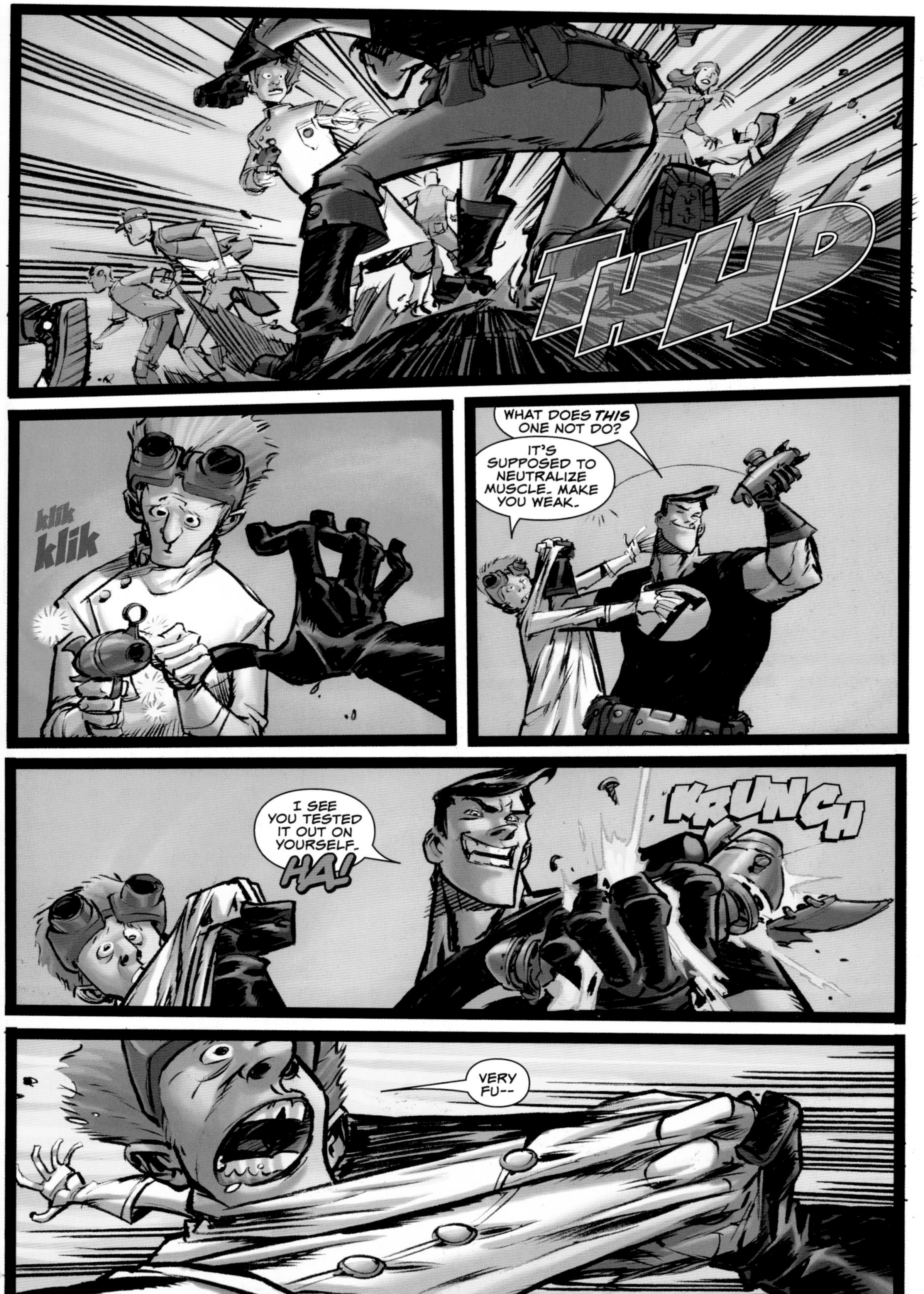
THUD
klik klik
WHAT DOES THIS ONE NOT DO?
IT'S SUPPOSED TO NEUTRALIZE MUSCLE. MAKE YOU WEAK.
I SEE YOU TESTED IT OUT ON YOURSELF.
HA!
KRUNCH
VERY FU--

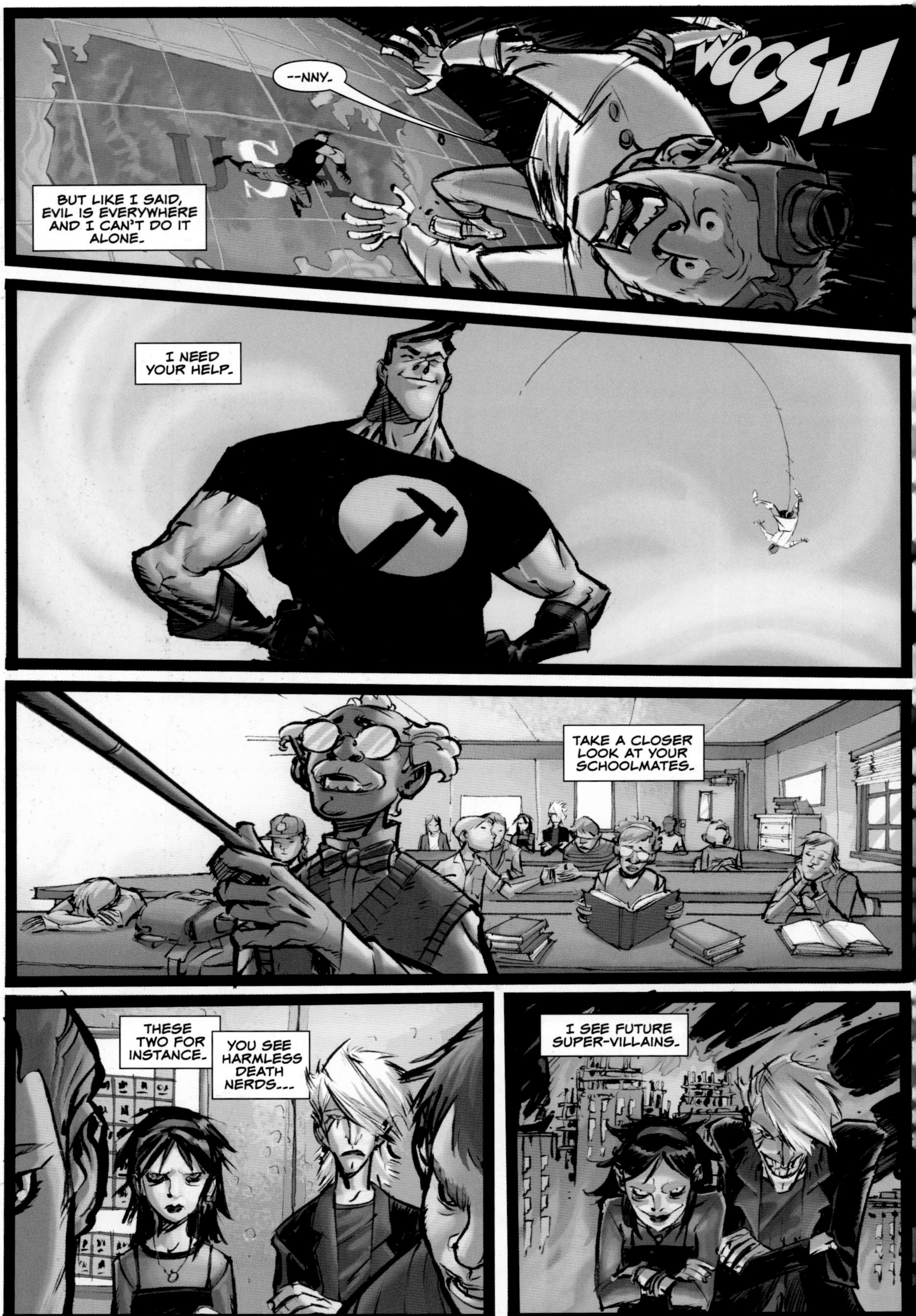
--NNY.
WOOSH
BUT LIKE I SAID, EVIL IS EVERYWHERE AND I CAN'T DO IT ALONE.
U.S.A.
I NEED YOUR HELP.
TAKE A CLOSER LOOK AT YOUR SCHOOLMATES.
THESE TWO FOR INSTANCE.
YOU SEE HARMLESS DEATH NERDS...
I SEE FUTURE SUPER-VILLAINS.

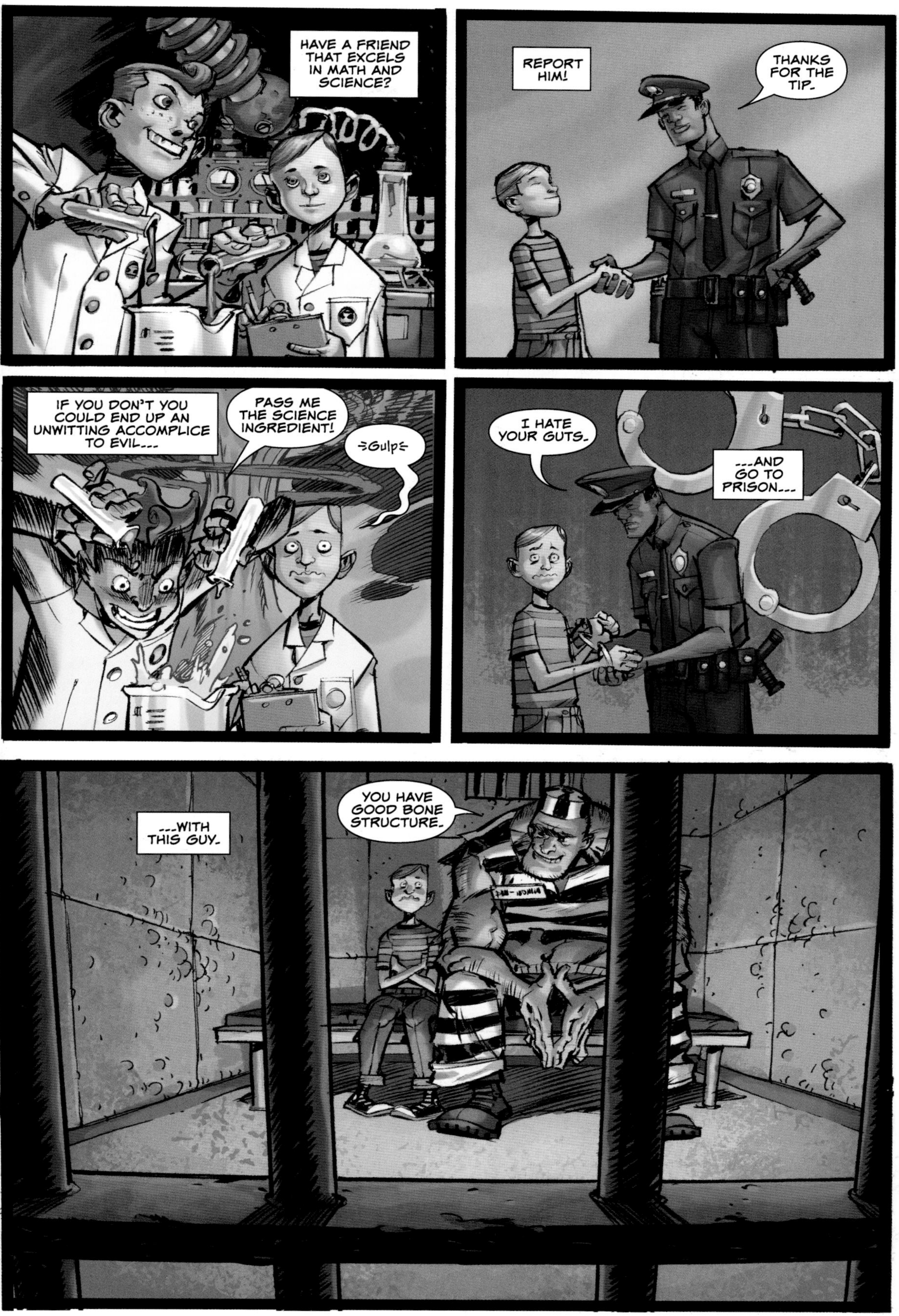
HAVE A FRIEND THAT EXCELS IN MATH AND SCIENCE?
REPORT HIM!
THANKS FOR THE TIP.
IF YOU DON'T YOU COULD END UP AN UNWITTING ACCOMPLICE TO EVIL...
PASS ME THE SCIENCE INGREDIENT!
=Gulp=
I HATE YOUR GUTS.
...AND GO TO PRISON...
...WITH THIS GUY.
YOU HAVE GOOD BONE STRUCTURE.

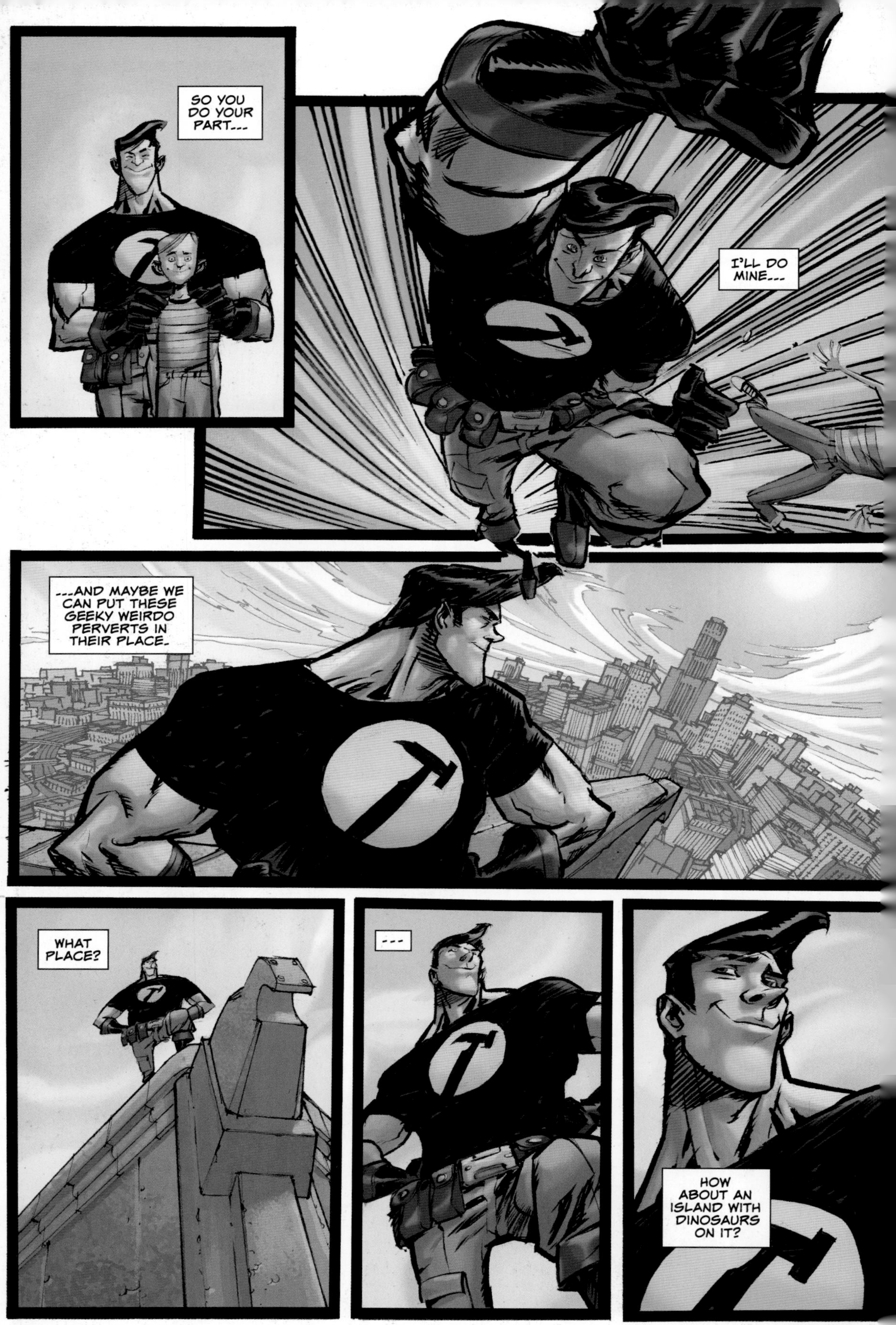
SO YOU DO YOUR PART...
I'LL DO MINE...
...AND MAYBE WE CAN PUT THESE GEEKY WEIRDO PERVERTS IN THEIR PLACE.
WHAT PLACE?
...
HOW ABOUT AN ISLAND WITH DINOSAURS ON IT?
THE END

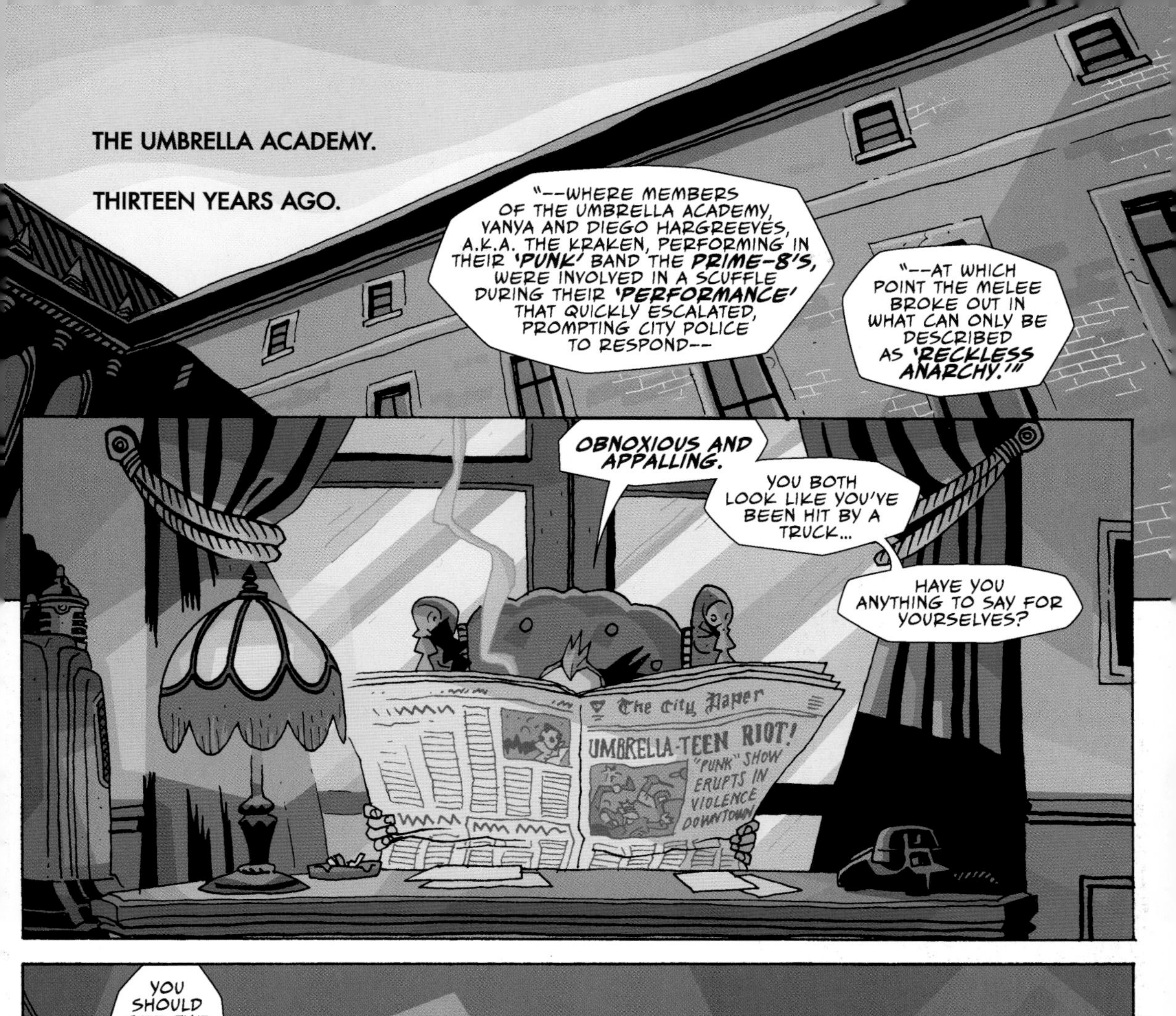

THE UMBRELLA ACADEMY.
THIRTEEN YEARS AGO.
"--WHERE MEMBERS OF THE UMBRELLA ACADEMY, VANYA AND DIEGO HARGREEVES, A.K.A. THE KRAKEN, PERFORMING IN THEIR 'PUNK' BAND THE PRIME-8'S, WERE INVOLVED IN A SCUFFLE DURING THEIR 'PERFORMANCE' THAT QUICKLY ESCALATED, PROMPTING CITY POLICE TO RESPOND--
"--AT WHICH POINT THE MELEE BROKE OUT IN WHAT CAN ONLY BE DESCRIBED AS 'RECKLESS ANARCHY.'"
OBNOXIOUS AND APPALLING.
YOU BOTH LOOK LIKE YOU'VE BEEN HIT BY A TRUCK...
HAVE YOU ANYTHING TO SAY FOR YOURSELVES?
The City Paper
UMBRELLA-TEEN RIOT!
"PUNK" SHOW ERUPTS IN VIOLENCE DOWNTOWN
YOU SHOULD SEE THE OTHER GUY.

THE UMBRELLA ACADEMY

ANYWHERE BUT HERE

By Gerard Way & Gabriel Bá
with Dave Stewart and Nate Piekos

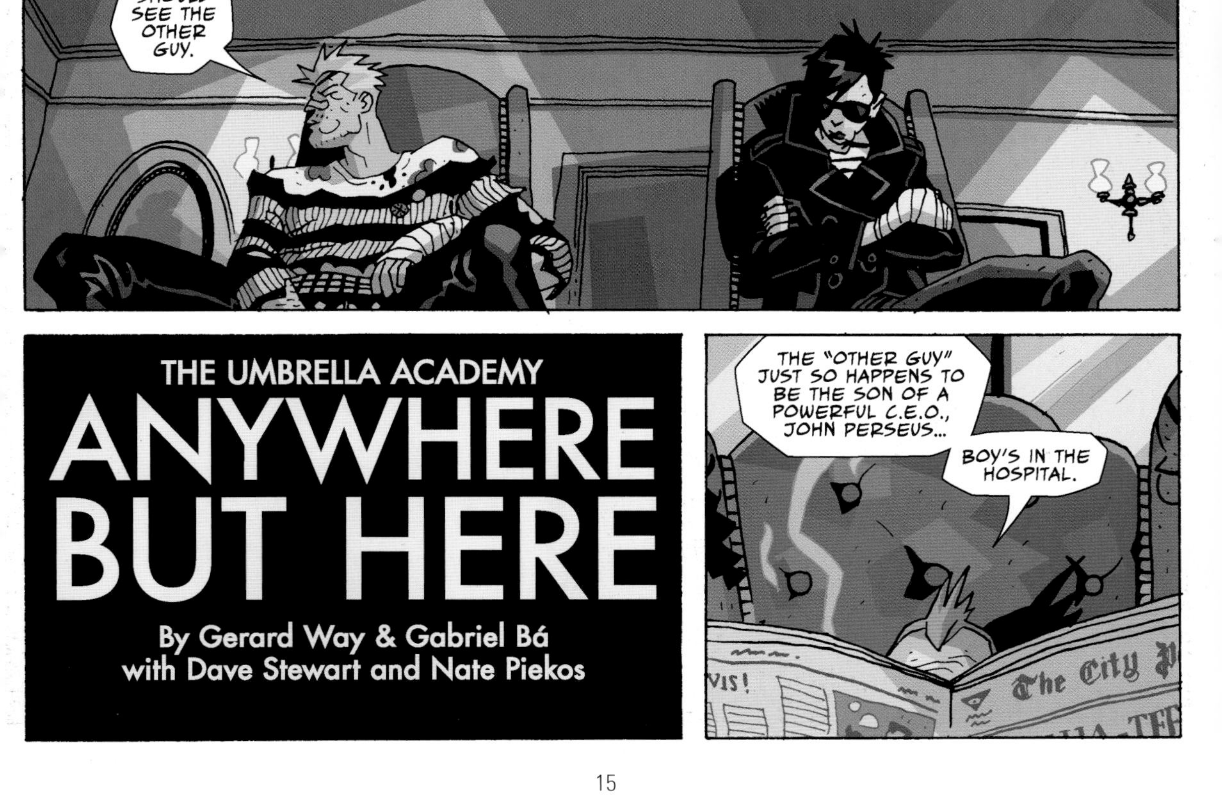

THE "OTHER GUY" JUST SO HAPPENS TO BE THE SON OF A POWERFUL C.E.O., JOHN PERSEUS...
BOY'S IN THE HOSPITAL.
The City

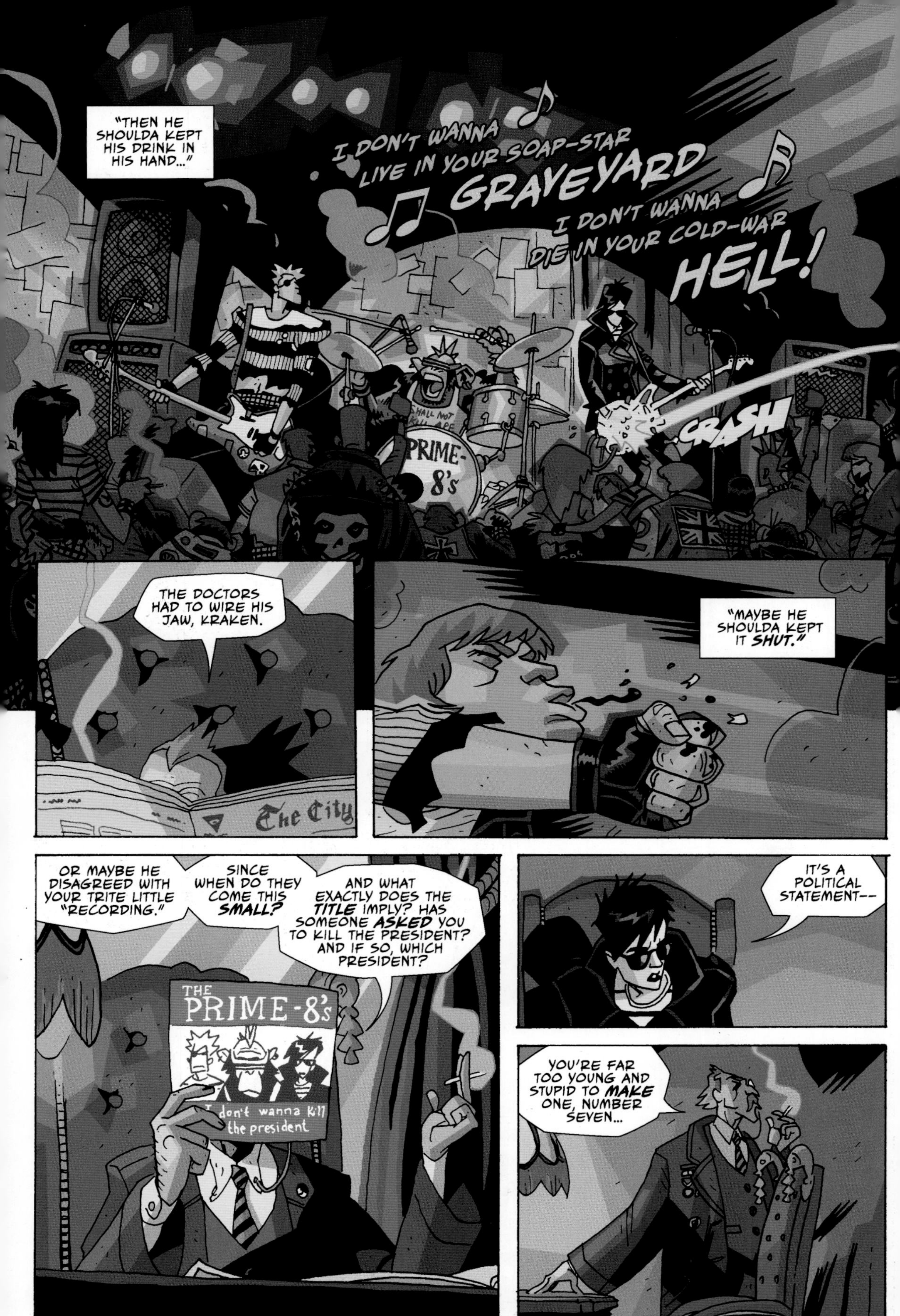
"THEN HE SHOULDA KEPT HIS DRINK IN HIS HAND..."
I DON'T WANNA LIVE IN YOUR SOAP-STAR GRAVEYARD
I DON'T WANNA DIE IN YOUR COLD-WAR HELL!
PRIME-8's
CRASH
THE DOCTORS HAD TO WIRE HIS JAW, KRAKEN.
The City
"MAYBE HE SHOULDA KEPT IT SHUT."
OR MAYBE HE DISAGREED WITH YOUR TRITE LITTLE "RECORDING."
SINCE WHEN DO THEY COME THIS SMALL?
AND WHAT EXACTLY DOES THE TITLE IMPLY? HAS SOMEONE ASKED YOU TO KILL THE PRESIDENT? AND IF SO, WHICH PRESIDENT?
THE PRIME-8's
I don't wanna kill the president
IT'S A POLITICAL STATEMENT--
YOU'RE FAR TOO YOUNG AND STUPID TO MAKE ONE, NUMBER SEVEN...

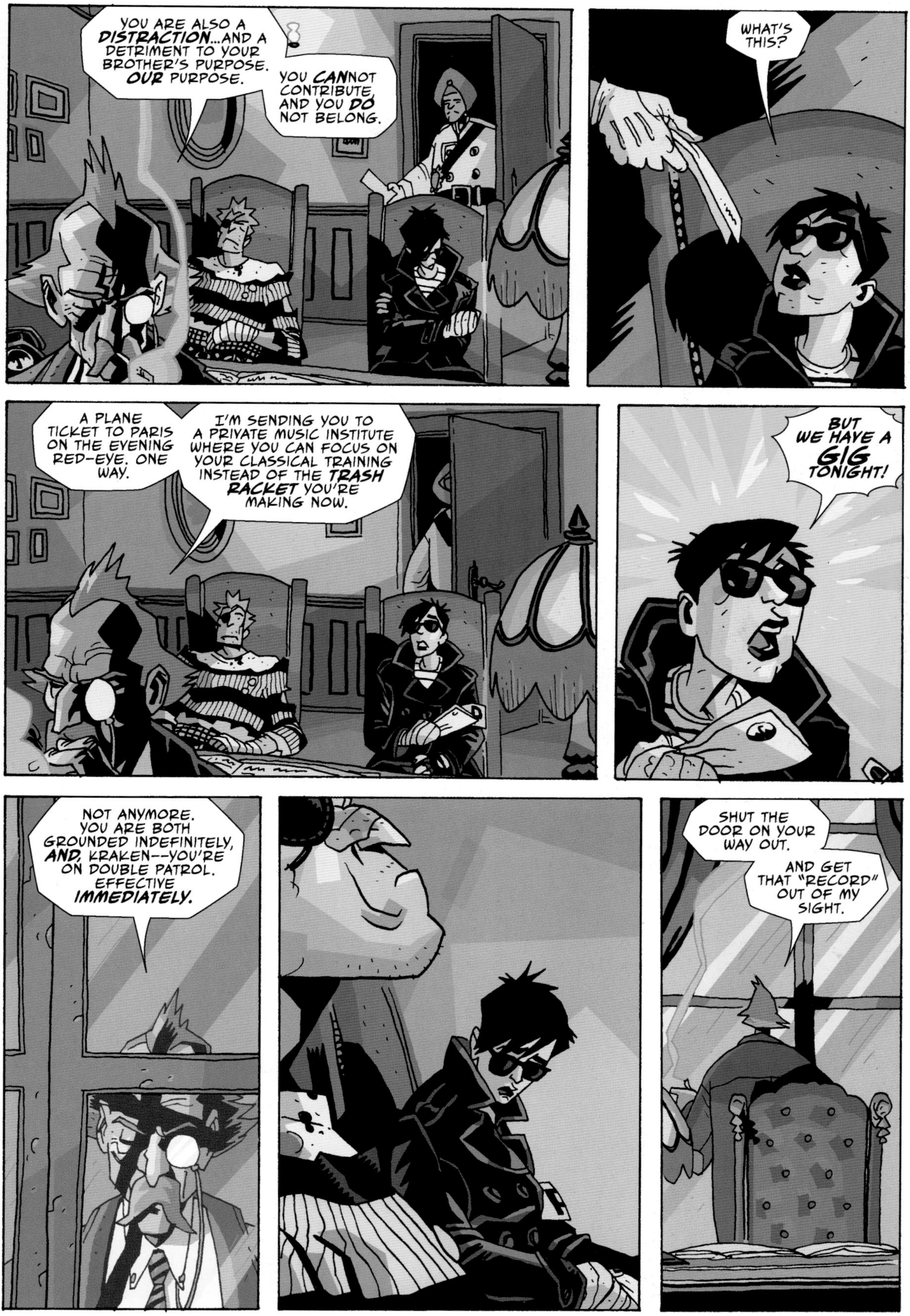
YOU ARE ALSO A DISTRACTION...AND A DETRIMENT TO YOUR BROTHER'S PURPOSE. OUR PURPOSE.
YOU CANNOT CONTRIBUTE, AND YOU DO NOT BELONG.
WHAT'S THIS?
A PLANE TICKET TO PARIS ON THE EVENING RED-EYE. ONE WAY.
I'M SENDING YOU TO A PRIVATE MUSIC INSTITUTE WHERE YOU CAN FOCUS ON YOUR CLASSICAL TRAINING INSTEAD OF THE TRASH RACKET YOU'RE MAKING NOW.
BUT WE HAVE A GIG TONIGHT!
NOT ANYMORE. YOU ARE BOTH GROUNDED INDEFINITELY, AND, KRAKEN--YOU'RE ON DOUBLE PATROL. EFFECTIVE IMMEDIATELY.
SHUT THE DOOR ON YOUR WAY OUT.
AND GET THAT "RECORD" OUT OF MY SIGHT.

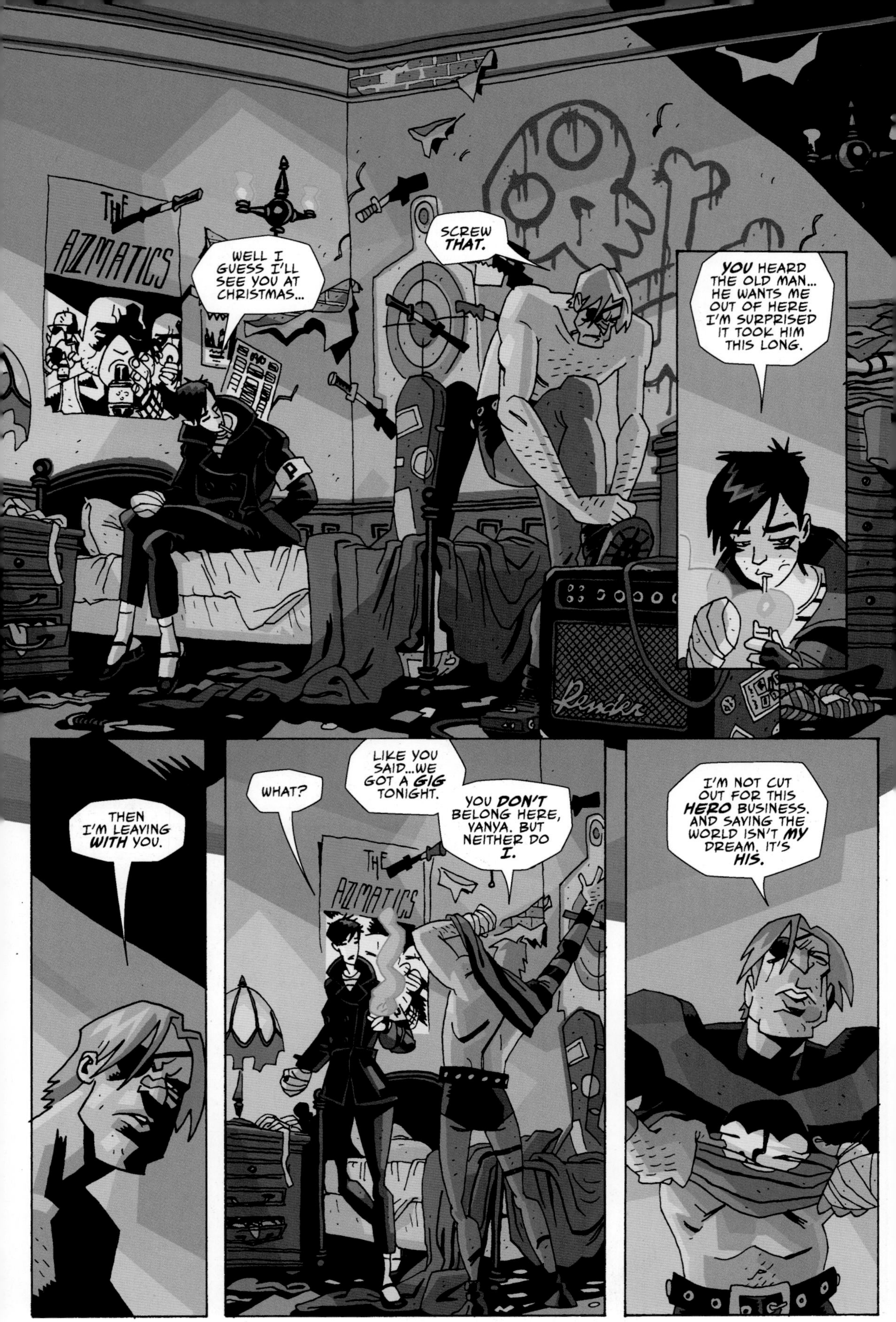
THE AZMATICS
WELL I GUESS I'LL SEE YOU AT CHRISTMAS...
SCREW THAT.
YOU HEARD THE OLD MAN... HE WANTS ME OUT OF HERE. I'M SURPRISED IT TOOK HIM THIS LONG.
Fender
THEN I'M LEAVING WITH YOU.
WHAT?
LIKE YOU SAID...WE GOT A GIG TONIGHT.
YOU DON'T BELONG HERE, VANYA. BUT NEITHER DO I.
THE AZMATICS
I'M NOT CUT OUT FOR THIS HERO BUSINESS. AND SAVING THE WORLD ISN'T MY DREAM. IT'S HIS.

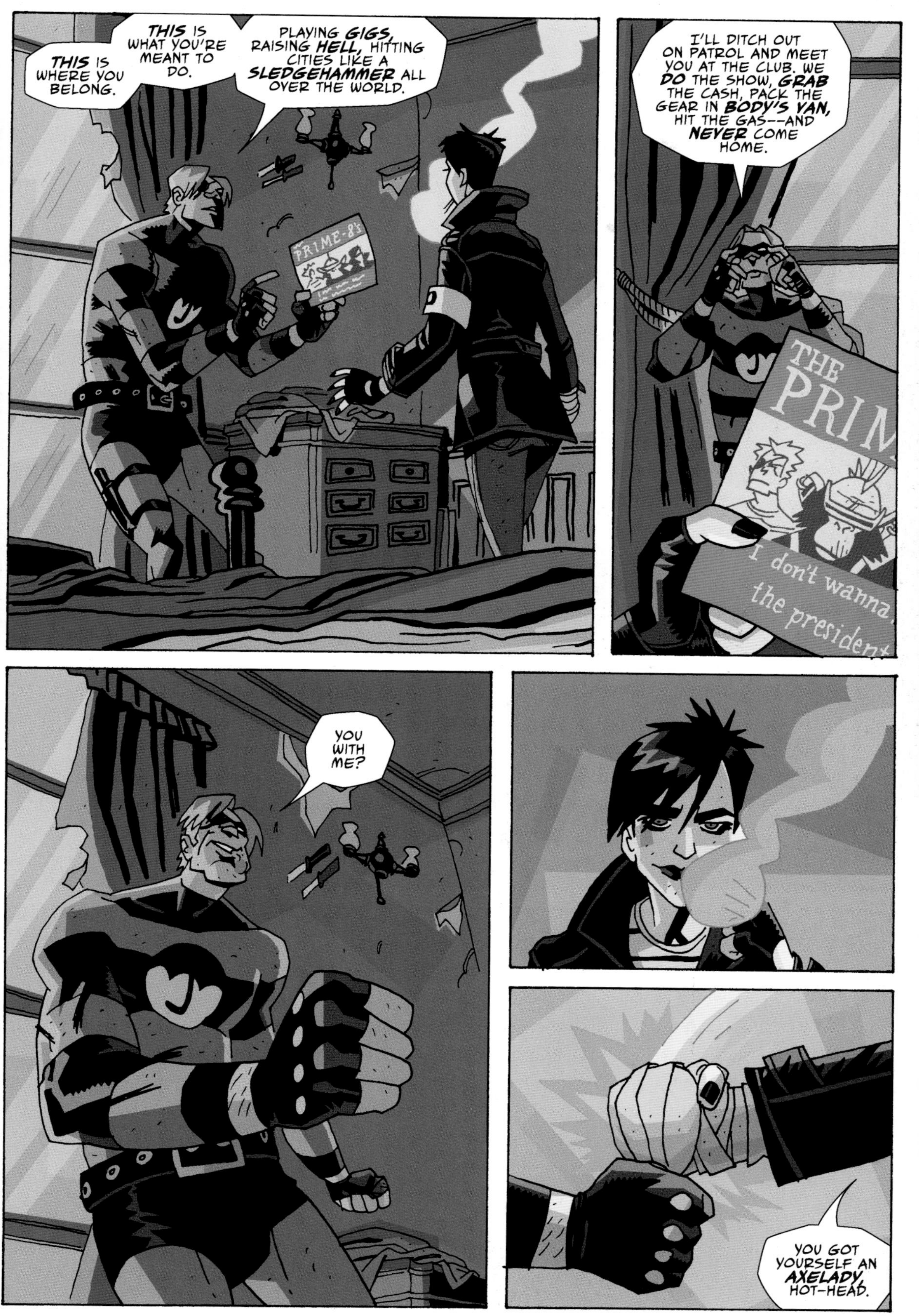
THIS IS WHERE YOU BELONG.
THIS IS WHAT YOU'RE MEANT TO DO.
PLAYING GIGS, RAISING HELL, HITTING CITIES LIKE A SLEDGEHAMMER ALL OVER THE WORLD.
PRIME-8's
I'LL DITCH OUT ON PATROL AND MEET YOU AT THE CLUB. WE DO THE SHOW, GRAB THE CASH, PACK THE GEAR IN BODY'S VAN, HIT THE GAS--AND NEVER COME HOME.
YOU WITH ME?
YOU GOT YOURSELF AN AXELADY, HOT-HEAD.

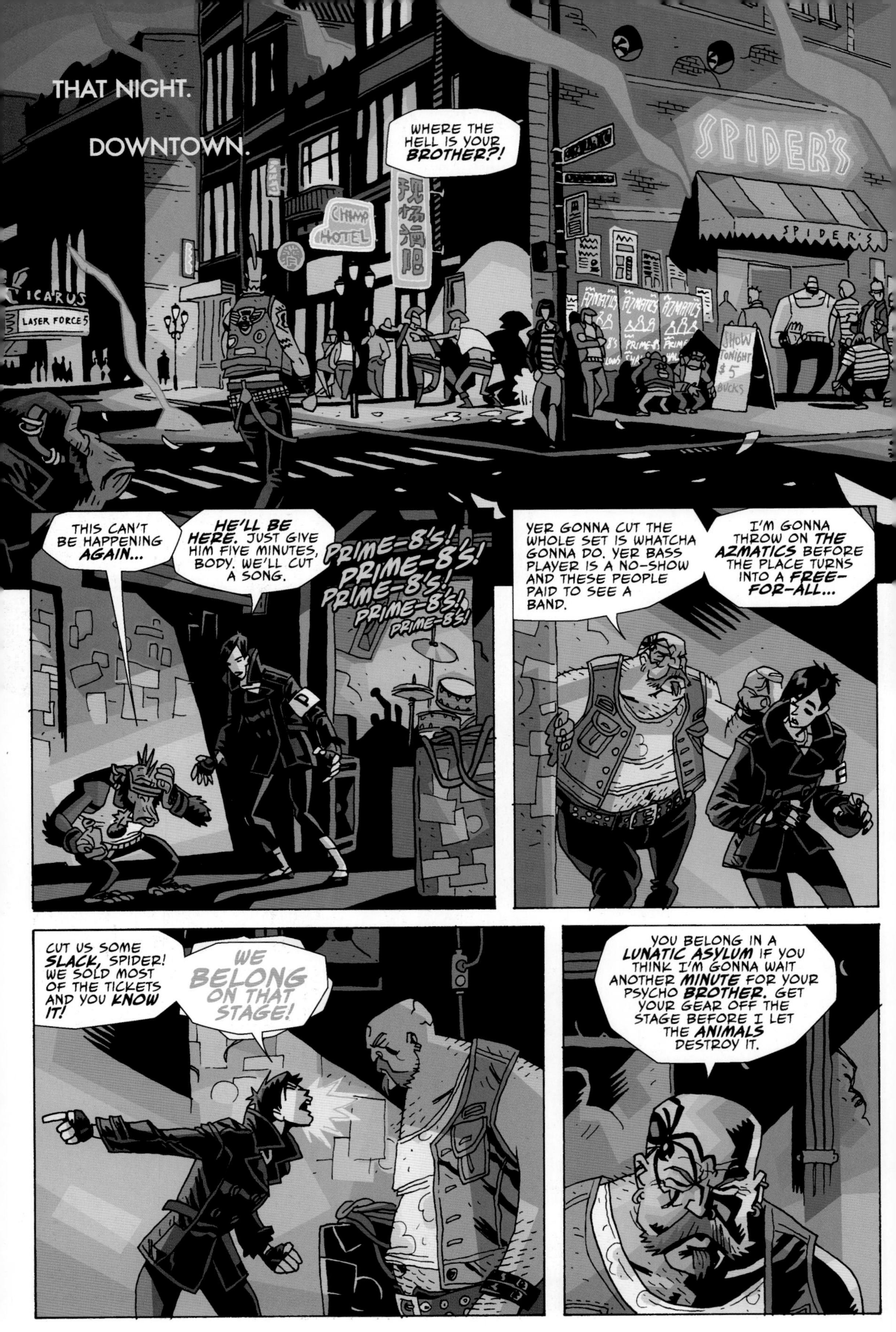
THAT NIGHT.
DOWNTOWN.
WHERE THE HELL IS YOUR BROTHER?!
SPIDER'S
ICARUS
LASER FORCE 5
SHOW TONIGHT $5 BUCKS
THIS CAN'T BE HAPPENING AGAIN...
HE'LL BE HERE. JUST GIVE HIM FIVE MINUTES, BODY. WE'LL CUT A SONG.
PRIME-8'S! PRIME-8'S! PRIME-8'S! PRIME-8'S! PRIME-8'S!
YER GONNA CUT THE WHOLE SET IS WHATCHA GONNA DO. YER BASS PLAYER IS A NO-SHOW AND THESE PEOPLE PAID TO SEE A BAND.
I'M GONNA THROW ON THE AZMATICS BEFORE THE PLACE TURNS INTO A FREE-FOR-ALL...
CUT US SOME SLACK, SPIDER! WE SOLD MOST OF THE TICKETS AND YOU KNOW IT!
WE BELONG ON THAT STAGE!
YOU BELONG IN A LUNATIC ASYLUM IF YOU THINK I'M GONNA WAIT ANOTHER MINUTE FOR YOUR PSYCHO BROTHER. GET YOUR GEAR OFF THE STAGE BEFORE I LET THE ANIMALS DESTROY IT.

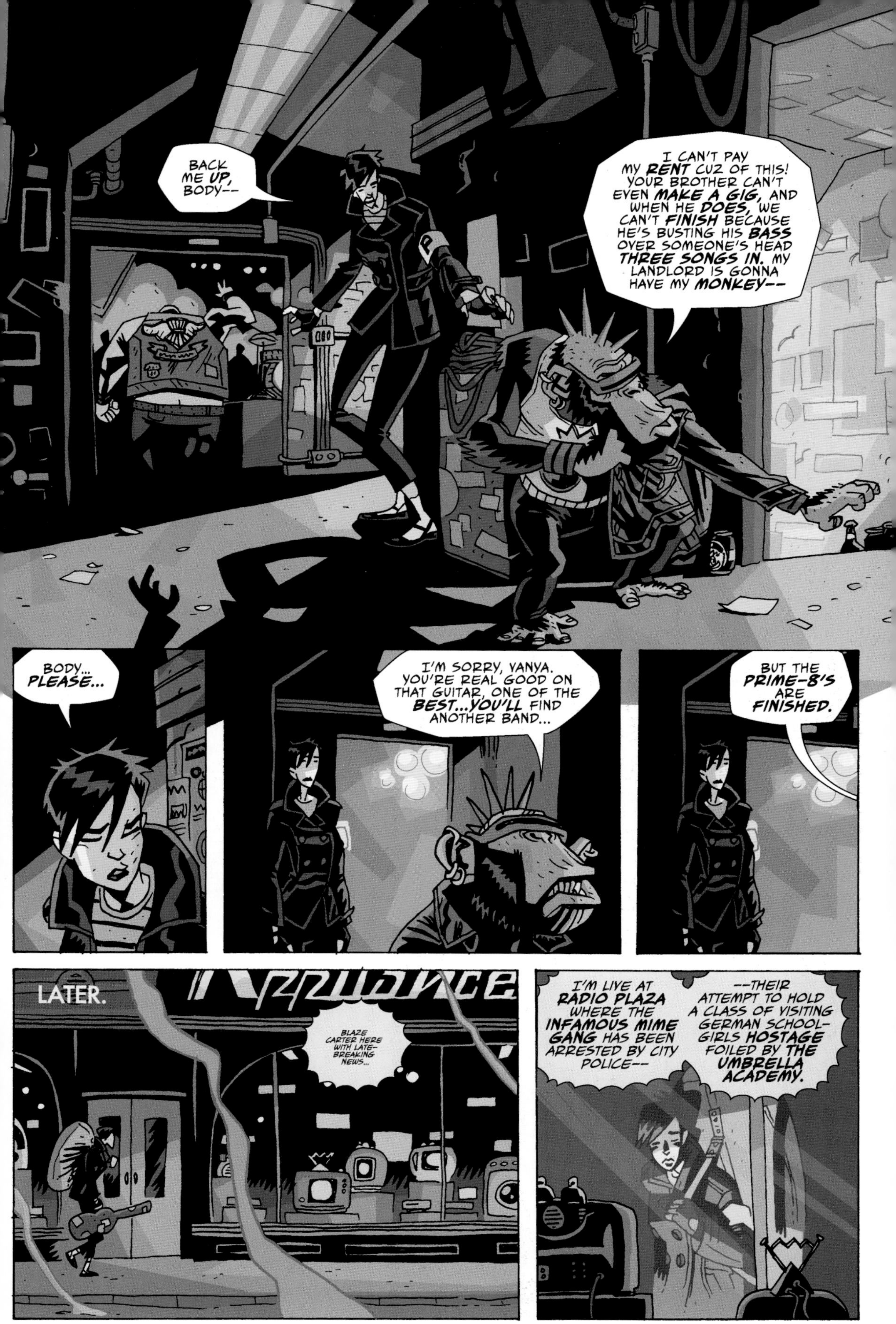
BACK ME UP, BODY--
I CAN'T PAY MY RENT CUZ OF THIS! YOUR BROTHER CAN'T EVEN MAKE A GIG, AND WHEN HE DOES, WE CAN'T FINISH BECAUSE HE'S BUSTING HIS BASS OVER SOMEONE'S HEAD THREE SONGS IN. MY LANDLORD IS GONNA HAVE MY MONKEY--
BODY... PLEASE...
I'M SORRY, VANYA. YOU'RE REAL GOOD ON THAT GUITAR, ONE OF THE BEST...YOU'LL FIND ANOTHER BAND...
BUT THE PRIME-8'S ARE FINISHED.
LATER.
BLAZE CARTER HERE WITH LATE-BREAKING NEWS...
I'M LIVE AT RADIO PLAZA WHERE THE INFAMOUS MIME GANG HAS BEEN ARRESTED BY CITY POLICE--
--THEIR ATTEMPT TO HOLD A CLASS OF VISITING GERMAN SCHOOL-GIRLS HOSTAGE FOILED BY THE UMBRELLA ACADEMY.

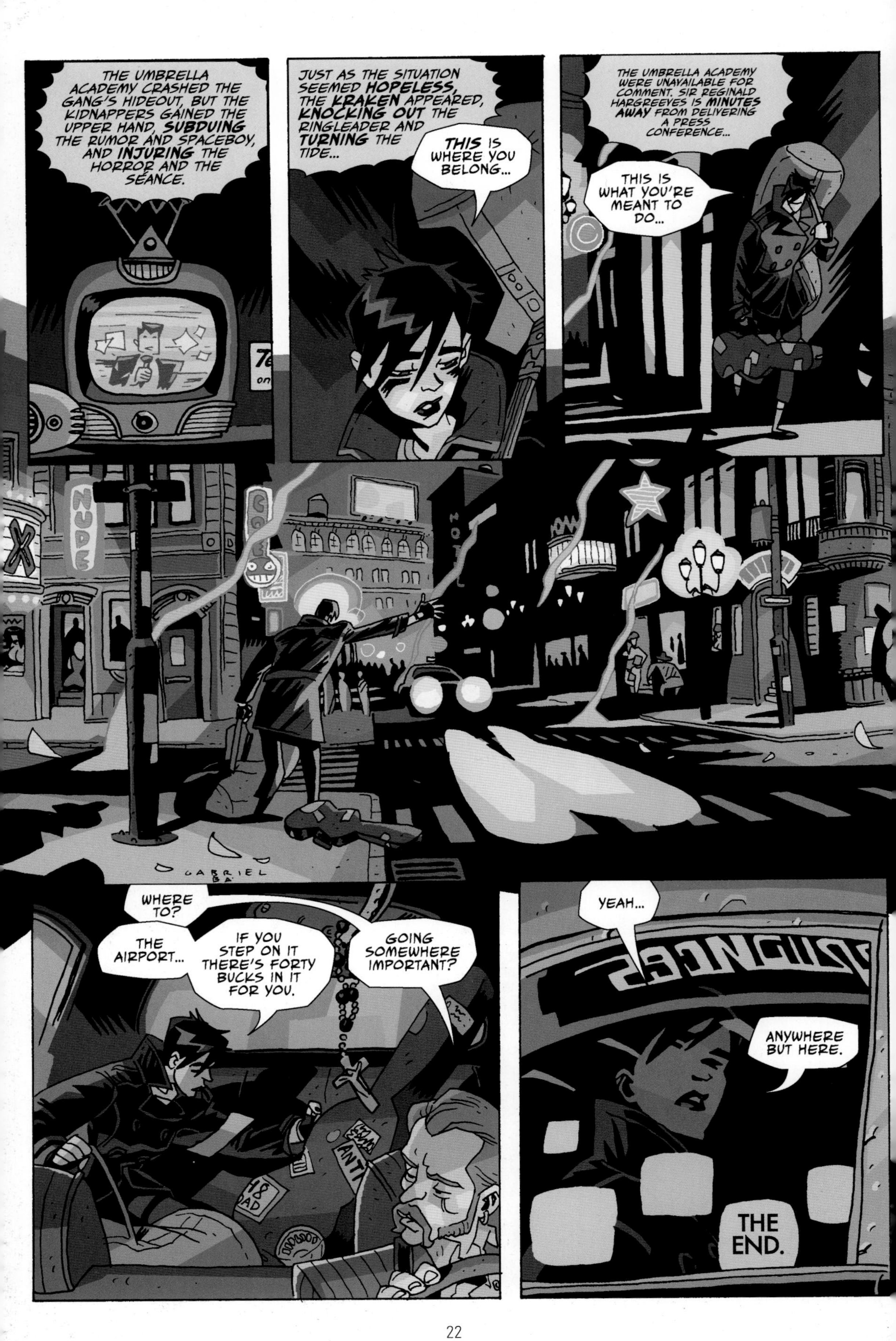
THE UMBRELLA ACADEMY CRASHED THE GANG'S HIDEOUT, BUT THE KIDNAPPERS GAINED THE UPPER HAND, SUBDUING THE RUMOR AND SPACEBOY, AND INJURING THE HORROR AND THE SÉANCE.
JUST AS THE SITUATION SEEMED HOPELESS, THE KRAKEN APPEARED, KNOCKING OUT THE RINGLEADER AND TURNING THE TIDE...
THIS IS WHERE YOU BELONG...
THE UMBRELLA ACADEMY WERE UNAVAILABLE FOR COMMENT. SIR REGINALD HARGREEVES IS MINUTES AWAY FROM DELIVERING A PRESS CONFERENCE...
THIS IS WHAT YOU'RE MEANT TO DO...
NUDE
GABRIEL BÁ
WHERE TO?
THE AIRPORT...
IF YOU STEP ON IT THERE'S FORTY BUCKS IN IT FOR YOU.
GOING SOMEWHERE IMPORTANT?
YEAH...
ANYWHERE BUT HERE.
THE END.

RETRO ROCKETS GO!

WORDS - IAN EDGINTON
PICTURES - I. N. J. CULBARD

GREAT GOOGLY-MOOGLY, GEAR-HEADS! THIS'S BEEN A RACE AN' A HALF AN' NO MISTAKE. TALK 'BOUT EDGE OF Y'SEAT STUFF! MY BUTT'S CLENCHED SO TIGHT, I COULD CRACK WALNUTS AN' CRAP DIAMONDS!

THE SOL SYSTEM SLALOM MAY BE JUST A SHORT RUN 'ROUND THE BLOCK, BUT THESE ROCKET JOCKS ARE PLAYIN' F'KEEPS!

IT'S THE FINAL STRETCH AN' THE TOP DOGS HAVE GOT VENUS IN THE REAR-VIEW AN' THE REST O'THE PACK EATIN' THEIR DUST!

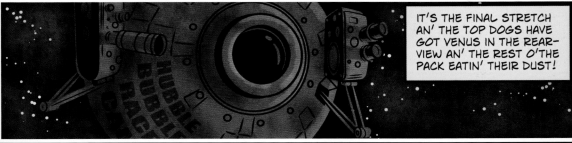

TAKIN' POINT'S THE HOTTEST HOT ROD ON THE CIRCUIT, JIM SWIFT, FLYIN' STICK IN THE *JAVELIN*, NAMED AFTER HIS OLD MAN, RED SWIFT'S, RIG.

THOSE O' YOU IN LONG PANTS WILL REMEMBER RED WENT MISSIN' PRESUMED DEAD, DURIN' THE INFAMOUS BIG-BANG BURN-OFF IN '66.

SNAPPIN' AT HIS HEELS IS THE ONLY SURVIVOR OF THAT METAL MONSTER MASH-- THE COUNT RIDIN' THE *COFFIN NAIL.*

IT'S WELL KNOWN THERE WAS NO LOVE LOST 'TWEEN RED AN' THE COUNT. LOOKS LIKE RED'S KID'S PICKED UP THE BATON!

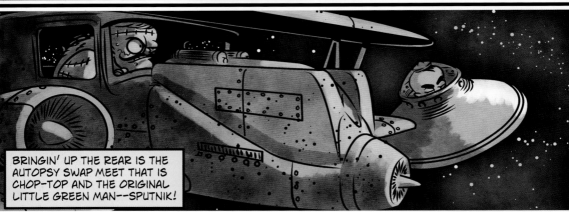

BRINGIN' UP THE REAR IS THE AUTOPSY SWAP MEET THAT IS CHOP-TOP AND THE ORIGINAL LITTLE GREEN MAN--SPUTNIK!

THO' AS THEY CLOSE ON THE CRUCIAL, CRISPY SLINGSHOT AROUND MERCURY, THE FIELD'S WIDE OPEN--!

--AN' THERE'S STILL ALL T'PLAY FOR!

I HEAR THAT! THIS ONE'S FOR YOU, POP!

GET ZAT JUNKER OUT'VE MY VAY, BOY! ZIS RACE IZ MINE!

COME ON AND TAKE IT, YOU CREEP!

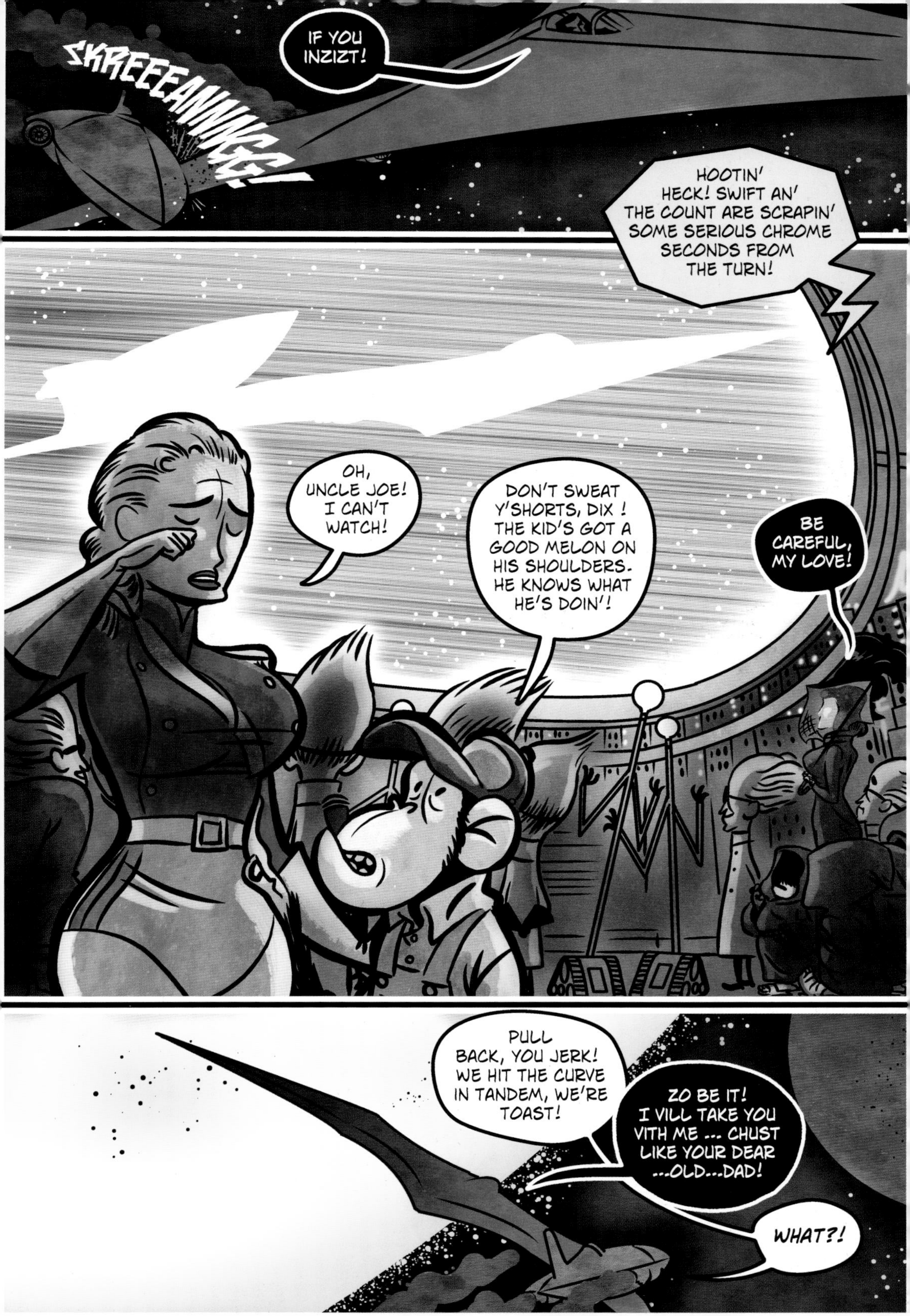
SKREEEANNKGG!
IF YOU INZIZT!
HOOTIN' HECK! SWIFT AN' THE COUNT ARE SCRAPIN' SOME SERIOUS CHROME SECONDS FROM THE TURN!
OH, UNCLE JOE! I CAN'T WATCH!
DON'T SWEAT Y'SHORTS, DIX ! THE KID'S GOT A GOOD MELON ON HIS SHOULDERS. HE KNOWS WHAT HE'S DOIN'!
BE CAREFUL, MY LOVE!
PULL BACK, YOU JERK! WE HIT THE CURVE IN TANDEM, WE'RE TOAST!
ZO BE IT! I VILL TAKE YOU VITH ME ... CHUST LIKE YOUR DEAR ...OLD...DAD!
WHAT?!

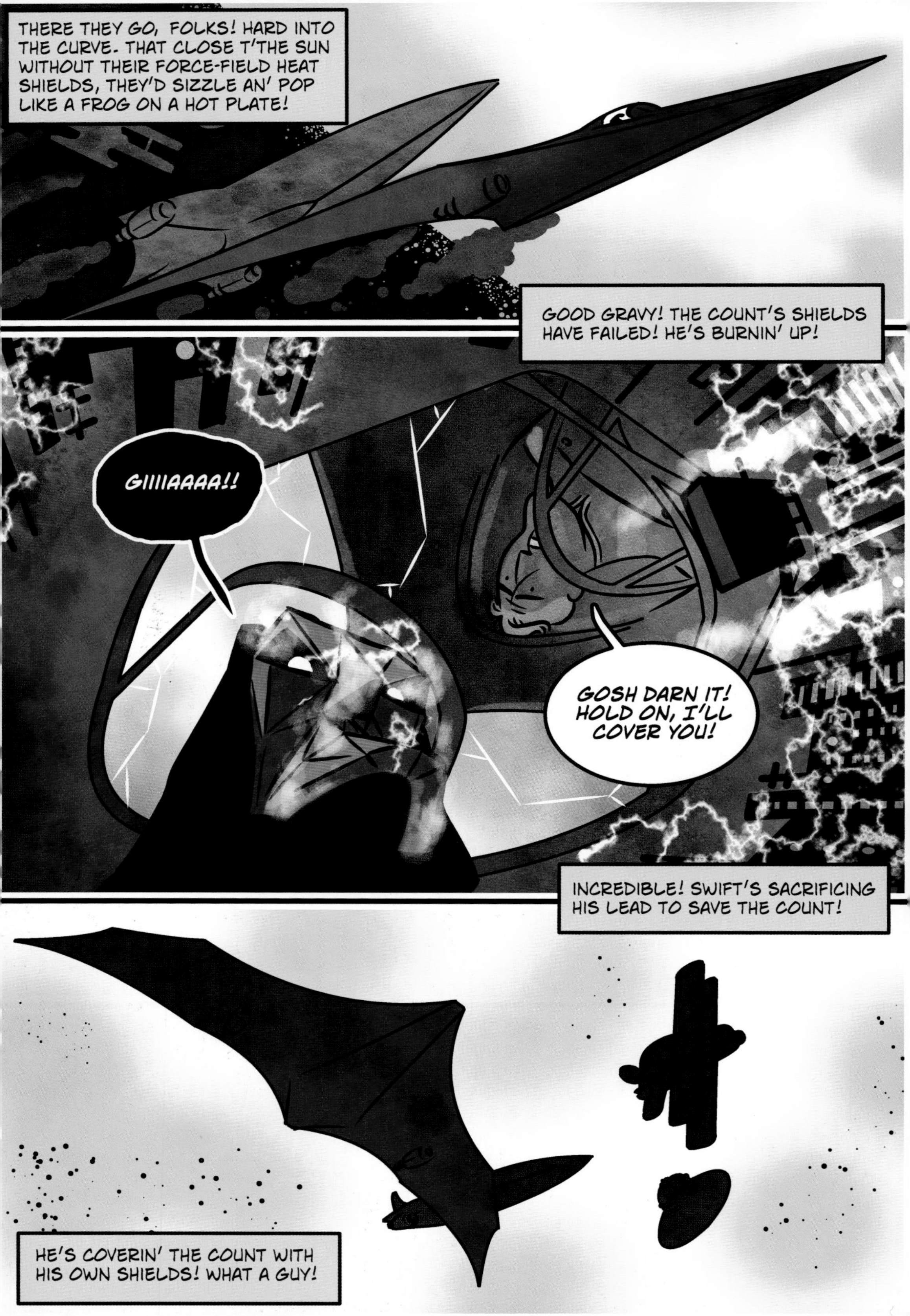
THERE THEY GO, FOLKS! HARD INTO THE CURVE. THAT CLOSE T'THE SUN WITHOUT THEIR FORCE-FIELD HEAT SHIELDS, THEY'D SIZZLE AN' POP LIKE A FROG ON A HOT PLATE!
GOOD GRAVY! THE COUNT'S SHIELDS HAVE FAILED! HE'S BURNIN' UP!
GIIIIAAAA!!
GOSH DARN IT! HOLD ON, I'LL COVER YOU!
INCREDIBLE! SWIFT'S SACRIFICING HIS LEAD TO SAVE THE COUNT!
HE'S COVERIN' THE COUNT WITH HIS OWN SHIELDS! WHAT A GUY!

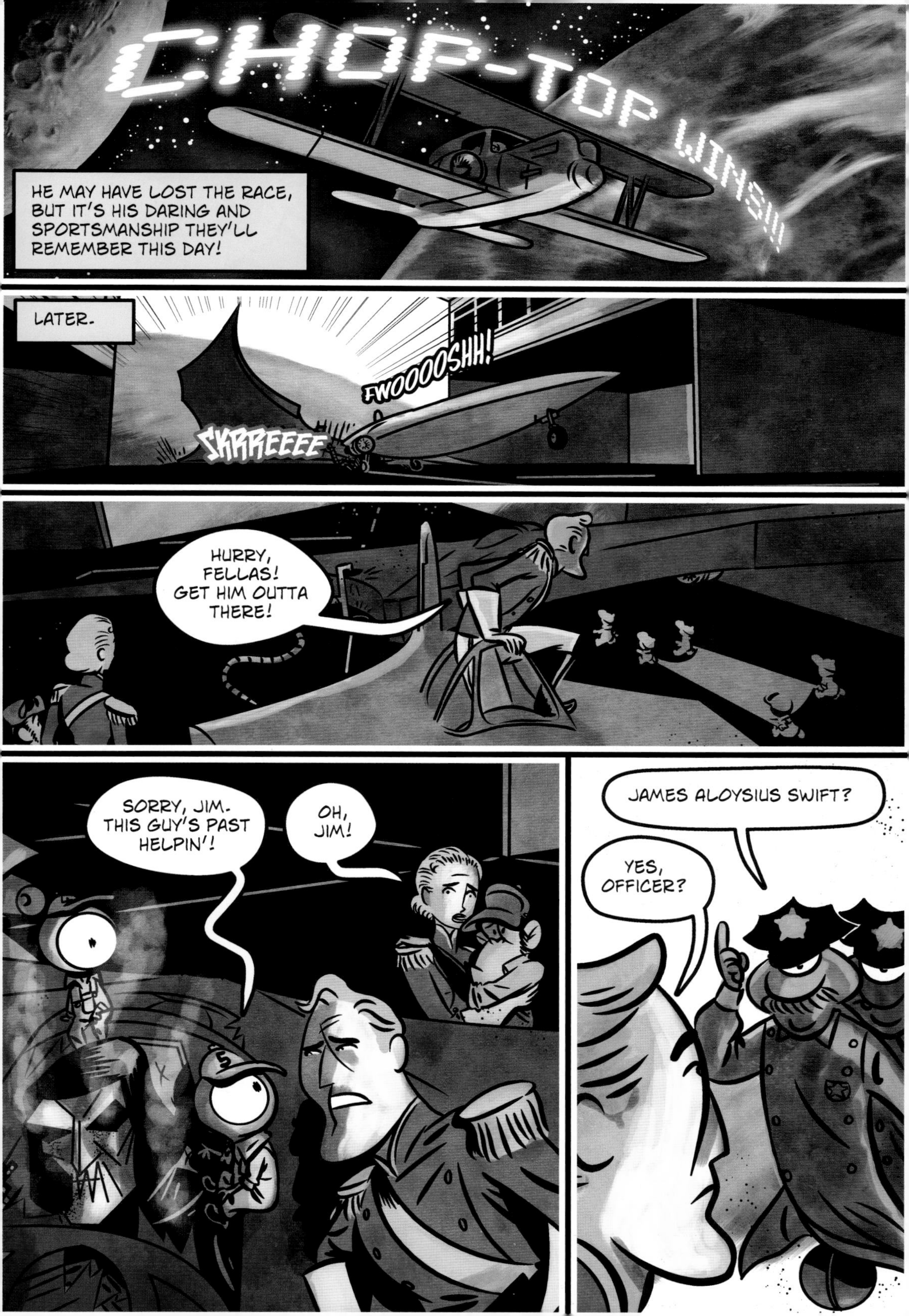
CHOP-TOP WINS!!!
HE MAY HAVE LOST THE RACE, BUT IT'S HIS DARING AND SPORTSMANSHIP THEY'LL REMEMBER THIS DAY!
LATER.
FWOOOOSHH!
SKRREEEEE
HURRY, FELLAS! GET HIM OUTTA THERE!
SORRY, JIM. THIS GUY'S PAST HELPIN'!
OH, JIM!
JAMES ALOYSIUS SWIFT?
YES, OFFICER?

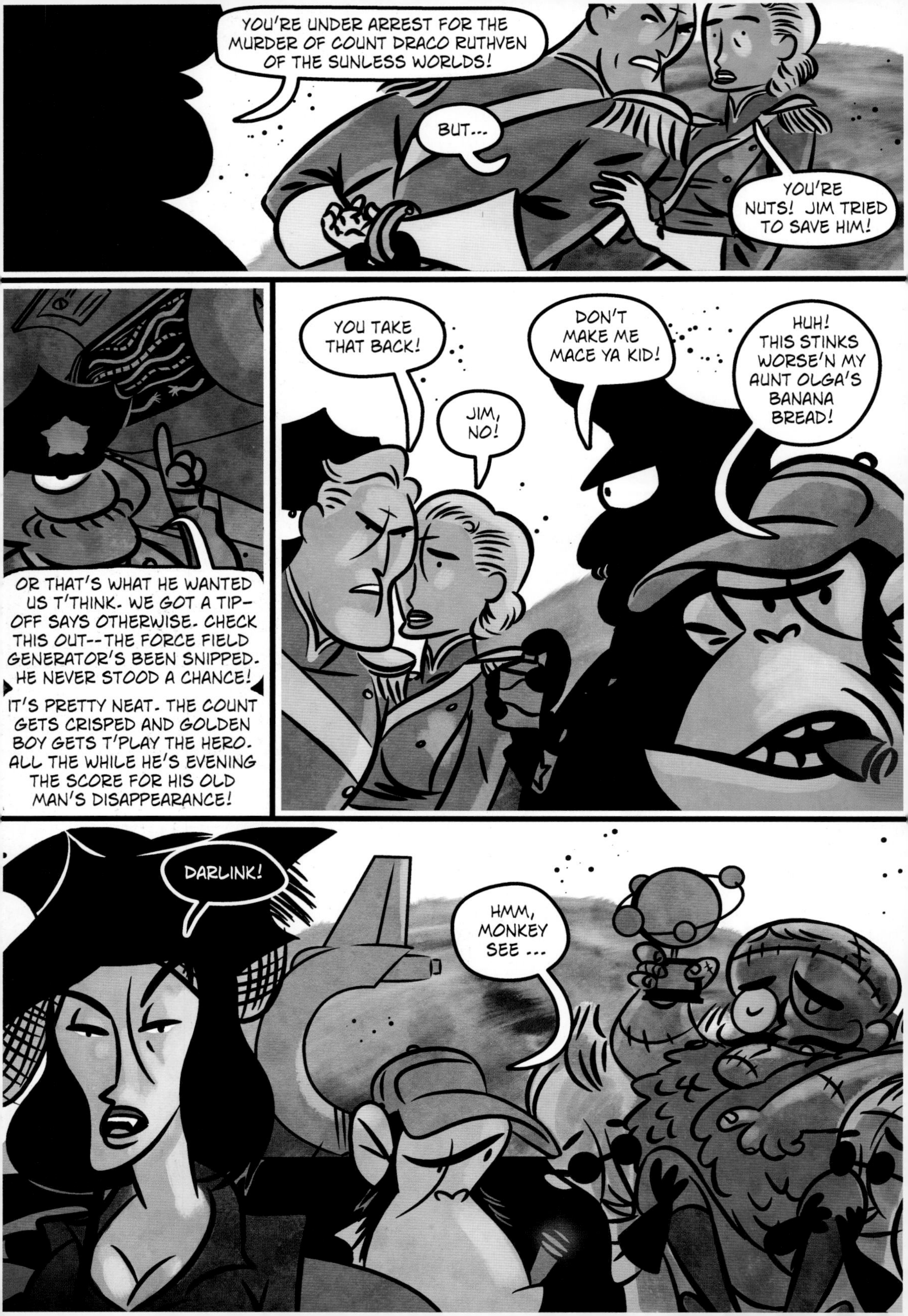
YOU'RE UNDER ARREST FOR THE MURDER OF COUNT DRACO RUTHVEN OF THE SUNLESS WORLDS!
BUT...
YOU'RE NUTS! JIM TRIED TO SAVE HIM!
OR THAT'S WHAT HE WANTED US T'THINK. WE GOT A TIP-OFF SAYS OTHERWISE. CHECK THIS OUT--THE FORCE FIELD GENERATOR'S BEEN SNIPPED. HE NEVER STOOD A CHANCE!
IT'S PRETTY NEAT. THE COUNT GETS CRISPED AND GOLDEN BOY GETS T'PLAY THE HERO. ALL THE WHILE HE'S EVENING THE SCORE FOR HIS OLD MAN'S DISAPPEARANCE!
YOU TAKE THAT BACK!
JIM, NO!
DON'T MAKE ME MACE YA KID!
HUH! THIS STINKS WORSE'N MY AUNT OLGA'S BANANA BREAD!
DARLINK!
HMM, MONKEY SEE ...

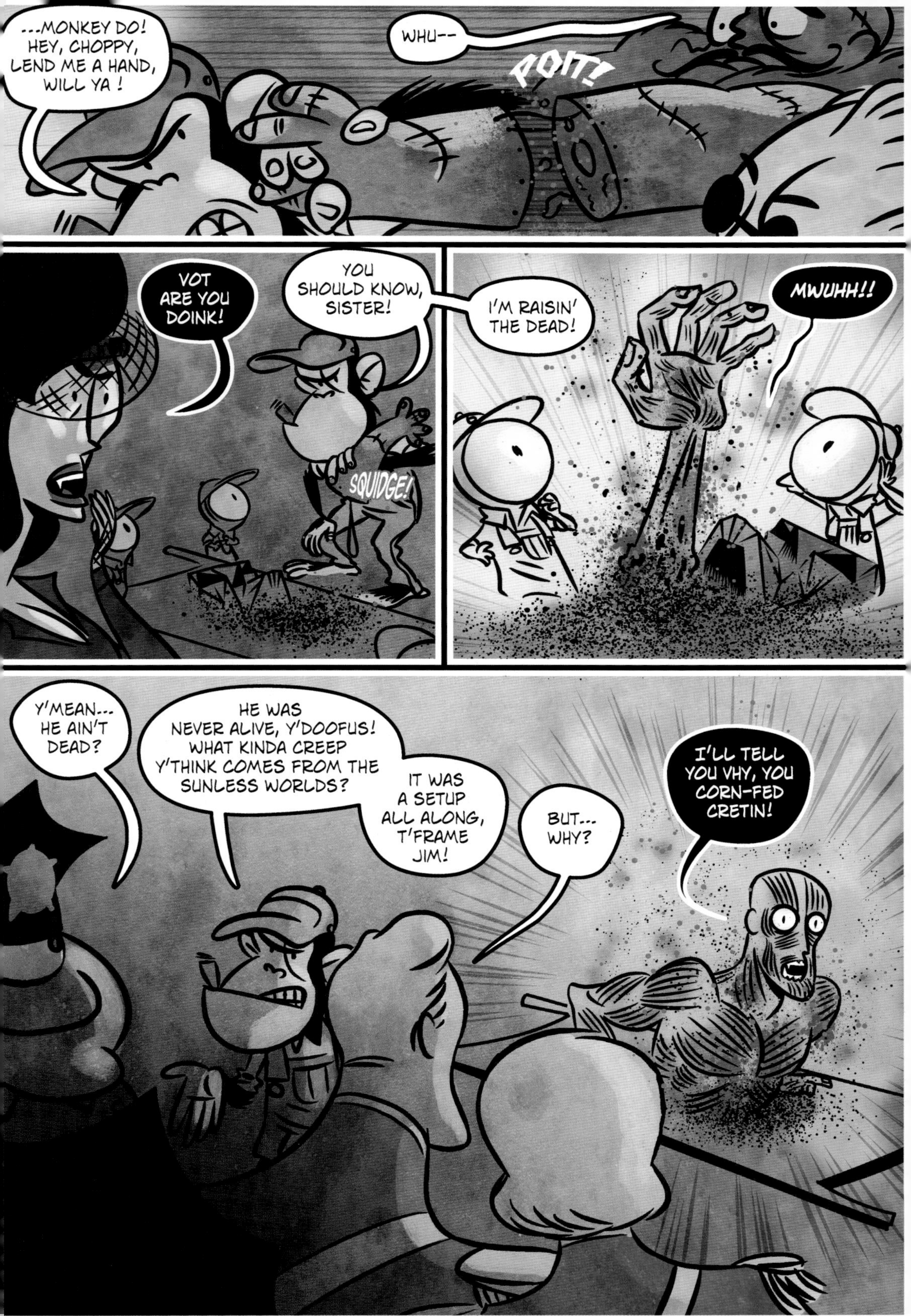

...MONKEY DO! HEY, CHOPPY, LEND ME A HAND, WILL YA !
WHU--
POIT!
VOT ARE YOU DOINK!
YOU SHOULD KNOW, SISTER!
SQUIDGE!
I'M RAISIN' THE DEAD!
MWUHH!!
Y'MEAN... HE AIN'T DEAD?
HE WAS NEVER ALIVE, Y'DOOFUS! WHAT KINDA CREEP Y'THINK COMES FROM THE SUNLESS WORLDS?
IT WAS A SETUP ALL ALONG, T'FRAME JIM!
BUT... WHY?
I'LL TELL YOU VHY, YOU CORN-FED CRETIN!

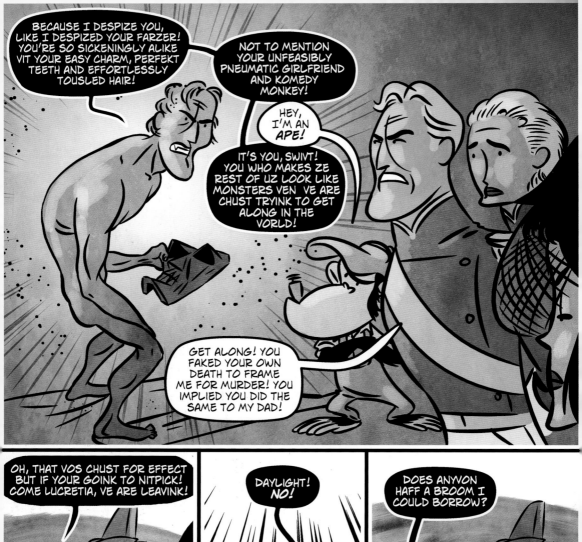

BECAUSE I DESPIZE YOU, LIKE I DESPIZED YOUR FARZER! YOU'RE SO SICKENINGLY ALIKE VIT YOUR EASY CHARM, PERFEKT TEETH AND EFFORTLESSLY TOUSLED HAIR!

NOT TO MENTION YOUR UNFEASIBLY PNEUMATIC GIRLFRIEND AND KOMEDY MONKEY!

HEY, I'M AN APE!

IT'S YOU, SWIVT! YOU WHO MAKES ZE REST OF UZ LOOK LIKE MONSTERS VEN VE ARE CHUST TRYINK TO GET ALONG IN THE VORLD!

GET ALONG! YOU FAKED YOUR OWN DEATH TO FRAME ME FOR MURDER! YOU IMPLIED YOU DID THE SAME TO MY DAD!

OH, THAT VOS CHUST FOR EFFECT BUT IF YOUR GOINK TO NITPICK! COME LUCRETIA, VE ARE LEAVINK!

BUT DARLINK, IT IS STILL--

DAYLIGHT! NO!

DOES ANYVON HAFF A BROOM I COULD BORROW?

THE END

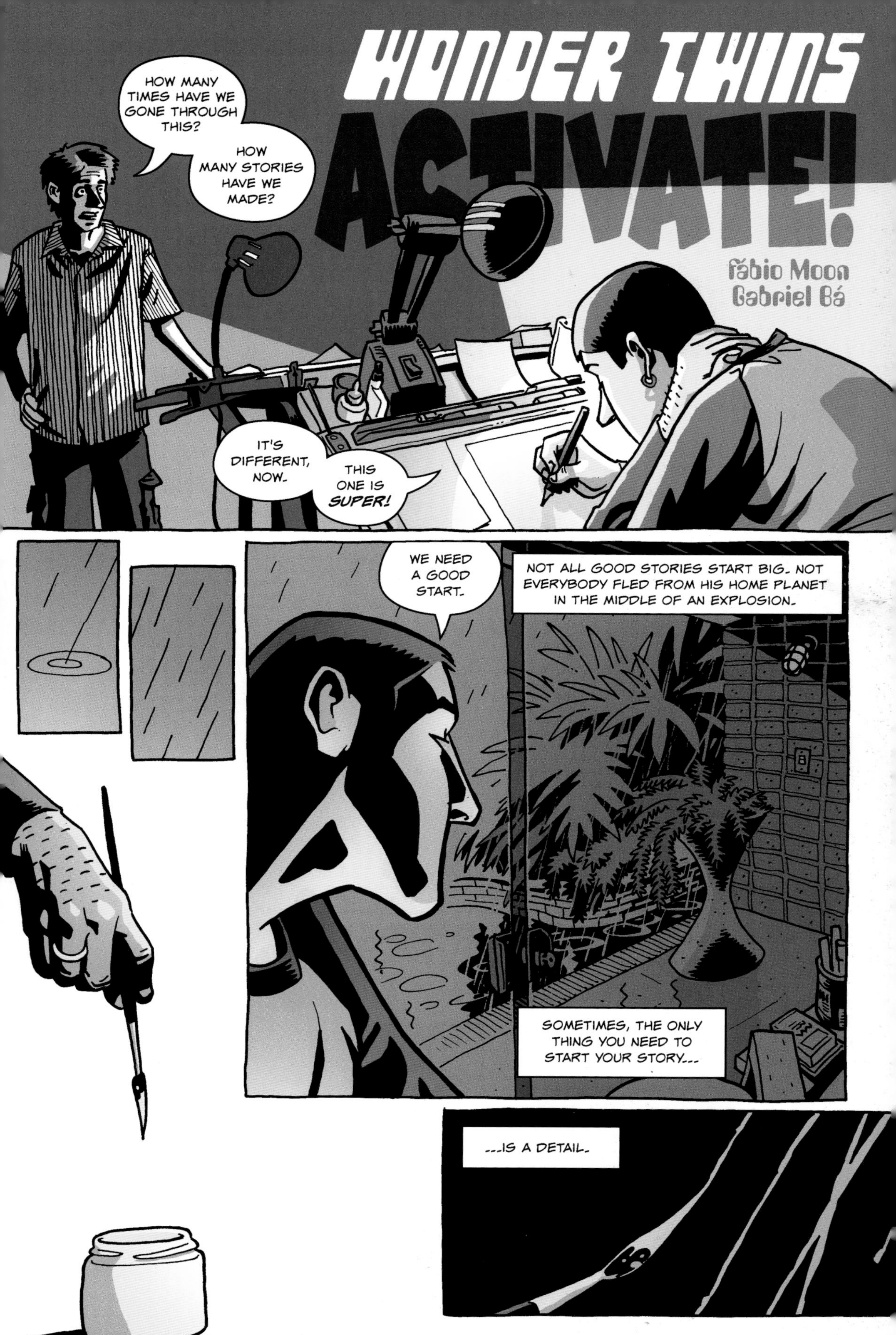
WONDER TWINS
ACTIVATE!
Fábio Moon
Gabriel Bá
HOW MANY TIMES HAVE WE GONE THROUGH THIS?
HOW MANY STORIES HAVE WE MADE?
IT'S DIFFERENT, NOW.
THIS ONE IS SUPER!
WE NEED A GOOD START.
NOT ALL GOOD STORIES START BIG. NOT EVERYBODY FLED FROM HIS HOME PLANET IN THE MIDDLE OF AN EXPLOSION.
SOMETIMES, THE ONLY THING YOU NEED TO START YOUR STORY...
...IS A DETAIL.

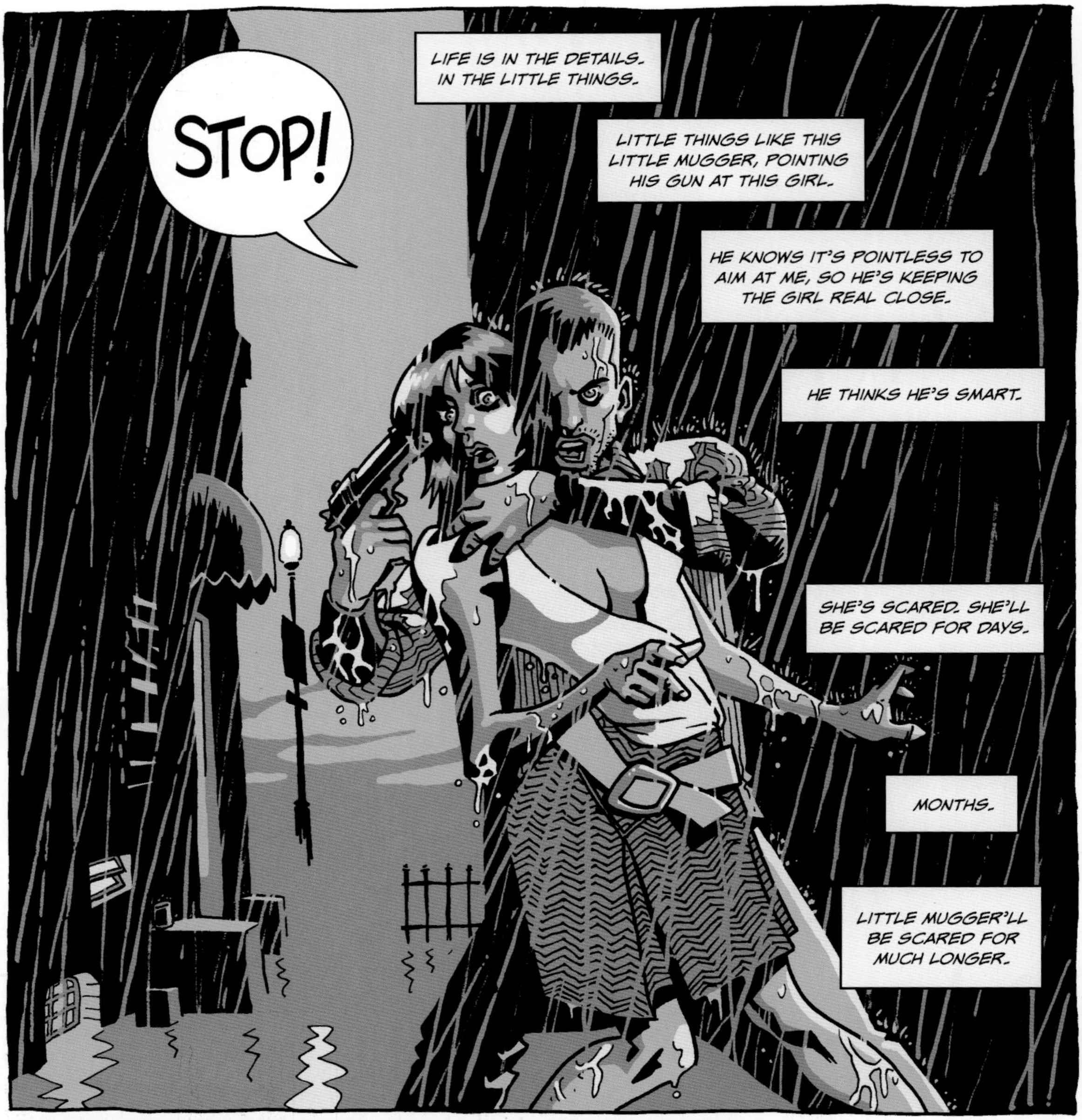
STOP!
LIFE IS IN THE DETAILS. IN THE LITTLE THINGS.
LITTLE THINGS LIKE THIS LITTLE MUGGER, POINTING HIS GUN AT THIS GIRL.
HE KNOWS IT'S POINTLESS TO AIM AT ME, SO HE'S KEEPING THE GIRL REAL CLOSE.
HE THINKS HE'S SMART.
SHE'S SCARED. SHE'LL BE SCARED FOR DAYS.
MONTHS.
LITTLE MUGGER'LL BE SCARED FOR MUCH LONGER.

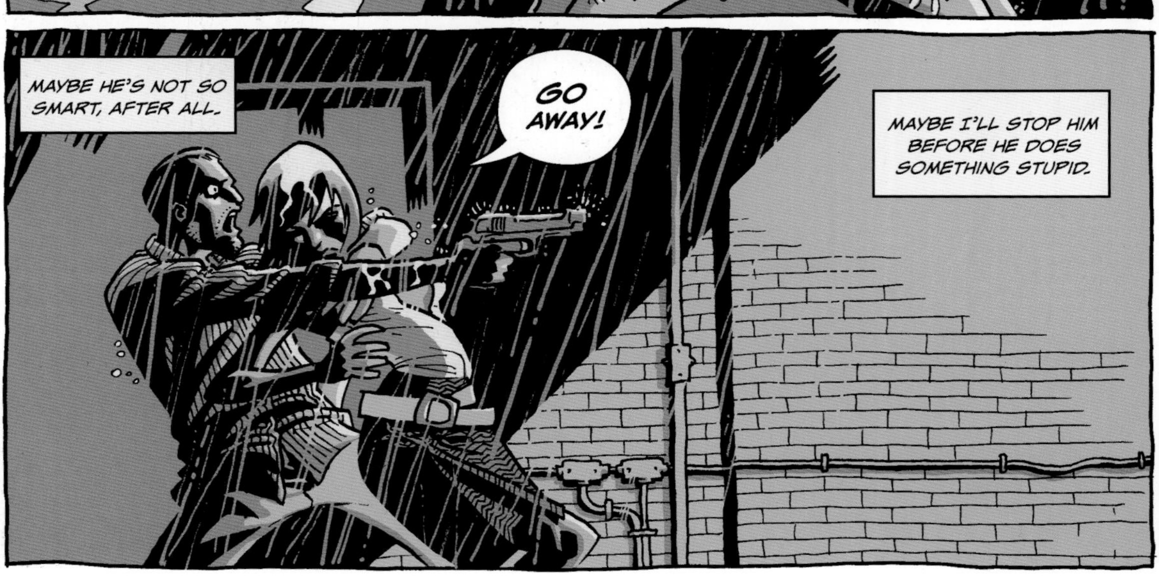
MAYBE HE'S NOT SO SMART, AFTER ALL.
GO AWAY!
MAYBE I'LL STOP HIM BEFORE HE DOES SOMETHING STUPID.

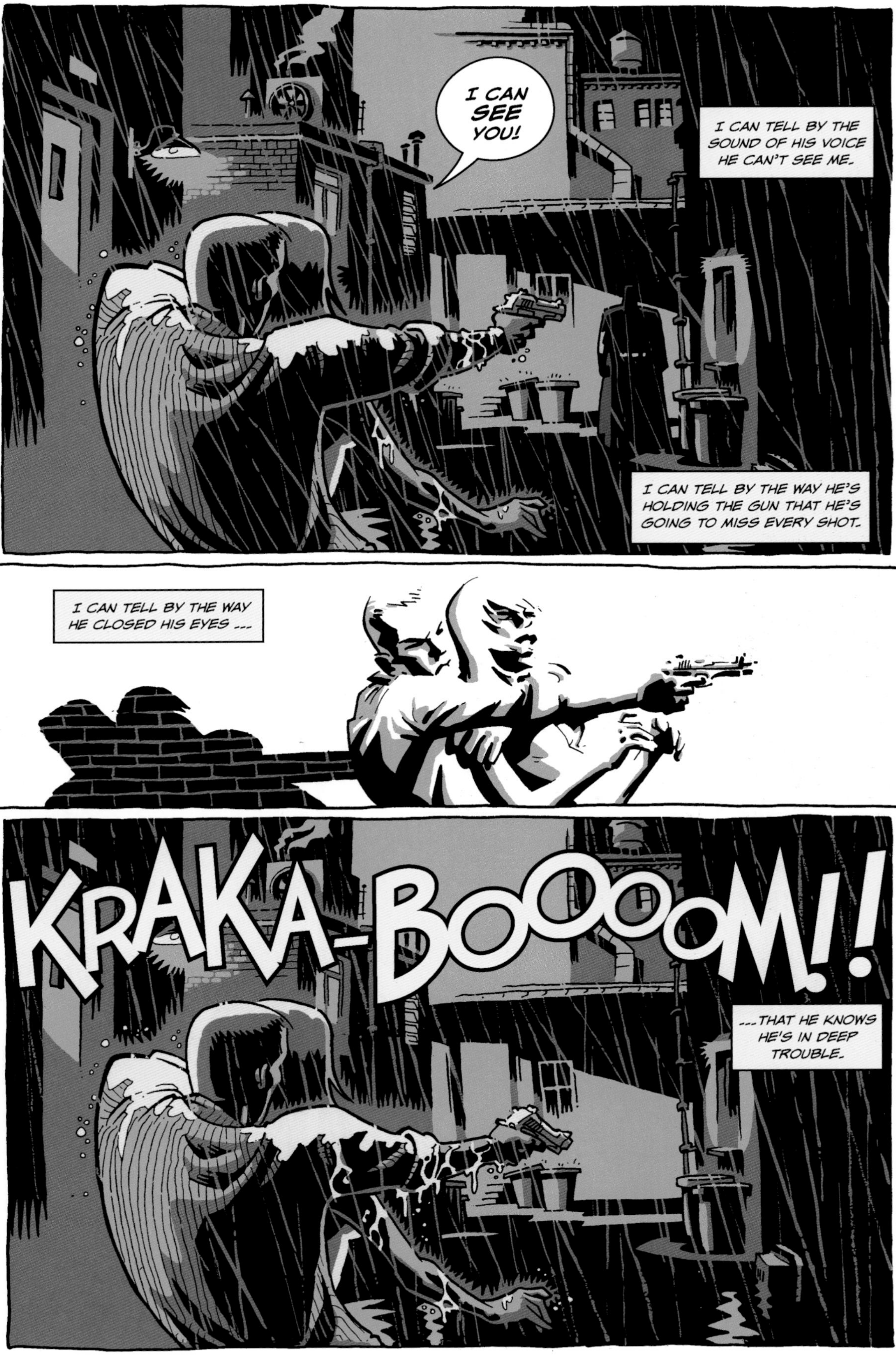
I CAN SEE YOU!
I CAN TELL BY THE SOUND OF HIS VOICE HE CAN'T SEE ME.
I CAN TELL BY THE WAY HE'S HOLDING THE GUN THAT HE'S GOING TO MISS EVERY SHOT.
I CAN TELL BY THE WAY HE CLOSED HIS EYES ---
KRAKA-BOOOOOM!!
---THAT HE KNOWS HE'S IN DEEP TROUBLE.

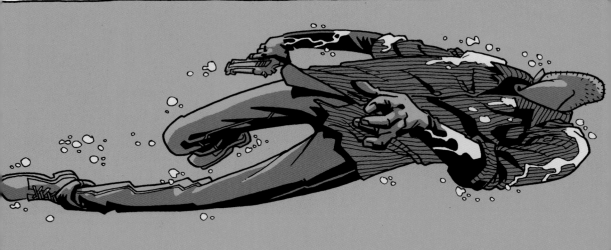

A PART OF ME HOPES I DIDN'T THROW THE LITTLE MUGGER TOO HARD.

I WOULDN'T WANT HIM UNCONSCIOUS AFTER THE FIRST PUNCH.

A PART OF ME SMILES WHEN HE FINALLY GETS UP.

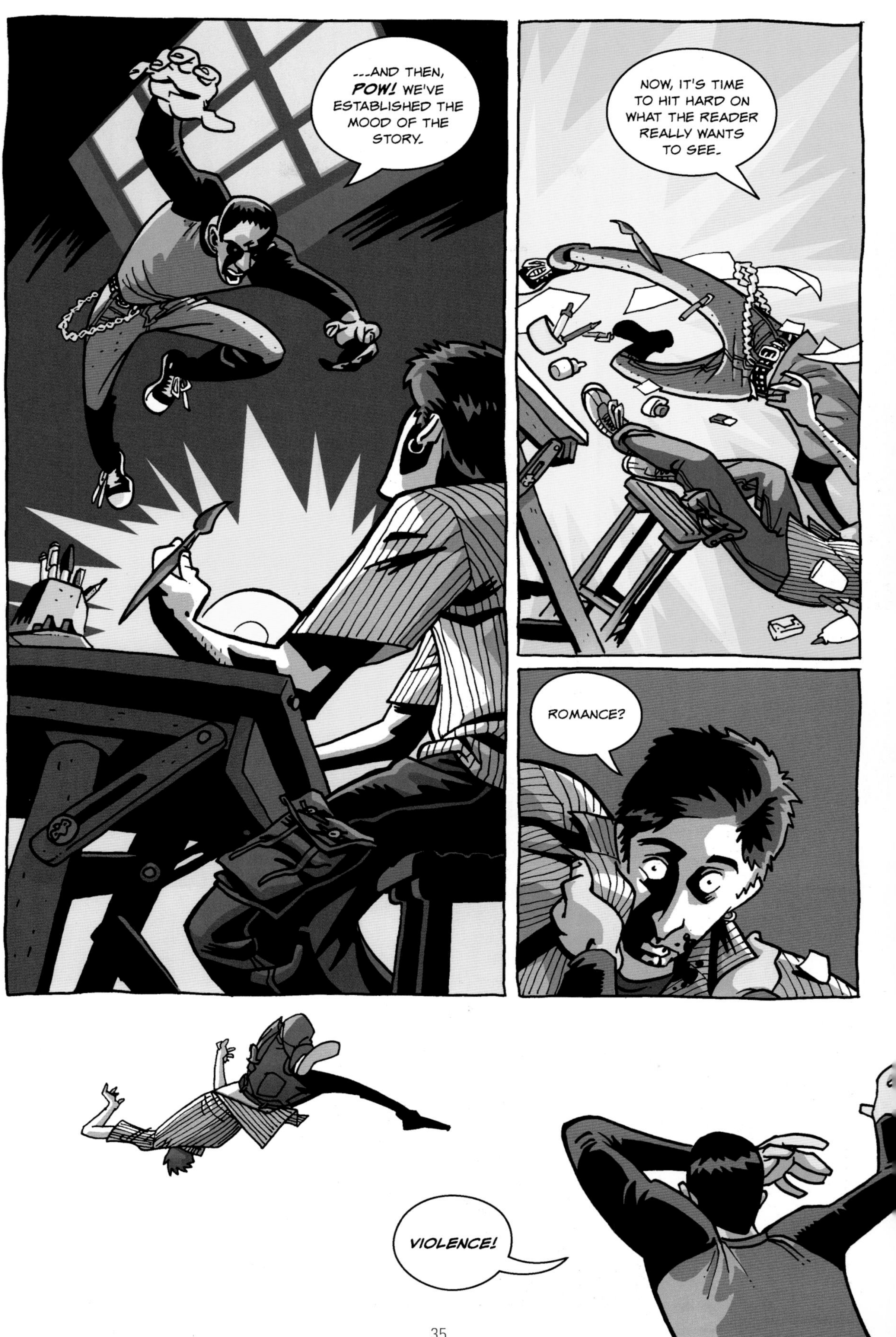
...AND THEN, POW! WE'VE ESTABLISHED THE MOOD OF THE STORY.
NOW, IT'S TIME TO HIT HARD ON WHAT THE READER REALLY WANTS TO SEE.
ROMANCE?
VIOLENCE!

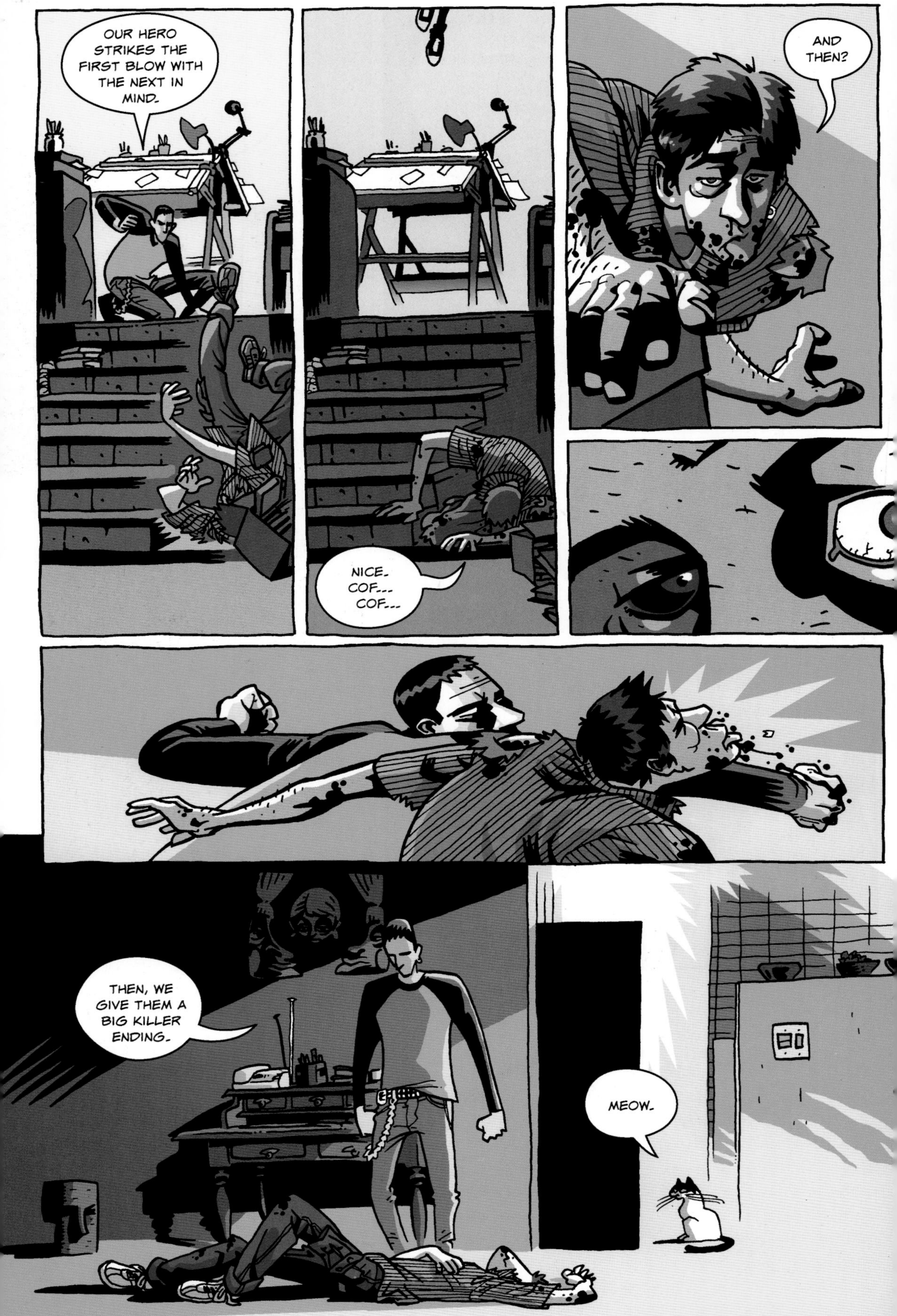
OUR HERO STRIKES THE FIRST BLOW WITH THE NEXT IN MIND.
NICE. COF... COF...
AND THEN?
THEN, WE GIVE THEM A BIG KILLER ENDING.
MEOW.

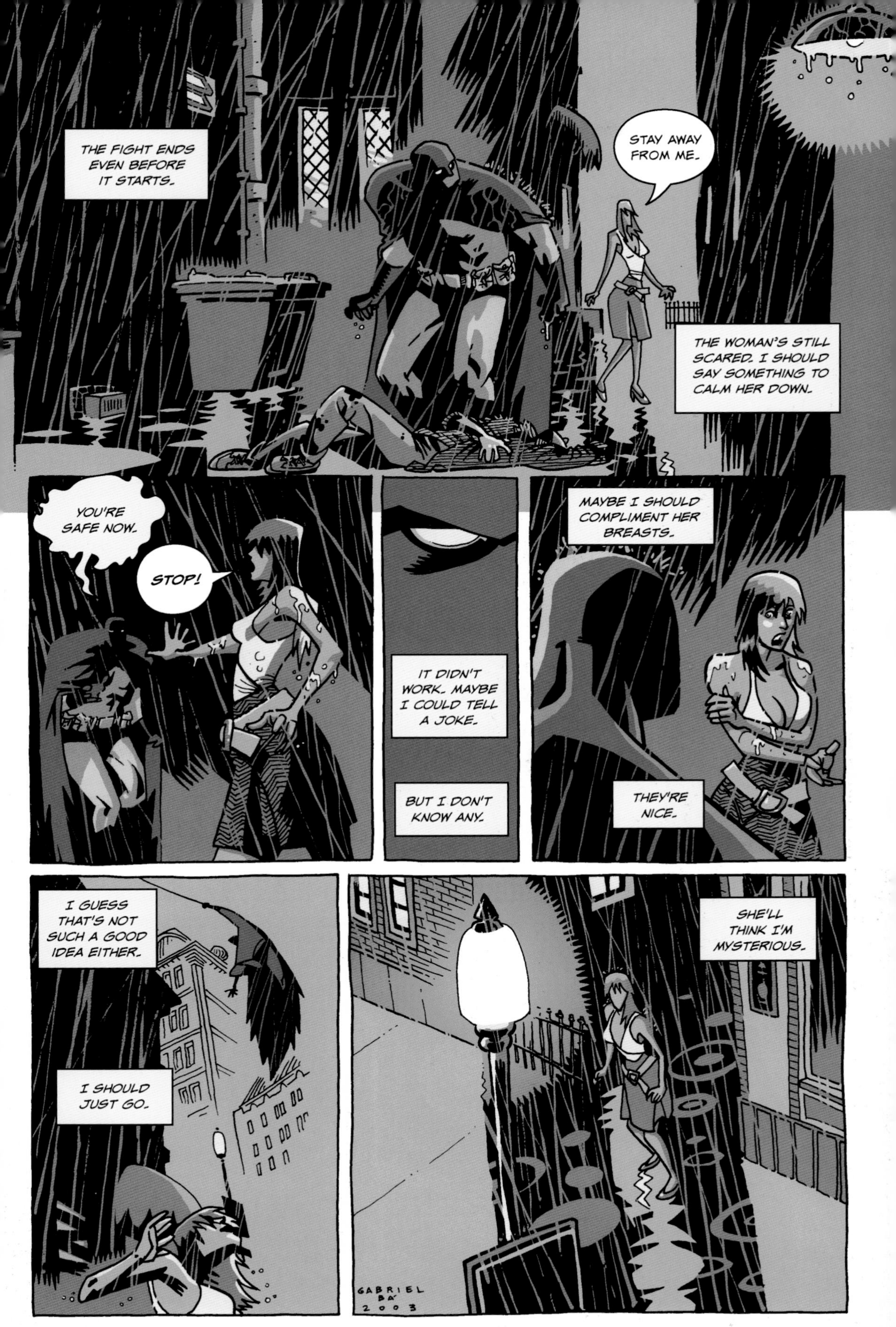
THE FIGHT ENDS EVEN BEFORE IT STARTS.
STAY AWAY FROM ME.
THE WOMAN'S STILL SCARED. I SHOULD SAY SOMETHING TO CALM HER DOWN.
YOU'RE SAFE NOW.
STOP!
IT DIDN'T WORK. MAYBE I COULD TELL A JOKE.
BUT I DON'T KNOW ANY.
MAYBE I SHOULD COMPLIMENT HER BREASTS.
THEY'RE NICE.
I GUESS THAT'S NOT SUCH A GOOD IDEA EITHER.
I SHOULD JUST GO.
SHE'LL THINK I'M MYSTERIOUS.
GABRIEL BÁ 2003

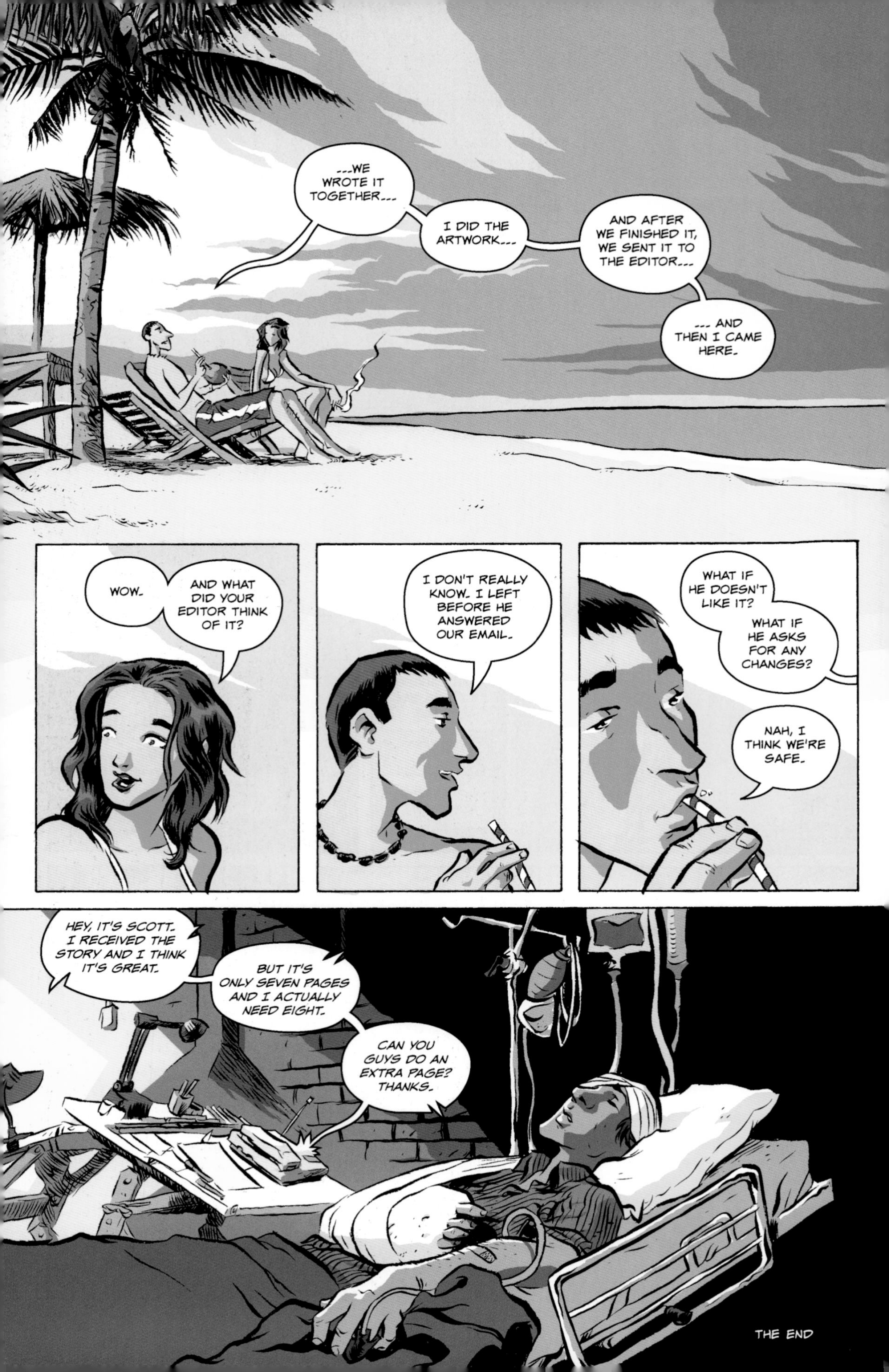
...WE WROTE IT TOGETHER...
I DID THE ARTWORK...
AND AFTER WE FINISHED IT, WE SENT IT TO THE EDITOR...
... AND THEN I CAME HERE.
WOW.
AND WHAT DID YOUR EDITOR THINK OF IT?
I DON'T REALLY KNOW. I LEFT BEFORE HE ANSWERED OUR EMAIL.
WHAT IF HE DOESN'T LIKE IT?
WHAT IF HE ASKS FOR ANY CHANGES?
NAH, I THINK WE'RE SAFE.
HEY, IT'S SCOTT. I RECEIVED THE STORY AND I THINK IT'S GREAT.
BUT IT'S ONLY SEVEN PAGES AND I ACTUALLY NEED EIGHT.
CAN YOU GUYS DO AN EXTRA PAGE? THANKS.
THE END

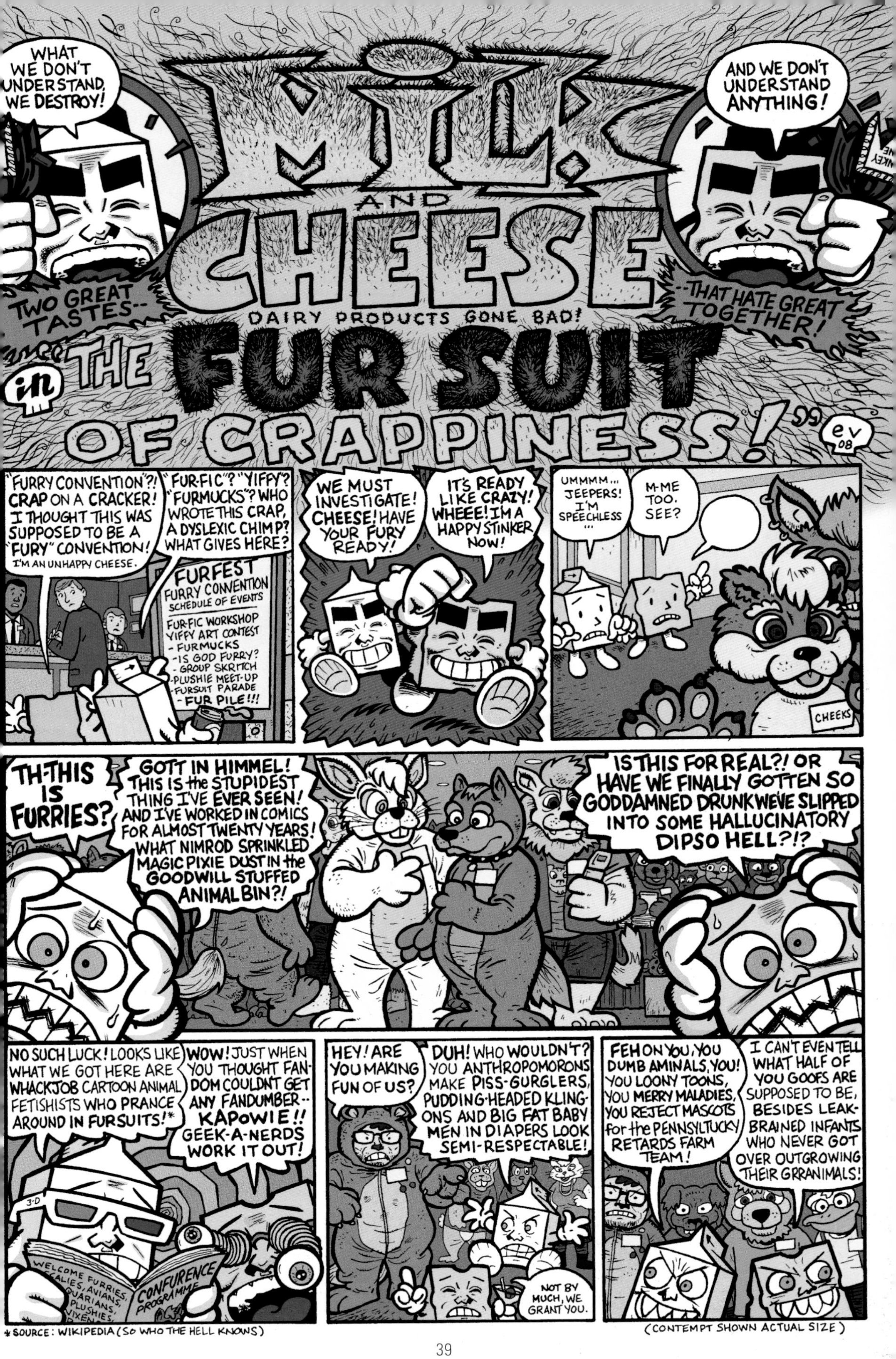
WHAT WE DON'T UNDERSTAND, WE DESTROY!
AND WE DON'T UNDERSTAND ANYTHING!
MILK AND CHEESE
TWO GREAT TASTES--
--THAT HATE GREAT TOGETHER!
DAIRY PRODUCTS GONE BAD!
in "THE FUR SUIT OF CRAPPINESS!"
ev 08
"FURRY CONVENTION"?! CRAP ON A CRACKER! I THOUGHT THIS WAS SUPPOSED TO BE A "FURY" CONVENTION! I'M AN UNHAPPY CHEESE.
"FUR-FIC"? "YIFFY"? "FURMUCKS"? WHO WROTE THIS CRAP, A DYSLEXIC CHIMP? WHAT GIVES HERE?
FURFEST FURRY CONVENTION SCHEDULE OF EVENTS
FUR-FIC WORKSHOP
YIFFY ART CONTEST
- FURMUCKS
- IS GOD FURRY?
- GROUP SKRITCH
- PLUSHIE MEET-UP
- FURSUIT PARADE
- FUR PILE!!!
WE MUST INVESTIGATE! CHEESE! HAVE YOUR FURY READY!
IT'S READY LIKE CRAZY! WHEEE! I'M A HAPPY STINKER NOW!
UMMMM... JEEPERS! I'M SPEECHLESS ...
M-ME TOO. SEE?
CHEEKS
TH-THIS IS FURRIES?
GOTT IN HIMMEL! THIS IS the STUPIDEST THING I'VE EVER SEEN! AND I'VE WORKED IN COMICS FOR ALMOST TWENTY YEARS! WHAT NIMROD SPRINKLED MAGIC PIXIE DUST IN the GOODWILL STUFFED ANIMAL BIN?!
IS THIS FOR REAL?! OR HAVE WE FINALLY GOTTEN SO GODDAMNED DRUNK WE'VE SLIPPED INTO SOME HALLUCINATORY DIPSO HELL?!?
NO SUCH LUCK! LOOKS LIKE WHAT WE GOT HERE ARE WHACKJOB CARTOON ANIMAL FETISHISTS WHO PRANCE AROUND IN FURSUITS!*
WOW! JUST WHEN YOU THOUGHT FANDOM COULDN'T GET ANY FANDUMBER-- KAPOWIE!! GEEK-A-NERDS WORK IT OUT!
3-D
WELCOME FURRIES, SCALIES, AVIANS, AQUARIANS, PLUSHIES, VIXENS,
CONFURENCE PROGRAMME
HEY! ARE YOU MAKING FUN OF US?
DUH! WHO WOULDN'T? YOU ANTHROPOMORONS MAKE PISS-GURGLERS, PUDDING-HEADED KLINGONS AND BIG FAT BABY MEN IN DIAPERS LOOK SEMI-RESPECTABLE!
NOT BY MUCH, WE GRANT YOU.
FEH ON YOU, YOU DUMB AMINALS, YOU! YOU LOONY TOONS, YOU MERRY MALADIES, YOU REJECT MASCOTS for the PENNSYLTUCKY RETARDS FARM TEAM!
I CAN'T EVEN TELL WHAT HALF OF YOU GOOFS ARE SUPPOSED TO BE, BESIDES LEAK-BRAINED INFANTS WHO NEVER GOT OVER OUTGROWING THEIR GRRANIMALS!

* SOURCE: WIKIPEDIA (SO WHO THE HELL KNOWS)

(CONTEMPT SHOWN ACTUAL SIZE)

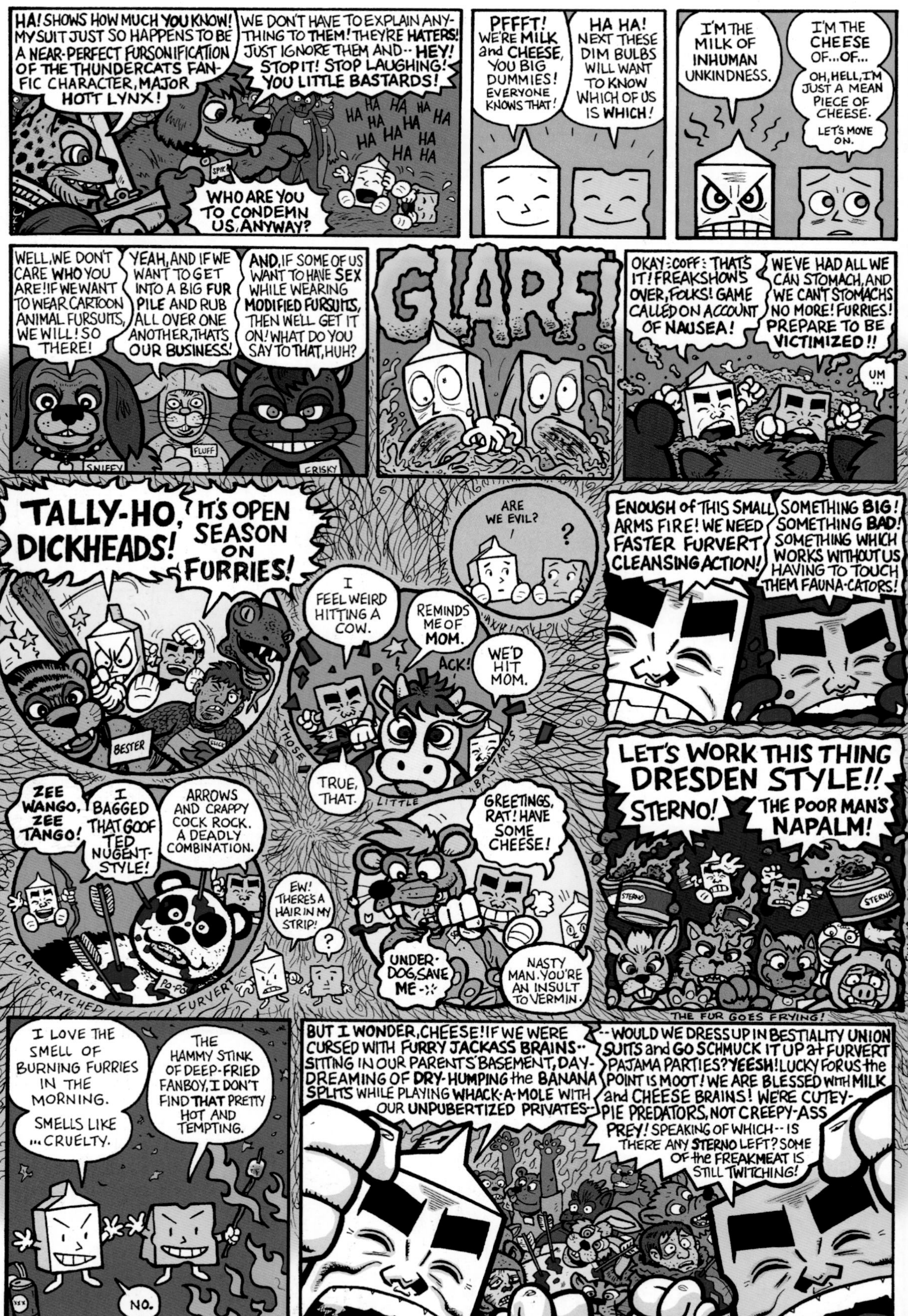
HA! SHOWS HOW MUCH YOU KNOW! MY SUIT JUST SO HAPPENS TO BE A NEAR-PERFECT FURSONIFICATION OF THE THUNDERCATS FAN-FIC CHARACTER, MAJOR HOTT LYNX!
WE DON'T HAVE TO EXPLAIN ANYTHING TO THEM! THEY'RE HATERS! JUST IGNORE THEM AND-- HEY! STOP IT! STOP LAUGHING! YOU LITTLE BASTARDS!
HA HA HA HA HA HA HA HA HA HA HA HA HA
WHO ARE YOU TO CONDEMN US, ANYWAY?
PFFFT! WE'RE MILK and CHEESE, YOU BIG DUMMIES! EVERYONE KNOWS THAT!
HA HA! NEXT THESE DIM BULBS WILL WANT TO KNOW WHICH OF US IS WHICH!
I'M THE MILK OF INHUMAN UNKINDNESS.
I'M THE CHEESE OF...OF...
OH, HELL, I'M JUST A MEAN PIECE OF CHEESE.
LET'S MOVE ON.
WELL, WE DON'T CARE WHO YOU ARE! IF WE WANT TO WEAR CARTOON ANIMAL FURSUITS, WE WILL! SO THERE!
YEAH, AND IF WE WANT TO GET INTO A BIG FUR PILE AND RUB ALL OVER ONE ANOTHER, THAT'S OUR BUSINESS!
AND, IF SOME OF US WANT TO HAVE SEX WHILE WEARING MODIFIED FURSUITS, THEN WE'LL GET IT ON! WHAT DO YOU SAY TO THAT, HUH?
SNIFFY
FLUFF
FRISKY
GLARF!
OKAY: COFF: THAT'S IT! FREAKSHOW'S OVER, FOLKS! GAME CALLED ON ACCOUNT OF NAUSEA!
WE'VE HAD ALL WE CAN STOMACH, AND WE CAN'T STOMACHS NO MORE! FURRIES! PREPARE TO BE VICTIMIZED!!
UM ...
TALLY-HO, DICKHEADS!
IT'S OPEN SEASON ON FURRIES!
BESTER
ARE WE EVIL?
?
I FEEL WEIRD HITTING A COW.
REMINDS ME OF MOM.
ACK!
WE'D HIT MOM.
TRUE, THAT.
THOSE LITTLE BASTARDS
ENOUGH OF THIS SMALL ARMS FIRE! WE NEED FASTER FURVERT CLEANSING ACTION!
SOMETHING BIG! SOMETHING BAD! SOMETHING WHICH WORKS WITHOUT US HAVING TO TOUCH THEM FAUNA-CATORS!
ZEE WANGO, ZEE TANGO!
I BAGGED THAT GOOF TED NUGENT-STYLE!
ARROWS AND CRAPPY COCK ROCK. A DEADLY COMBINATION.
PO-PO
CAT-SCRATCHED FURVERT
EW! THERE'S A HAIR IN MY STRIP!
?
GREETINGS, RAT! HAVE SOME CHEESE!
UNDER-DOG, SAVE ME
NASTY MAN. YOU'RE AN INSULT TO VERMIN.
LET'S WORK THIS THING DRESDEN STYLE!!
STERNO!
THE POOR MAN'S NAPALM!
STERNO
STERNO
THE FUR GOES FRYING!
I LOVE THE SMELL OF BURNING FURRIES IN THE MORNING.
SMELLS LIKE ...CRUELTY.
THE HAMMY STINK OF DEEP-FRIED FANBOY, I DON'T FIND THAT PRETTY HOT AND TEMPTING.
NO.
BUT I WONDER, CHEESE! IF WE WERE CURSED WITH FURRY JACKASS BRAINS-- SITTING IN OUR PARENTS' BASEMENT, DAY-DREAMING OF DRY-HUMPING the BANANA SPLITS WHILE PLAYING WHACK-A-MOLE WITH OUR UNPUBERTIZED PRIVATES--
--WOULD WE DRESS UP IN BESTIALITY UNION SUITS and GO SCHMUCK IT UP at FURVERT PAJAMA PARTIES? YEESH! LUCKY FOR US the POINT IS MOOT! WE ARE BLESSED WITH MILK and CHEESE BRAINS! WE'RE CUTEY-PIE PREDATORS, NOT CREEPY-ASS PREY! SPEAKING OF WHICH-- IS THERE ANY STERNO LEFT? SOME OF the FREAKMEAT IS STILL TWITCHING!

REMEMBER: ONLY YOU CAN PREVENT FOREST FURRIES.

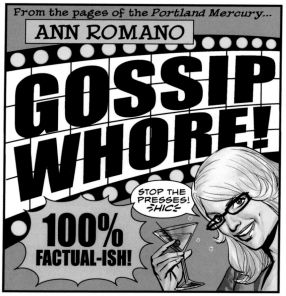

From the pages of the *Portland Mercury*...

ANN ROMANO

GOSSIP WHORE!

100% FACTUAL-ISH!

STOP THE PRESSES! ÷HIC÷

When? JANUARY 2008! Where? HOLLYWEIRD! What? NUDE SHOPPING TIRADE! Who? BRITNEY SPEARS! (Like you're surprised.)

GOTCHA!

It always begins INNOCENTLY, doesn't it? Britney and her L.D.B. went wardrobe shopping...

...But little did this store's unsuspecting employees know that Brit's NOT THAT INNOCENT! (Get it?!)

LATEST DOUCHEBAG BOYFRIEND

Entirely too soon afterward...

TA-DAH, Y'ALL!

There's nothing under here you haven't seen before.

Tragically, an unwitting SALESCLERK took the full brunt of the blast.

VA-VA-VAHEENAAA!

Sorry, Salesclerk! Dropping out of college doesn't seem like such a brilliant idea now, does it?

B-B-BUH-BRITNEY'S PRIVATES WERE R-R-RIGHT THERE! I COULDN'T ESCAPE! ÷SOB÷

Uh-huh. SURE. THERE, THERE....

Oooh! TWENTY PERCENT OFF!

BY ANN ROMANO AND PAUL LEE
LETTERS: NATE PIEKOS

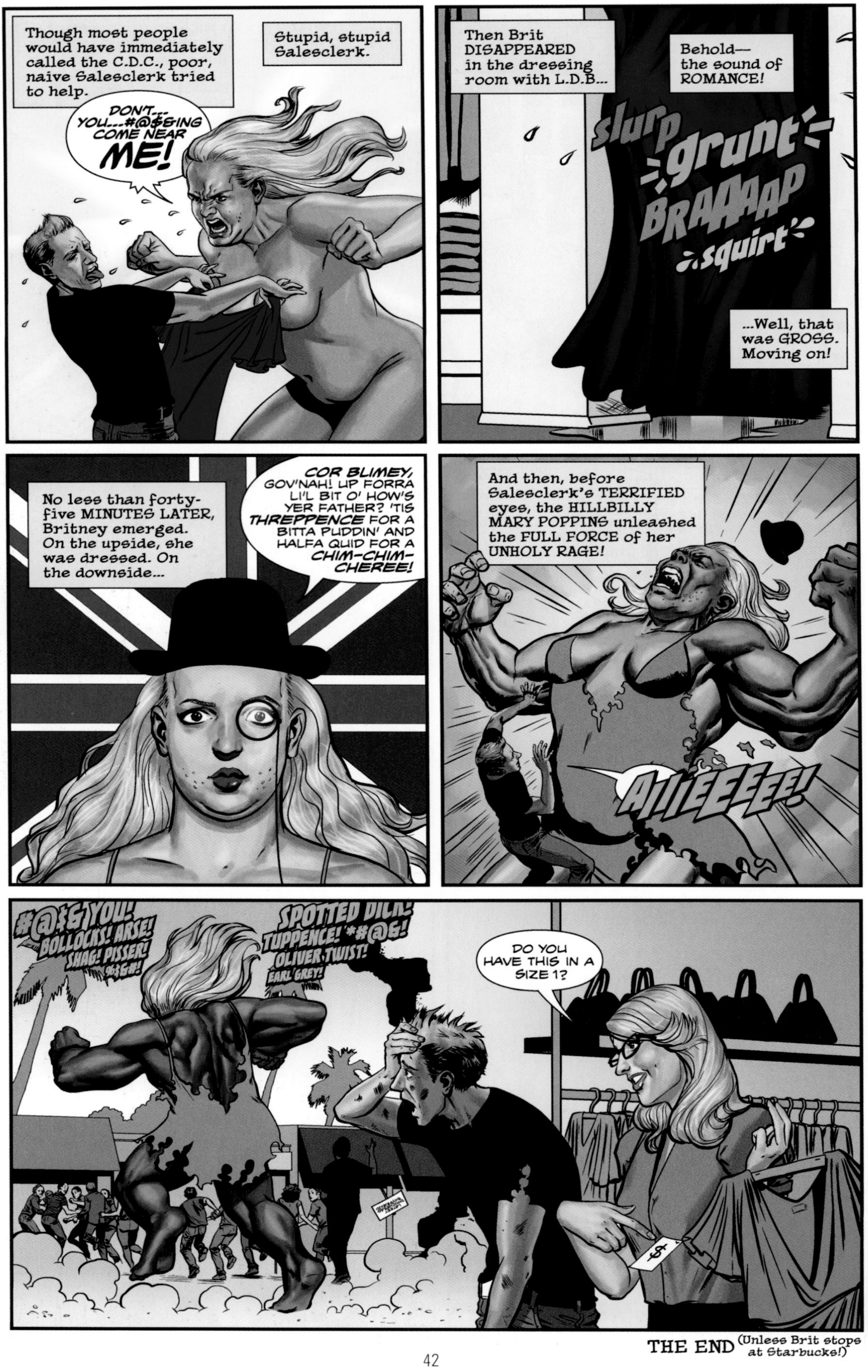

Though most people would have immediately called the C.D.C., poor, naive Salesclerk tried to help.
Stupid, stupid Salesclerk.
DON'T... YOU...#@$&ING COME NEAR ME!
Then Brit DISAPPEARED in the dressing room with L.D.B...
Behold— the sound of ROMANCE!
slurp
grunt
BRAAAAP
squirt
...Well, that was GROSS. Moving on!
No less than forty-five MINUTES LATER, Britney emerged. On the upside, she was dressed. On the downside...
COR BLIMEY, GOV'NAH! UP FORRA LI'L BIT O' HOW'S YER FATHER? 'TIS THREPPENCE FOR A BITTA PUDDIN' AND HALFA QUID FOR A CHIM-CHIM-CHEREE!
And then, before Salesclerk's TERRIFIED eyes, the HILLBILLY MARY POPPINS unleashed the FULL FORCE of her UNHOLY RAGE!
AIIEEEEE!
#@$& YOU! BOLLOCKS! ARSE! SHAG! PISSER! %$&#!
SPOTTED DICK! TUPPENCE! *#@&! OLIVER TWIST! EARL GREY!
DO YOU HAVE THIS IN A SIZE 1?

THE END (Unless Brit stops at Starbucks!)

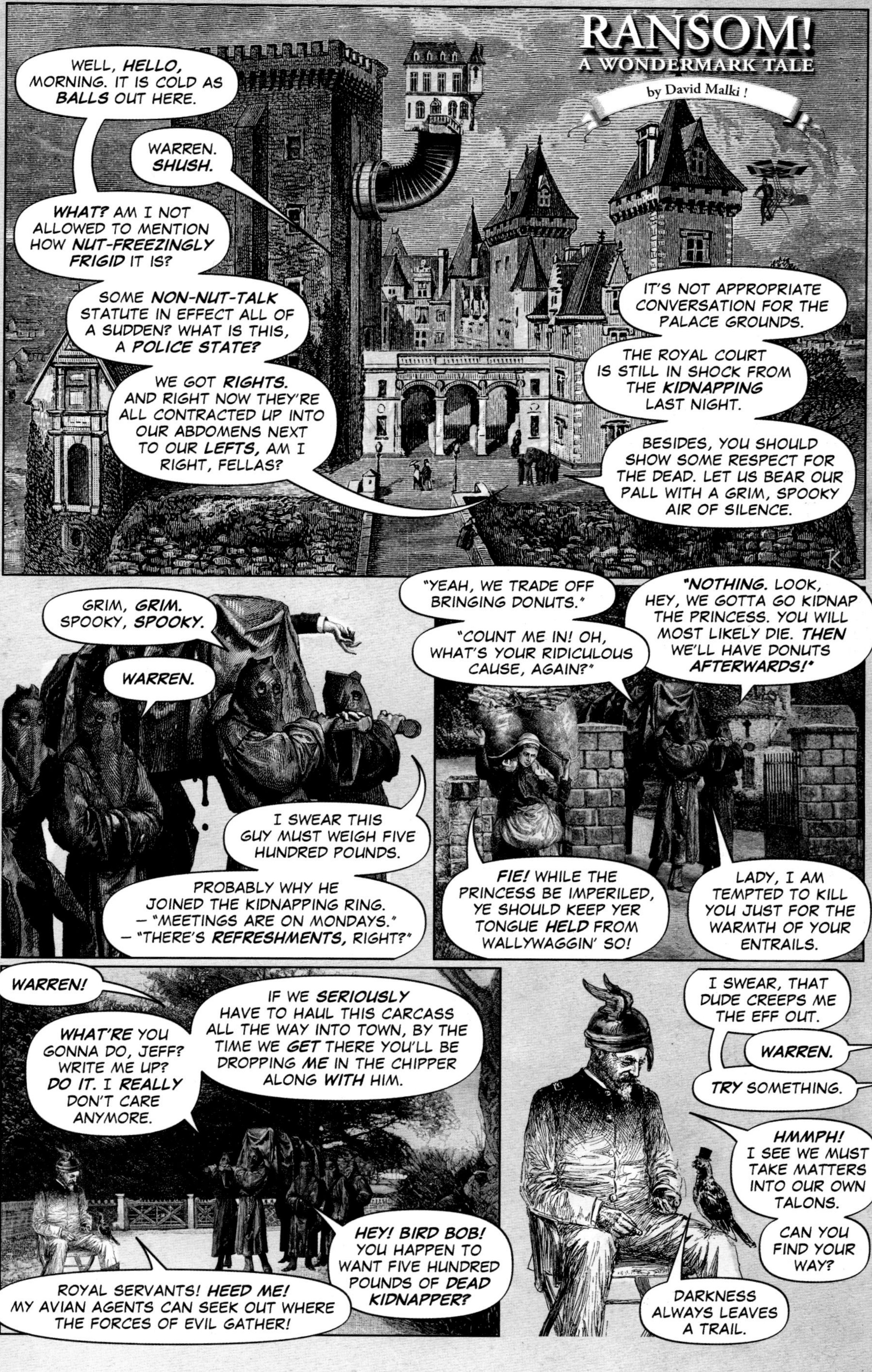
RANSOM!
A WONDERMARK TALE
by David Malki !
WELL, HELLO, MORNING. IT IS COLD AS BALLS OUT HERE.
WARREN. SHUSH.
WHAT? AM I NOT ALLOWED TO MENTION HOW NUT-FREEZINGLY FRIGID IT IS?
SOME NON-NUT-TALK STATUTE IN EFFECT ALL OF A SUDDEN? WHAT IS THIS, A POLICE STATE?
WE GOT RIGHTS. AND RIGHT NOW THEY'RE ALL CONTRACTED UP INTO OUR ABDOMENS NEXT TO OUR LEFTS, AM I RIGHT, FELLAS?
IT'S NOT APPROPRIATE CONVERSATION FOR THE PALACE GROUNDS.
THE ROYAL COURT IS STILL IN SHOCK FROM THE KIDNAPPING LAST NIGHT.
BESIDES, YOU SHOULD SHOW SOME RESPECT FOR THE DEAD. LET US BEAR OUR PALL WITH A GRIM, SPOOKY AIR OF SILENCE.
GRIM, GRIM. SPOOKY, SPOOKY.
WARREN.
I SWEAR THIS GUY MUST WEIGH FIVE HUNDRED POUNDS.
PROBABLY WHY HE JOINED THE KIDNAPPING RING. – "MEETINGS ARE ON MONDAYS." – "THERE'S REFRESHMENTS, RIGHT?"
"YEAH, WE TRADE OFF BRINGING DONUTS."
"COUNT ME IN! OH, WHAT'S YOUR RIDICULOUS CAUSE, AGAIN?"
"NOTHING. LOOK, HEY, WE GOTTA GO KIDNAP THE PRINCESS. YOU WILL MOST LIKELY DIE. THEN WE'LL HAVE DONUTS AFTERWARDS!"
FIE! WHILE THE PRINCESS BE IMPERILED, YE SHOULD KEEP YER TONGUE HELD FROM WALLYWAGGIN' SO!
LADY, I AM TEMPTED TO KILL YOU JUST FOR THE WARMTH OF YOUR ENTRAILS.
WARREN!
WHAT'RE YOU GONNA DO, JEFF? WRITE ME UP? DO IT. I REALLY DON'T CARE ANYMORE.
IF WE SERIOUSLY HAVE TO HAUL THIS CARCASS ALL THE WAY INTO TOWN, BY THE TIME WE GET THERE YOU'LL BE DROPPING ME IN THE CHIPPER ALONG WITH HIM.
ROYAL SERVANTS! HEED ME! MY AVIAN AGENTS CAN SEEK OUT WHERE THE FORCES OF EVIL GATHER!
HEY! BIRD BOB! YOU HAPPEN TO WANT FIVE HUNDRED POUNDS OF DEAD KIDNAPPER?
I SWEAR, THAT DUDE CREEPS ME THE EFF OUT.
WARREN.
TRY SOMETHING.
HMMPH! I SEE WE MUST TAKE MATTERS INTO OUR OWN TALONS.
CAN YOU FIND YOUR WAY?
DARKNESS ALWAYS LEAVES A TRAIL.

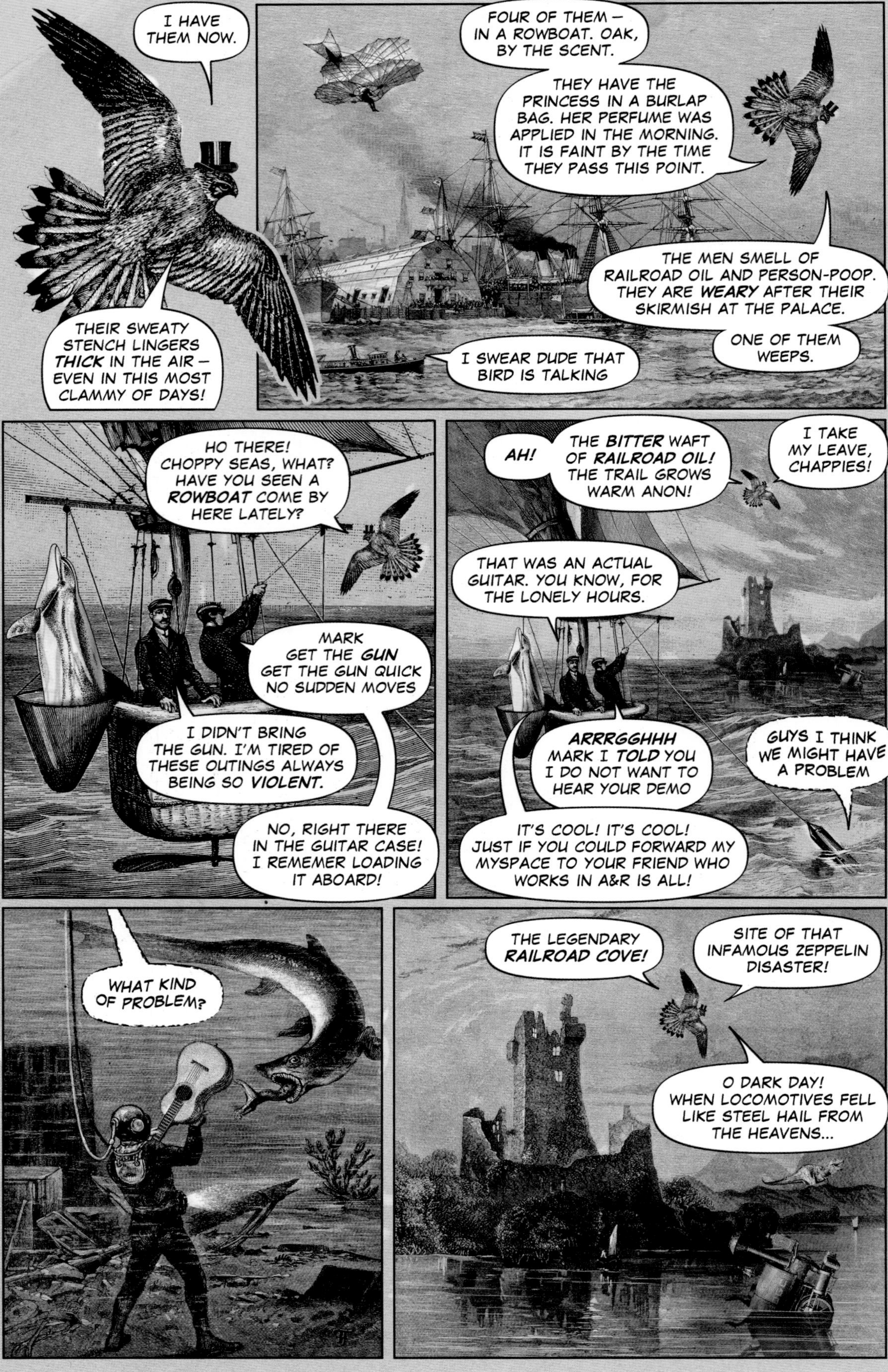
I HAVE THEM NOW.
THEIR SWEATY STENCH LINGERS THICK IN THE AIR — EVEN IN THIS MOST CLAMMY OF DAYS!
FOUR OF THEM — IN A ROWBOAT. OAK, BY THE SCENT.
THEY HAVE THE PRINCESS IN A BURLAP BAG. HER PERFUME WAS APPLIED IN THE MORNING. IT IS FAINT BY THE TIME THEY PASS THIS POINT.
THE MEN SMELL OF RAILROAD OIL AND PERSON-POOP. THEY ARE WEARY AFTER THEIR SKIRMISH AT THE PALACE.
ONE OF THEM WEEPS.
I SWEAR DUDE THAT BIRD IS TALKING
HO THERE! CHOPPY SEAS, WHAT? HAVE YOU SEEN A ROWBOAT COME BY HERE LATELY?
MARK GET THE GUN GET THE GUN QUICK NO SUDDEN MOVES
I DIDN'T BRING THE GUN. I'M TIRED OF THESE OUTINGS ALWAYS BEING SO VIOLENT.
NO, RIGHT THERE IN THE GUITAR CASE! I REMEMER LOADING IT ABOARD!
AH!
THE BITTER WAFT OF RAILROAD OIL! THE TRAIL GROWS WARM ANON!
I TAKE MY LEAVE, CHAPPIES!
THAT WAS AN ACTUAL GUITAR. YOU KNOW, FOR THE LONELY HOURS.
ARRRGGHHH MARK I TOLD YOU I DO NOT WANT TO HEAR YOUR DEMO
IT'S COOL! IT'S COOL! JUST IF YOU COULD FORWARD MY MYSPACE TO YOUR FRIEND WHO WORKS IN A&R IS ALL!
GUYS I THINK WE MIGHT HAVE A PROBLEM
WHAT KIND OF PROBLEM?
THE LEGENDARY RAILROAD COVE!
SITE OF THAT INFAMOUS ZEPPELIN DISASTER!
O DARK DAY! WHEN LOCOMOTIVES FELL LIKE STEEL HAIL FROM THE HEAVENS...

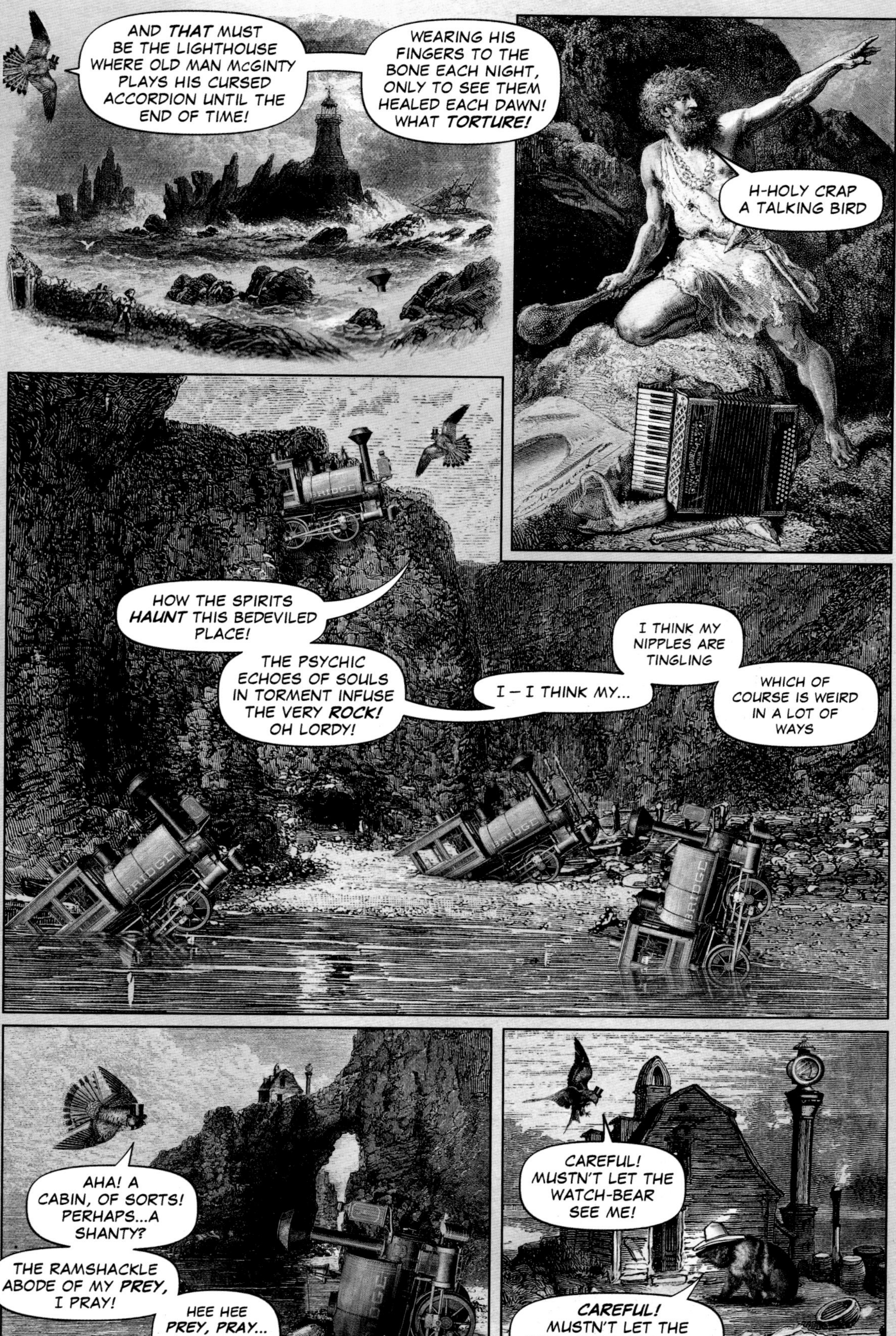
AND THAT MUST BE THE LIGHTHOUSE WHERE OLD MAN McGINTY PLAYS HIS CURSED ACCORDION UNTIL THE END OF TIME!
WEARING HIS FINGERS TO THE BONE EACH NIGHT, ONLY TO SEE THEM HEALED EACH DAWN! WHAT TORTURE!
H-HOLY CRAP A TALKING BIRD
HOW THE SPIRITS HAUNT THIS BEDEVILED PLACE!
THE PSYCHIC ECHOES OF SOULS IN TORMENT INFUSE THE VERY ROCK! OH LORDY!
I — I THINK MY...
I THINK MY NIPPLES ARE TINGLING
WHICH OF COURSE IS WEIRD IN A LOT OF WAYS
AHA! A CABIN, OF SORTS! PERHAPS...A SHANTY?
THE RAMSHACKLE ABODE OF MY PREY, I PRAY!
HEE HEE PREY, PRAY... GOTTA WRITE THAT ONE DOWN
CAREFUL! MUSTN'T LET THE WATCH-BEAR SEE ME!
CAREFUL! MUSTN'T LET THE BIRD KNOW HE'S BEING FRIKKIN LOUD

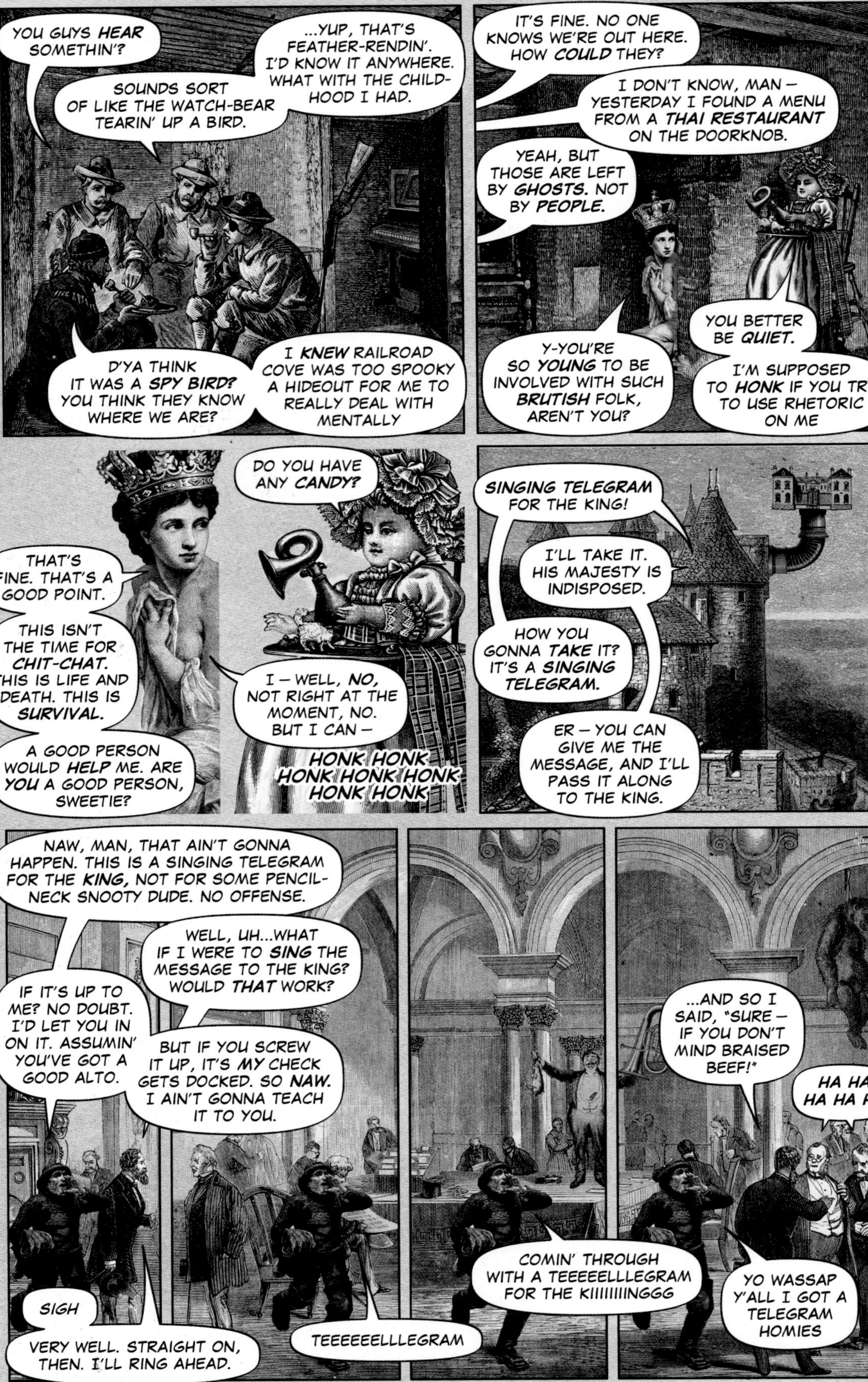
YOU GUYS HEAR SOMETHIN'?
SOUNDS SORT OF LIKE THE WATCH-BEAR TEARIN' UP A BIRD.
...YUP, THAT'S FEATHER-RENDIN'. I'D KNOW IT ANYWHERE. WHAT WITH THE CHILD-HOOD I HAD.
D'YA THINK IT WAS A SPY BIRD? YOU THINK THEY KNOW WHERE WE ARE?
I KNEW RAILROAD COVE WAS TOO SPOOKY A HIDEOUT FOR ME TO REALLY DEAL WITH MENTALLY
IT'S FINE. NO ONE KNOWS WE'RE OUT HERE. HOW COULD THEY?
I DON'T KNOW, MAN — YESTERDAY I FOUND A MENU FROM A THAI RESTAURANT ON THE DOORKNOB.
YEAH, BUT THOSE ARE LEFT BY GHOSTS. NOT BY PEOPLE.
Y-YOU'RE SO YOUNG TO BE INVOLVED WITH SUCH BRUTISH FOLK, AREN'T YOU?
YOU BETTER BE QUIET.
I'M SUPPOSED TO HONK IF YOU TRY TO USE RHETORIC ON ME
DO YOU HAVE ANY CANDY?
THAT'S FINE. THAT'S A GOOD POINT.
THIS ISN'T THE TIME FOR CHIT-CHAT. THIS IS LIFE AND DEATH. THIS IS SURVIVAL.
A GOOD PERSON WOULD HELP ME. ARE YOU A GOOD PERSON, SWEETIE?
I — WELL, NO, NOT RIGHT AT THE MOMENT, NO. BUT I CAN —
HONK HONK HONK HONK HONK HONK HONK
SINGING TELEGRAM FOR THE KING!
I'LL TAKE IT. HIS MAJESTY IS INDISPOSED.
HOW YOU GONNA TAKE IT? IT'S A SINGING TELEGRAM.
ER — YOU CAN GIVE ME THE MESSAGE, AND I'LL PASS IT ALONG TO THE KING.
NAW, MAN, THAT AIN'T GONNA HAPPEN. THIS IS A SINGING TELEGRAM FOR THE KING, NOT FOR SOME PENCIL-NECK SNOOTY DUDE. NO OFFENSE.
WELL, UH...WHAT IF I WERE TO SING THE MESSAGE TO THE KING? WOULD THAT WORK?
IF IT'S UP TO ME? NO DOUBT. I'D LET YOU IN ON IT. ASSUMIN' YOU'VE GOT A GOOD ALTO.
BUT IF YOU SCREW IT UP, IT'S MY CHECK GETS DOCKED. SO NAW. I AIN'T GONNA TEACH IT TO YOU.
SIGH
VERY WELL. STRAIGHT ON, THEN. I'LL RING AHEAD.
TEEEEEELLLEGRAM
COMIN' THROUGH WITH A TEEEEELLLEGRAM FOR THE KIIIIIIINGGG
...AND SO I SAID, "SURE — IF YOU DON'T MIND BRAISED BEEF!"
HA HA HA HA HA
YO WASSAP Y'ALL I GOT A TELEGRAM HOMIES

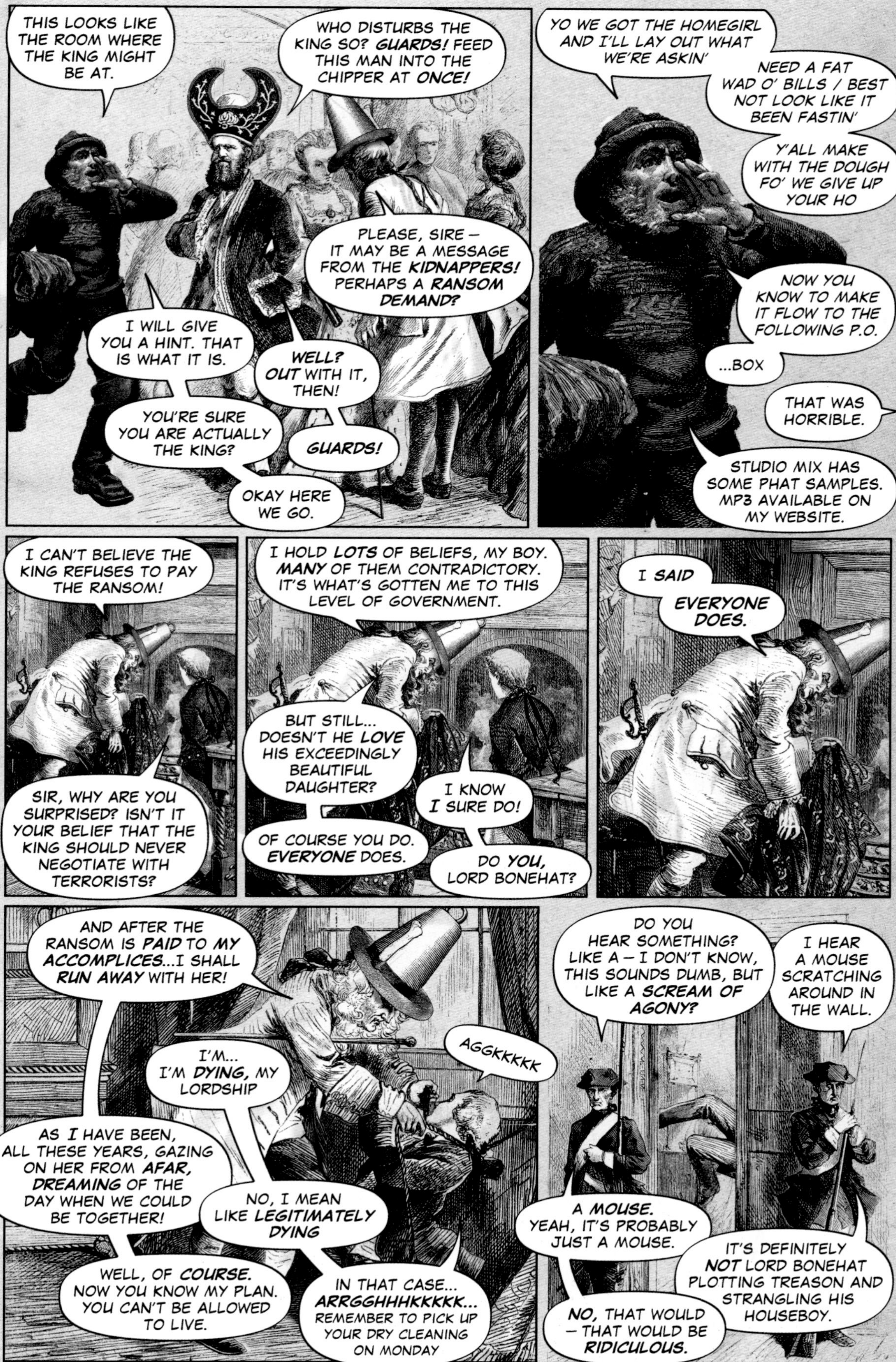
THIS LOOKS LIKE THE ROOM WHERE THE KING MIGHT BE AT.
WHO DISTURBS THE KING SO? GUARDS! FEED THIS MAN INTO THE CHIPPER AT ONCE!
PLEASE, SIRE — IT MAY BE A MESSAGE FROM THE KIDNAPPERS! PERHAPS A RANSOM DEMAND?
I WILL GIVE YOU A HINT. THAT IS WHAT IT IS.
WELL? OUT WITH IT, THEN!
YOU'RE SURE YOU ARE ACTUALLY THE KING?
GUARDS!
OKAY HERE WE GO.
YO WE GOT THE HOMEGIRL AND I'LL LAY OUT WHAT WE'RE ASKIN'
NEED A FAT WAD O' BILLS / BEST NOT LOOK LIKE IT BEEN FASTIN'
Y'ALL MAKE WITH THE DOUGH FO' WE GIVE UP YOUR HO
NOW YOU KNOW TO MAKE IT FLOW TO THE FOLLOWING P.O.
...BOX
THAT WAS HORRIBLE.
STUDIO MIX HAS SOME PHAT SAMPLES. MP3 AVAILABLE ON MY WEBSITE.
I CAN'T BELIEVE THE KING REFUSES TO PAY THE RANSOM!
SIR, WHY ARE YOU SURPRISED? ISN'T IT YOUR BELIEF THAT THE KING SHOULD NEVER NEGOTIATE WITH TERRORISTS?
I HOLD LOTS OF BELIEFS, MY BOY. MANY OF THEM CONTRADICTORY. IT'S WHAT'S GOTTEN ME TO THIS LEVEL OF GOVERNMENT.
BUT STILL... DOESN'T HE LOVE HIS EXCEEDINGLY BEAUTIFUL DAUGHTER?
OF COURSE YOU DO. EVERYONE DOES.
I KNOW I SURE DO!
DO YOU, LORD BONEHAT?
I SAID EVERYONE DOES.
AND AFTER THE RANSOM IS PAID TO MY ACCOMPLICES...I SHALL RUN AWAY WITH HER!
I'M... I'M DYING, MY LORDSHIP
AGGKKKKK
AS I HAVE BEEN, ALL THESE YEARS, GAZING ON HER FROM AFAR, DREAMING OF THE DAY WHEN WE COULD BE TOGETHER!
NO, I MEAN LIKE LEGITIMATELY DYING
WELL, OF COURSE. NOW YOU KNOW MY PLAN. YOU CAN'T BE ALLOWED TO LIVE.
IN THAT CASE... ARRGGHHHKKKKK... REMEMBER TO PICK UP YOUR DRY CLEANING ON MONDAY
DO YOU HEAR SOMETHING? LIKE A — I DON'T KNOW, THIS SOUNDS DUMB, BUT LIKE A SCREAM OF AGONY?
I HEAR A MOUSE SCRATCHING AROUND IN THE WALL.
A MOUSE. YEAH, IT'S PROBABLY JUST A MOUSE.
IT'S DEFINITELY NOT LORD BONEHAT PLOTTING TREASON AND STRANGLING HIS HOUSEBOY.
NO, THAT WOULD — THAT WOULD BE RIDICULOUS.

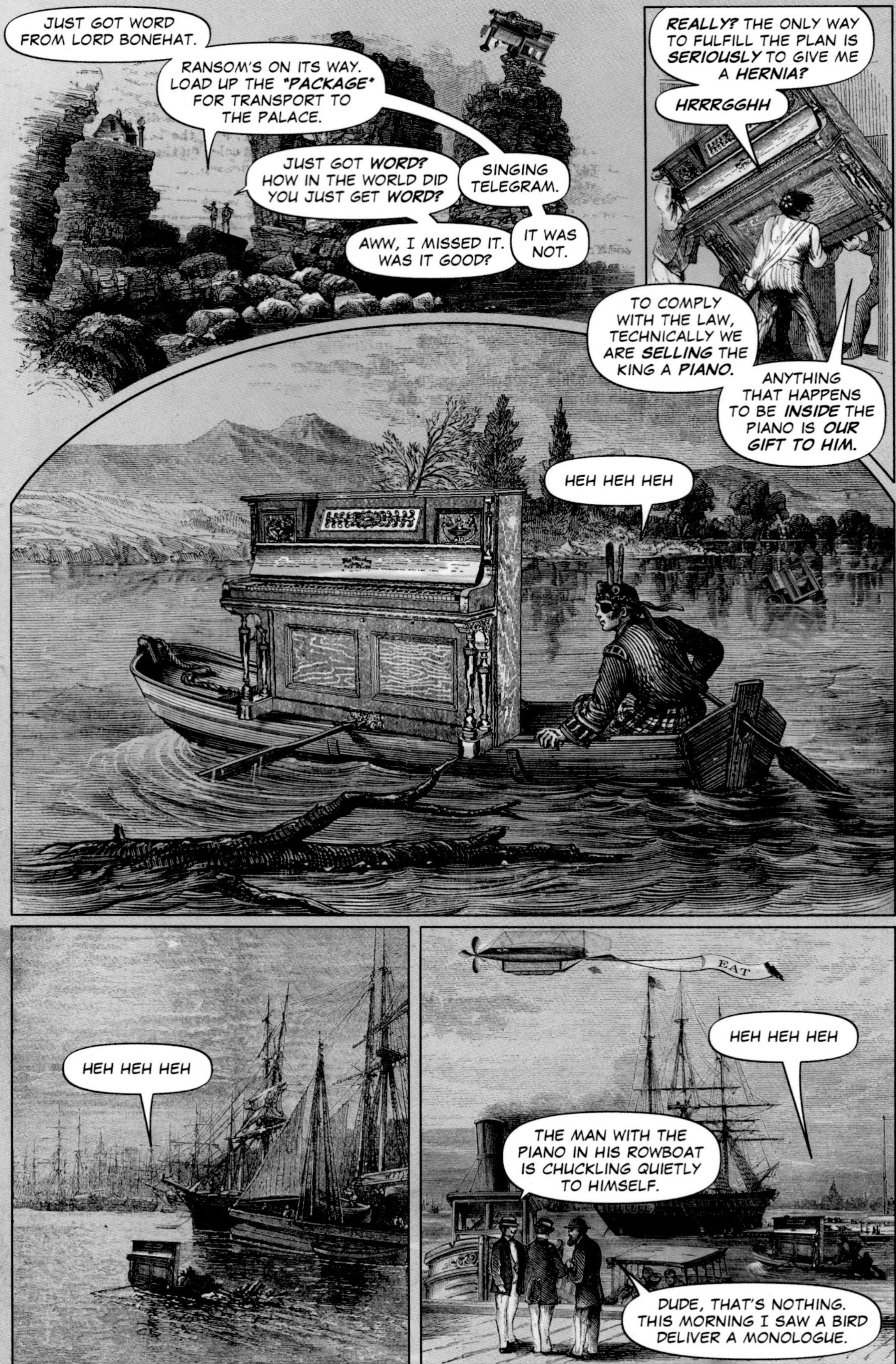
JUST GOT WORD FROM LORD BONEHAT.
RANSOM'S ON ITS WAY. LOAD UP THE "PACKAGE" FOR TRANSPORT TO THE PALACE.
JUST GOT WORD? HOW IN THE WORLD DID YOU JUST GET WORD?
SINGING TELEGRAM.
AWW, I MISSED IT. WAS IT GOOD?
IT WAS NOT.
REALLY? THE ONLY WAY TO FULFILL THE PLAN IS SERIOUSLY TO GIVE ME A HERNIA?
HRRRGGHH
TO COMPLY WITH THE LAW, TECHNICALLY WE ARE SELLING THE KING A PIANO.
ANYTHING THAT HAPPENS TO BE INSIDE THE PIANO IS OUR GIFT TO HIM.
HEH HEH HEH
HEH HEH HEH
EAT
HEH HEH HEH
THE MAN WITH THE PIANO IN HIS ROWBOAT IS CHUCKLING QUIETLY TO HIMSELF.
DUDE, THAT'S NOTHING. THIS MORNING I SAW A BIRD DELIVER A MONOLOGUE.

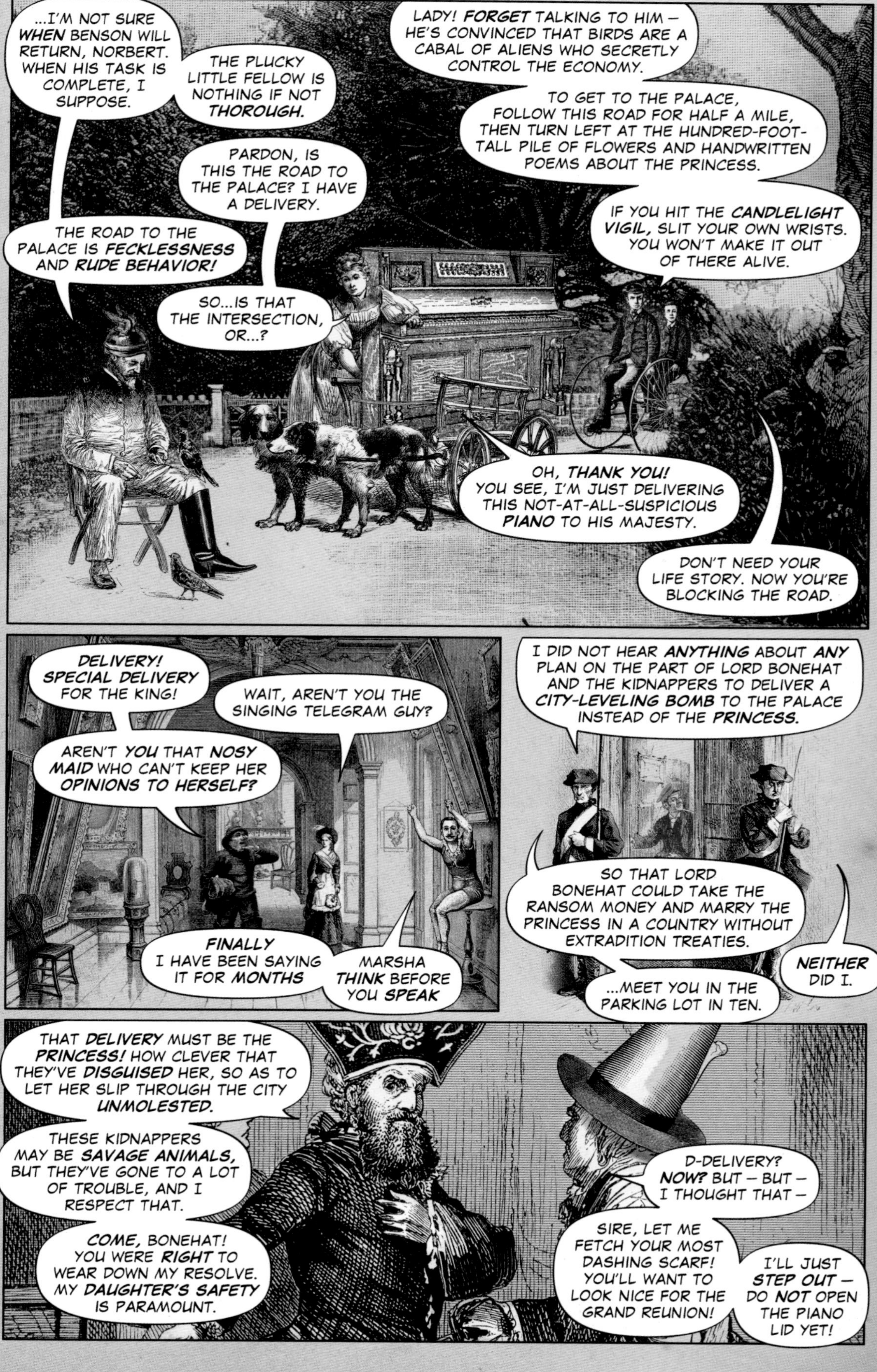
...I'M NOT SURE WHEN BENSON WILL RETURN, NORBERT. WHEN HIS TASK IS COMPLETE, I SUPPOSE.
THE PLUCKY LITTLE FELLOW IS NOTHING IF NOT THOROUGH.
PARDON, IS THIS THE ROAD TO THE PALACE? I HAVE A DELIVERY.
THE ROAD TO THE PALACE IS FECKLESSNESS AND RUDE BEHAVIOR!
SO...IS THAT THE INTERSECTION, OR...?
LADY! FORGET TALKING TO HIM – HE'S CONVINCED THAT BIRDS ARE A CABAL OF ALIENS WHO SECRETLY CONTROL THE ECONOMY.
TO GET TO THE PALACE, FOLLOW THIS ROAD FOR HALF A MILE, THEN TURN LEFT AT THE HUNDRED-FOOT-TALL PILE OF FLOWERS AND HANDWRITTEN POEMS ABOUT THE PRINCESS.
IF YOU HIT THE CANDLELIGHT VIGIL, SLIT YOUR OWN WRISTS. YOU WON'T MAKE IT OUT OF THERE ALIVE.
OH, THANK YOU! YOU SEE, I'M JUST DELIVERING THIS NOT-AT-ALL-SUSPICIOUS PIANO TO HIS MAJESTY.
DON'T NEED YOUR LIFE STORY. NOW YOU'RE BLOCKING THE ROAD.
DELIVERY! SPECIAL DELIVERY FOR THE KING!
WAIT, AREN'T YOU THE SINGING TELEGRAM GUY?
AREN'T YOU THAT NOSY MAID WHO CAN'T KEEP HER OPINIONS TO HERSELF?
FINALLY I HAVE BEEN SAYING IT FOR MONTHS
MARSHA THINK BEFORE YOU SPEAK
I DID NOT HEAR ANYTHING ABOUT ANY PLAN ON THE PART OF LORD BONEHAT AND THE KIDNAPPERS TO DELIVER A CITY-LEVELING BOMB TO THE PALACE INSTEAD OF THE PRINCESS.
SO THAT LORD BONEHAT COULD TAKE THE RANSOM MONEY AND MARRY THE PRINCESS IN A COUNTRY WITHOUT EXTRADITION TREATIES.
NEITHER DID I.
...MEET YOU IN THE PARKING LOT IN TEN.
THAT DELIVERY MUST BE THE PRINCESS! HOW CLEVER THAT THEY'VE DISGUISED HER, SO AS TO LET HER SLIP THROUGH THE CITY UNMOLESTED.
THESE KIDNAPPERS MAY BE SAVAGE ANIMALS, BUT THEY'VE GONE TO A LOT OF TROUBLE, AND I RESPECT THAT.
COME, BONEHAT! YOU WERE RIGHT TO WEAR DOWN MY RESOLVE. MY DAUGHTER'S SAFETY IS PARAMOUNT.
D-DELIVERY? NOW? BUT – BUT – I THOUGHT THAT –
SIRE, LET ME FETCH YOUR MOST DASHING SCARF! YOU'LL WANT TO LOOK NICE FOR THE GRAND REUNION!
I'LL JUST STEP OUT – DO NOT OPEN THE PIANO LID YET!

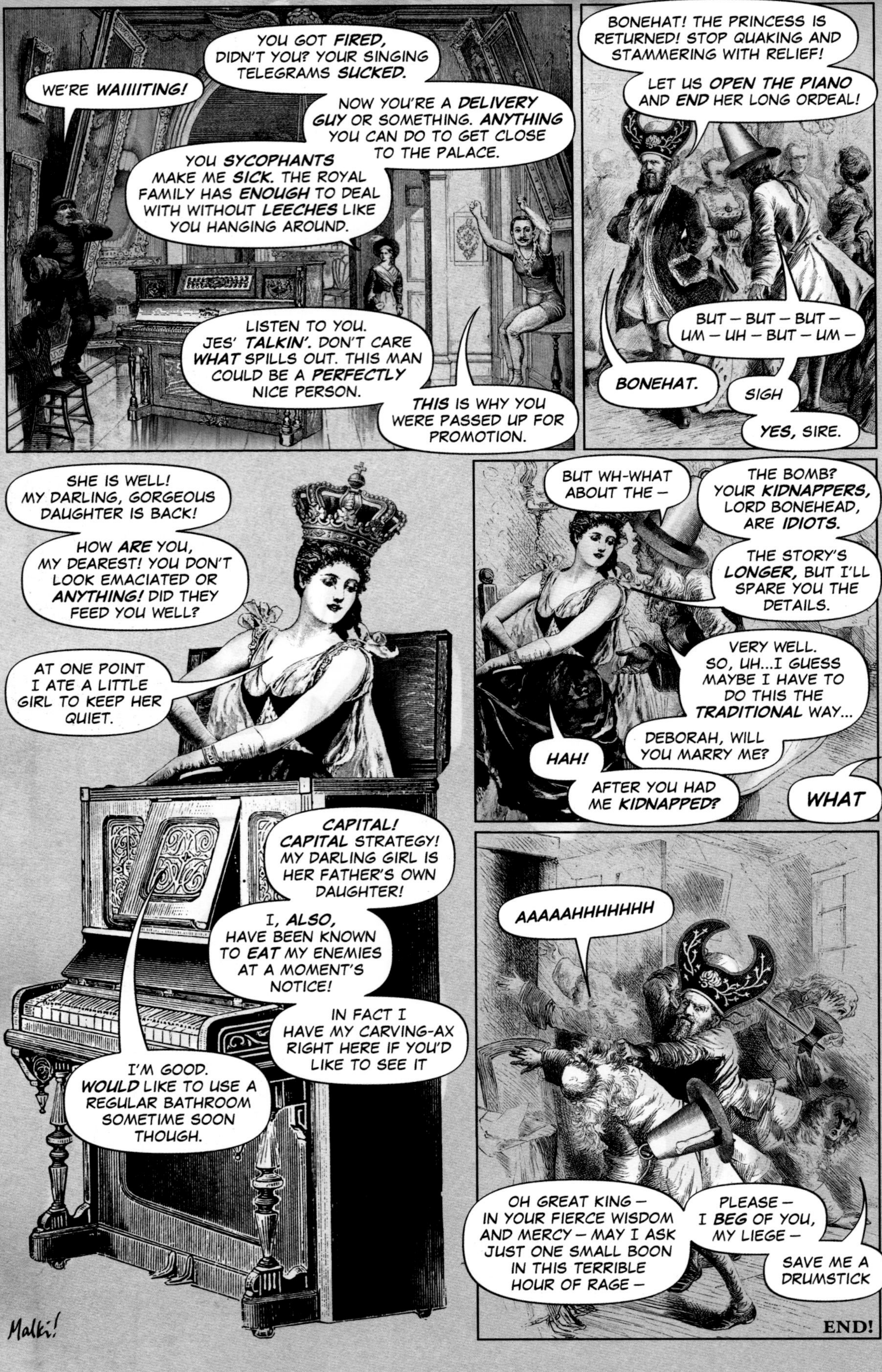

WE'RE WAIIIITING!
YOU GOT FIRED, DIDN'T YOU? YOUR SINGING TELEGRAMS SUCKED.
NOW YOU'RE A DELIVERY GUY OR SOMETHING. ANYTHING YOU CAN DO TO GET CLOSE TO THE PALACE.
YOU SYCOPHANTS MAKE ME SICK. THE ROYAL FAMILY HAS ENOUGH TO DEAL WITH WITHOUT LEECHES LIKE YOU HANGING AROUND.
LISTEN TO YOU. JES' TALKIN'. DON'T CARE WHAT SPILLS OUT. THIS MAN COULD BE A PERFECTLY NICE PERSON.
THIS IS WHY YOU WERE PASSED UP FOR PROMOTION.
BONEHAT! THE PRINCESS IS RETURNED! STOP QUAKING AND STAMMERING WITH RELIEF!
LET US OPEN THE PIANO AND END HER LONG ORDEAL!
BUT — BUT — BUT — UM — UH — BUT — UM —
BONEHAT.
SIGH
YES, SIRE.
SHE IS WELL! MY DARLING, GORGEOUS DAUGHTER IS BACK!
HOW ARE YOU, MY DEAREST! YOU DON'T LOOK EMACIATED OR ANYTHING! DID THEY FEED YOU WELL?
AT ONE POINT I ATE A LITTLE GIRL TO KEEP HER QUIET.
CAPITAL! CAPITAL STRATEGY! MY DARLING GIRL IS HER FATHER'S OWN DAUGHTER!
I, ALSO, HAVE BEEN KNOWN TO EAT MY ENEMIES AT A MOMENT'S NOTICE!
IN FACT I HAVE MY CARVING-AX RIGHT HERE IF YOU'D LIKE TO SEE IT
I'M GOOD. WOULD LIKE TO USE A REGULAR BATHROOM SOMETIME SOON THOUGH.
BUT WH-WHAT ABOUT THE —
THE BOMB? YOUR KIDNAPPERS, LORD BONEHEAD, ARE IDIOTS.
THE STORY'S LONGER, BUT I'LL SPARE YOU THE DETAILS.
VERY WELL. SO, UH...I GUESS MAYBE I HAVE TO DO THIS THE TRADITIONAL WAY...
DEBORAH, WILL YOU MARRY ME?
HAH!
AFTER YOU HAD ME KIDNAPPED?
WHAT
AAAAAHHHHHH
OH GREAT KING — IN YOUR FIERCE WISDOM AND MERCY — MAY I ASK JUST ONE SMALL BOON IN THIS TERRIBLE HOUR OF RAGE —
PLEASE — I BEG OF YOU, MY LIEGE —
SAVE ME A DRUMSTICK
Malki!
END!

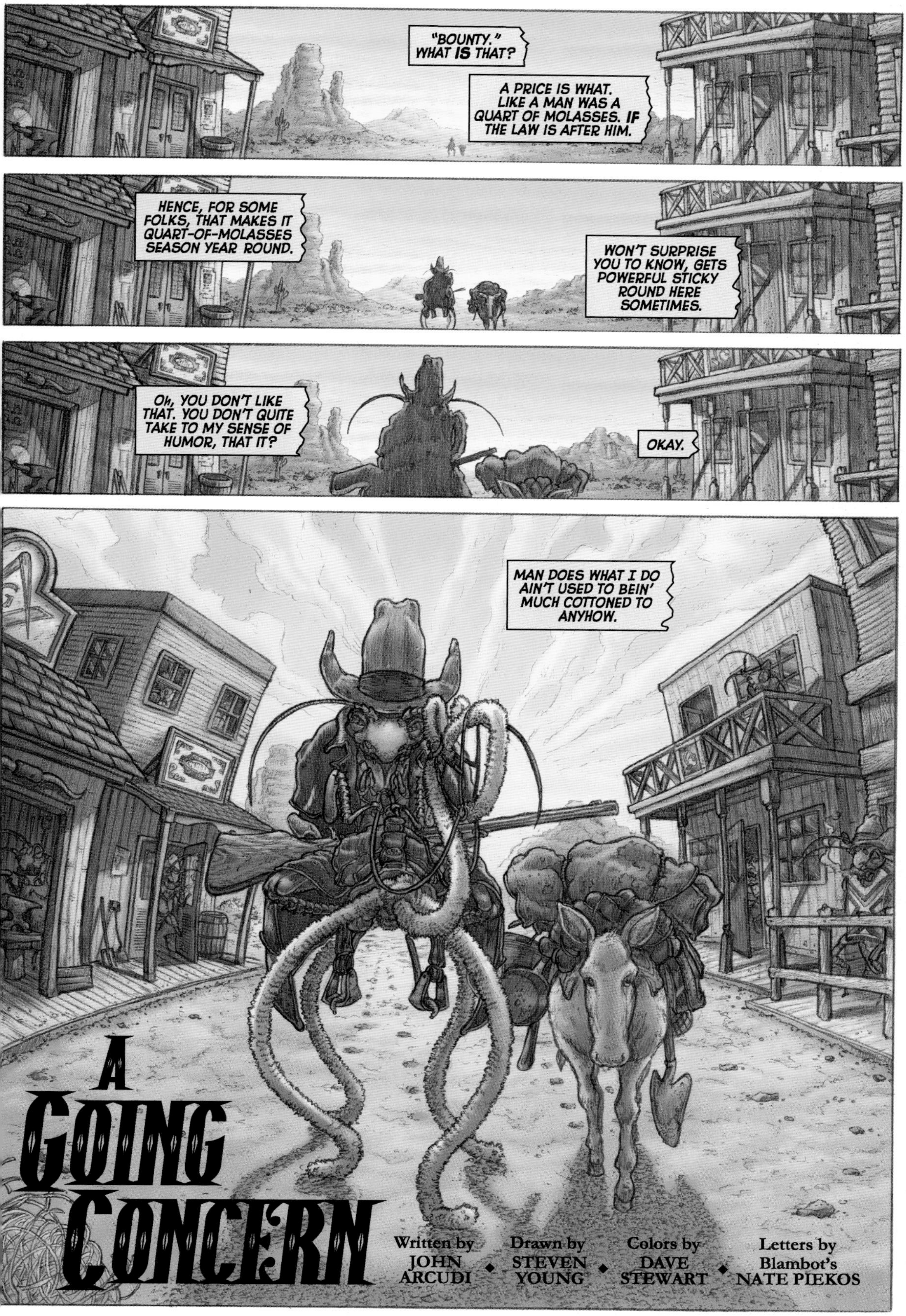
"BOUNTY." WHAT IS THAT?
A PRICE IS WHAT. LIKE A MAN WAS A QUART OF MOLASSES. IF THE LAW IS AFTER HIM.
HENCE, FOR SOME FOLKS, THAT MAKES IT QUART-OF-MOLASSES SEASON YEAR ROUND.
WON'T SURPRISE YOU TO KNOW, GETS POWERFUL STICKY ROUND HERE SOMETIMES.
Oh, YOU DON'T LIKE THAT. YOU DON'T QUITE TAKE TO MY SENSE OF HUMOR, THAT IT?
OKAY.
MAN DOES WHAT I DO AIN'T USED TO BEIN' MUCH COTTONED TO ANYHOW.
A GOING CONCERN
Written by JOHN ARCUDI
Drawn by STEVEN YOUNG
Colors by DAVE STEWART
Letters by Blambot's NATE PIEKOS

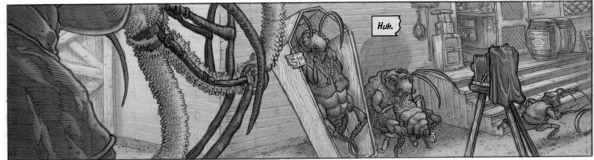

Huh.

QUITE A MESSAGE YOU MEAN TO SEND WOULD-BE ROGUES. WHAT BEFELL HIM?

SHOULD HAVE BEEN NOTHING. HE HAD TO HAVE IT HIS WAY, THOUGH.

STARTED A SET-TO IN YONDER SALOON. PUNCHING, KICKING, SPILLED OUT ONTO THE STREET. SHERIFF BROKE IT UP, BUT--SMART FELLA HERE, HE PULLED HIS GUN.

AND THAT WAS *THAT,* huh?

SO YOU KNOW, THIS IS NO MESSAGE. WE'RE CIVILIZED HERE IN PECOS. BOY'S A STRANGER. DISPLAYING HIM THIS WAY, PEOPLE PASSING THROUGH MIGHT RECOGNIZE HIM. GET HIM TO HOME.

DOLLAR. CIVILIZED-ENOUGH PRICE.

BROTHER, I *BUILT* THIS CASKET.

I DON'T WANT TROUBLE, BUT I CAN'T SEE HOW MY MAKING AN HONEST PROFIT SHOULD BOTHER ANYBODY.

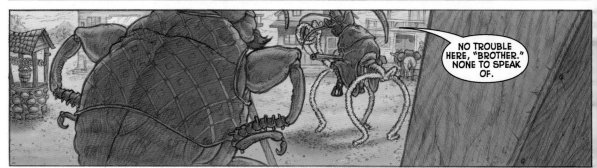

NO TROUBLE HERE, "BROTHER." NONE TO SPEAK OF.

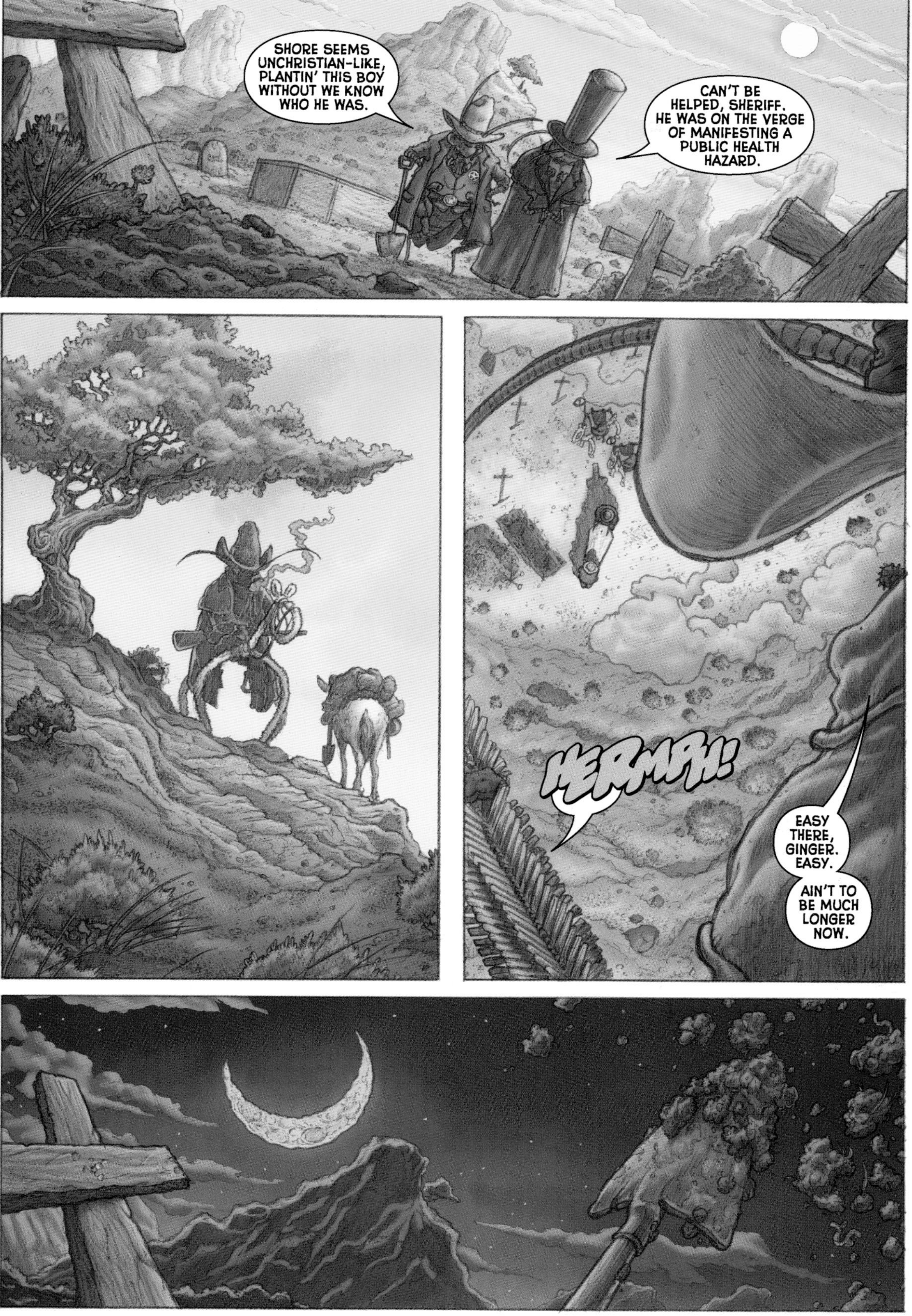
SHORE SEEMS UNCHRISTIAN-LIKE, PLANTIN' THIS BOY WITHOUT WE KNOW WHO HE WAS.
CAN'T BE HELPED, SHERIFF. HE WAS ON THE VERGE OF MANIFESTING A PUBLIC HEALTH HAZARD.
HERMPH!
EASY THERE, GINGER. EASY.
AIN'T TO BE MUCH LONGER NOW.

SO WHAT DO YOU SAY THERE, HOMER? WHAT WE GON' TALK 'BOUT?

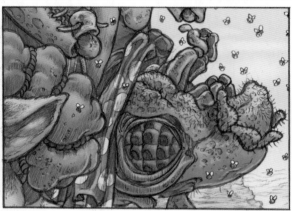

Aww, NOW LOOK, I AIN'T A BAD SORT.

YOU DIDN'T WANNA STAY IN PECOS NO WAYS, FOLKS NOT EVEN KNOWIN' WHO YOU WAS.

AND ME, I CAN'T HELP IT IF IT'S MY BUSINESS TO KNOW.

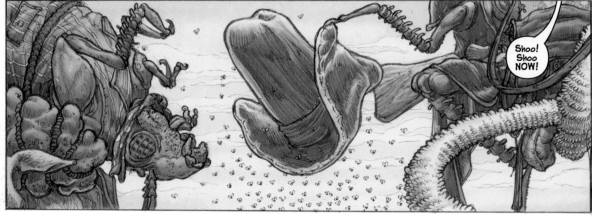

Shoo! Shoo NOW!

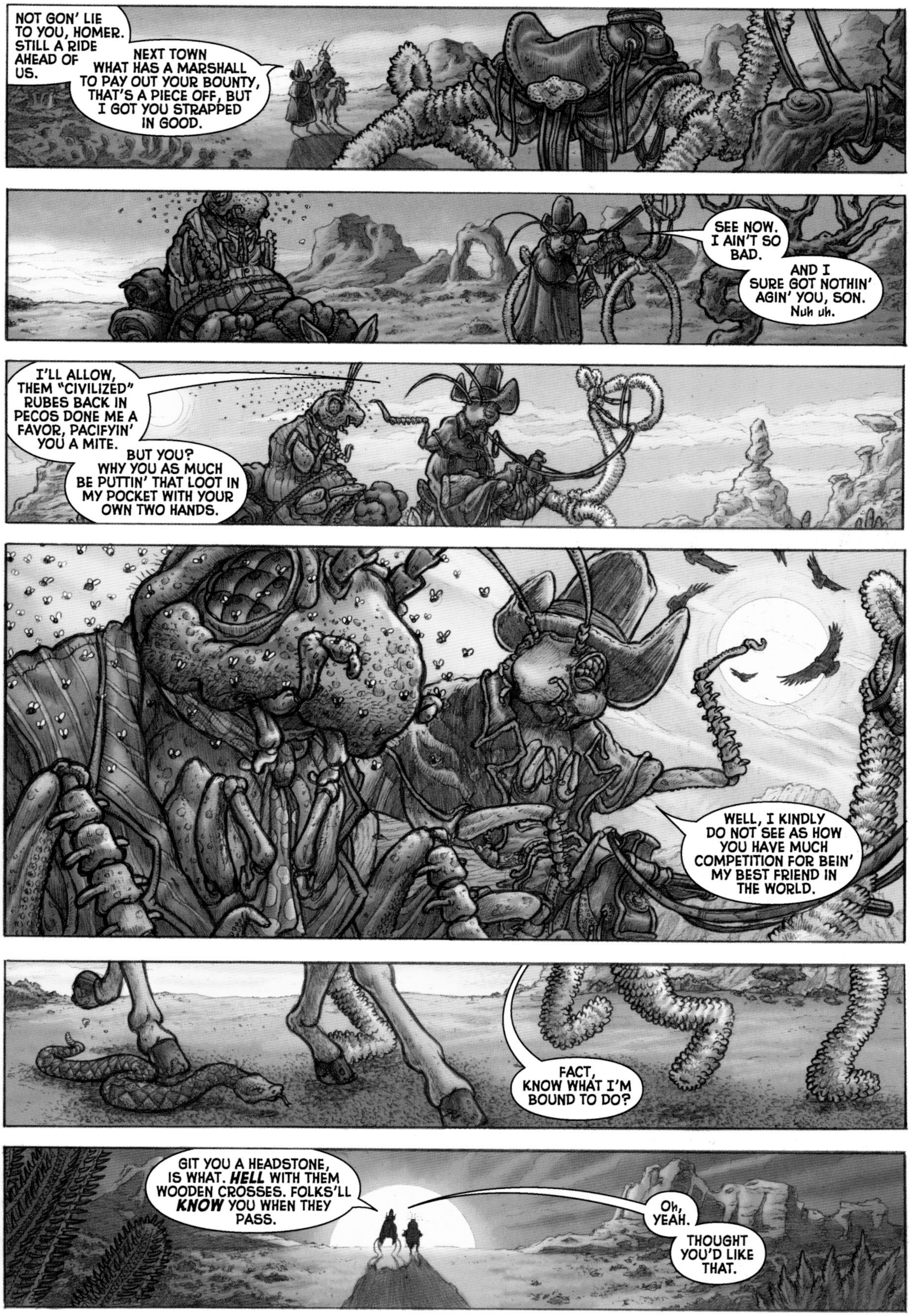
NOT GON' LIE TO YOU, HOMER. STILL A RIDE AHEAD OF US.
NEXT TOWN WHAT HAS A MARSHALL TO PAY OUT YOUR BOUNTY, THAT'S A PIECE OFF, BUT I GOT YOU STRAPPED IN GOOD.
SEE NOW. I AIN'T SO BAD.
AND I SURE GOT NOTHIN' AGIN' YOU, SON. Nuh uh.
I'LL ALLOW, THEM "CIVILIZED" RUBES BACK IN PECOS DONE ME A FAVOR, PACIFYIN' YOU A MITE.
BUT YOU? WHY YOU AS MUCH BE PUTTIN' THAT LOOT IN MY POCKET WITH YOUR OWN TWO HANDS.
WELL, I KINDLY DO NOT SEE AS HOW YOU HAVE MUCH COMPETITION FOR BEIN' MY BEST FRIEND IN THE WORLD.
FACT, KNOW WHAT I'M BOUND TO DO?
GIT YOU A HEADSTONE, IS WHAT. HELL WITH THEM WOODEN CROSSES. FOLKS'LL KNOW YOU WHEN THEY PASS.
Oh, YEAH.
THOUGHT YOU'D LIKE THAT.

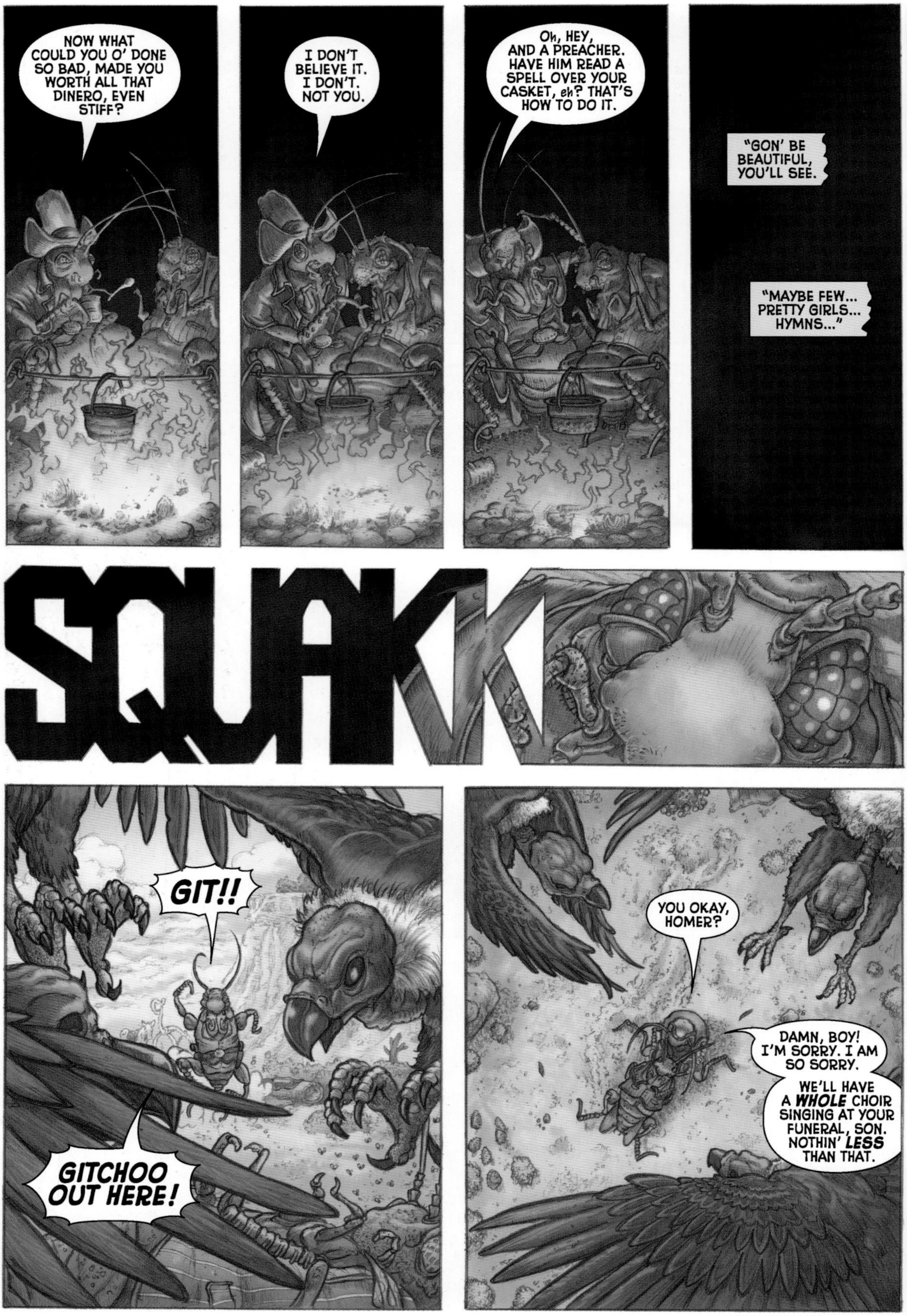
NOW WHAT COULD YOU O' DONE SO BAD, MADE YOU WORTH ALL THAT DINERO, EVEN STIFF?
I DON'T BELIEVE IT. I DON'T. NOT YOU.
Oh, HEY, AND A PREACHER. HAVE HIM READ A SPELL OVER YOUR CASKET, eh? THAT'S HOW TO DO IT.
"GON' BE BEAUTIFUL, YOU'LL SEE.
"MAYBE FEW... PRETTY GIRLS... HYMNS..."
SQUAKK
GIT!!
GITCHOO OUT HERE!
YOU OKAY, HOMER?
DAMN, BOY! I'M SORRY. I AM SO SORRY.
WE'LL HAVE A WHOLE CHOIR SINGING AT YOUR FUNERAL, SON. NOTHIN' LESS THAN THAT.

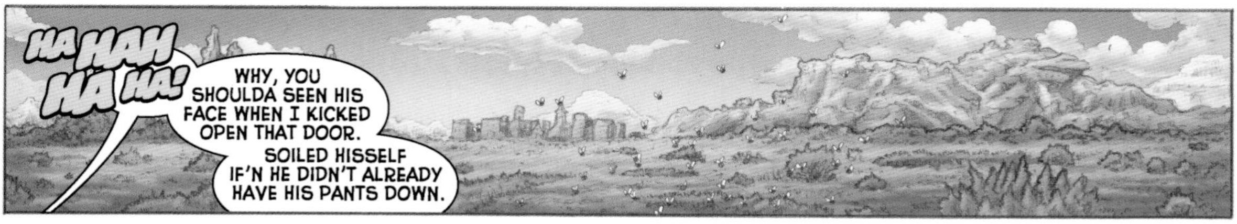
HA HAH HA HA!
WHY, YOU SHOULDA SEEN HIS FACE WHEN I KICKED OPEN THAT DOOR.
SOILED HISSELF IF'N HE DIDN'T ALREADY HAVE HIS PANTS DOWN.

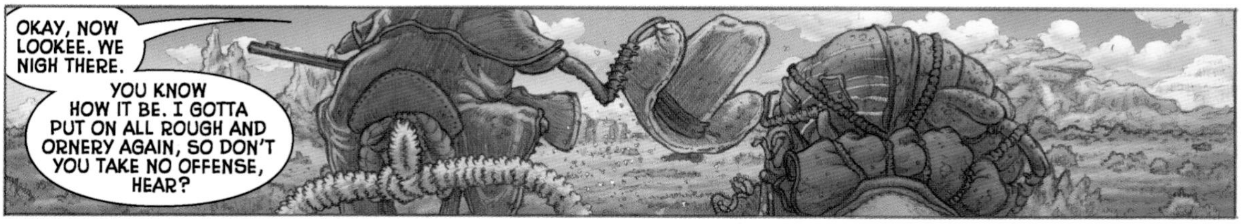
OKAY, NOW LOOKEE. WE NIGH THERE.
YOU KNOW HOW IT BE. I GOTTA PUT ON ALL ROUGH AND ORNERY AGAIN, SO DON'T YOU TAKE NO OFFENSE, HEAR?

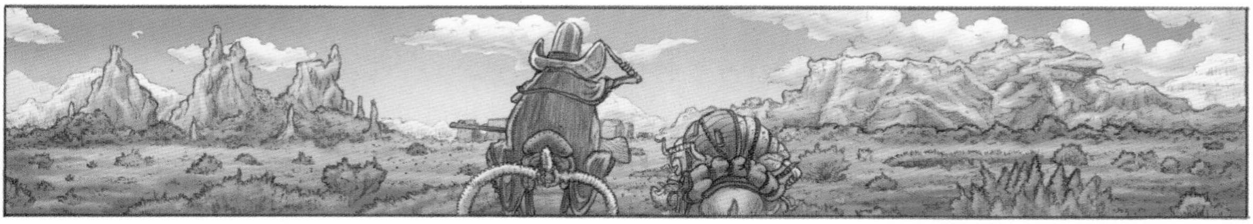

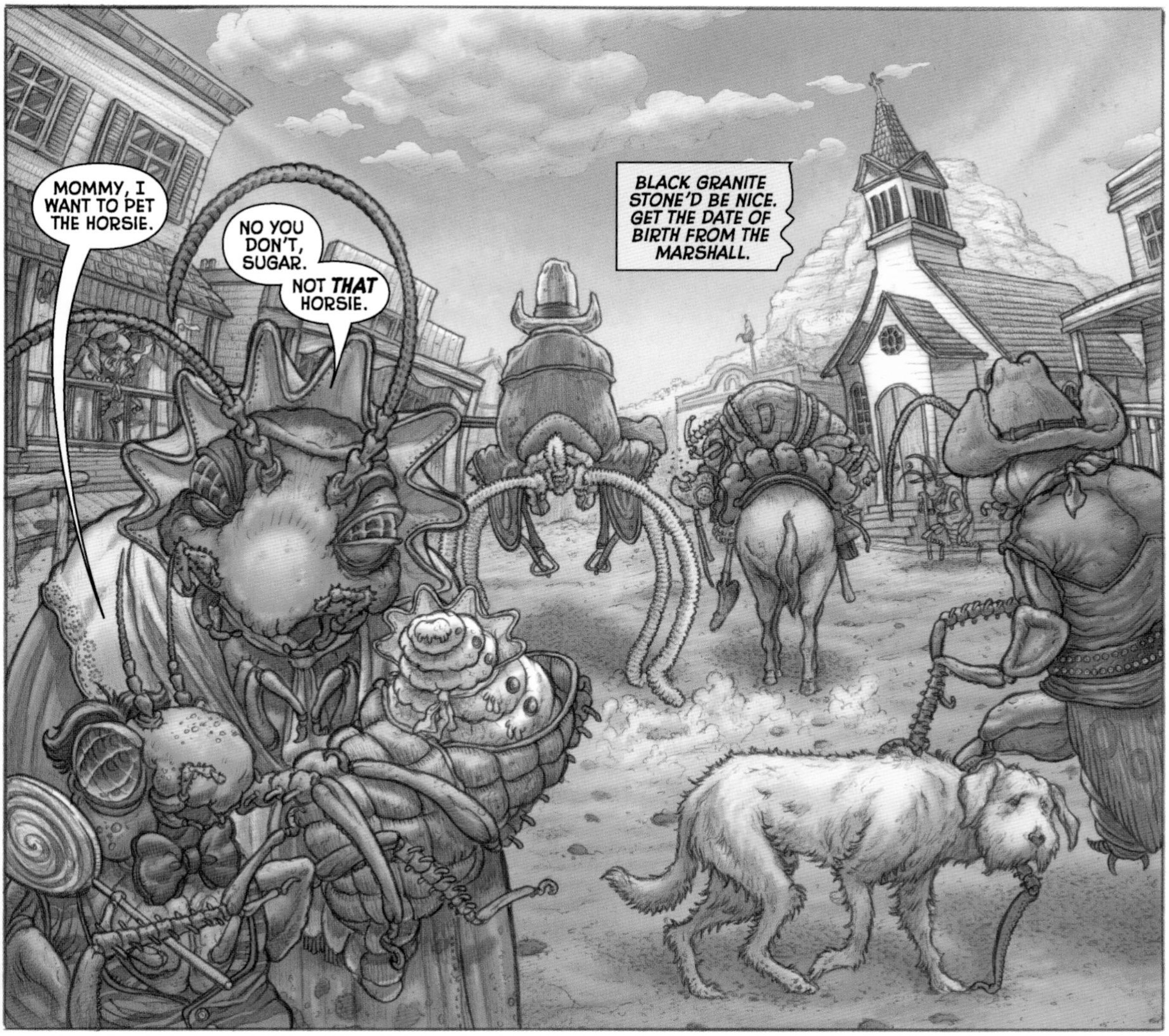
MOMMY, I WANT TO PET THE HORSIE.
NO YOU DON'T, SUGAR.
NOT **THAT** HORSIE.
BLACK GRANITE STONE'D BE NICE. GET THE DATE OF BIRTH FROM THE MARSHALL.

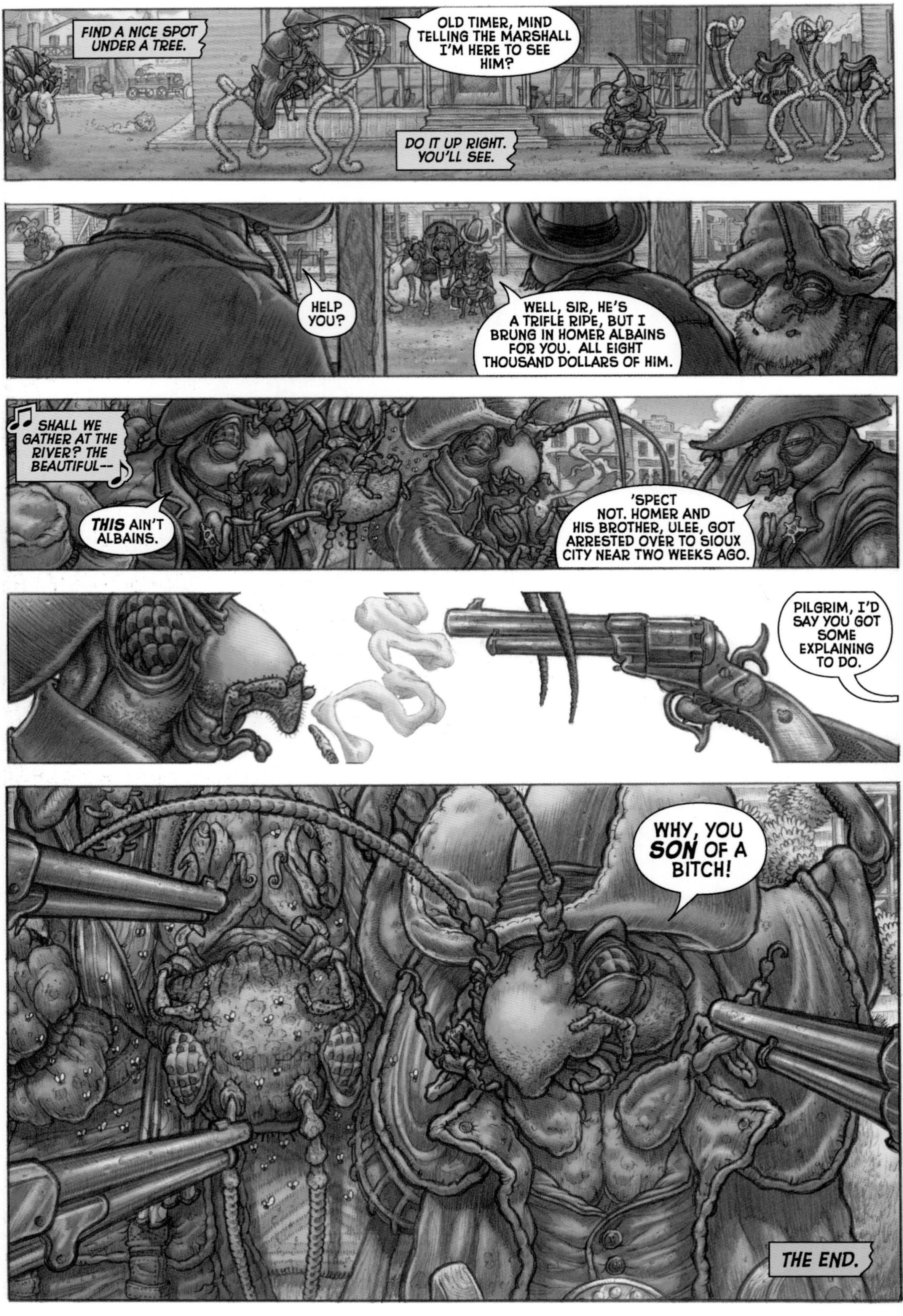
FIND A NICE SPOT UNDER A TREE.
OLD TIMER, MIND TELLING THE MARSHALL I'M HERE TO SEE HIM?
DO IT UP RIGHT. YOU'LL SEE.
HELP YOU?
WELL, SIR, HE'S A TRIFLE RIPE, BUT I BRUNG IN HOMER ALBAINS FOR YOU. ALL EIGHT THOUSAND DOLLARS OF HIM.
♪ SHALL WE GATHER AT THE RIVER? THE BEAUTIFUL-- ♪
THIS AIN'T ALBAINS.
'SPECT NOT. HOMER AND HIS BROTHER, ULEE, GOT ARRESTED OVER TO SIOUX CITY NEAR TWO WEEKS AGO.
PILGRIM, I'D SAY YOU GOT SOME EXPLAINING TO DO.
WHY, YOU SON OF A BITCH!
THE END.

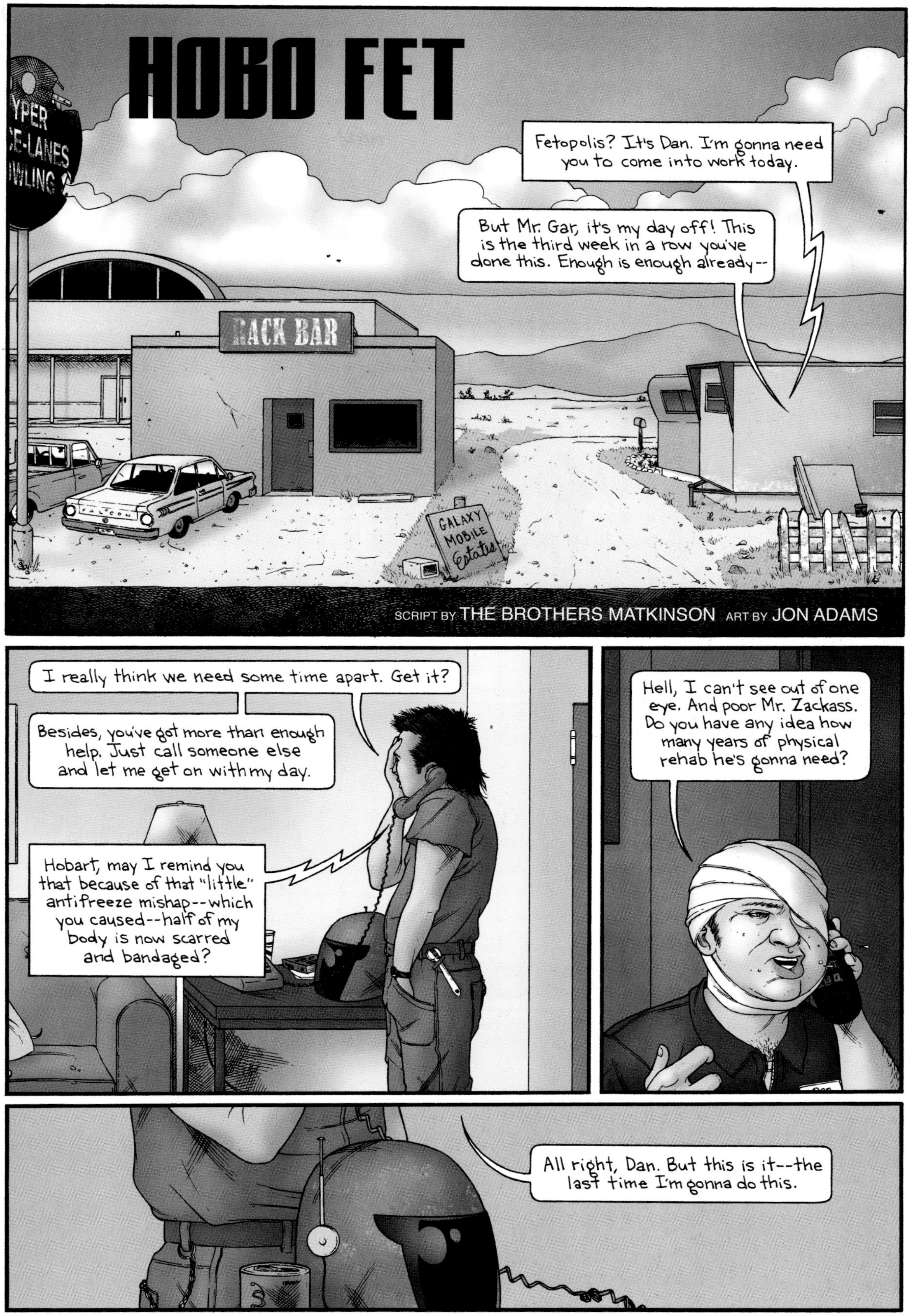
HOBO FET
YPER
CE-LANES
WLING
Fetopolis? It's Dan. I'm gonna need you to come into work today.
But Mr. Gar, it's my day off! This is the third week in a row you've done this. Enough is enough already--
RACK BAR
FALCON
GALAXY MOBILE Estates
SCRIPT BY THE BROTHERS MATKINSON ART BY JON ADAMS
I really think we need some time apart. Get it?
Besides, you've got more than enough help. Just call someone else and let me get on with my day.
Hobart, may I remind you that because of that "little" antifreeze mishap--which you caused--half of my body is now scarred and bandaged?
Hell, I can't see out of one eye. And poor Mr. Zackass. Do you have any idea how many years of physical rehab he's gonna need?
All right, Dan. But this is it--the last time I'm gonna do this.

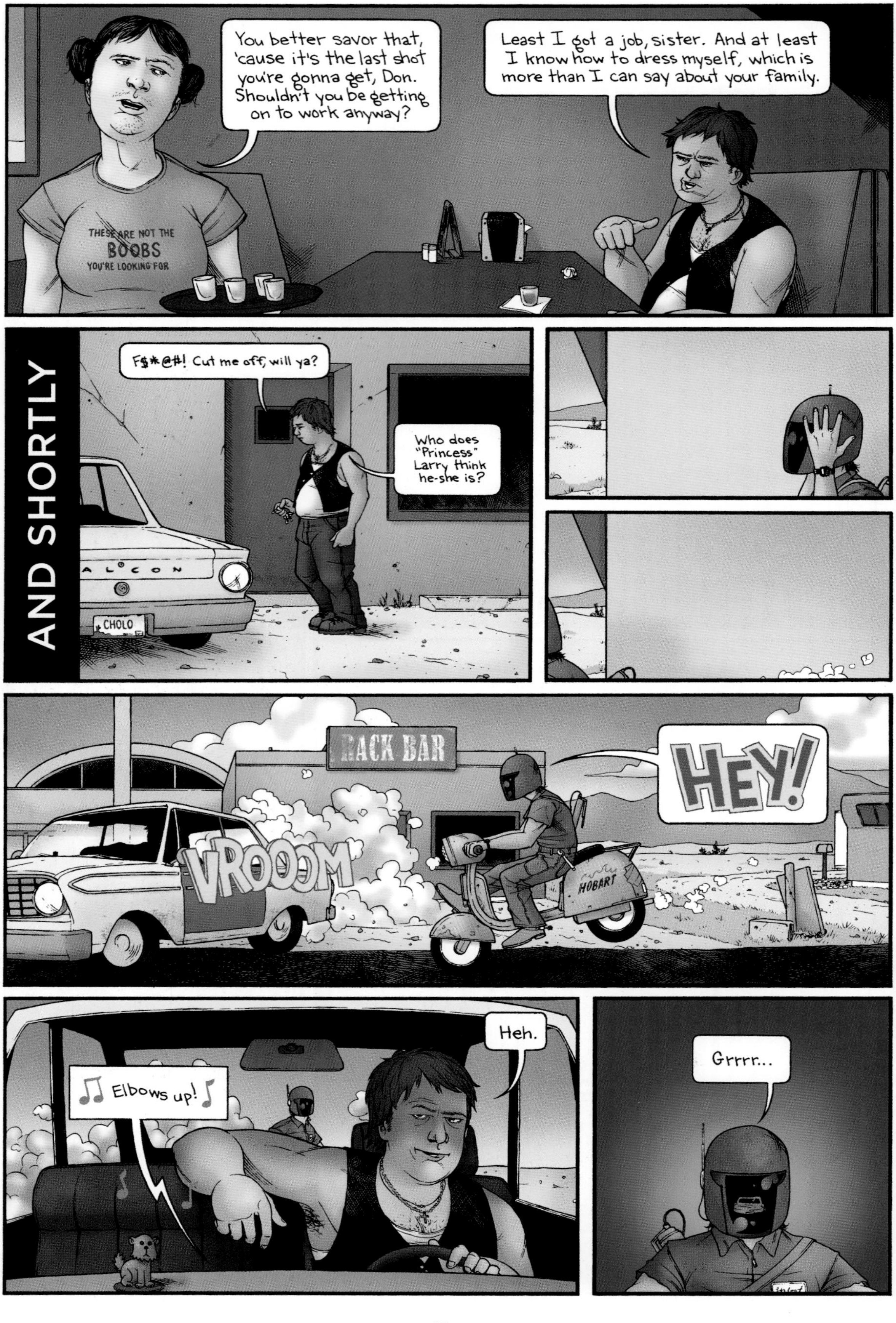
THESE ARE NOT THE BOOBS YOU'RE LOOKING FOR
You better savor that, 'cause it's the last shot you're gonna get, Don. Shouldn't you be getting on to work anyway?
Least I got a job, sister. And at least I know how to dress myself, which is more than I can say about your family.
AND SHORTLY
F$*@#! Cut me off, will ya?
Who does "Princess" Larry think he-she is?
CHOLO
RACK BAR
HEY!
VROOOM
HOBART
Heh.
Elbows up!
Grrrr...

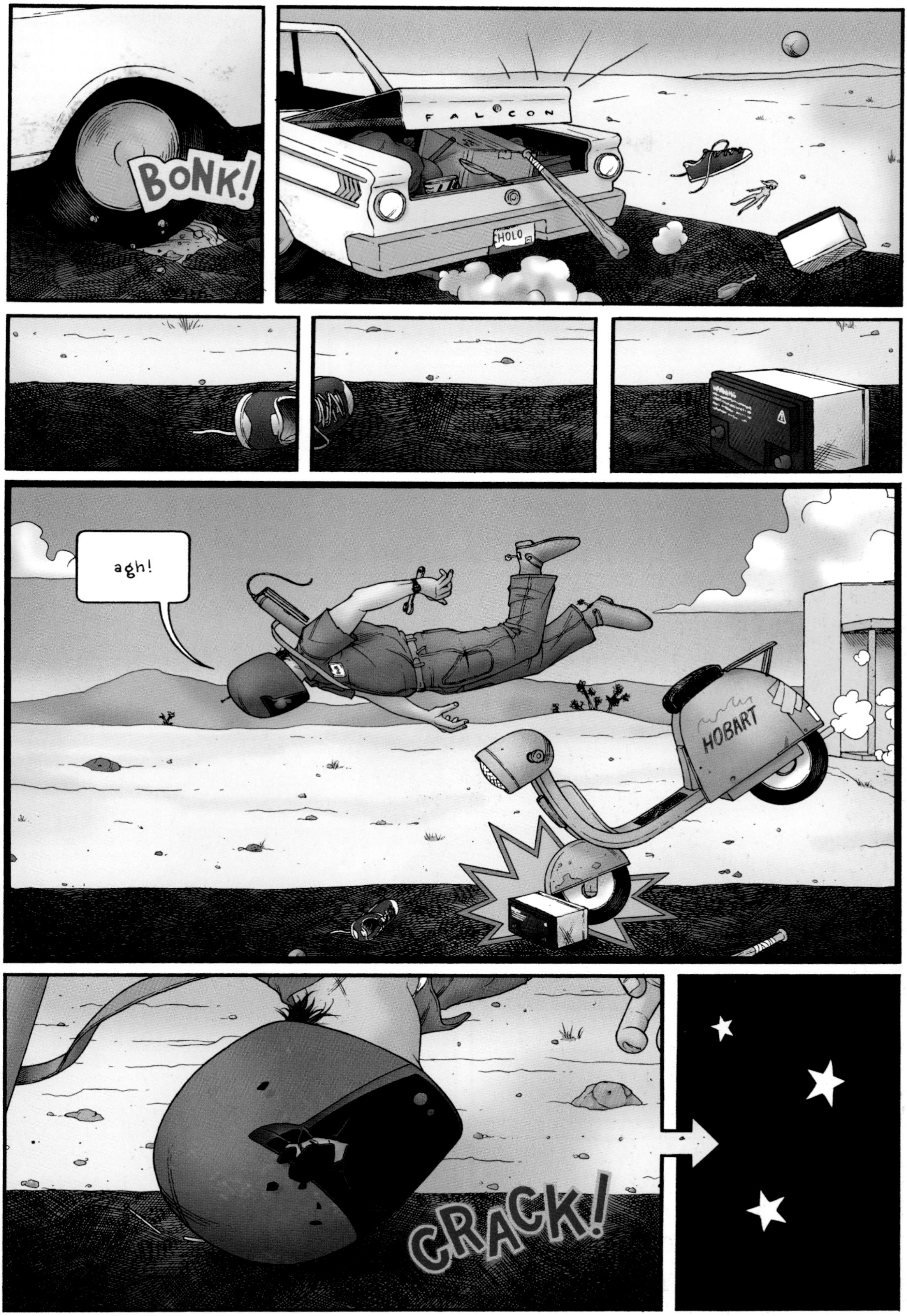
BONK!
FALCON
HOLO
agh!
HOBART
CRACK!

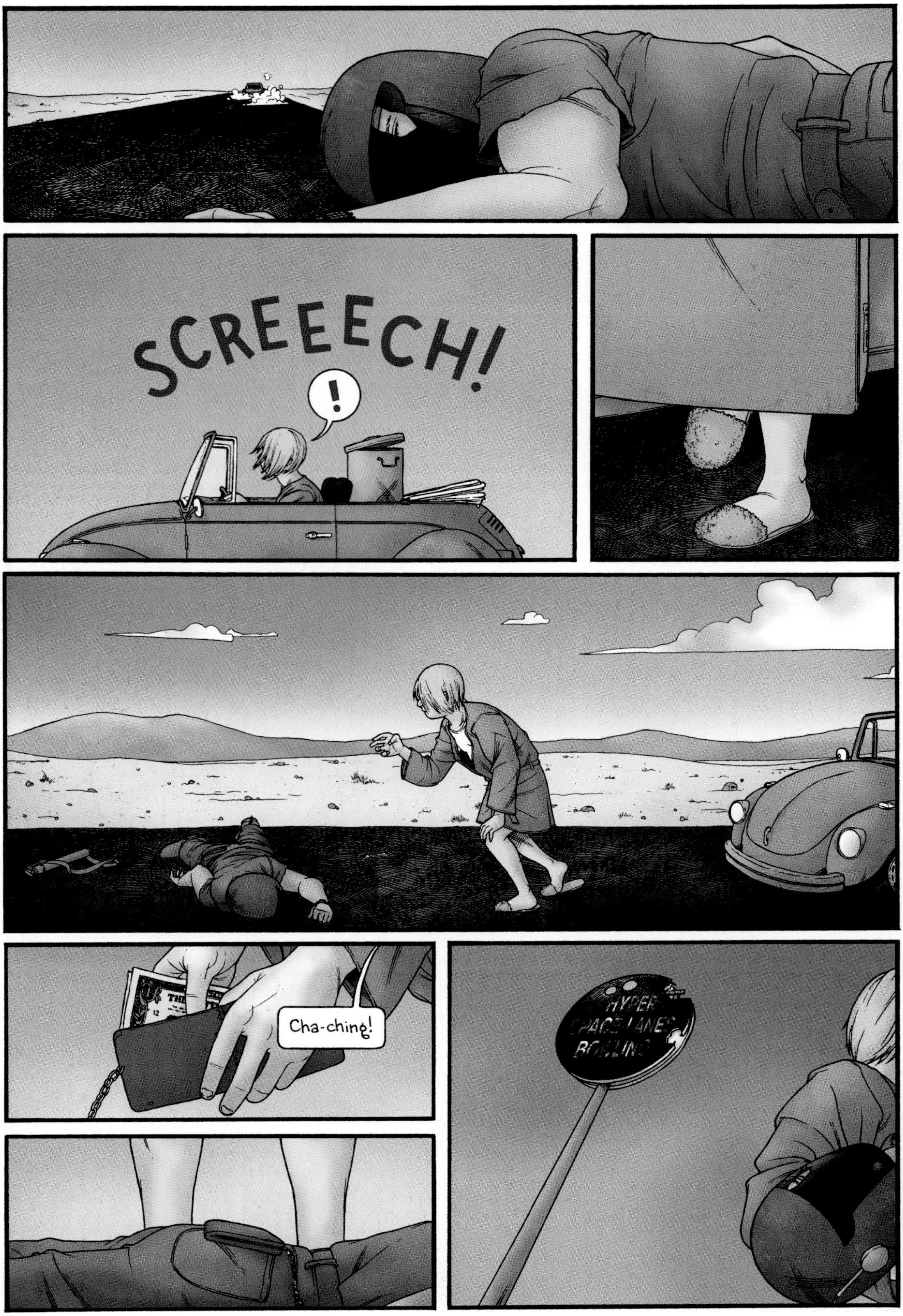
SCREEECH!
!
Cha-ching!
HYPER SPACE LANES BOWLING

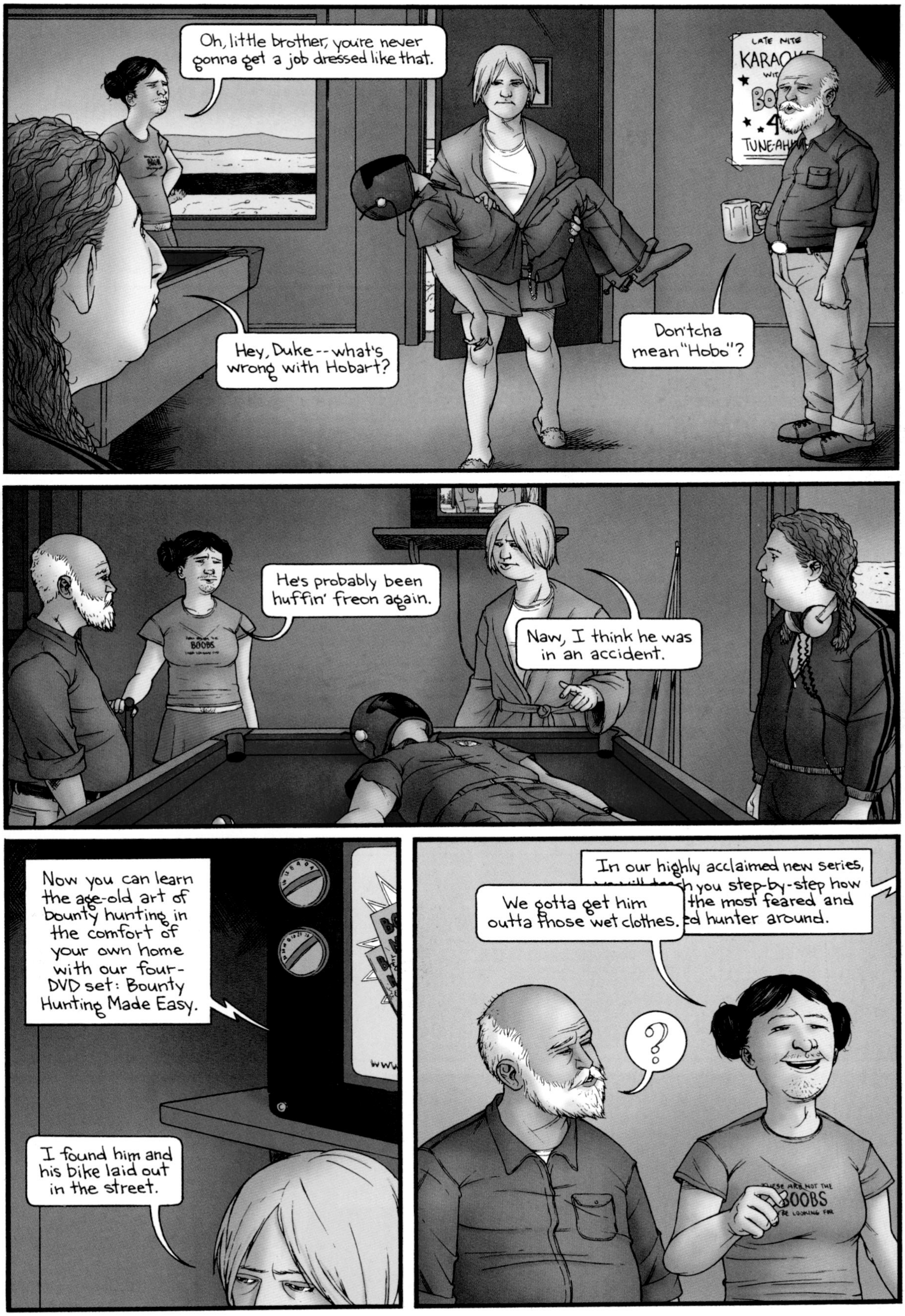

Oh, little brother, you're never gonna get a job dressed like that.
LATE NITE
Hey, Duke--what's wrong with Hobart?
Don'tcha mean "Hobo"?
He's probably been huffin' freon again.
BOOBS
Naw, I think he was in an accident.
Now you can learn the age-old art of bounty hunting in the comfort of your own home with our four-DVD set: Bounty Hunting Made Easy.
I found him and his bike laid out in the street.
In our highly acclaimed new series,
you step-by-step how
the most feared and
hunter around.
We gotta get him outta those wet clothes.
?
BOOBS

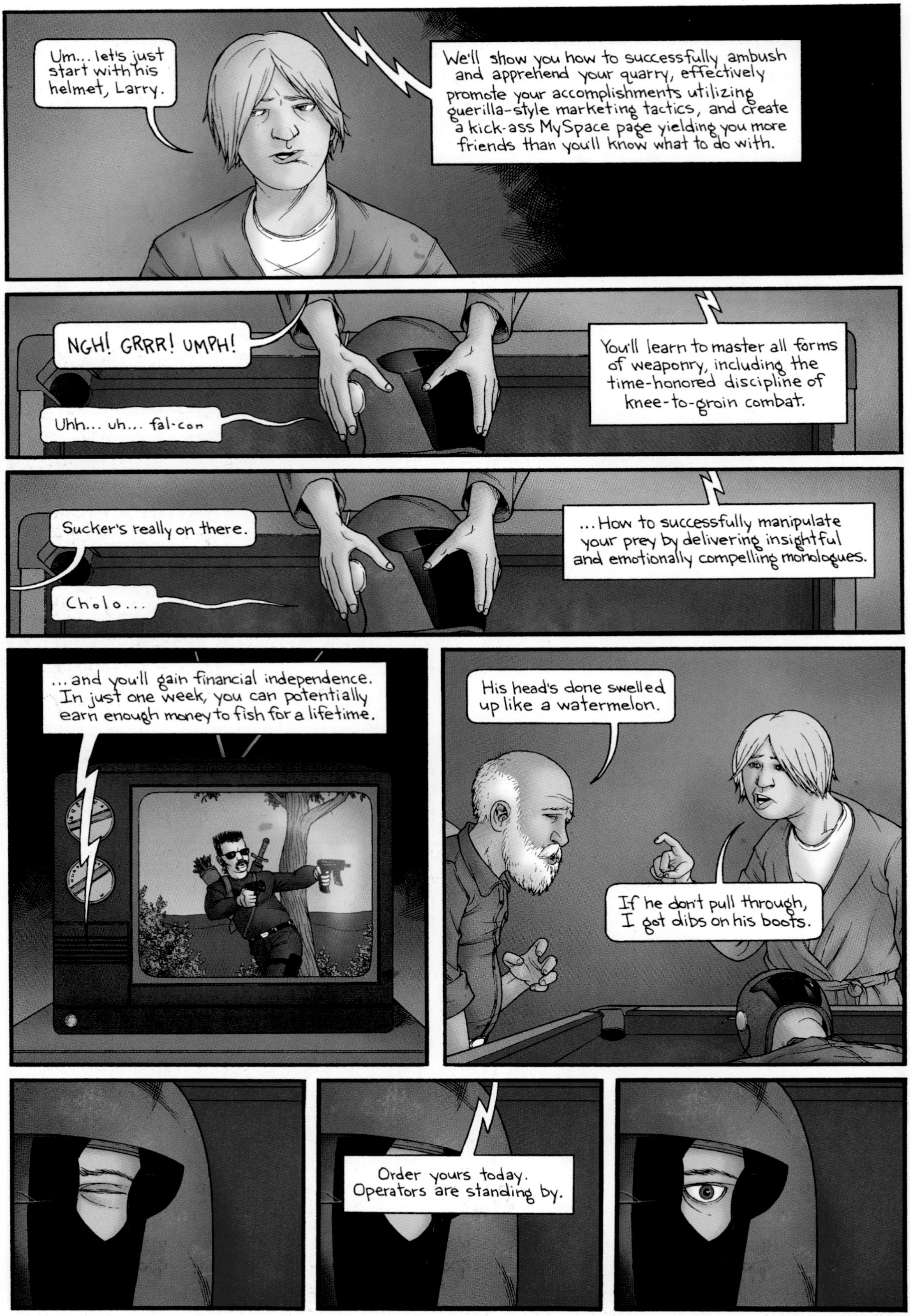
Um... let's just start with his helmet, Larry.
We'll show you how to successfully ambush and apprehend your quarry, effectively promote your accomplishments utilizing guerilla-style marketing tactics, and create a kick-ass MySpace page yielding you more friends than you'll know what to do with.
NGH! GRRR! UMPH!
Uhh... uh... fal-con
You'll learn to master all forms of weaponry, including the time-honored discipline of knee-to-groin combat.
Sucker's really on there.
Cholo...
...How to successfully manipulate your prey by delivering insightful and emotionally compelling monologues.
...and you'll gain financial independence. In just one week, you can potentially earn enough money to fish for a lifetime.
His head's done swelled up like a watermelon.
If he don't pull through, I got dibs on his boots.
Order yours today. Operators are standing by.

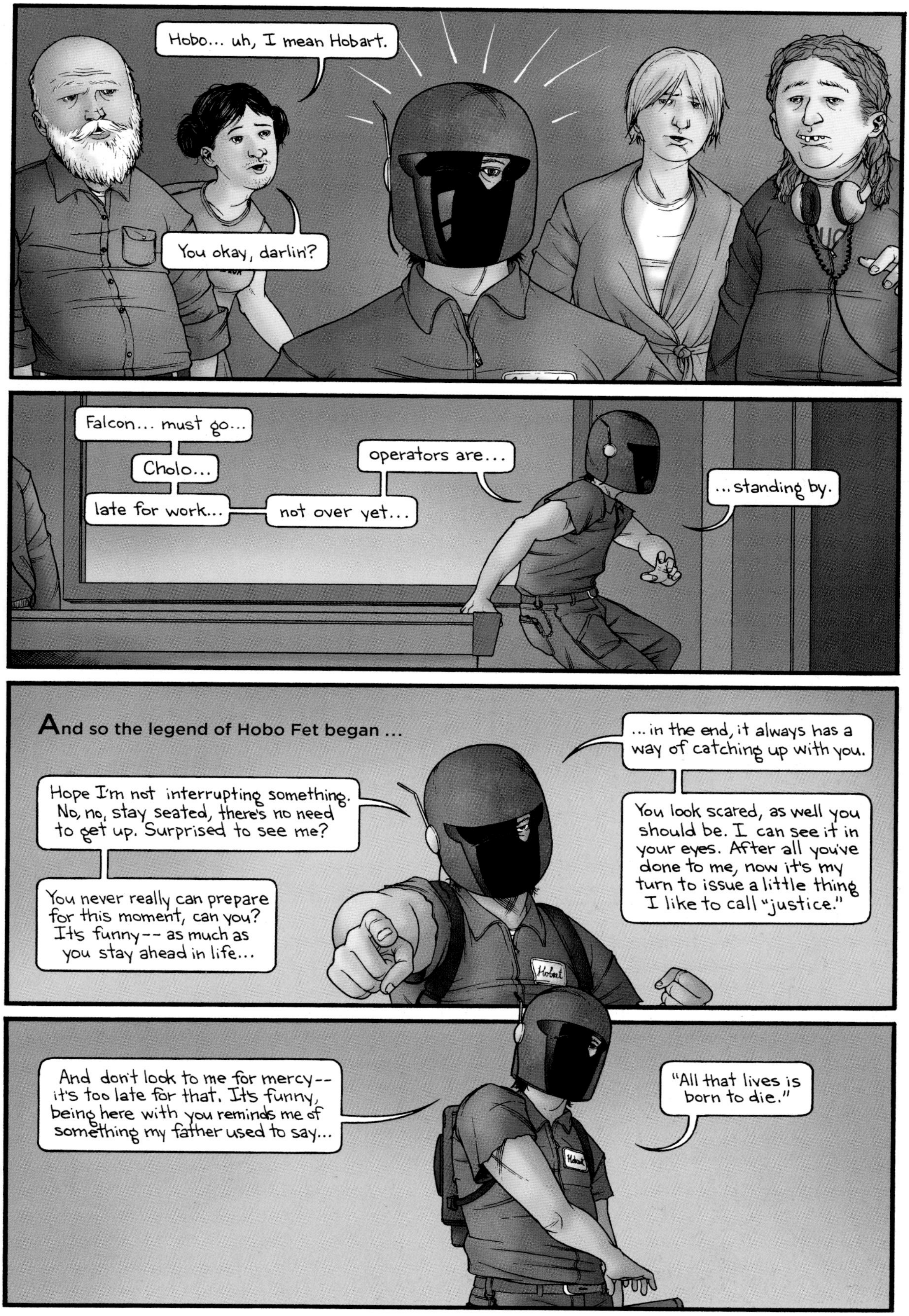
Hobo... uh, I mean Hobart.
You okay, darlin'?
Falcon... must go...
Cholo...
late for work...
not over yet...
operators are...
...standing by.
And so the legend of Hobo Fet began ...
Hope I'm not interrupting something. No, no, stay seated, there's no need to get up. Surprised to see me?
You never really can prepare for this moment, can you? It's funny-- as much as you stay ahead in life...
...in the end, it always has a way of catching up with you.
You look scared, as well you should be. I can see it in your eyes. After all you've done to me, now it's my turn to issue a little thing I like to call "justice."
And don't look to me for mercy-- it's too late for that. It's funny, being here with you reminds me of something my father used to say...
"All that lives is born to die."

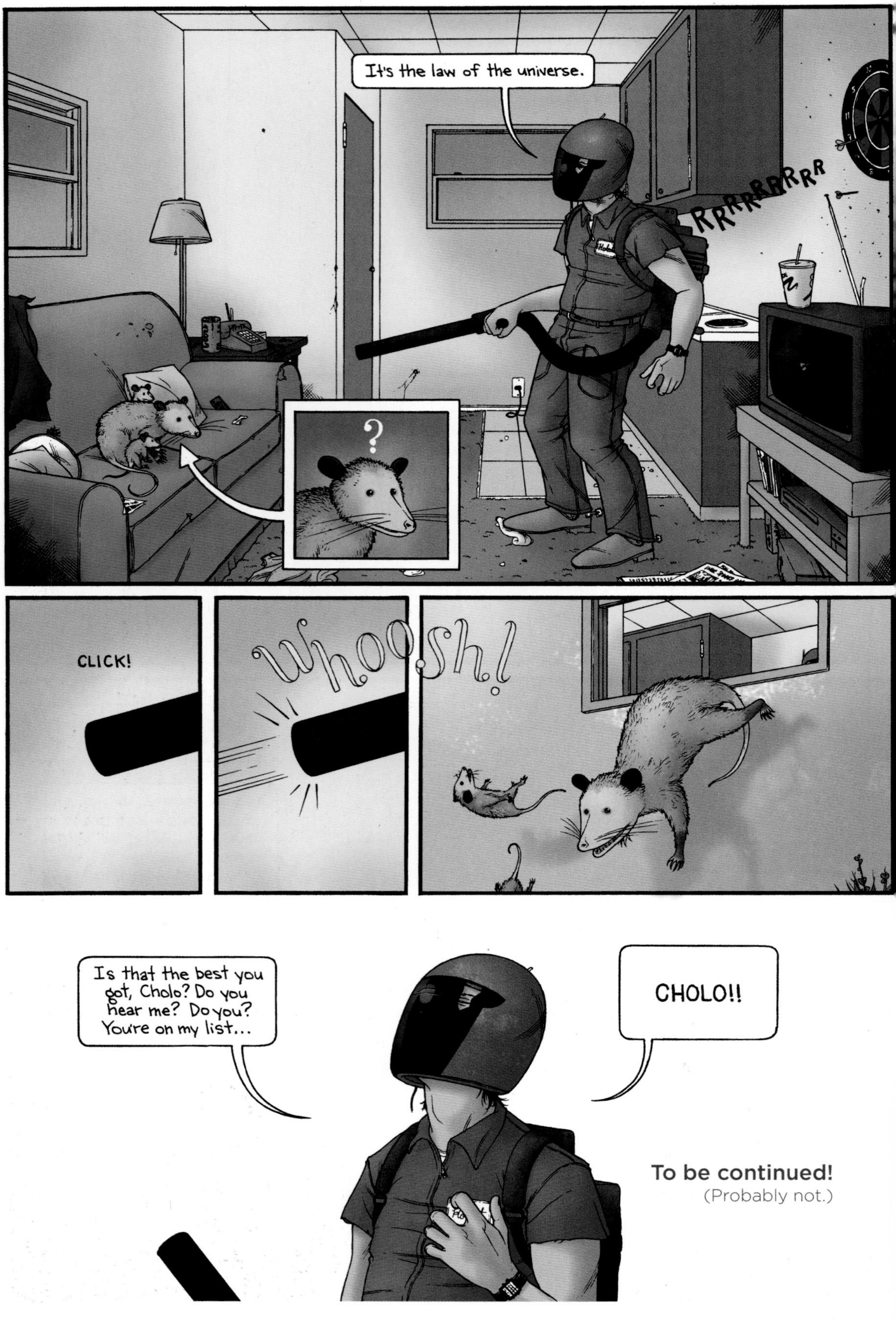
It's the law of the universe.
RRRRRRRRRR
?
CLICK!
WHOOSH!
Is that the best you got, Cholo? Do you hear me? Do you? You're on my list...
CHOLO!!
To be continued!
(Probably not.)

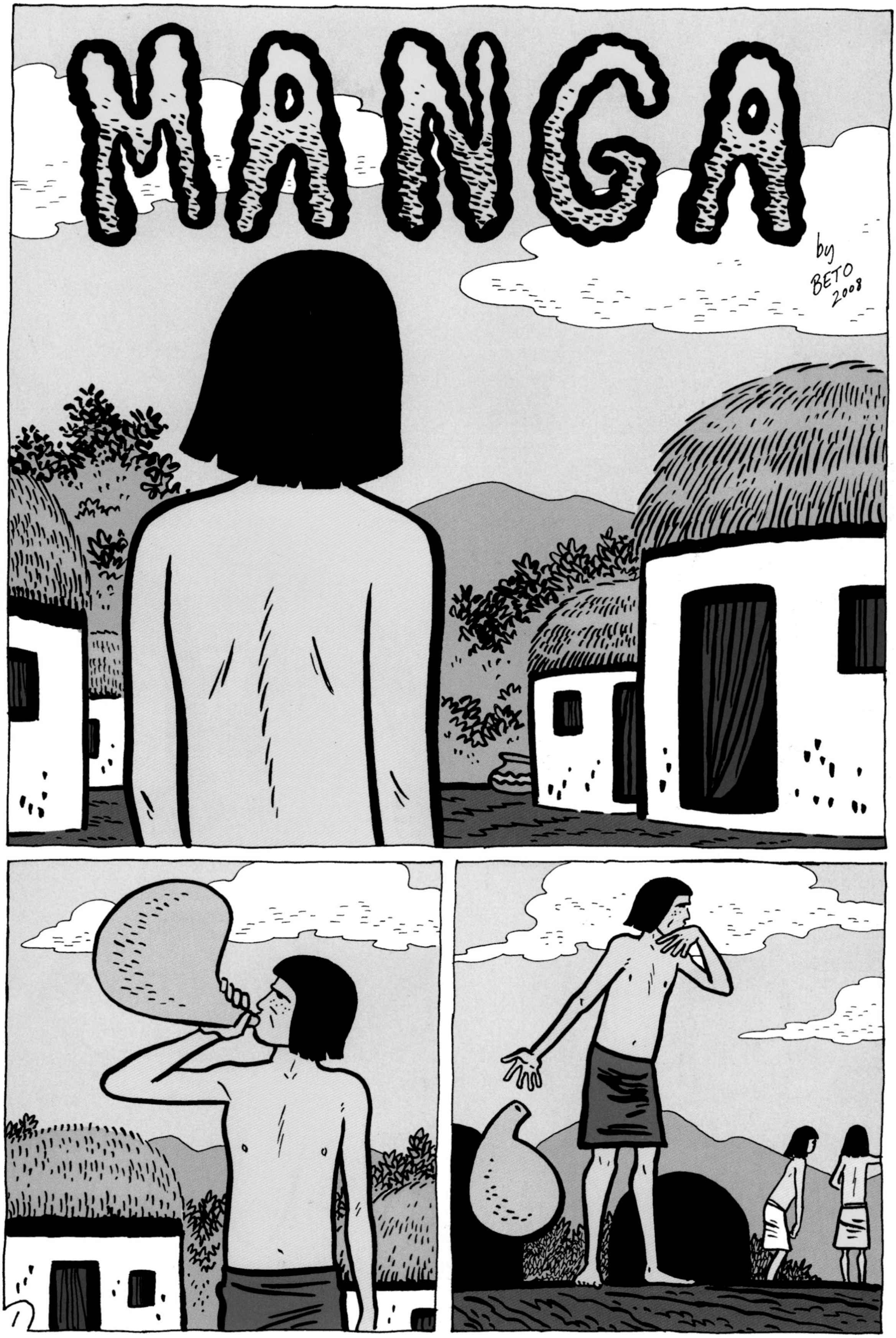
MANGA
by BETO 2008

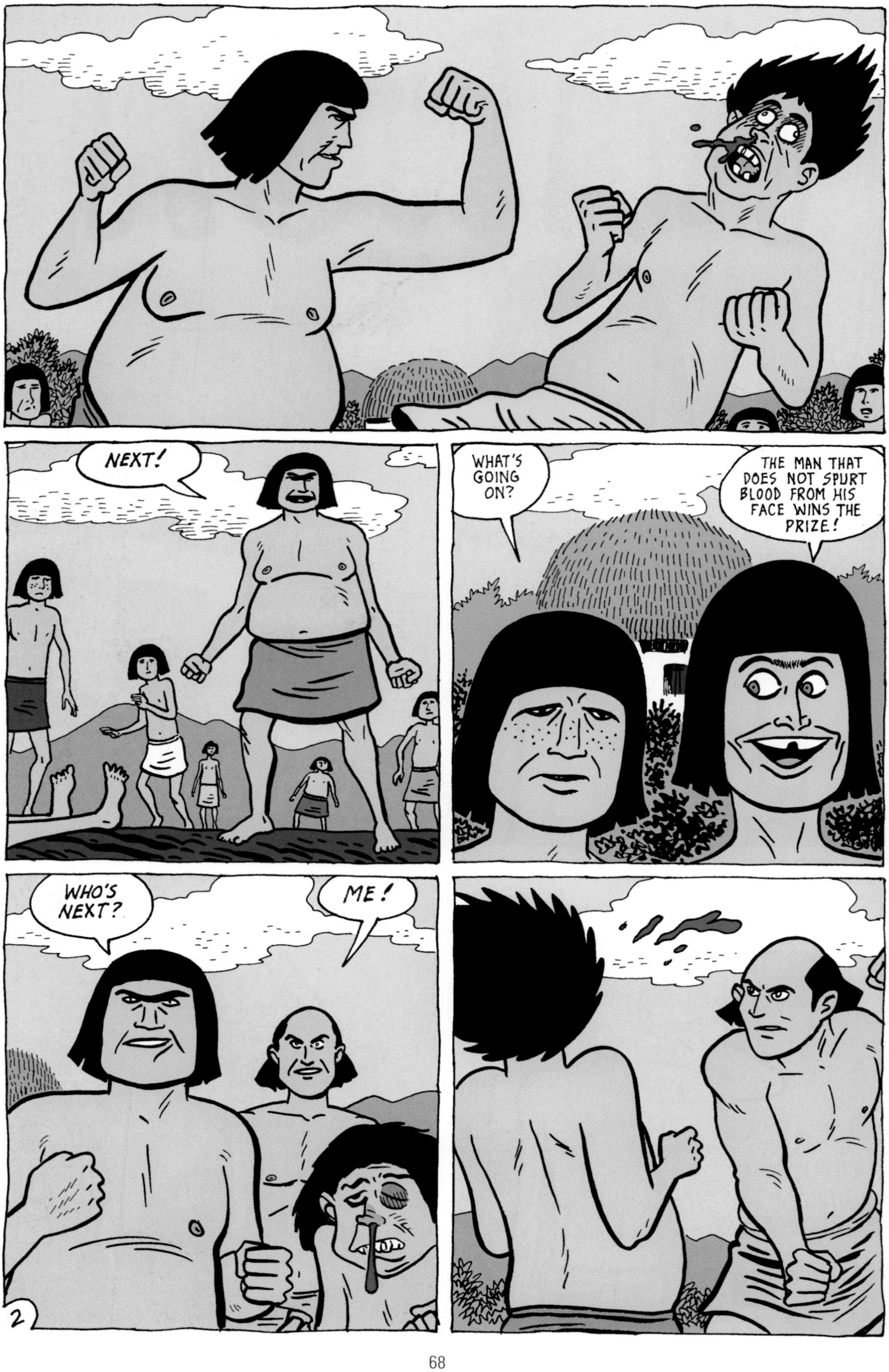
NEXT!
WHAT'S GOING ON?
THE MAN THAT DOES NOT SPURT BLOOD FROM HIS FACE WINS THE PRIZE!
WHO'S NEXT?
ME!
2

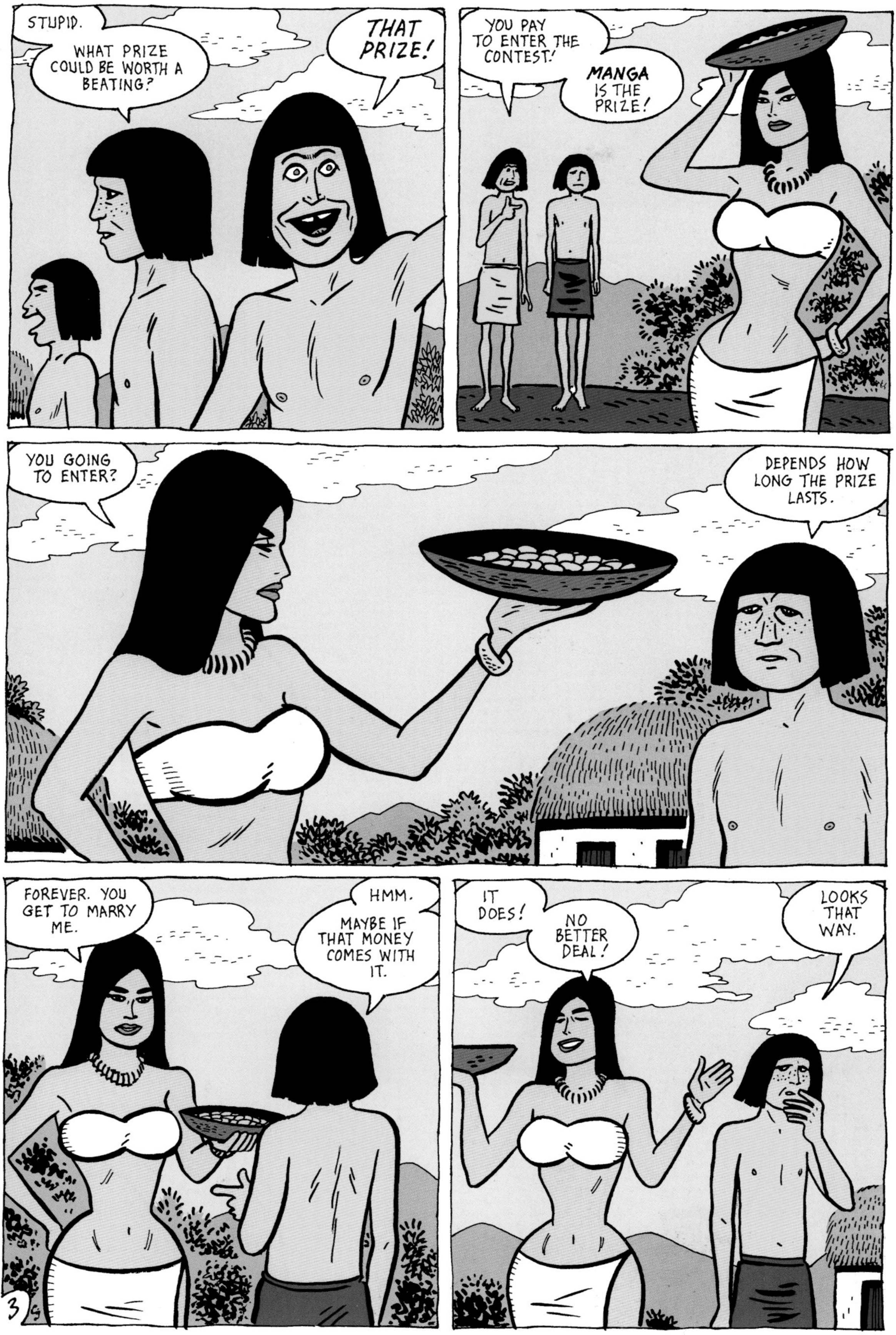
STUPID.
WHAT PRIZE COULD BE WORTH A BEATING?
THAT PRIZE!
YOU PAY TO ENTER THE CONTEST!
MANGA IS THE PRIZE!
YOU GOING TO ENTER?
DEPENDS HOW LONG THE PRIZE LASTS.
FOREVER. YOU GET TO MARRY ME.
HMM.
MAYBE IF THAT MONEY COMES WITH IT.
IT DOES!
NO BETTER DEAL!
LOOKS THAT WAY.
3

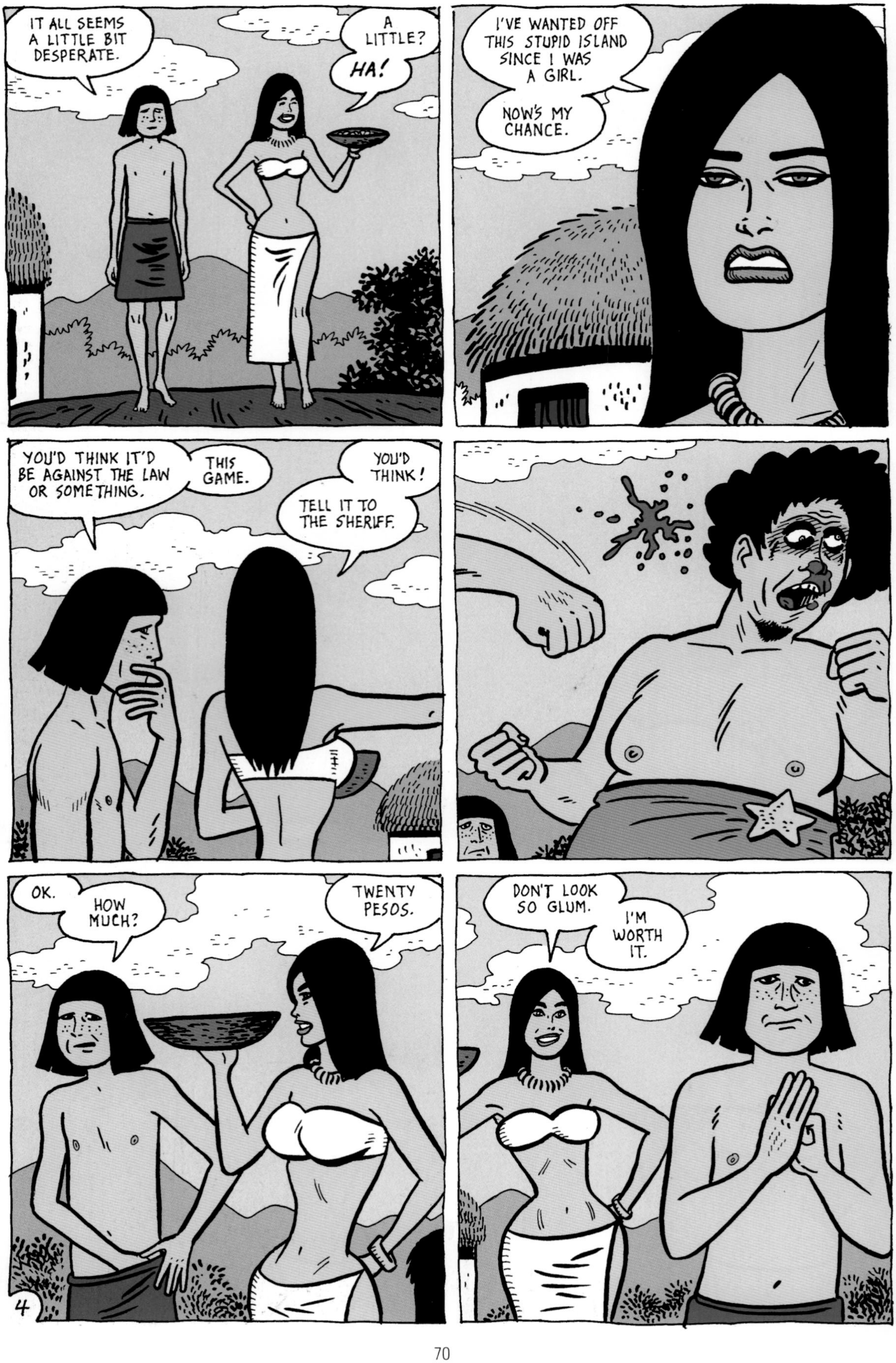
IT ALL SEEMS A LITTLE BIT DESPERATE.
A LITTLE?
HA!
I'VE WANTED OFF THIS STUPID ISLAND SINCE I WAS A GIRL.
NOW'S MY CHANCE.
YOU'D THINK IT'D BE AGAINST THE LAW OR SOMETHING.
THIS GAME.
YOU'D THINK!
TELL IT TO THE SHERIFF.
OK.
HOW MUCH?
TWENTY PESOS.
4
DON'T LOOK SO GLUM.
I'M WORTH IT.

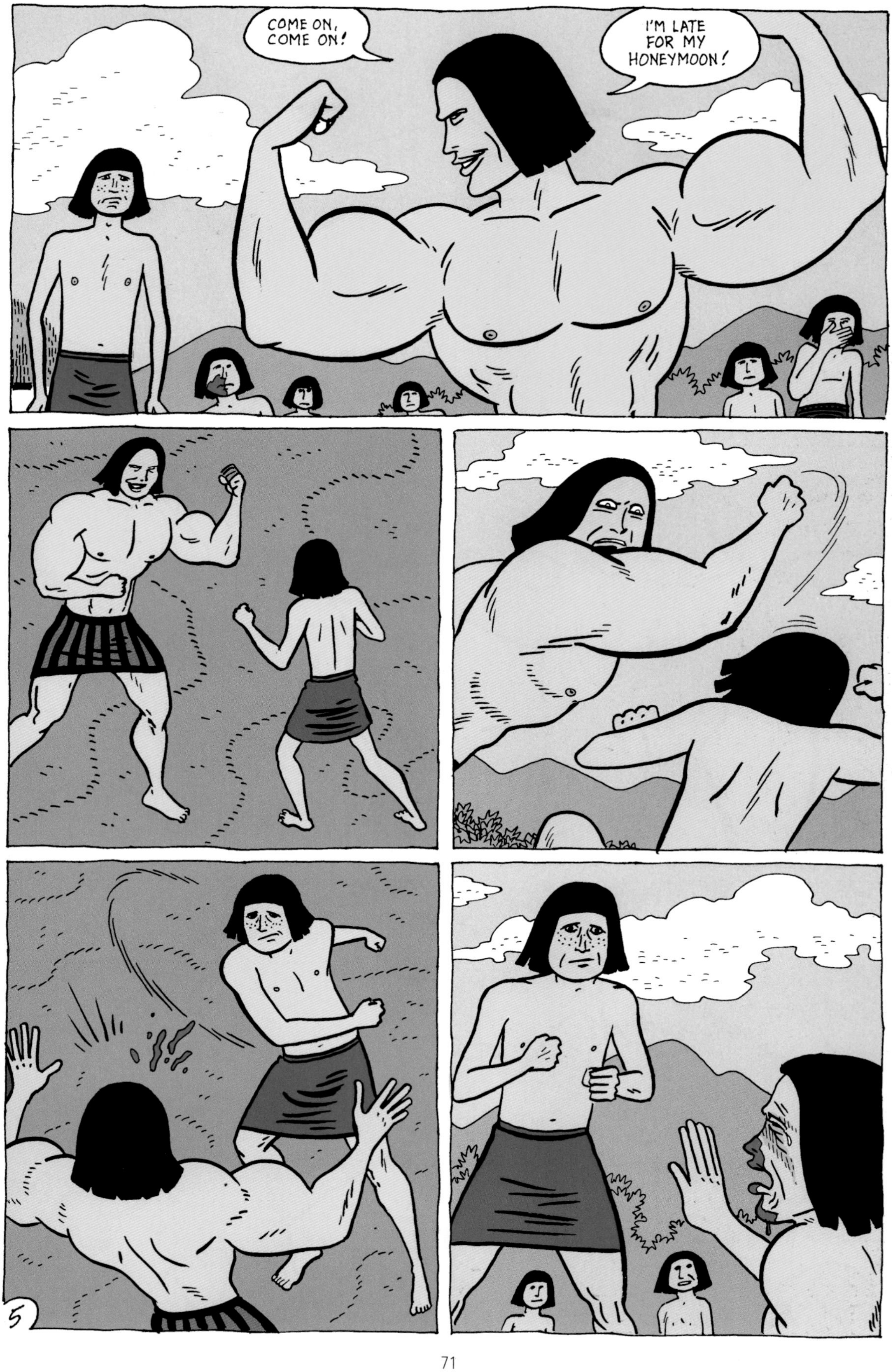
COME ON,
COME ON!
I'M LATE
FOR MY
HONEYMOON!

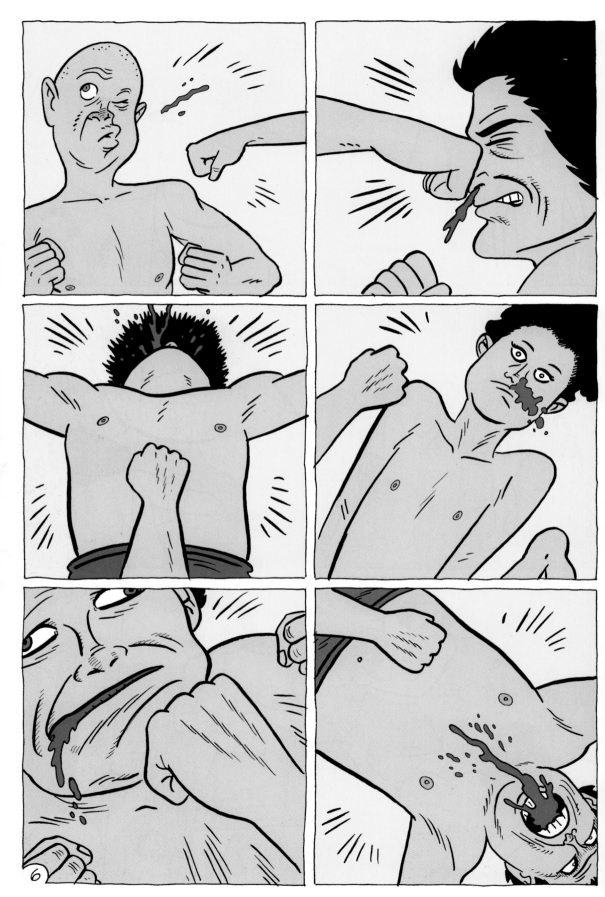

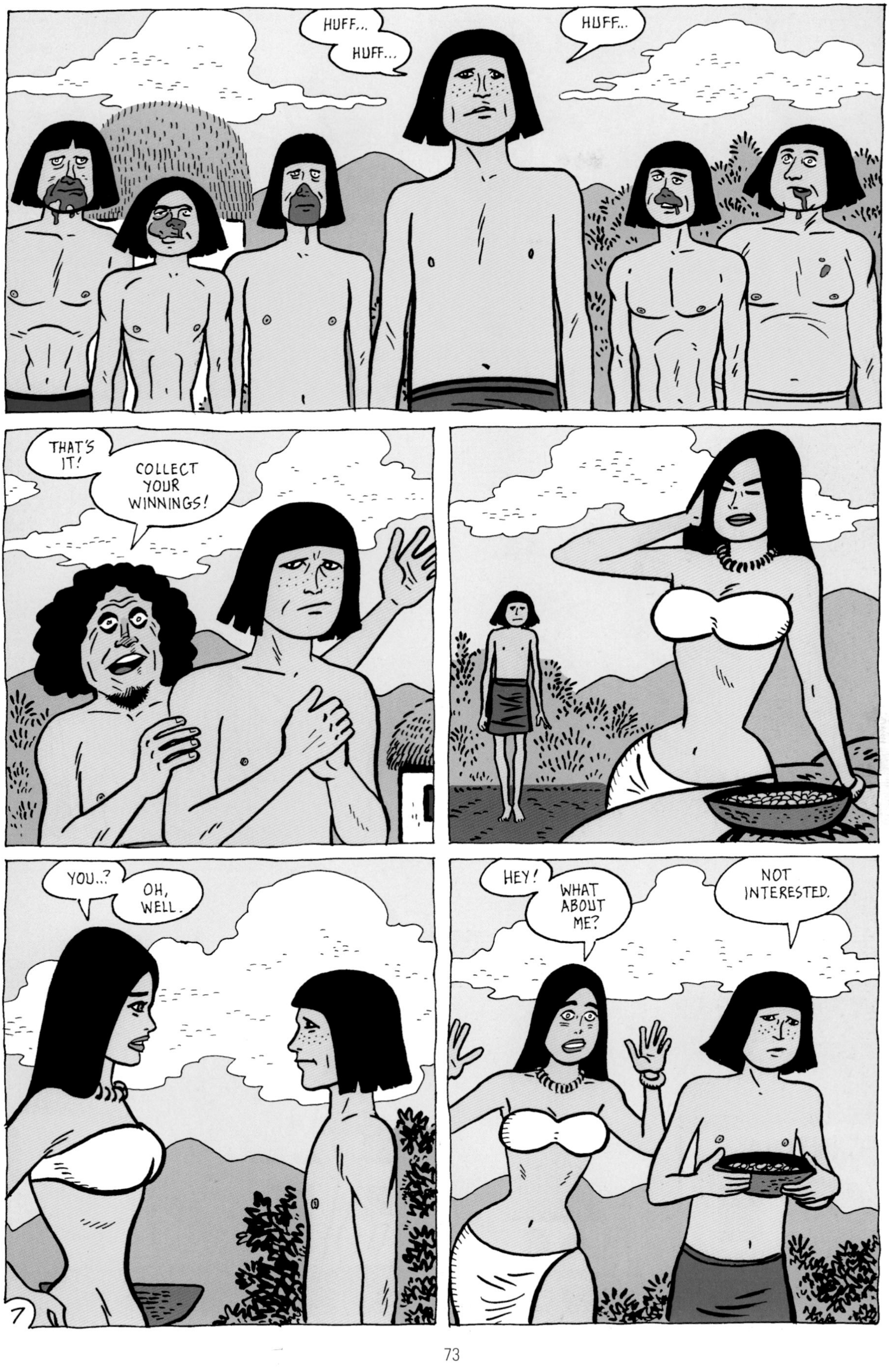

HUFF...
HUFF...
HUFF...
THAT'S IT!
COLLECT YOUR WINNINGS!
YOU..?
OH, WELL.
HEY!
WHAT ABOUT ME?
NOT INTERESTED.

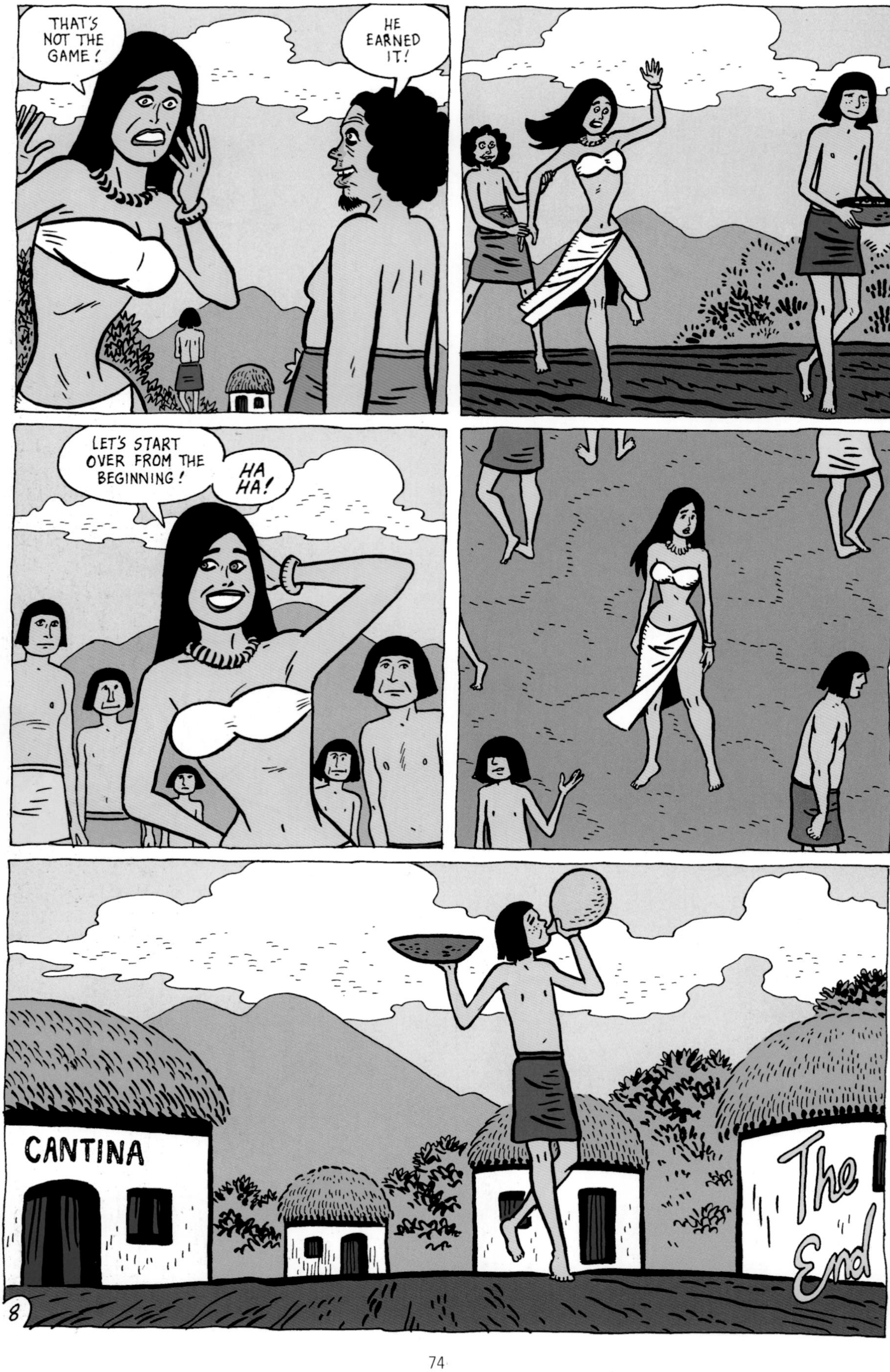
THAT'S NOT THE GAME!
HE EARNED IT!
LET'S START OVER FROM THE BEGINNING!
HA HA!
CANTINA
The End
8

JARED

BY ILIAS KYRIAZIS

LETTERING BY BLAMBOT'S NATE PIEKOS

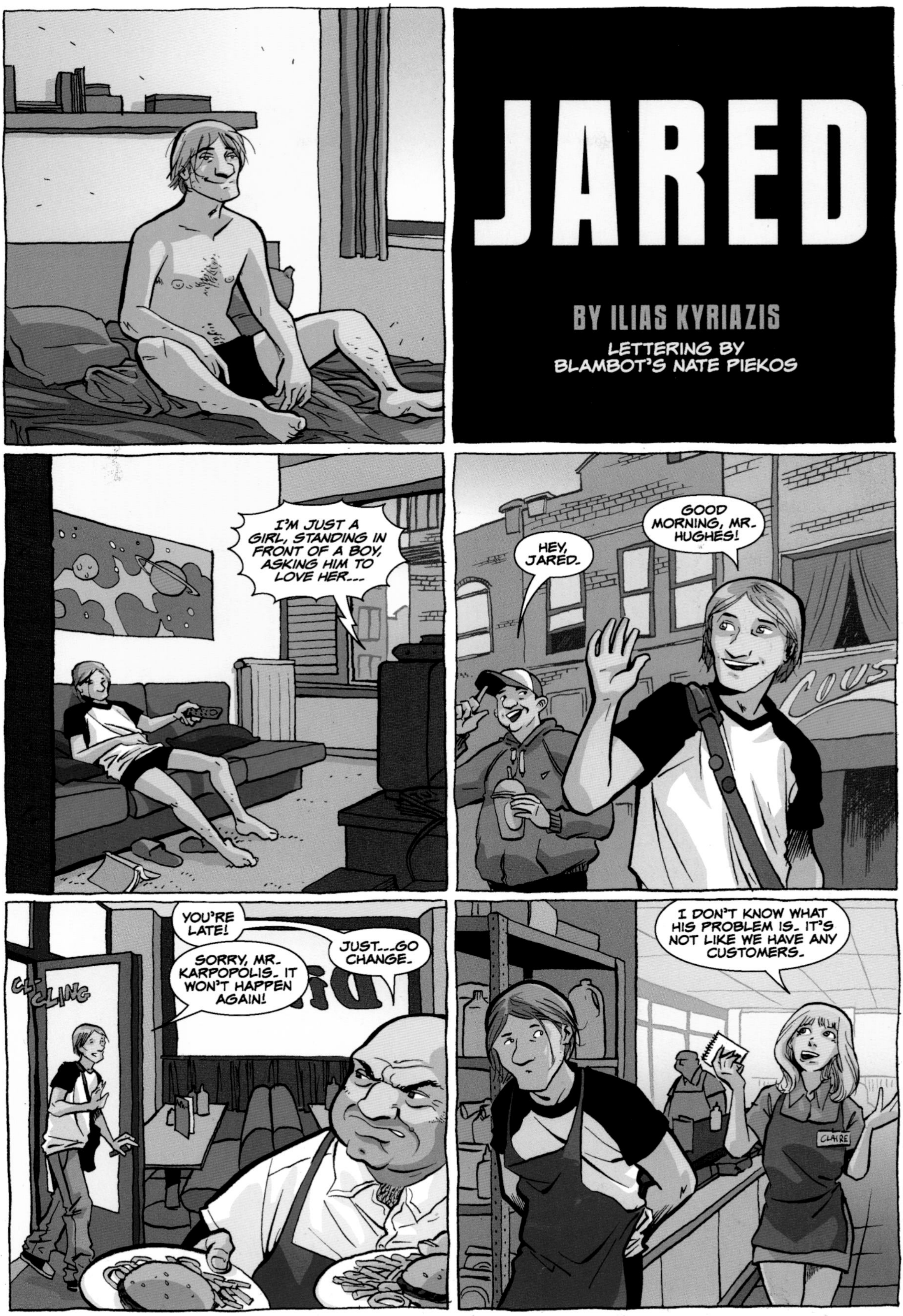
I'M JUST A GIRL, STANDING IN FRONT OF A BOY, ASKING HIM TO LOVE HER...
HEY, JARED.
GOOD MORNING, MR. HUGHES!
COUS
CL-CLING
YOU'RE LATE!
SORRY, MR. KARPOPOLIS. IT WON'T HAPPEN AGAIN!
JUST...GO CHANGE.
I DON'T KNOW WHAT HIS PROBLEM IS. IT'S NOT LIKE WE HAVE ANY CUSTOMERS.
CLAIRE

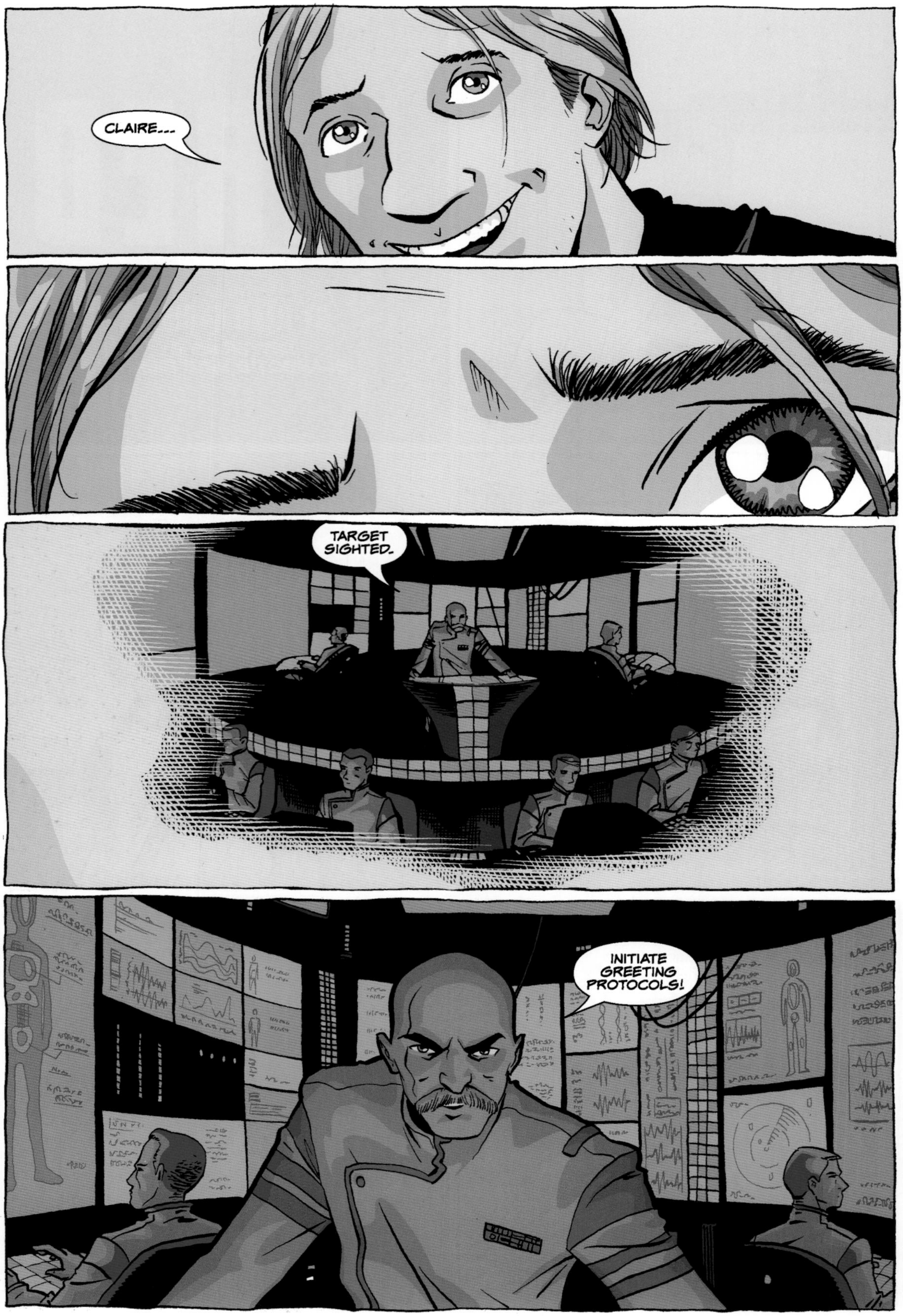
CLAIRE...
TARGET SIGHTED.
INITIATE GREETING PROTOCOLS!

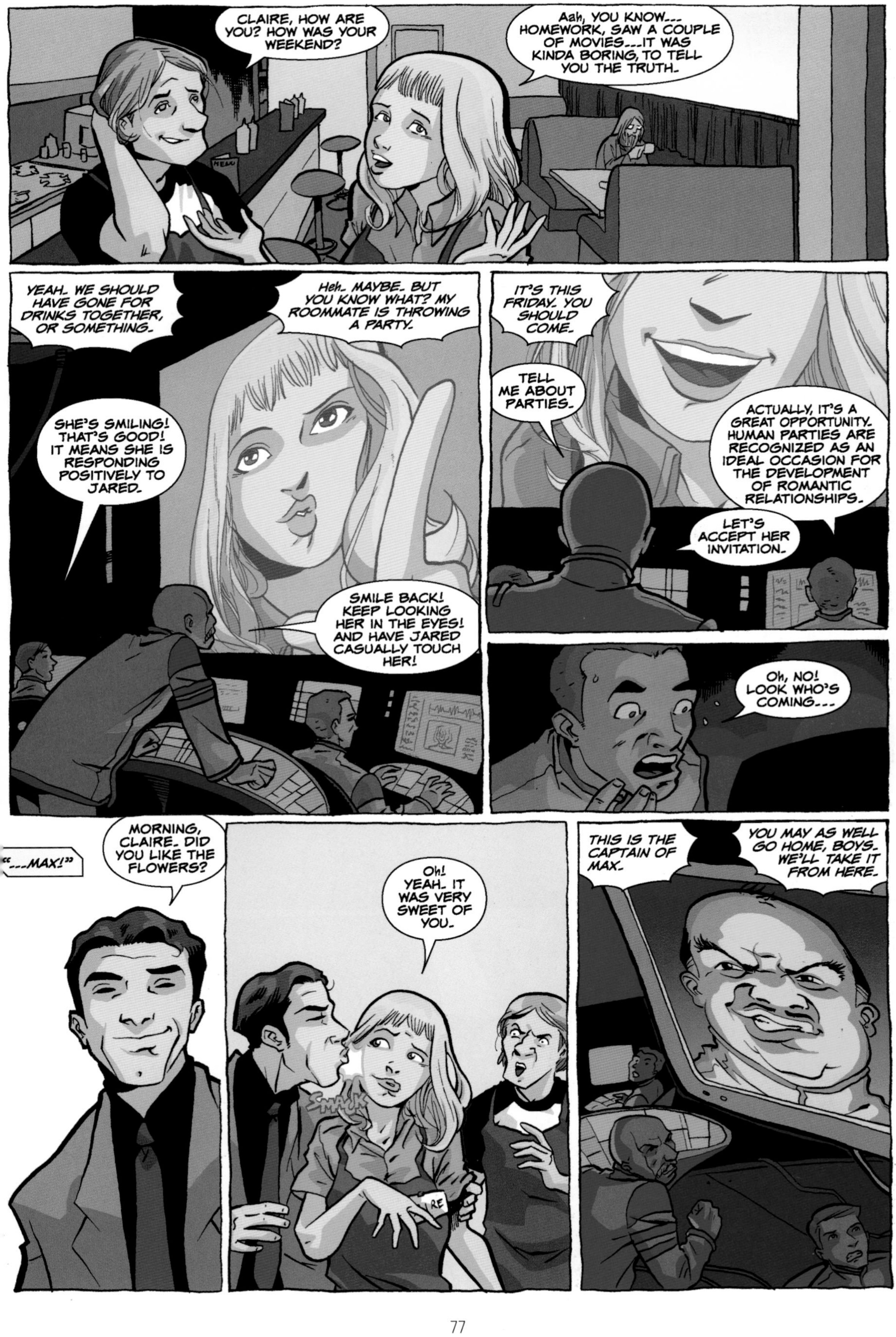
CLAIRE, HOW ARE YOU? HOW WAS YOUR WEEKEND?
Aah, YOU KNOW... HOMEWORK, SAW A COUPLE OF MOVIES...IT WAS KINDA BORING, TO TELL YOU THE TRUTH.
YEAH. WE SHOULD HAVE GONE FOR DRINKS TOGETHER, OR SOMETHING.
Heh. MAYBE. BUT YOU KNOW WHAT? MY ROOMMATE IS THROWING A PARTY.
SHE'S SMILING! THAT'S GOOD! IT MEANS SHE IS RESPONDING POSITIVELY TO JARED.
SMILE BACK! KEEP LOOKING HER IN THE EYES! AND HAVE JARED CASUALLY TOUCH HER!
IT'S THIS FRIDAY. YOU SHOULD COME.
TELL ME ABOUT PARTIES.
ACTUALLY, IT'S A GREAT OPPORTUNITY. HUMAN PARTIES ARE RECOGNIZED AS AN IDEAL OCCASION FOR THE DEVELOPMENT OF ROMANTIC RELATIONSHIPS.
LET'S ACCEPT HER INVITATION.
Oh, NO! LOOK WHO'S COMING...
"...MAX!"
MORNING, CLAIRE. DID YOU LIKE THE FLOWERS?
Oh! YEAH. IT WAS VERY SWEET OF YOU.
SMACK
THIS IS THE CAPTAIN OF MAX.
YOU MAY AS WELL GO HOME, BOYS. WE'LL TAKE IT FROM HERE.

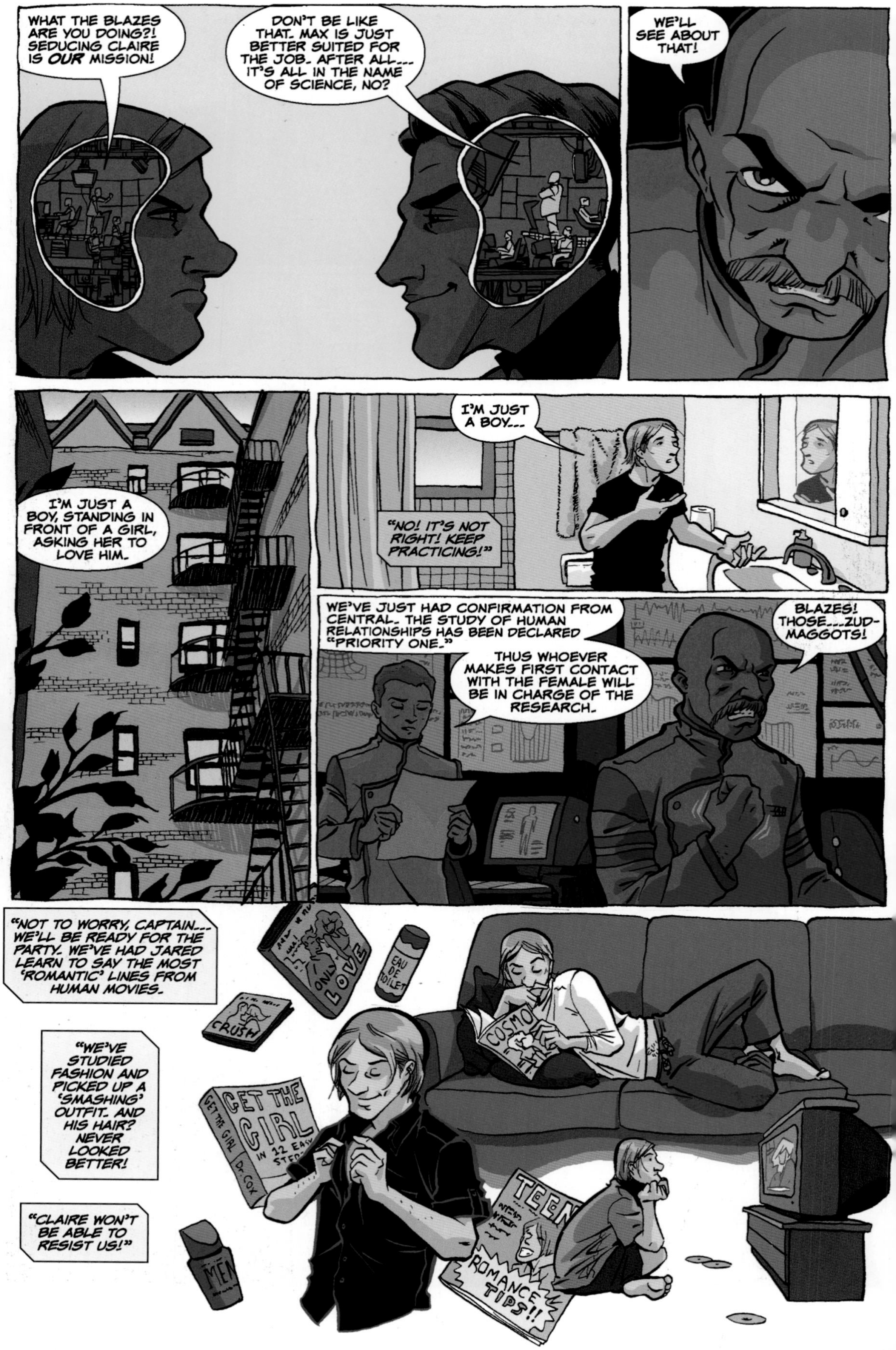
WHAT THE BLAZES ARE YOU DOING?! SEDUCING CLAIRE IS *OUR* MISSION!
DON'T BE LIKE THAT. MAX IS JUST BETTER SUITED FOR THE JOB. AFTER ALL... IT'S ALL IN THE NAME OF SCIENCE, NO?
WE'LL SEE ABOUT THAT!
I'M JUST A BOY, STANDING IN FRONT OF A GIRL, ASKING HER TO LOVE HIM.
I'M JUST A BOY...
"NO! IT'S NOT RIGHT! KEEP PRACTICING!"
WE'VE JUST HAD CONFIRMATION FROM CENTRAL. THE STUDY OF HUMAN RELATIONSHIPS HAS BEEN DECLARED "PRIORITY ONE."
THUS WHOEVER MAKES FIRST CONTACT WITH THE FEMALE WILL BE IN CHARGE OF THE RESEARCH.
BLAZES! THOSE... ZUD-MAGGOTS!
"NOT TO WORRY, CAPTAIN... WE'LL BE READY FOR THE PARTY. WE'VE HAD JARED LEARN TO SAY THE MOST 'ROMANTIC' LINES FROM HUMAN MOVIES.
"WE'VE STUDIED FASHION AND PICKED UP A 'SMASHING' OUTFIT. AND HIS HAIR? NEVER LOOKED BETTER!
"CLAIRE WON'T BE ABLE TO RESIST US!"
ONLY LOVE
EAU DE TOILET
CRUSH
COSMO
GET THE GIRL IN 12 EASY STEPS
DR. COX
TEEN
ROMANCE TIPS!!
MEN

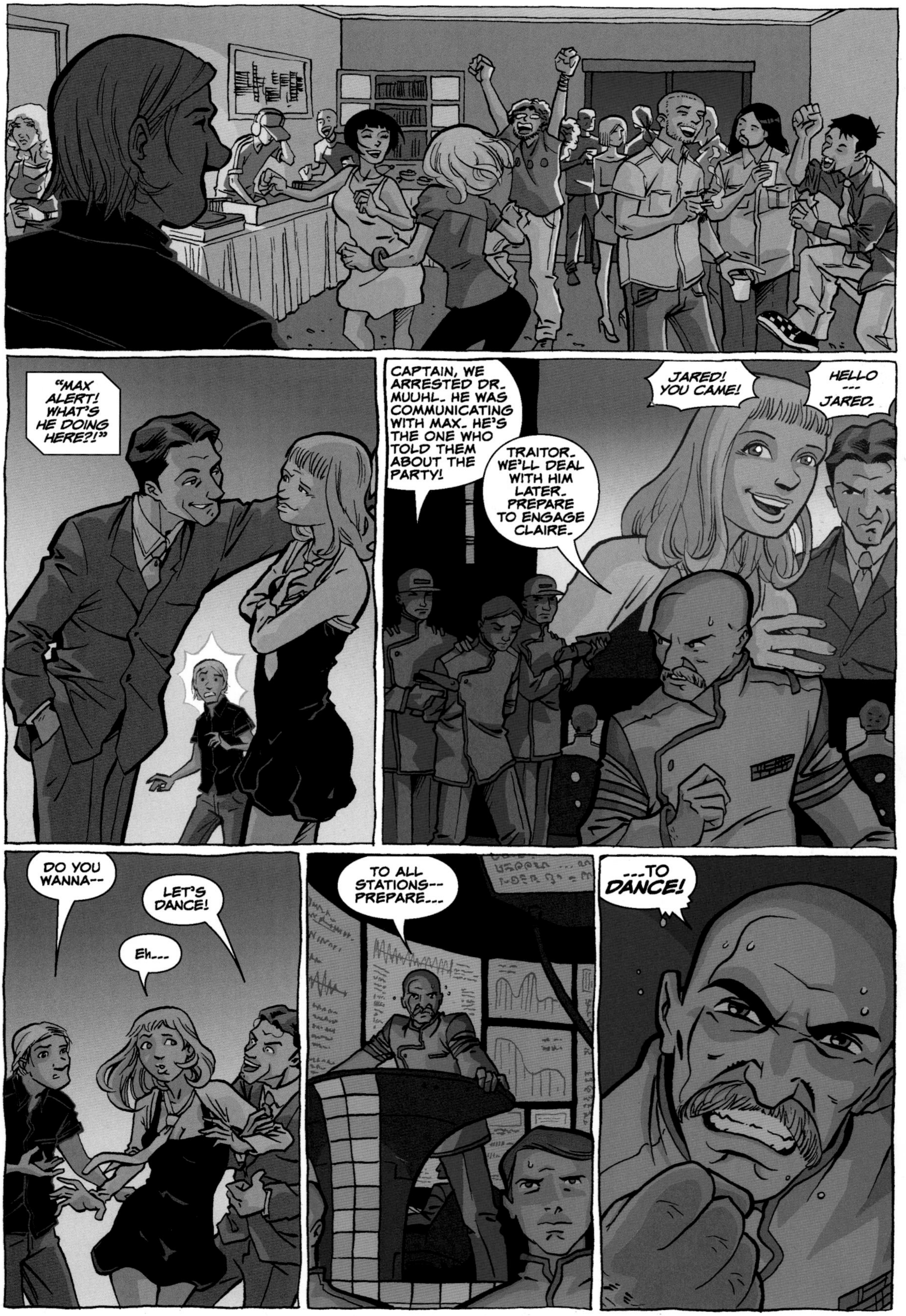
"MAX ALERT! WHAT'S HE DOING HERE?!"
CAPTAIN, WE ARRESTED DR. MUUHL. HE WAS COMMUNICATING WITH MAX. HE'S THE ONE WHO TOLD THEM ABOUT THE PARTY!
TRAITOR. WE'LL DEAL WITH HIM LATER. PREPARE TO ENGAGE CLAIRE.
JARED! YOU CAME!
HELLO --- JARED.
DO YOU WANNA--
LET'S DANCE!
Eh---
TO ALL STATIONS-- PREPARE---
---TO DANCE!

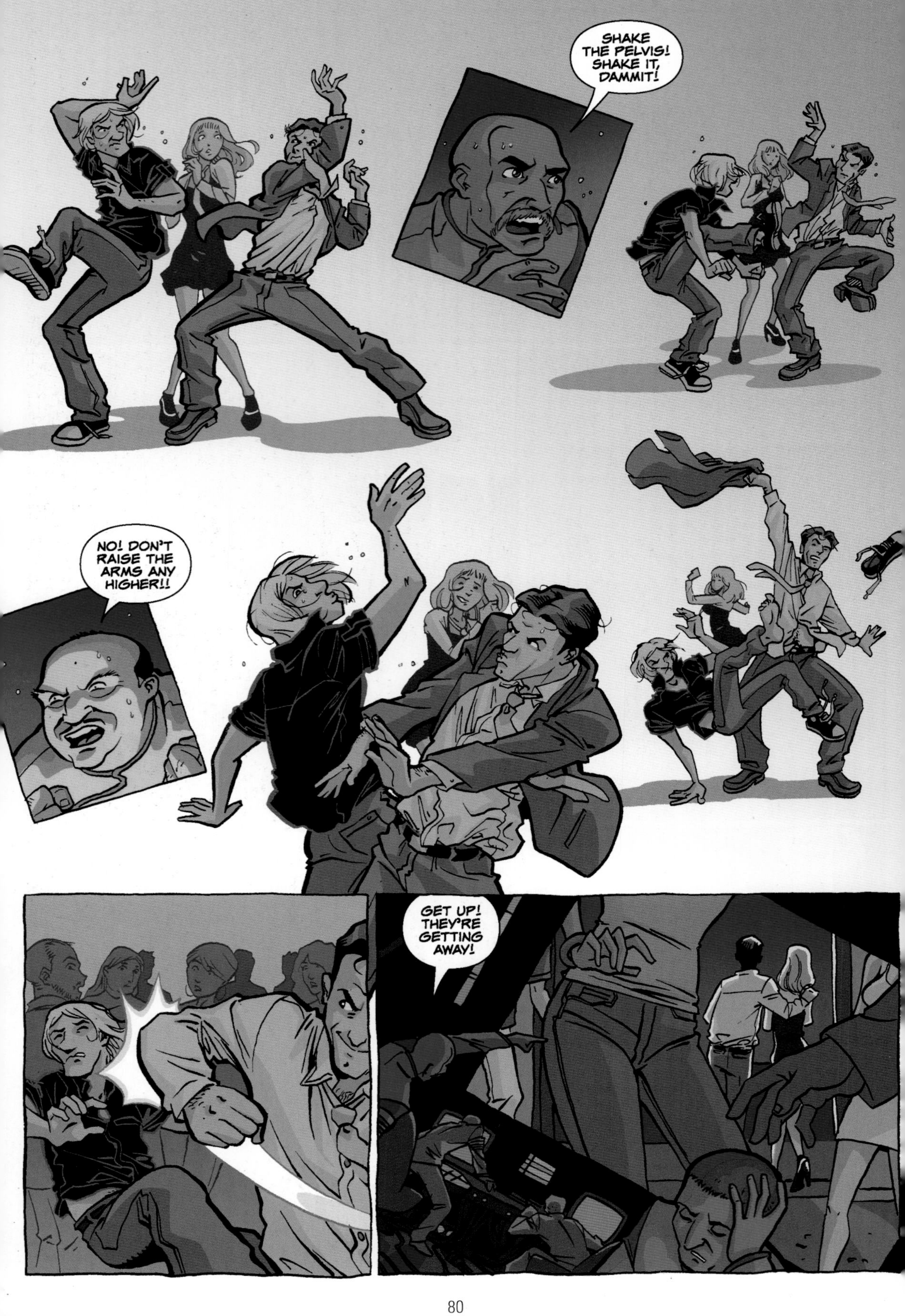
SHAKE THE PELVIS! SHAKE IT, DAMMIT!
NO! DON'T RAISE THE ARMS ANY HIGHER!!
GET UP! THEY'RE GETTING AWAY!

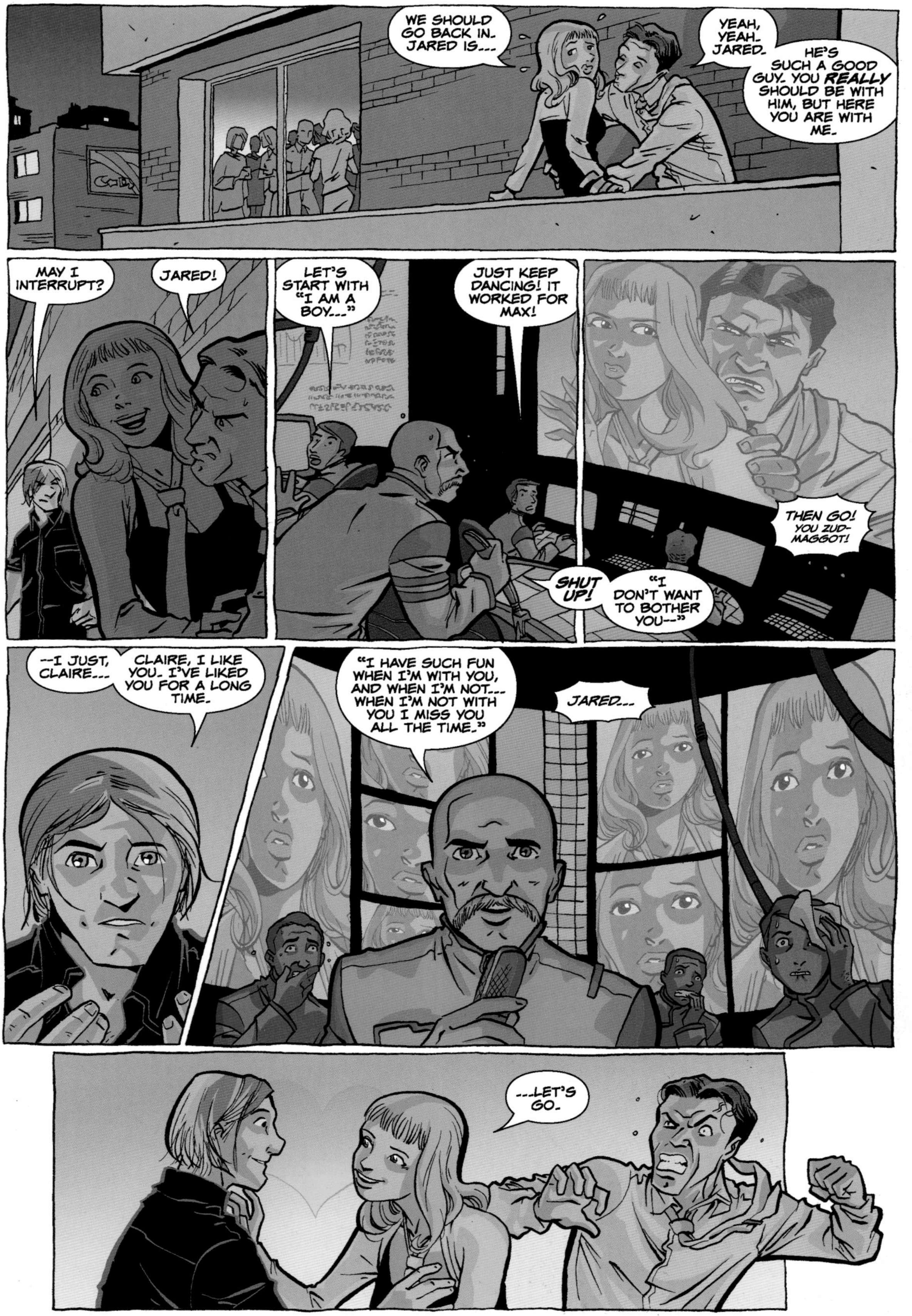
WE SHOULD GO BACK IN. JARED IS...
YEAH, YEAH. JARED.
HE'S SUCH A GOOD GUY. YOU **REALLY** SHOULD BE WITH HIM, BUT HERE YOU ARE WITH ME.
MAY I INTERRUPT?
JARED!
LET'S START WITH "I AM A BOY..."
JUST KEEP DANCING! IT WORKED FOR MAX!
THEN GO! YOU ZUD-MAGGOT!
SHUT UP!
"I DON'T WANT TO BOTHER YOU--"
--I JUST, CLAIRE...
CLAIRE, I LIKE YOU. I'VE LIKED YOU FOR A LONG TIME.
"I HAVE SUCH FUN WHEN I'M WITH YOU, AND WHEN I'M NOT... WHEN I'M NOT WITH YOU I MISS YOU ALL THE TIME."
JARED...
...LET'S GO.

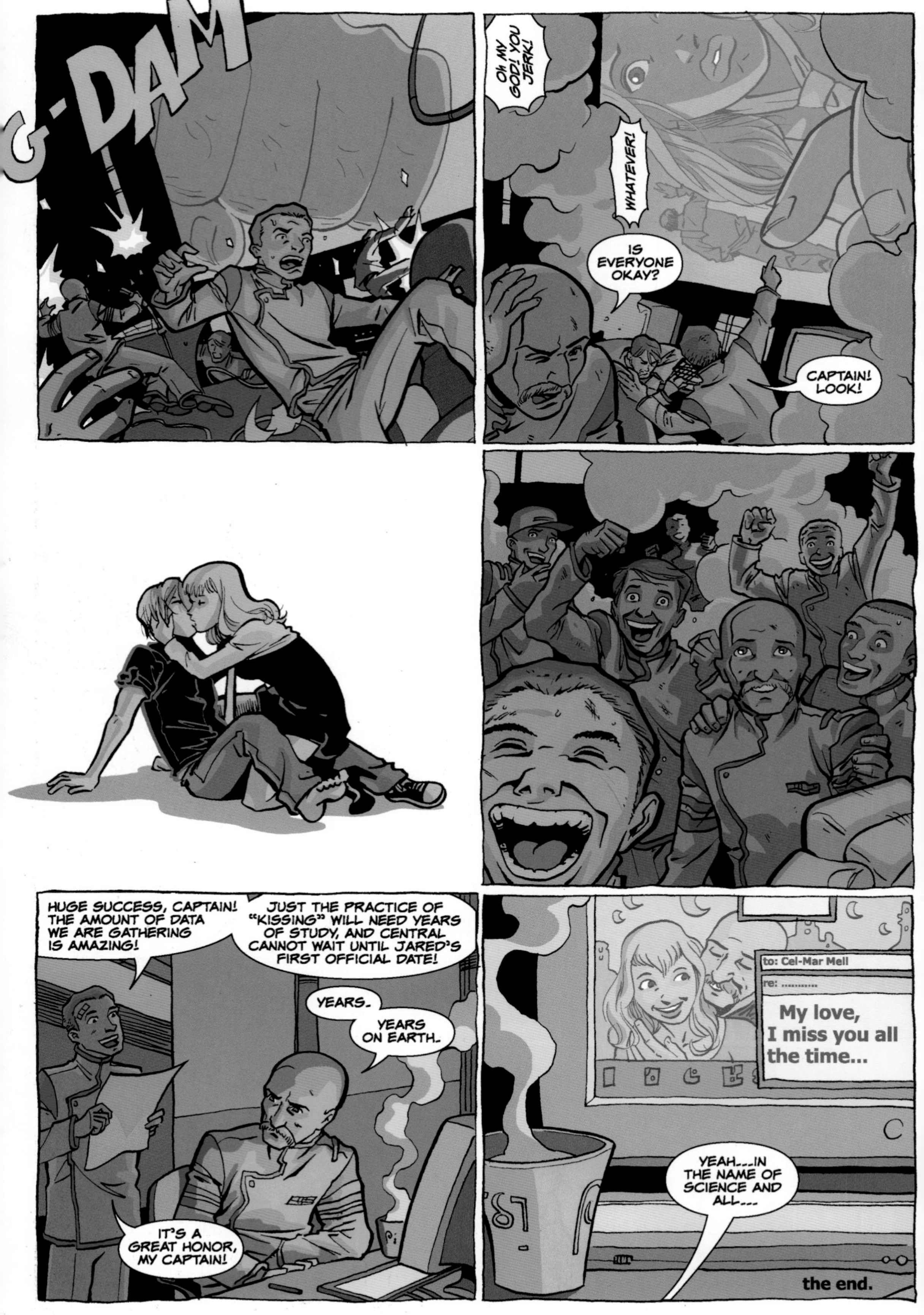
G-DAM
Oh MY GOD! YOU JERK!
WHATEVER!
IS EVERYONE OKAY?
CAPTAIN! LOOK!
HUGE SUCCESS, CAPTAIN! THE AMOUNT OF DATA WE ARE GATHERING IS AMAZING!
JUST THE PRACTICE OF "KISSING" WILL NEED YEARS OF STUDY, AND CENTRAL CANNOT WAIT UNTIL JARED'S FIRST OFFICIAL DATE!
YEARS.
YEARS ON EARTH.
IT'S A GREAT HONOR, MY CAPTAIN!
to: Cel-Mar Mell
re:
My love, I miss you all the time...
YEAH...IN THE NAME OF SCIENCE AND ALL...
the end.

How to Heal a Broken Heart: Method 37

by Tara McPherson

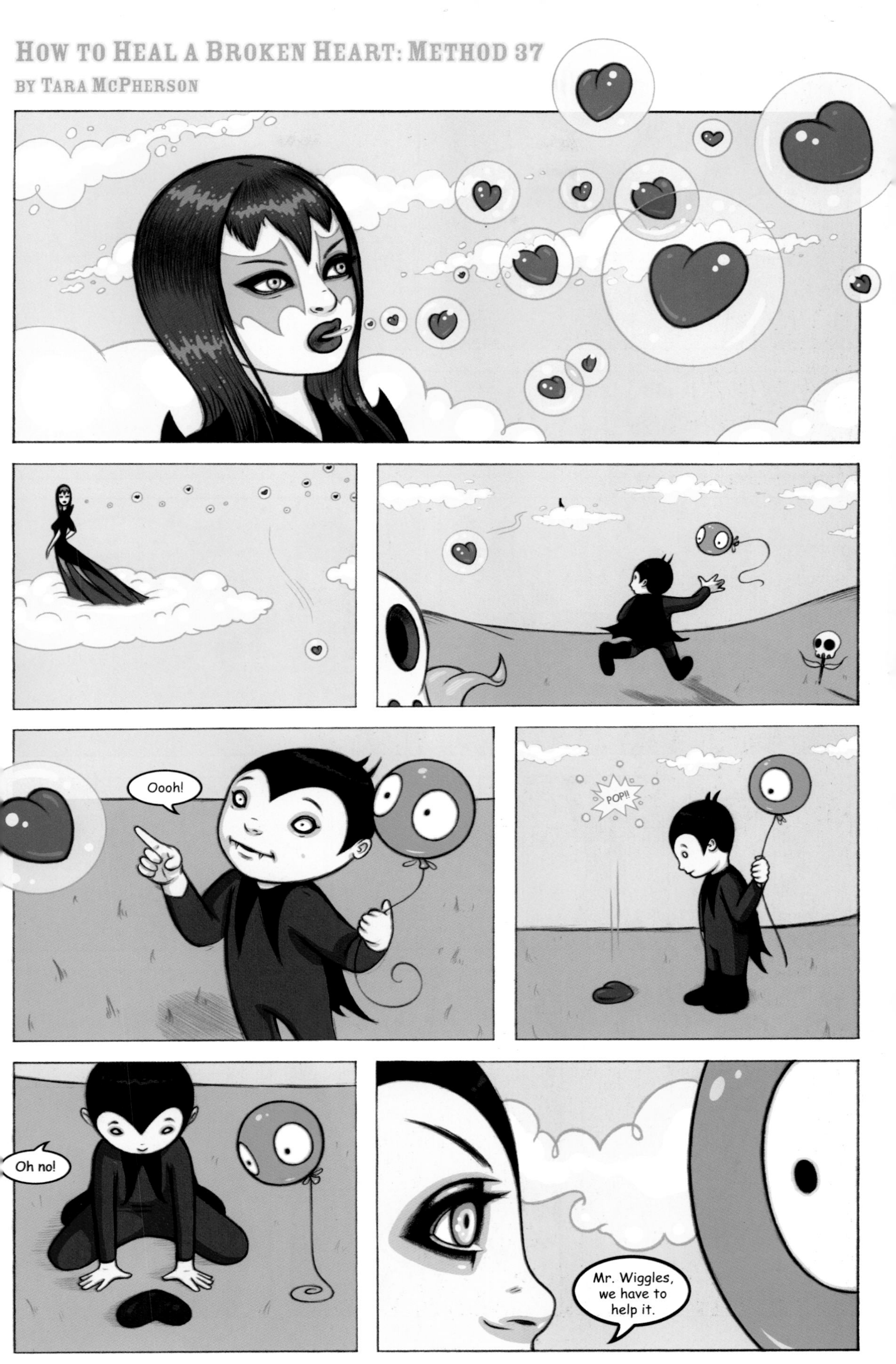
Oooh!
POP!!
Oh no!
Mr. Wiggles, we have to help it.

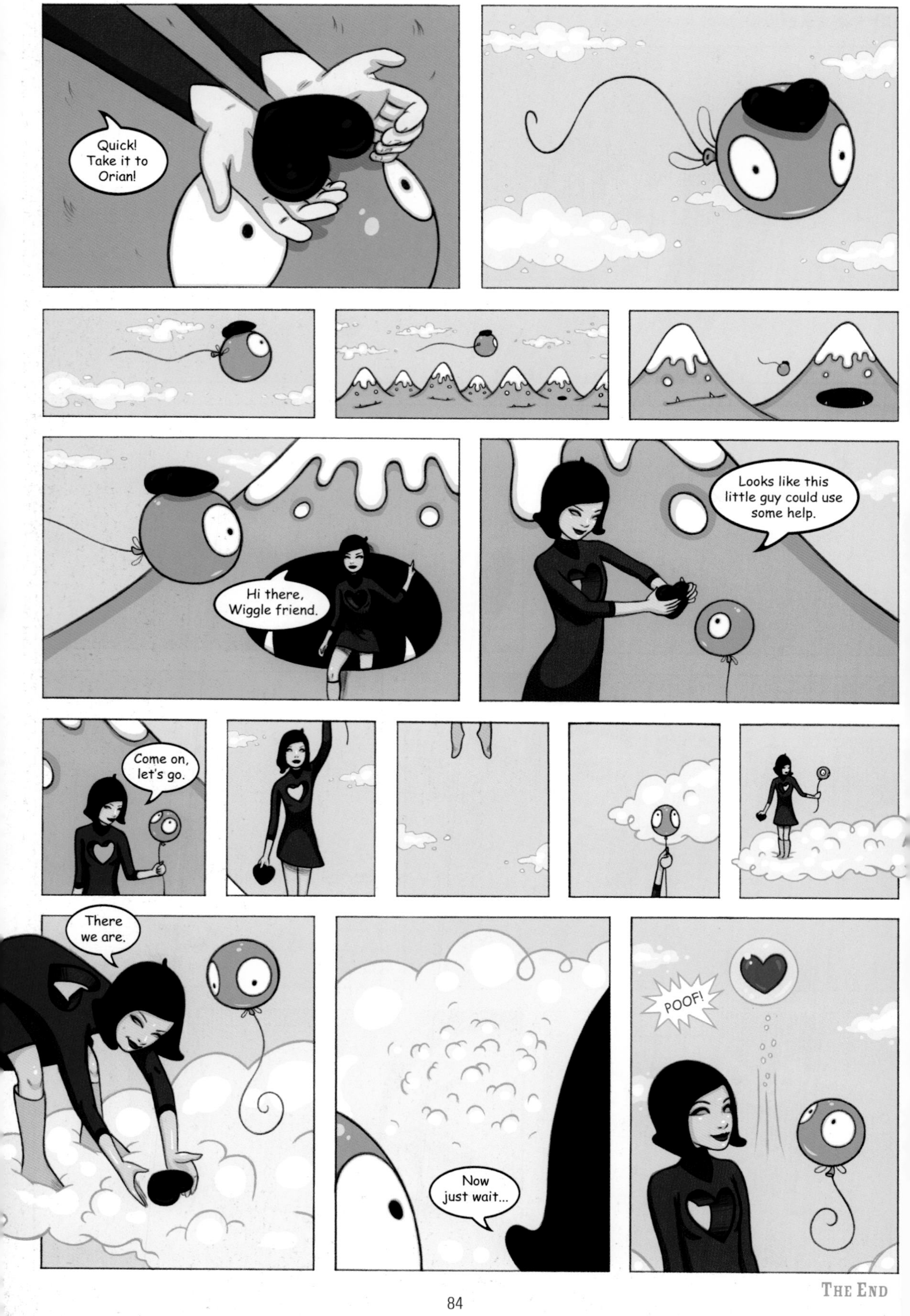
Quick! Take it to Orian!
Hi there, Wiggle friend.
Looks like this little guy could use some help.
Come on, let's go.
There we are.
Now just wait...
POOF!

THE END

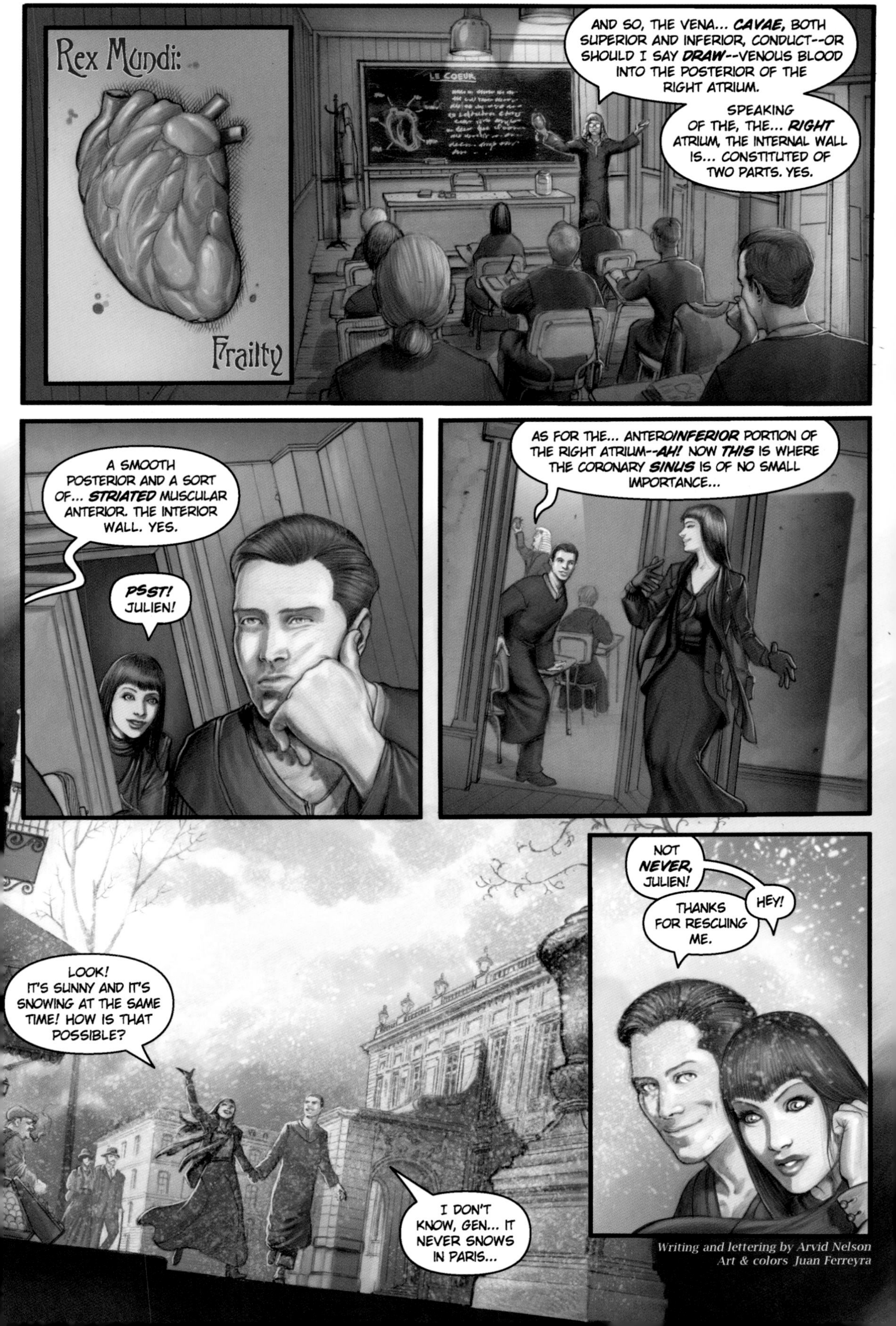
Rex Mundi:
Frailty
LE COEUR
AND SO, THE VENA... CAVAE, BOTH SUPERIOR AND INFERIOR, CONDUCT--OR SHOULD I SAY DRAW--VENOUS BLOOD INTO THE POSTERIOR OF THE RIGHT ATRIUM.
SPEAKING OF THE, THE... RIGHT ATRIUM, THE INTERNAL WALL IS... CONSTITUTED OF TWO PARTS. YES.
A SMOOTH POSTERIOR AND A SORT OF... STRIATED MUSCULAR ANTERIOR. THE INTERIOR WALL. YES.
PSST! JULIEN!
AS FOR THE... ANTEROINFERIOR PORTION OF THE RIGHT ATRIUM--AH! NOW THIS IS WHERE THE CORONARY SINUS IS OF NO SMALL IMPORTANCE...
LOOK! IT'S SUNNY AND IT'S SNOWING AT THE SAME TIME! HOW IS THAT POSSIBLE?
I DON'T KNOW, GEN... IT NEVER SNOWS IN PARIS...
NOT NEVER, JULIEN!
HEY!
THANKS FOR RESCUING ME.
Writing and lettering by Arvid Nelson
Art & colors Juan Ferreyra

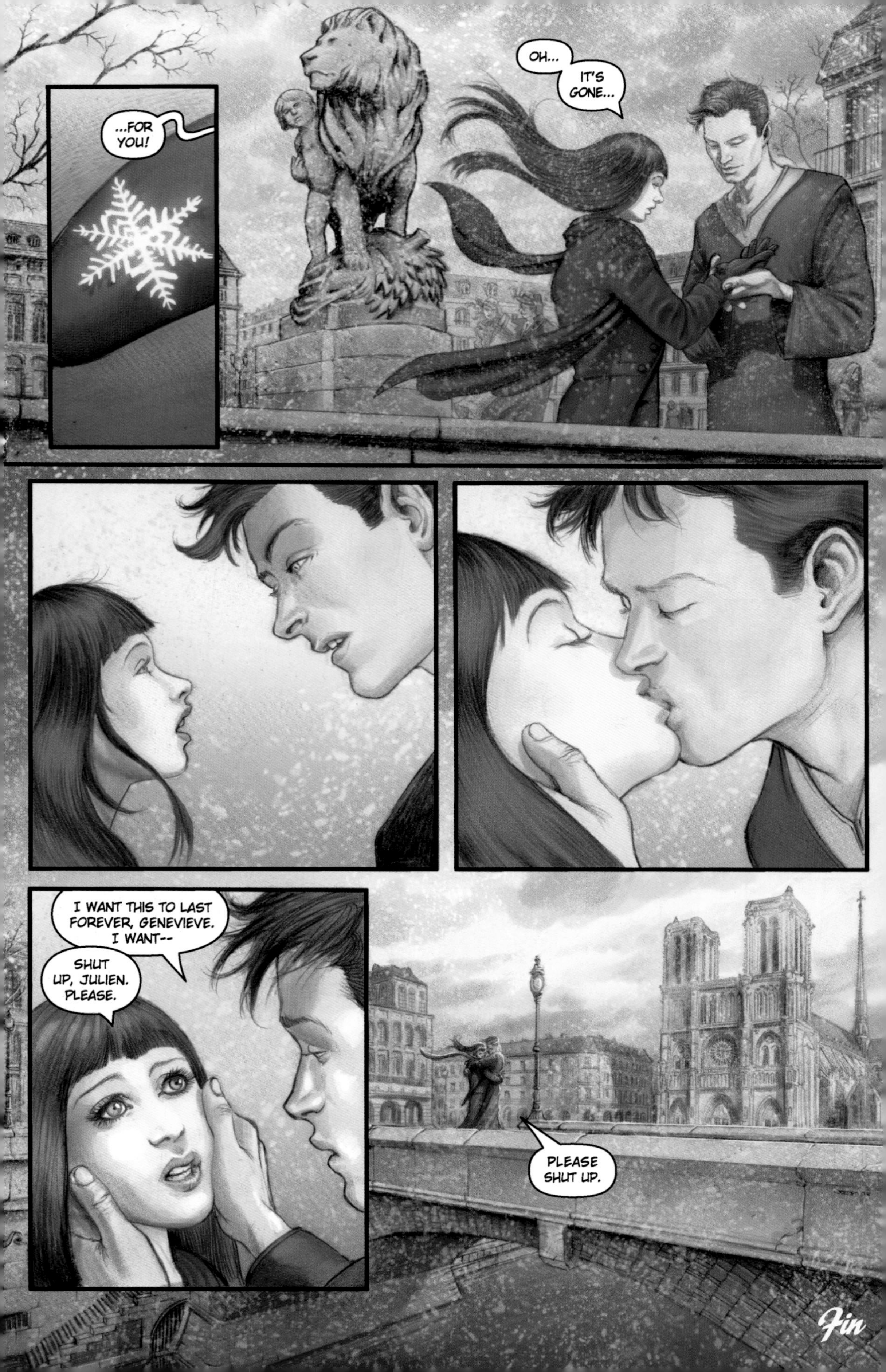
...FOR YOU!
OH...
IT'S GONE...
I WANT THIS TO LAST FOREVER, GENEVIEVE. I WANT--
SHUT UP, JULIEN. PLEASE.
PLEASE SHUT UP.
Fin

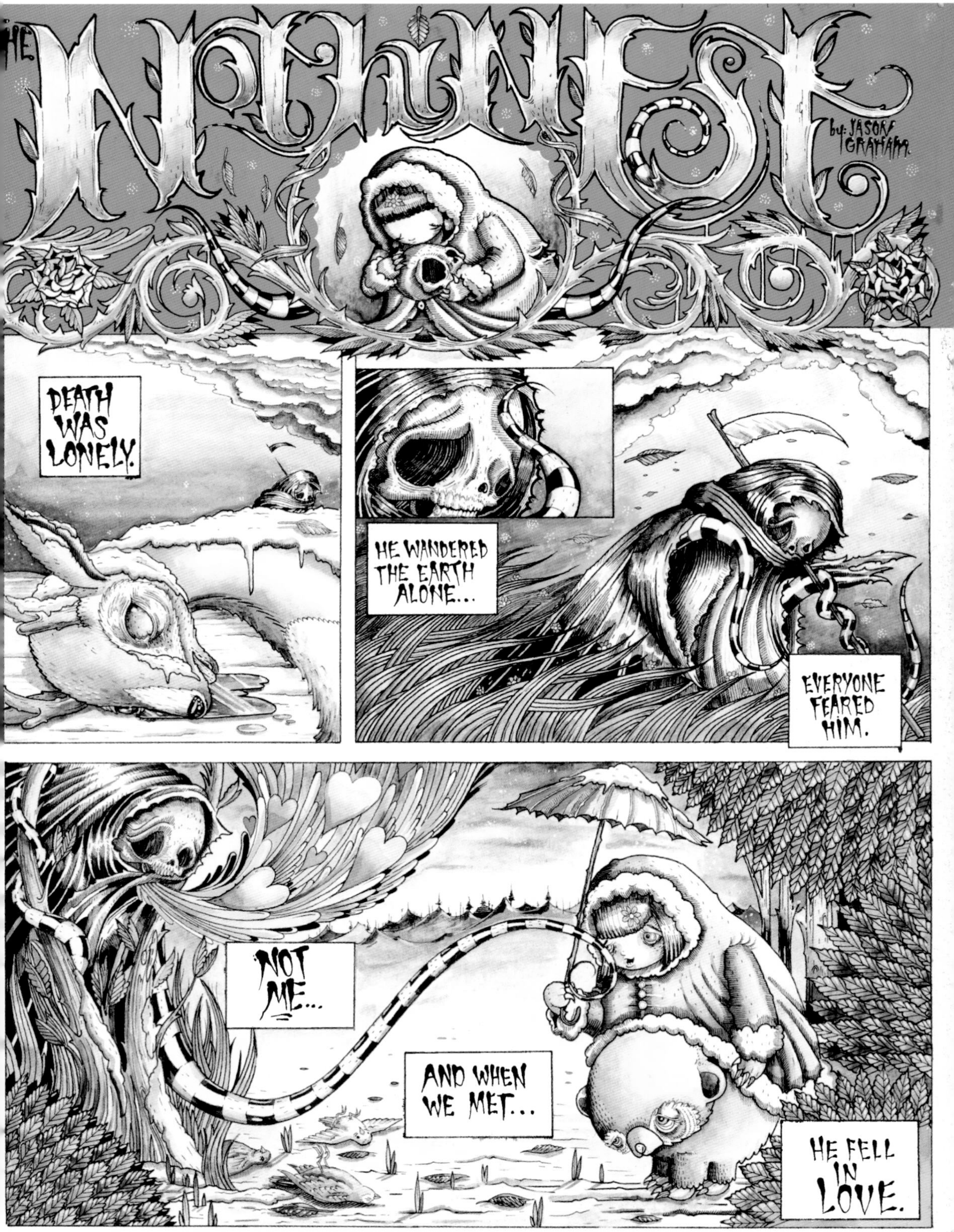
THE
by: JASON GRAHAM.
DEATH WAS LONELY.
HE WANDERED THE EARTH ALONE...
EVERYONE FEARED HIM.
NOT ME...
AND WHEN WE MET...
HE FELL IN LOVE.

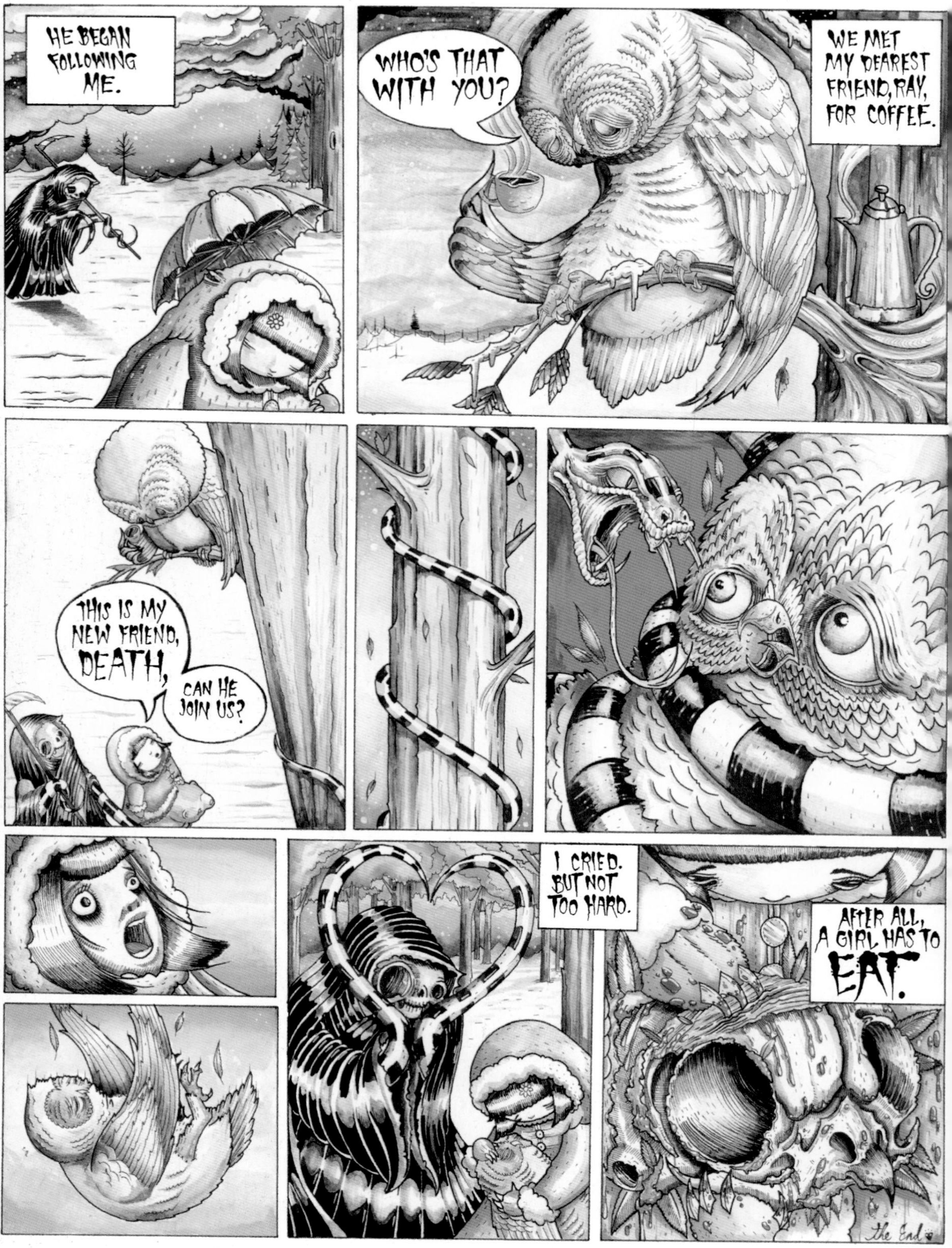
HE BEGAN FOLLOWING ME.
WHO'S THAT WITH YOU?
WE MET MY DEAREST FRIEND, RAY, FOR COFFEE.
THIS IS MY NEW FRIEND, DEATH,
CAN HE JOIN US?
I CRIED. BUT NOT TOO HARD.
AFTER ALL, A GIRL HAS TO EAT.
the End

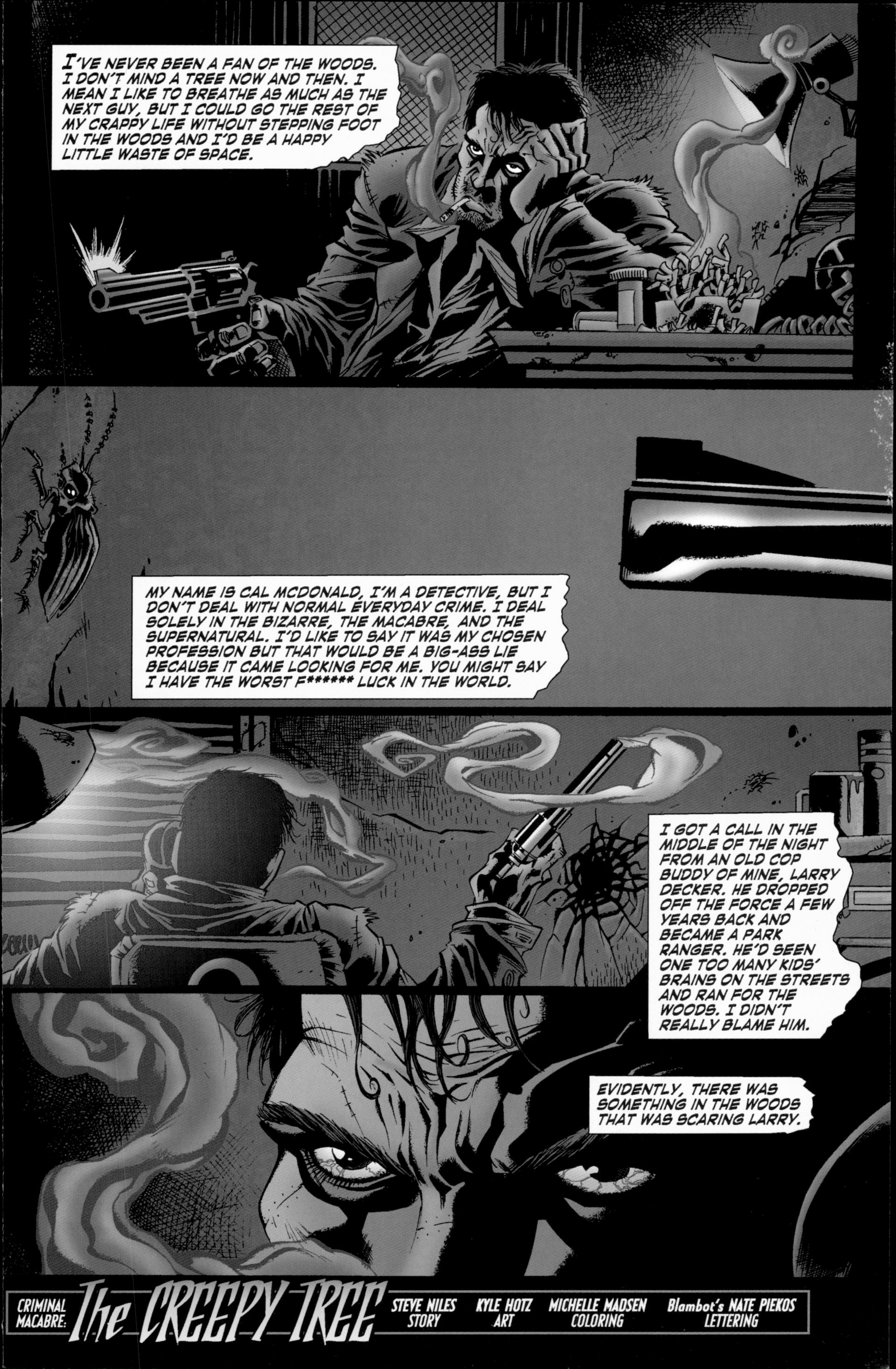
I'VE NEVER BEEN A FAN OF THE WOODS. I DON'T MIND A TREE NOW AND THEN. I MEAN I LIKE TO BREATHE AS MUCH AS THE NEXT GUY, BUT I COULD GO THE REST OF MY CRAPPY LIFE WITHOUT STEPPING FOOT IN THE WOODS AND I'D BE A HAPPY LITTLE WASTE OF SPACE.
MY NAME IS CAL MCDONALD, I'M A DETECTIVE, BUT I DON'T DEAL WITH NORMAL EVERYDAY CRIME. I DEAL SOLELY IN THE BIZARRE, THE MACABRE, AND THE SUPERNATURAL. I'D LIKE TO SAY IT WAS MY CHOSEN PROFESSION BUT THAT WOULD BE A BIG-ASS LIE BECAUSE IT CAME LOOKING FOR ME. YOU MIGHT SAY I HAVE THE WORST F****** LUCK IN THE WORLD.
I GOT A CALL IN THE MIDDLE OF THE NIGHT FROM AN OLD COP BUDDY OF MINE, LARRY DECKER. HE DROPPED OFF THE FORCE A FEW YEARS BACK AND BECAME A PARK RANGER. HE'D SEEN ONE TOO MANY KIDS' BRAINS ON THE STREETS AND RAN FOR THE WOODS. I DIDN'T REALLY BLAME HIM.
EVIDENTLY, THERE WAS SOMETHING IN THE WOODS THAT WAS SCARING LARRY.
CRIMINAL MACABRE: The CREEPY TREE
STEVE NILES STORY
KYLE HOTZ ART
MICHELLE MADSEN COLORING
Blambot's NATE PIEKOS LETTERING

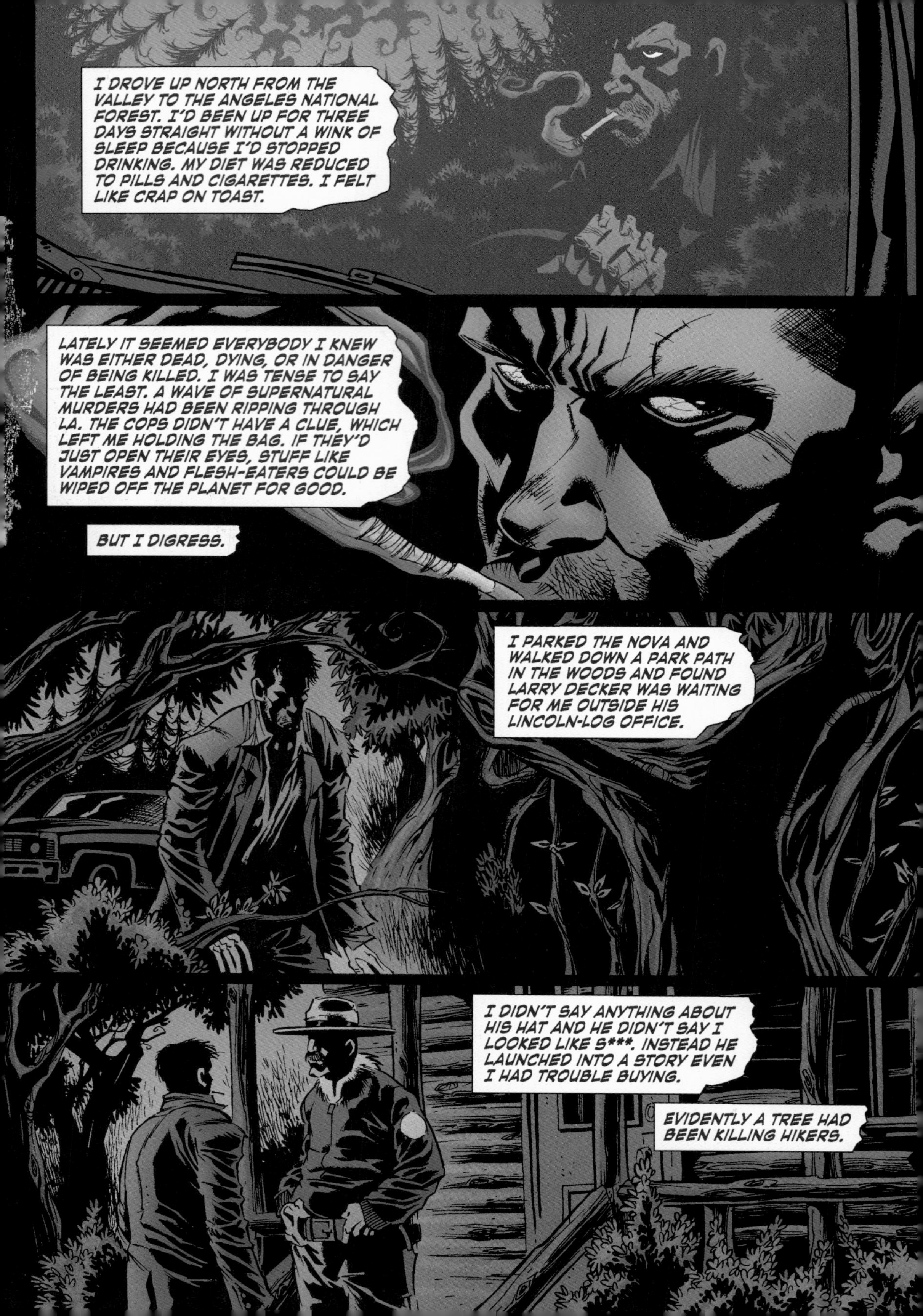
I DROVE UP NORTH FROM THE VALLEY TO THE ANGELES NATIONAL FOREST. I'D BEEN UP FOR THREE DAYS STRAIGHT WITHOUT A WINK OF SLEEP BECAUSE I'D STOPPED DRINKING. MY DIET WAS REDUCED TO PILLS AND CIGARETTES. I FELT LIKE CRAP ON TOAST.
LATELY IT SEEMED EVERYBODY I KNEW WAS EITHER DEAD, DYING, OR IN DANGER OF BEING KILLED. I WAS TENSE TO SAY THE LEAST. A WAVE OF SUPERNATURAL MURDERS HAD BEEN RIPPING THROUGH LA. THE COPS DIDN'T HAVE A CLUE, WHICH LEFT ME HOLDING THE BAG. IF THEY'D JUST OPEN THEIR EYES, STUFF LIKE VAMPIRES AND FLESH-EATERS COULD BE WIPED OFF THE PLANET FOR GOOD.
BUT I DIGRESS.
I PARKED THE NOVA AND WALKED DOWN A PARK PATH IN THE WOODS AND FOUND LARRY DECKER WAS WAITING FOR ME OUTSIDE HIS LINCOLN-LOG OFFICE.
I DIDN'T SAY ANYTHING ABOUT HIS HAT AND HE DIDN'T SAY I LOOKED LIKE S***. INSTEAD HE LAUNCHED INTO A STORY EVEN I HAD TROUBLE BUYING.
EVIDENTLY A TREE HAD BEEN KILLING HIKERS.

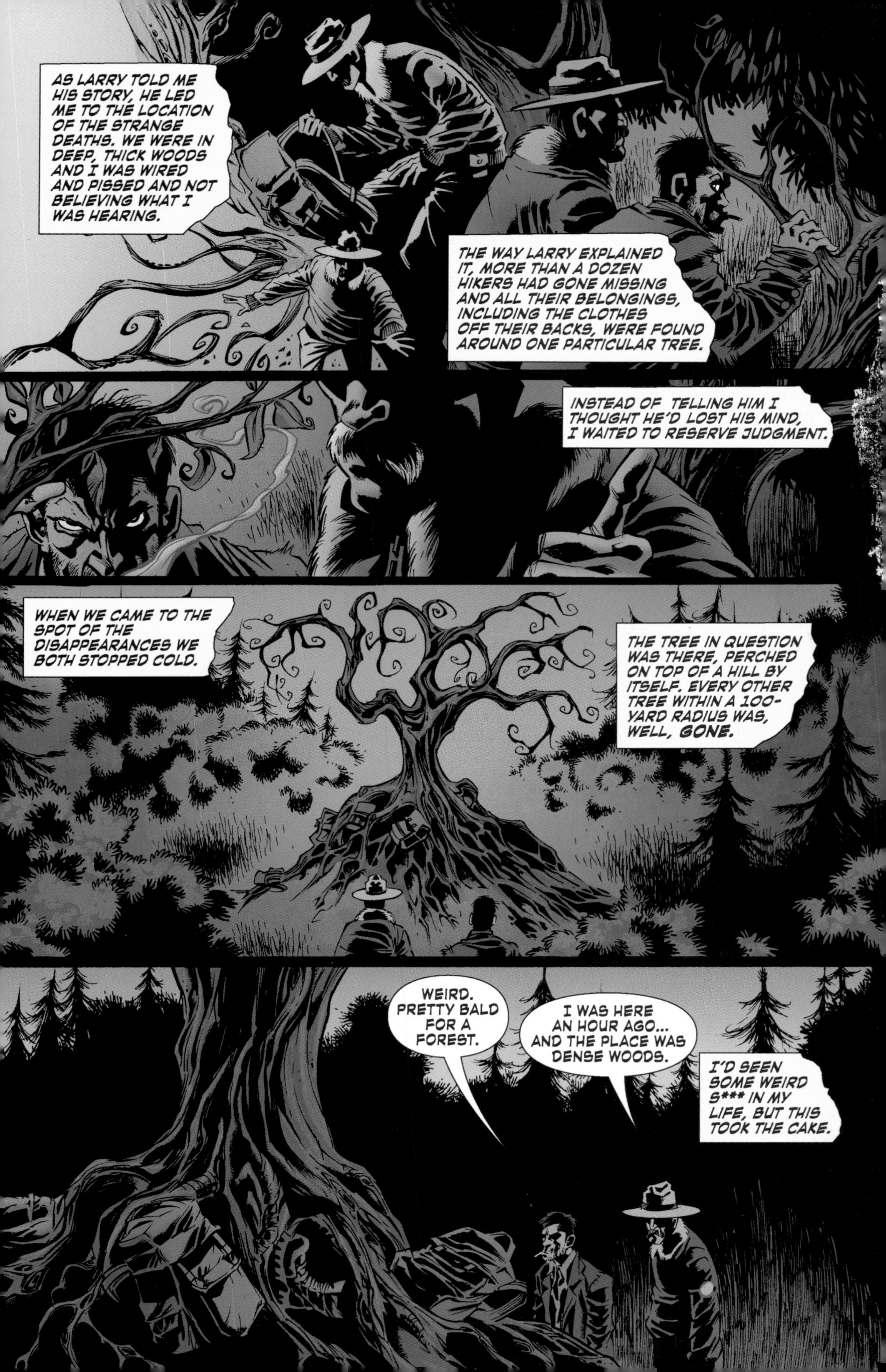
AS LARRY TOLD ME HIS STORY, HE LED ME TO THE LOCATION OF THE STRANGE DEATHS. WE WERE IN DEEP, THICK WOODS AND I WAS WIRED AND PISSED AND NOT BELIEVING WHAT I WAS HEARING.
THE WAY LARRY EXPLAINED IT, MORE THAN A DOZEN HIKERS HAD GONE MISSING AND ALL THEIR BELONGINGS, INCLUDING THE CLOTHES OFF THEIR BACKS, WERE FOUND AROUND ONE PARTICULAR TREE.
INSTEAD OF TELLING HIM I THOUGHT HE'D LOST HIS MIND, I WAITED TO RESERVE JUDGMENT.
WHEN WE CAME TO THE SPOT OF THE DISAPPEARANCES WE BOTH STOPPED COLD.
THE TREE IN QUESTION WAS THERE, PERCHED ON TOP OF A HILL BY ITSELF. EVERY OTHER TREE WITHIN A 100-YARD RADIUS WAS, WELL, GONE.
WEIRD. PRETTY BALD FOR A FOREST.
I WAS HERE AN HOUR AGO... AND THE PLACE WAS DENSE WOODS.
I'D SEEN SOME WEIRD S*** IN MY LIFE, BUT THIS TOOK THE CAKE.

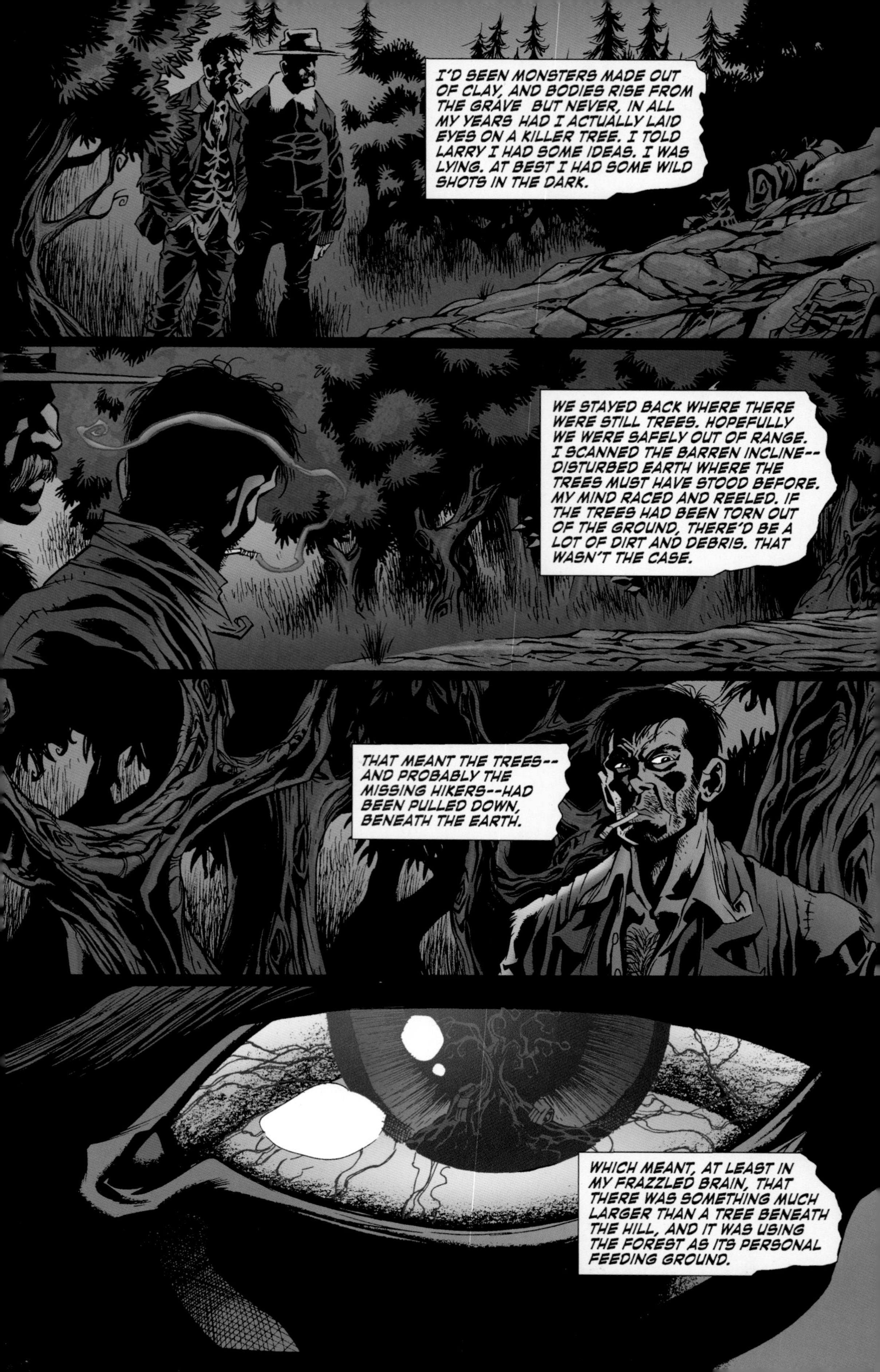
I'D SEEN MONSTERS MADE OUT OF CLAY, AND BODIES RISE FROM THE GRAVE BUT NEVER, IN ALL MY YEARS HAD I ACTUALLY LAID EYES ON A KILLER TREE. I TOLD LARRY I HAD SOME IDEAS. I WAS LYING. AT BEST I HAD SOME WILD SHOTS IN THE DARK.
WE STAYED BACK WHERE THERE WERE STILL TREES. HOPEFULLY WE WERE SAFELY OUT OF RANGE. I SCANNED THE BARREN INCLINE--DISTURBED EARTH WHERE THE TREES MUST HAVE STOOD BEFORE. MY MIND RACED AND REELED. IF THE TREES HAD BEEN TORN OUT OF THE GROUND, THERE'D BE A LOT OF DIRT AND DEBRIS. THAT WASN'T THE CASE.
THAT MEANT THE TREES--AND PROBABLY THE MISSING HIKERS--HAD BEEN PULLED DOWN, BENEATH THE EARTH.
WHICH MEANT, AT LEAST IN MY FRAZZLED BRAIN, THAT THERE WAS SOMETHING MUCH LARGER THAN A TREE BENEATH THE HILL, AND IT WAS USING THE FOREST AS ITS PERSONAL FEEDING GROUND.

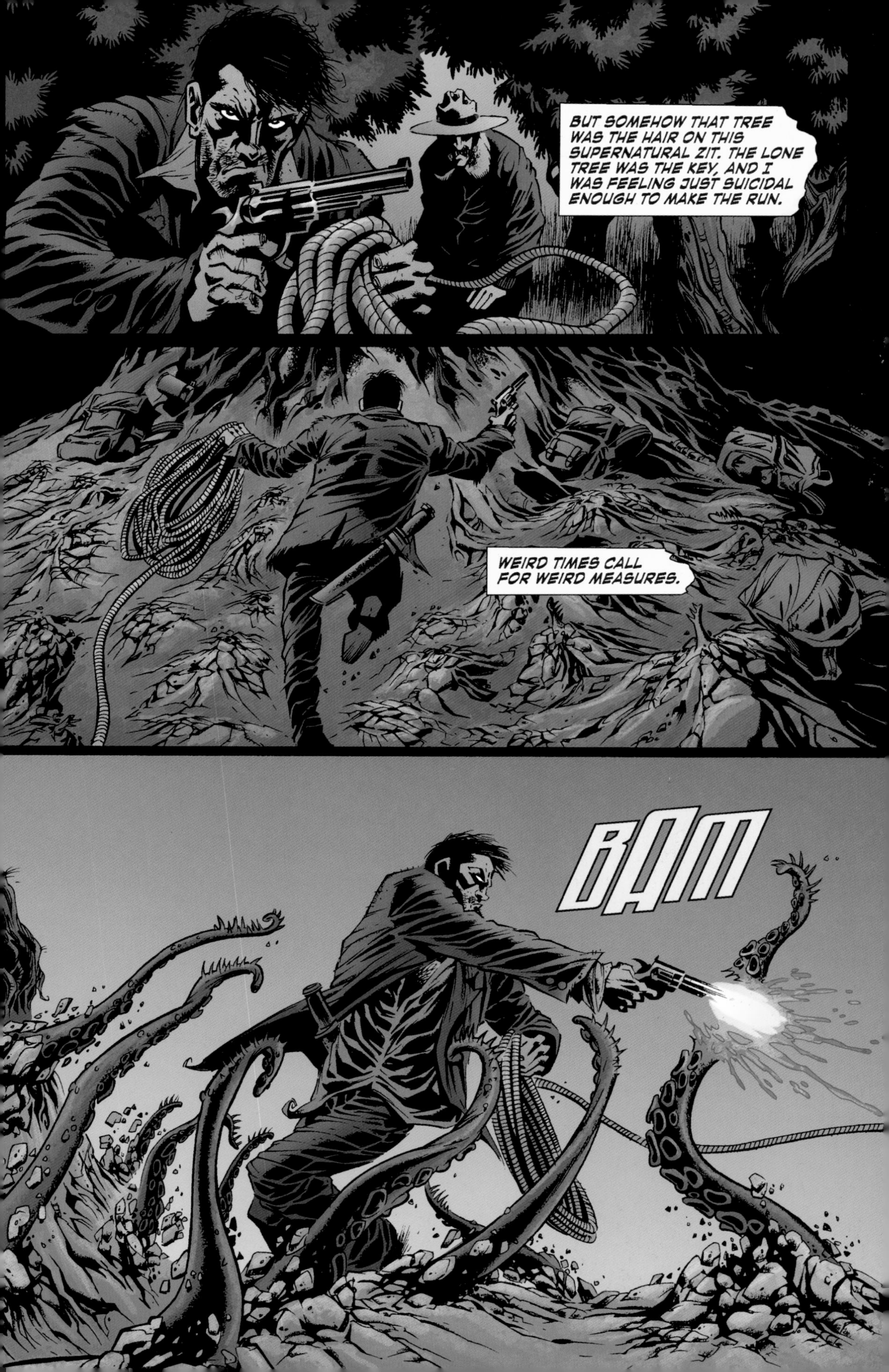
BUT SOMEHOW THAT TREE WAS THE HAIR ON THIS SUPERNATURAL ZIT. THE LONE TREE WAS THE KEY, AND I WAS FEELING JUST SUICIDAL ENOUGH TO MAKE THE RUN.
WEIRD TIMES CALL FOR WEIRD MEASURES.
BAM

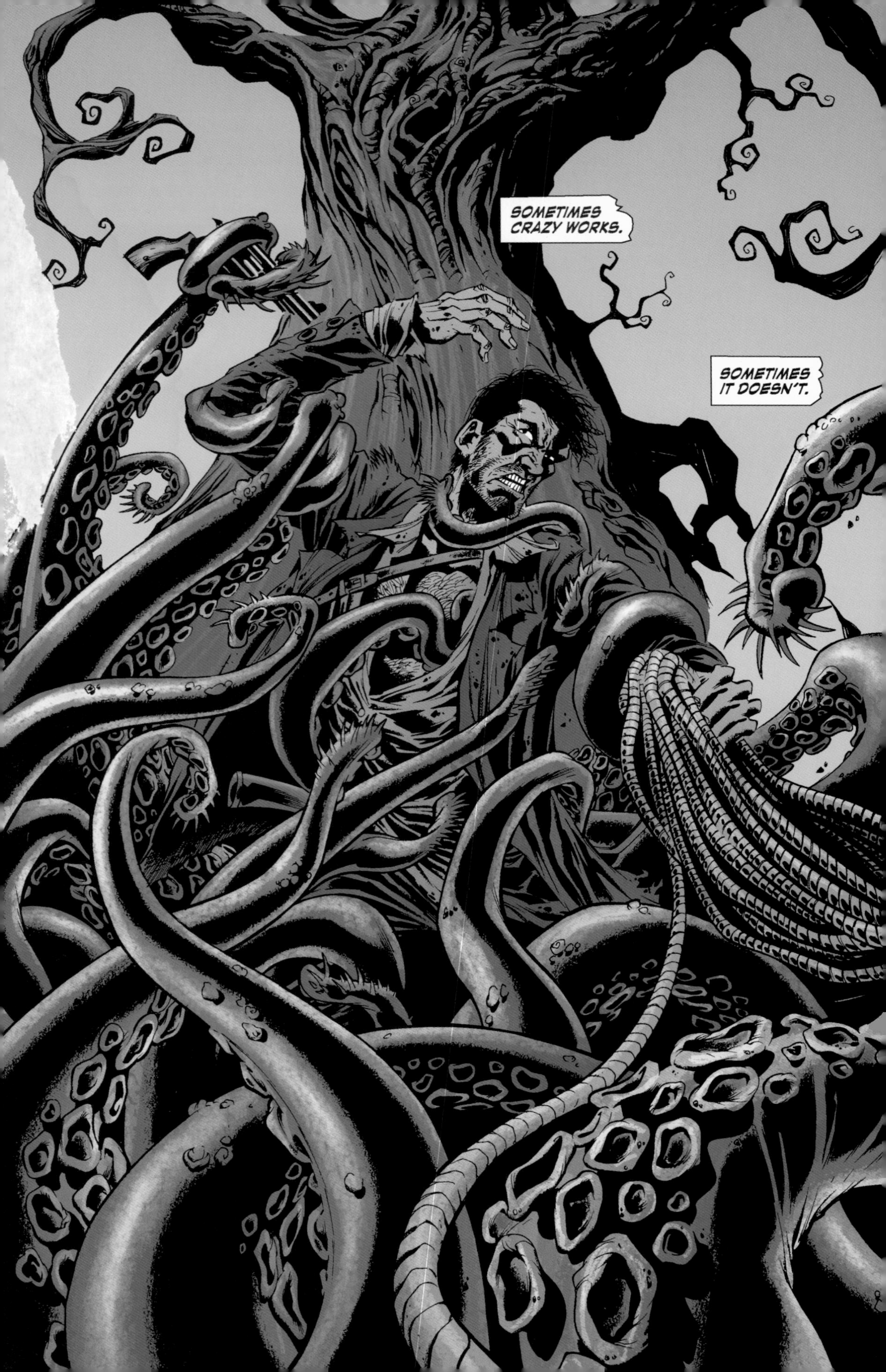
SOMETIMES CRAZY WORKS.
SOMETIMES IT DOESN'T.

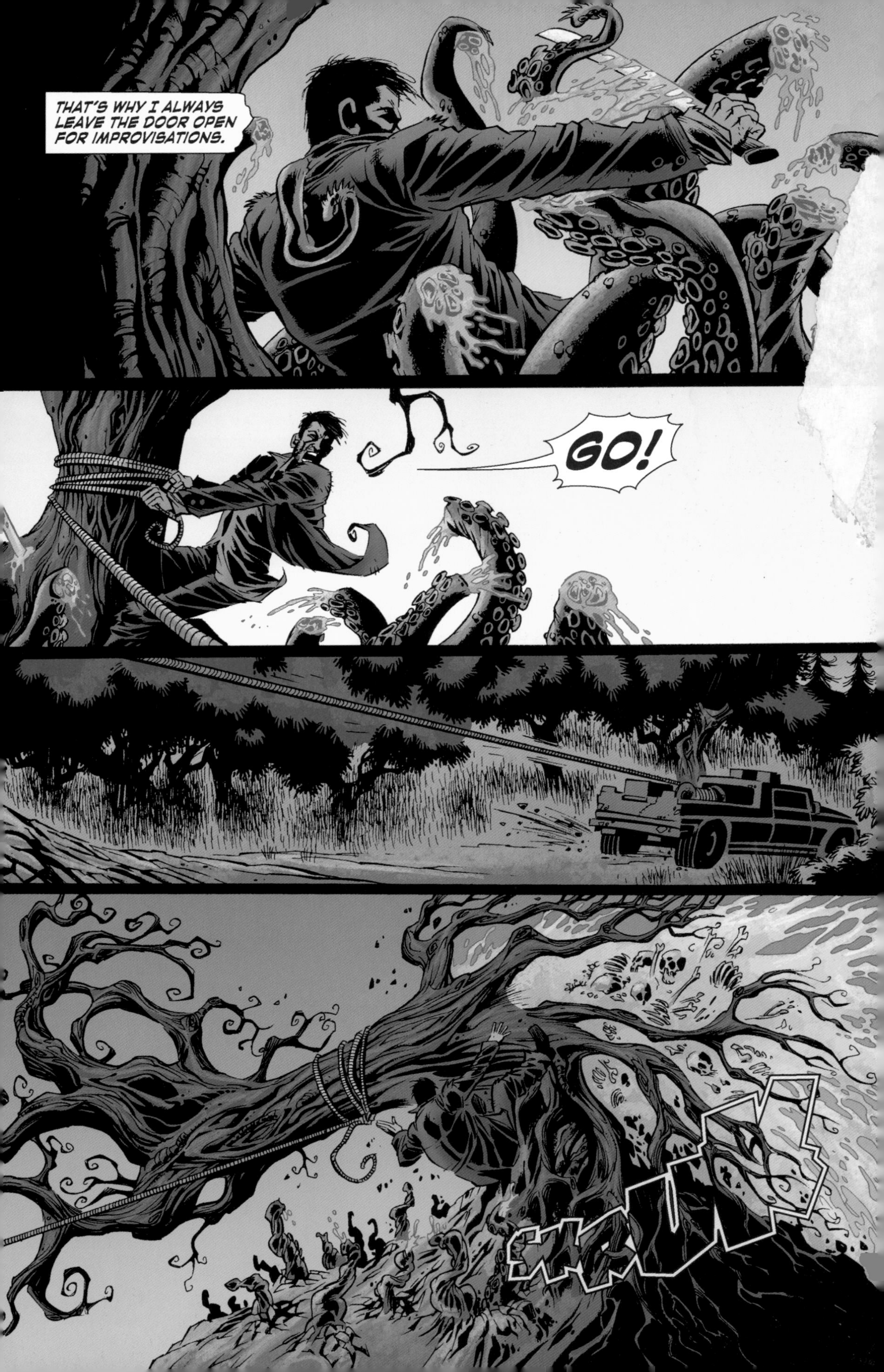
THAT'S WHY I ALWAYS LEAVE THE DOOR OPEN FOR IMPROVISATIONS.
GO!

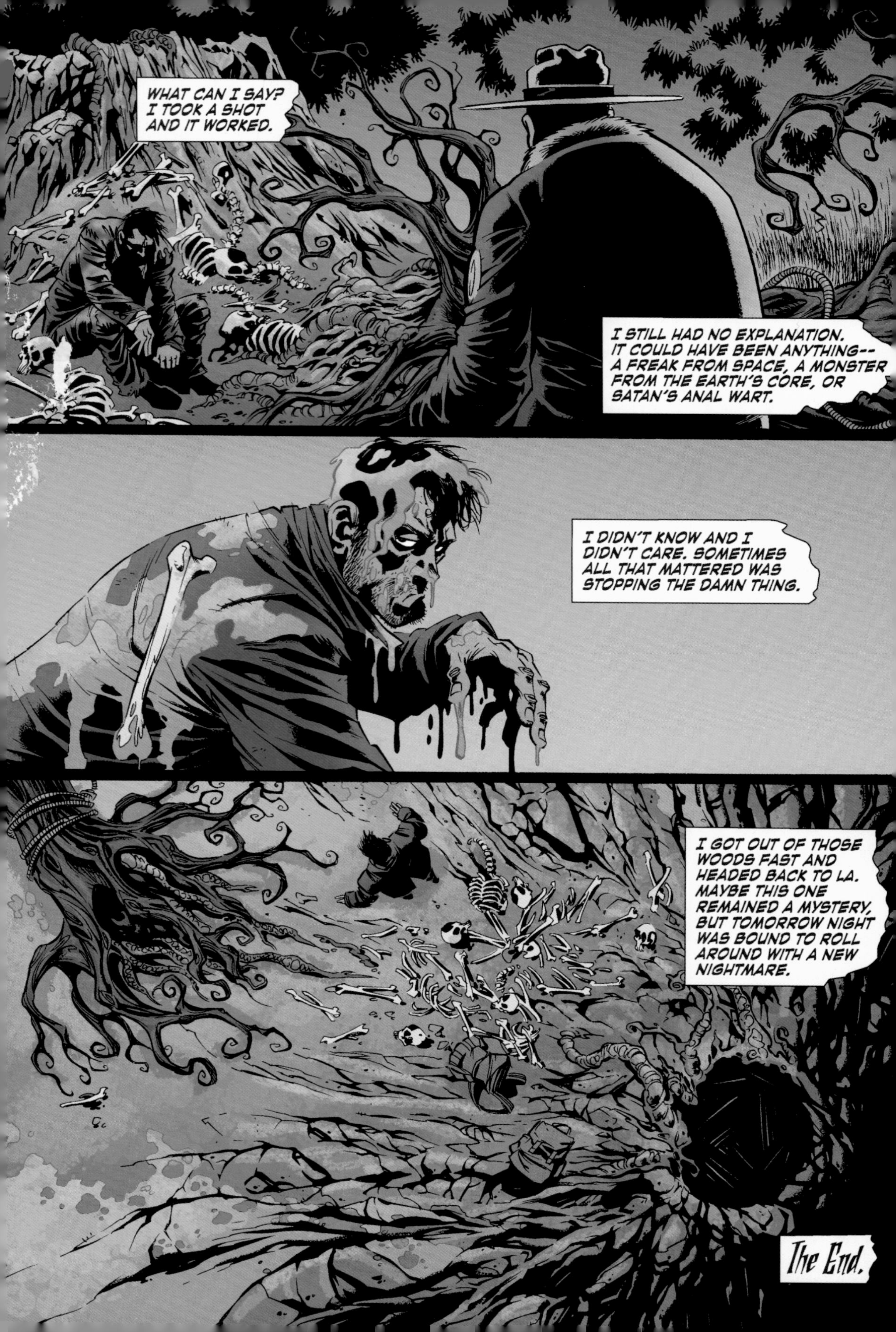
WHAT CAN I SAY? I TOOK A SHOT AND IT WORKED.
I STILL HAD NO EXPLANATION. IT COULD HAVE BEEN ANYTHING-- A FREAK FROM SPACE, A MONSTER FROM THE EARTH'S CORE, OR SATAN'S ANAL WART.
I DIDN'T KNOW AND I DIDN'T CARE. SOMETIMES ALL THAT MATTERED WAS STOPPING THE DAMN THING.
I GOT OUT OF THOSE WOODS FAST AND HEADED BACK TO LA. MAYBE THIS ONE REMAINED A MYSTERY, BUT TOMORROW NIGHT WAS BOUND TO ROLL AROUND WITH A NEW NIGHTMARE.
The End.

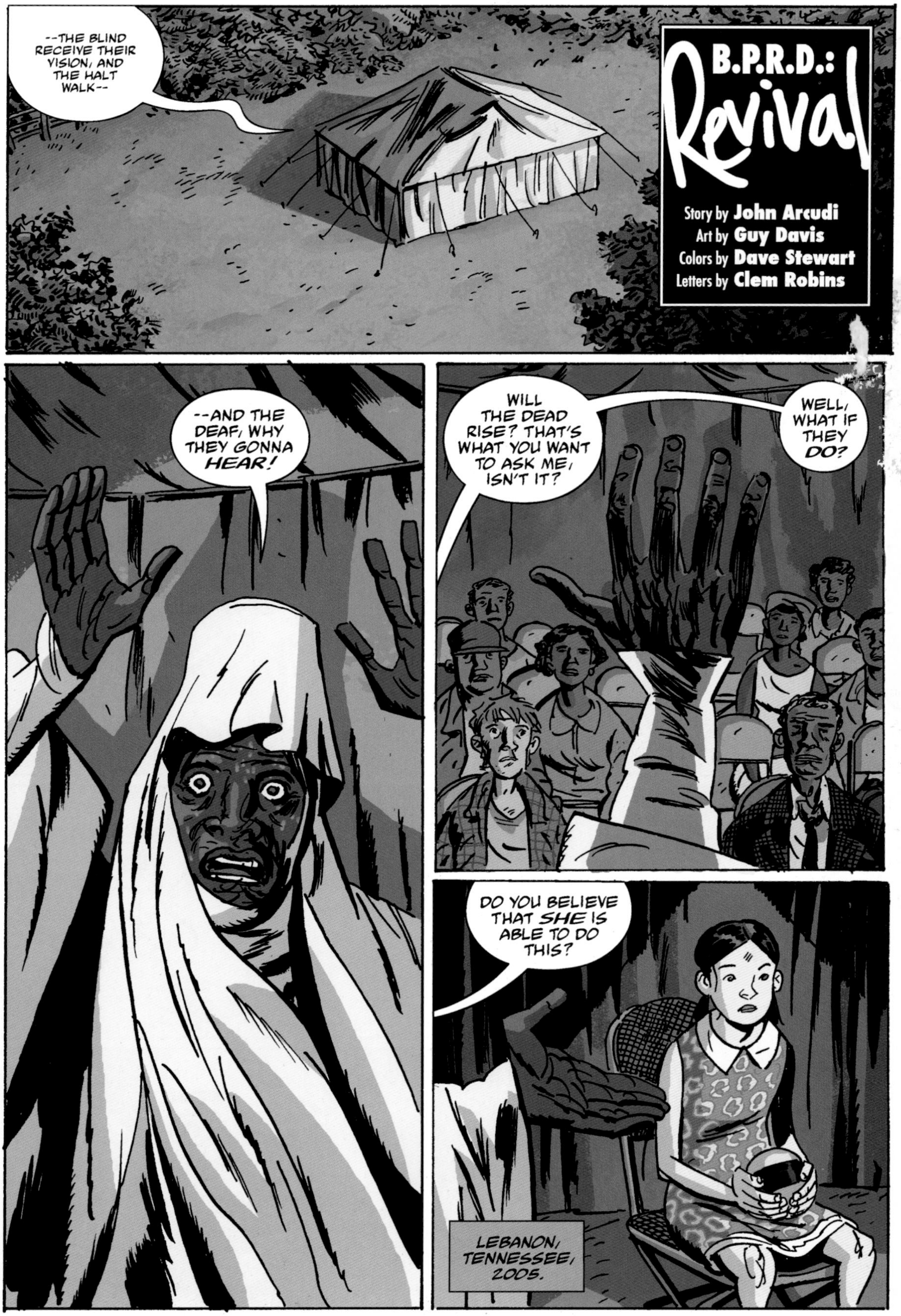
--THE BLIND RECEIVE THEIR VISION, AND THE HALT WALK--
B.P.R.D.: Revival
Story by John Arcudi
Art by Guy Davis
Colors by Dave Stewart
Letters by Clem Robins
--AND THE DEAF, WHY THEY GONNA HEAR!
WILL THE DEAD RISE? THAT'S WHAT YOU WANT TO ASK ME, ISN'T IT?
WELL, WHAT IF THEY DO?
DO YOU BELIEVE THAT SHE IS ABLE TO DO THIS?
LEBANON, TENNESSEE, 2005.

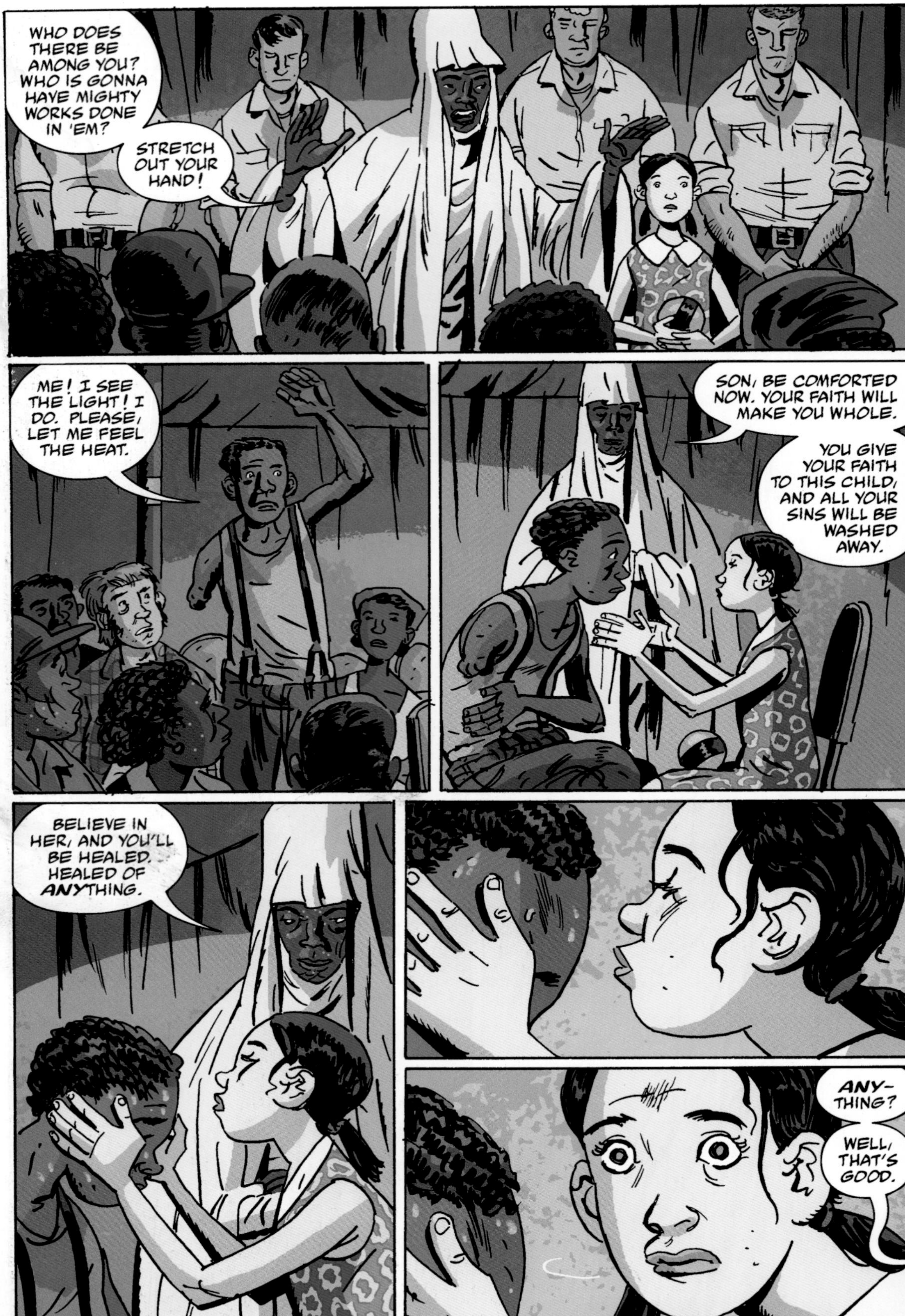
WHO DOES THERE BE AMONG YOU? WHO IS GONNA HAVE MIGHTY WORKS DONE IN 'EM?
STRETCH OUT YOUR HAND!
ME! I SEE THE LIGHT! I DO. PLEASE, LET ME FEEL THE HEAT.
SON, BE COMFORTED NOW. YOUR FAITH WILL MAKE YOU WHOLE.
YOU GIVE YOUR FAITH TO THIS CHILD, AND ALL YOUR SINS WILL BE WASHED AWAY.
BELIEVE IN HER, AND YOU'LL BE HEALED. HEALED OF ANYTHING.
ANY-THING?
WELL, THAT'S GOOD.

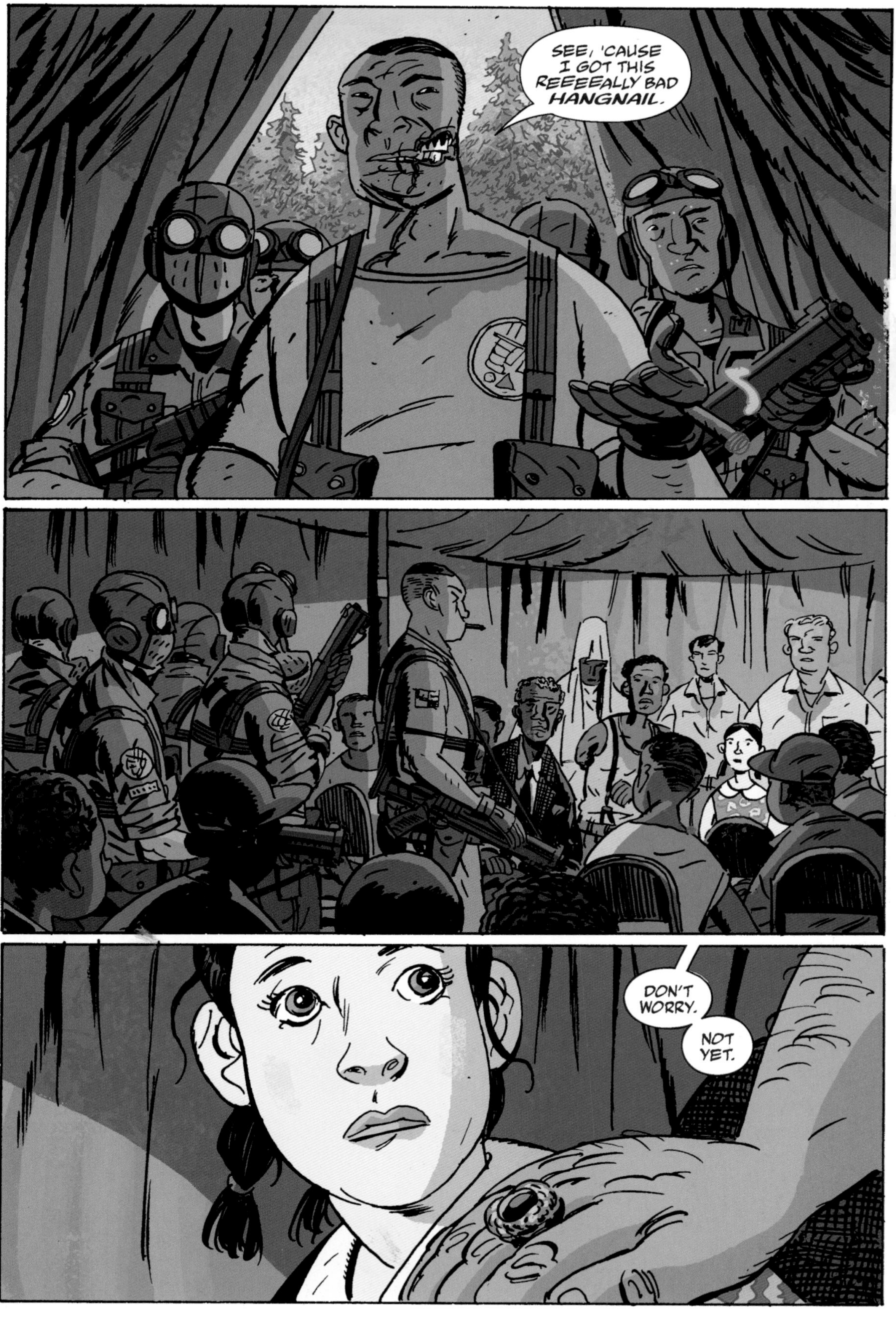
SEE, 'CAUSE I GOT THIS REEEEALLY BAD HANGNAIL.
DON'T WORRY.
NOT YET.

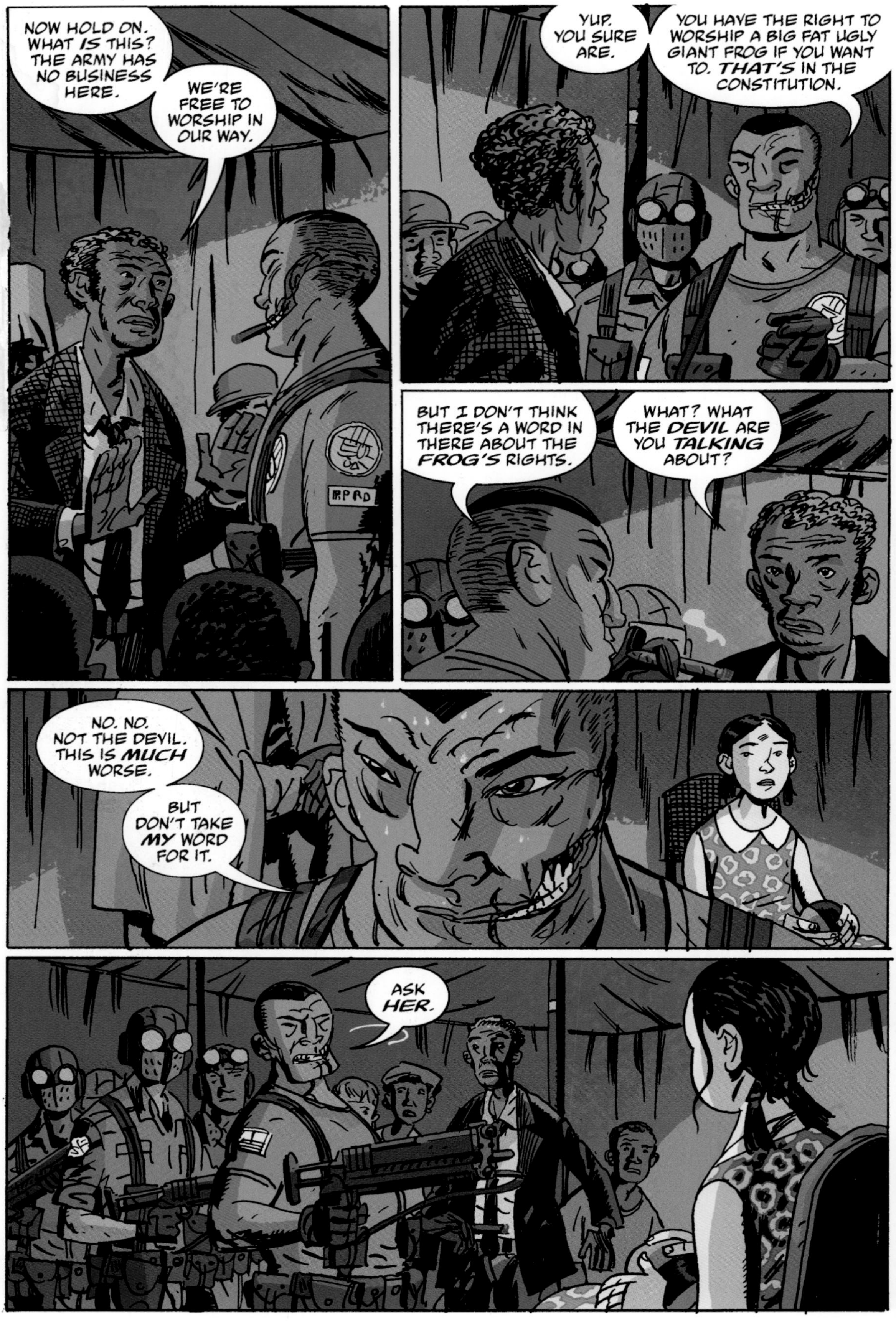
NOW HOLD ON. WHAT *IS* THIS? THE ARMY HAS NO BUSINESS HERE.
WE'RE FREE TO WORSHIP IN OUR WAY.
YUP. YOU SURE ARE.
YOU HAVE THE RIGHT TO WORSHIP A BIG FAT UGLY GIANT FROG IF YOU WANT TO. *THAT'S* IN THE CONSTITUTION.
BUT I DON'T THINK THERE'S A WORD IN THERE ABOUT THE *FROG'S* RIGHTS.
WHAT? WHAT THE *DEVIL* ARE YOU *TALKING* ABOUT?
NO. NO. NOT THE DEVIL. THIS IS *MUCH* WORSE.
BUT DON'T TAKE *MY* WORD FOR IT.
ASK *HER*.

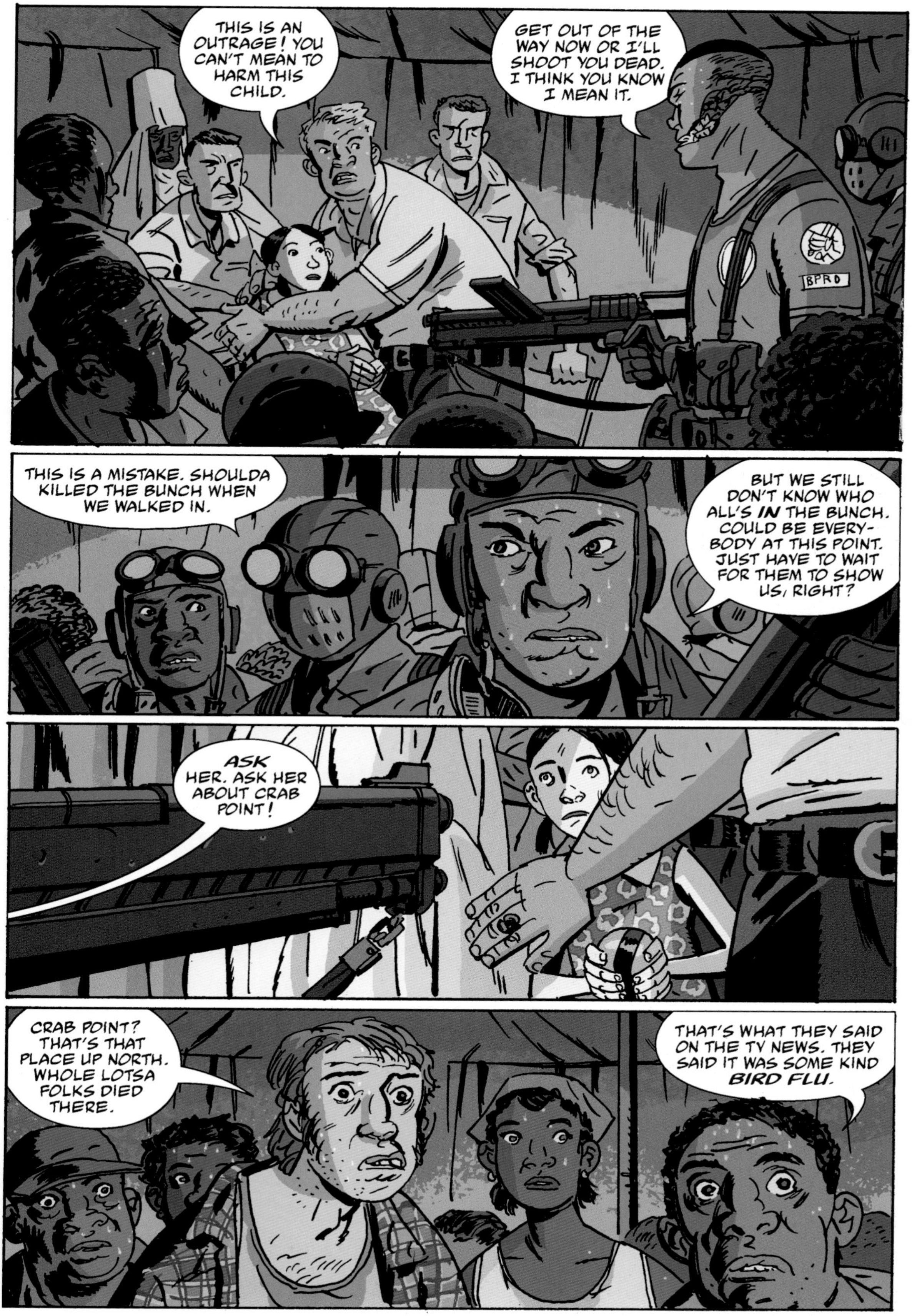

THIS IS AN OUTRAGE! YOU CAN'T MEAN TO HARM THIS CHILD.
GET OUT OF THE WAY NOW OR I'LL SHOOT YOU DEAD. I THINK YOU KNOW I MEAN IT.
BPRD
THIS IS A MISTAKE. SHOULDA KILLED THE BUNCH WHEN WE WALKED IN.
BUT WE STILL DON'T KNOW WHO ALL'S *IN* THE BUNCH. COULD BE EVERY-BODY AT THIS POINT. JUST HAVE TO WAIT FOR THEM TO SHOW US, RIGHT?
ASK HER. ASK HER ABOUT CRAB POINT!
CRAB POINT? THAT'S THAT PLACE UP NORTH. WHOLE LOTSA FOLKS DIED THERE.
THAT'S WHAT THEY SAID ON THE TV NEWS. THEY SAID IT WAS SOME KIND *BIRD FLU*.

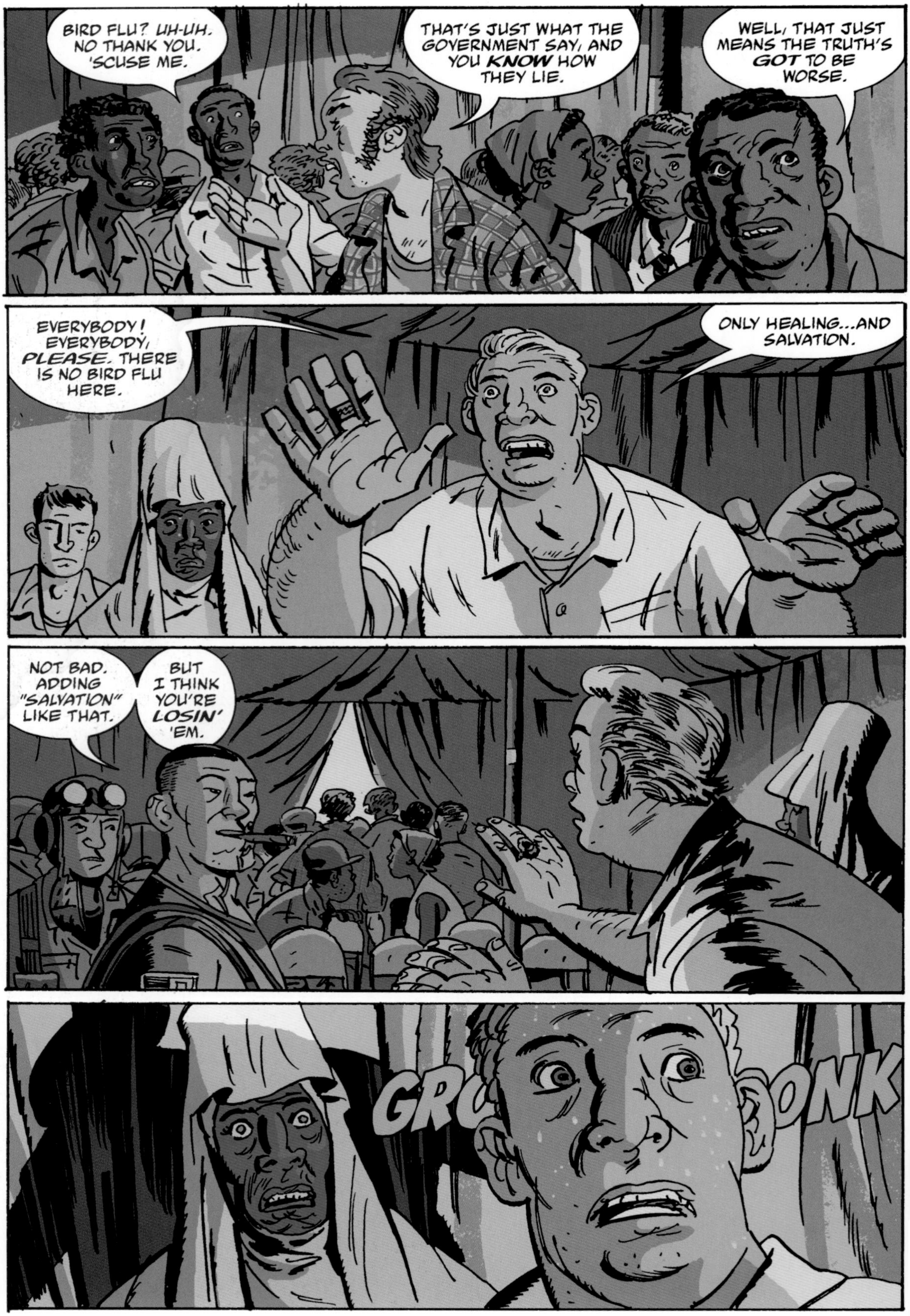
BIRD FLU? UH-UH. NO THANK YOU. 'SCUSE ME.
THAT'S JUST WHAT THE GOVERNMENT SAY, AND YOU **KNOW** HOW THEY LIE.
WELL, THAT JUST MEANS THE TRUTH'S **GOT** TO BE WORSE.
EVERYBODY! EVERYBODY, **PLEASE**. THERE IS NO BIRD FLU HERE.
ONLY HEALING...AND SALVATION.
NOT BAD. ADDING "SALVATION" LIKE THAT.
BUT I THINK YOU'RE **LOSIN'** 'EM.
GRO
ONK

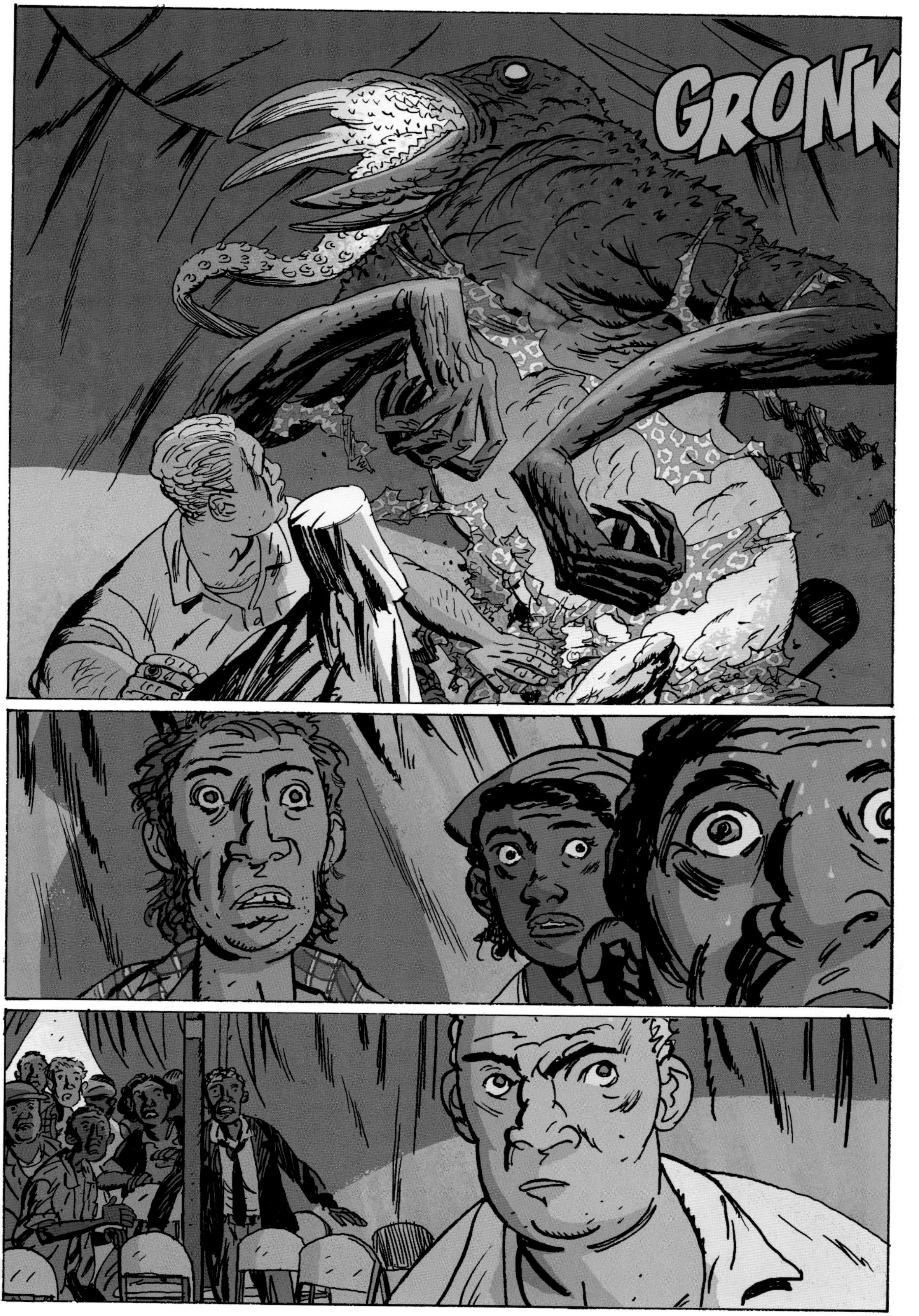
GRONK

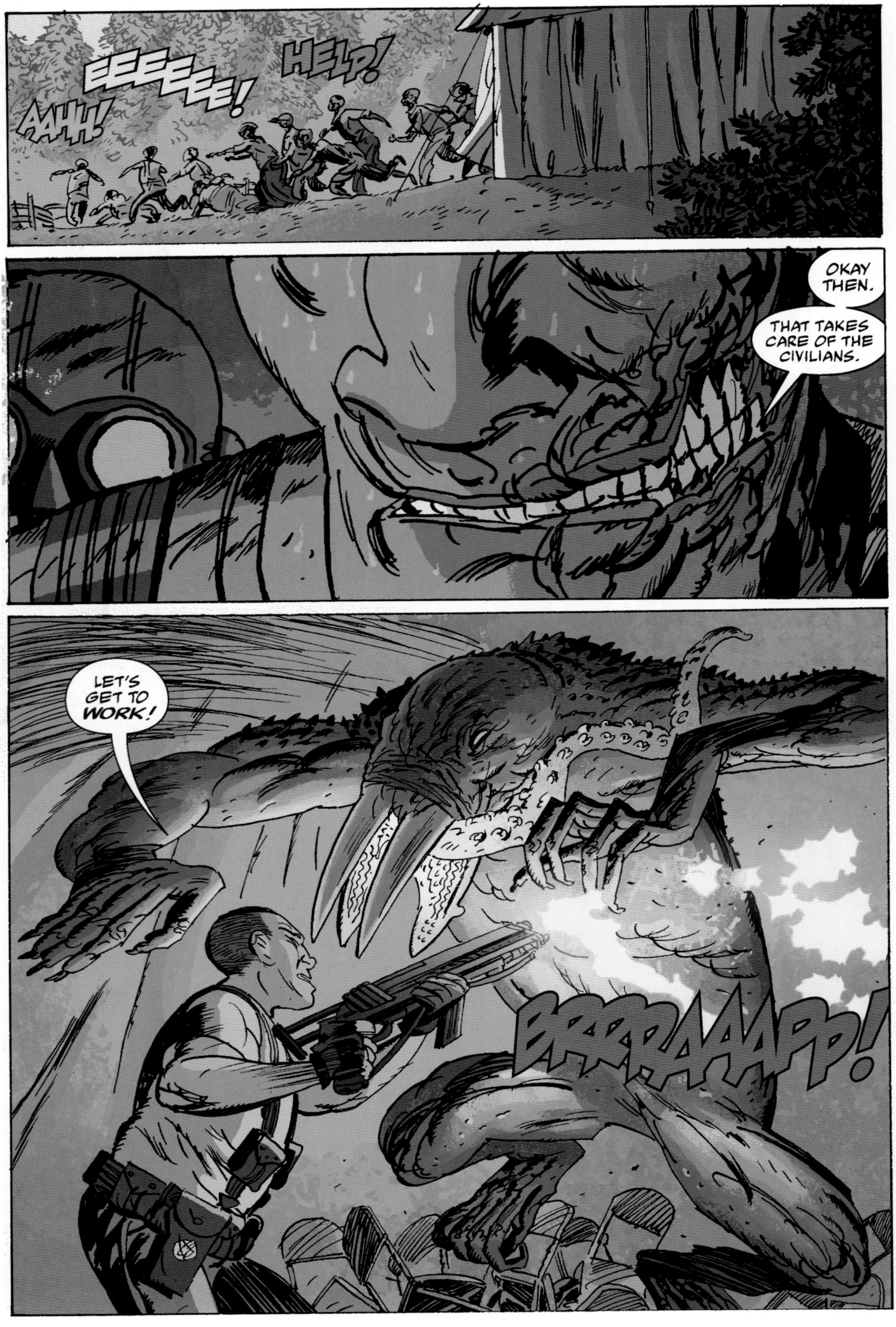
EEEEEEE!
HELP!
AAHH!
OKAY THEN.
THAT TAKES CARE OF THE CIVILIANS.
LET'S GET TO **WORK**!
BRRRAAAPP!

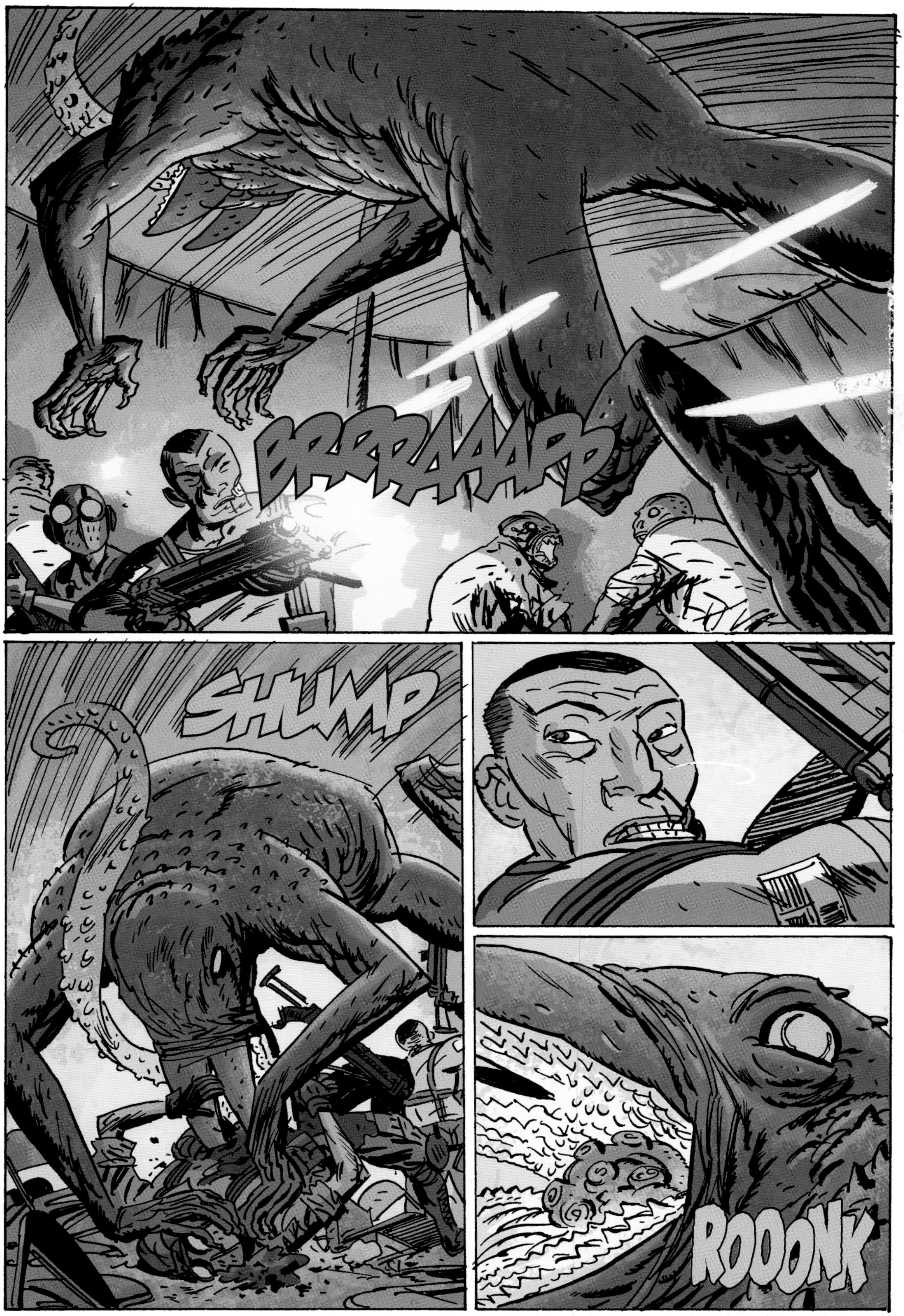
BRRRAAAPP
SHUMP
ROOONK

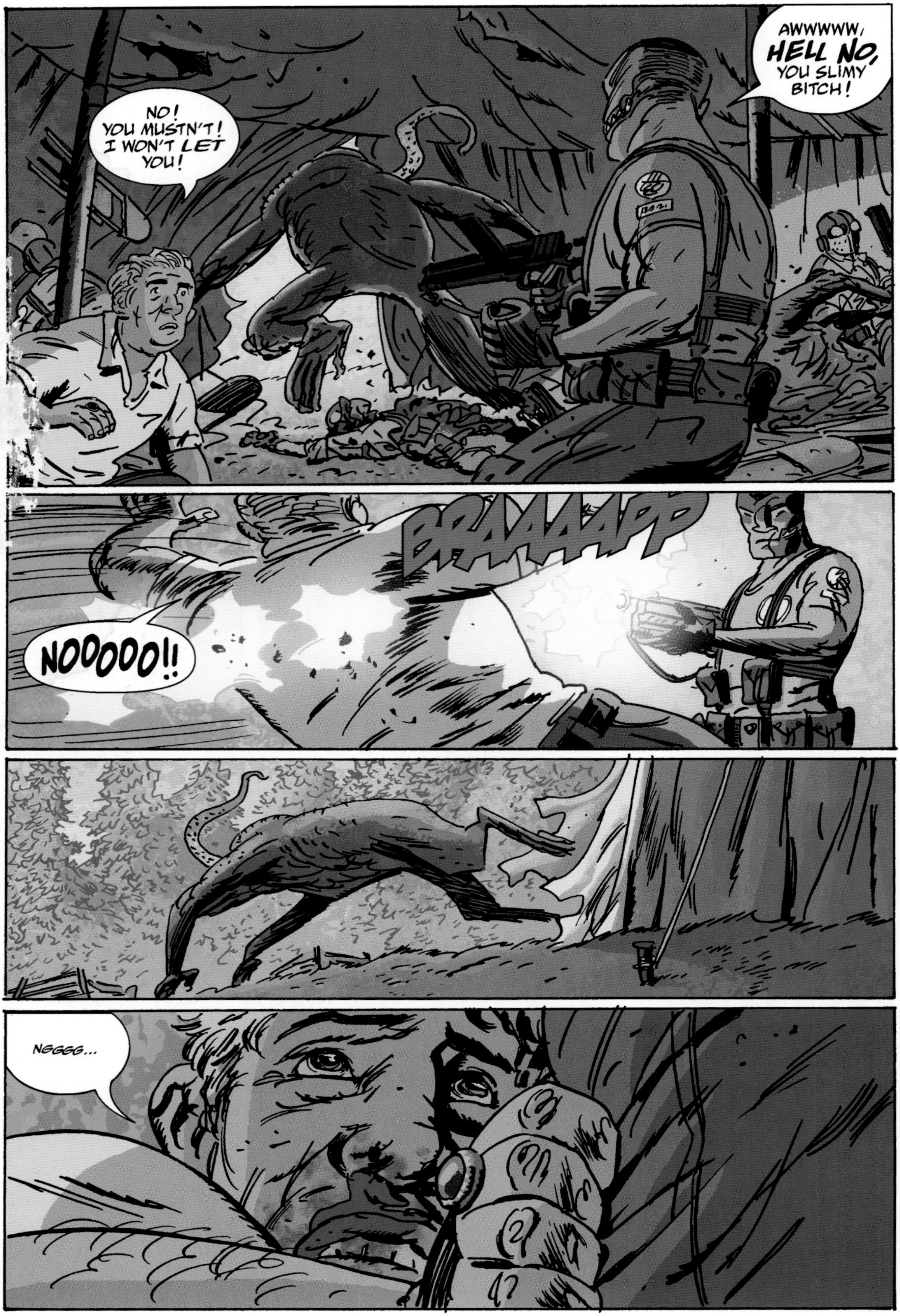
NO! YOU MUSTN'T! I WON'T LET YOU!
AWWWWW, HELL NO, YOU SLIMY BITCH!
BRAAAAPP
NOOOOO!!
NGGGG...

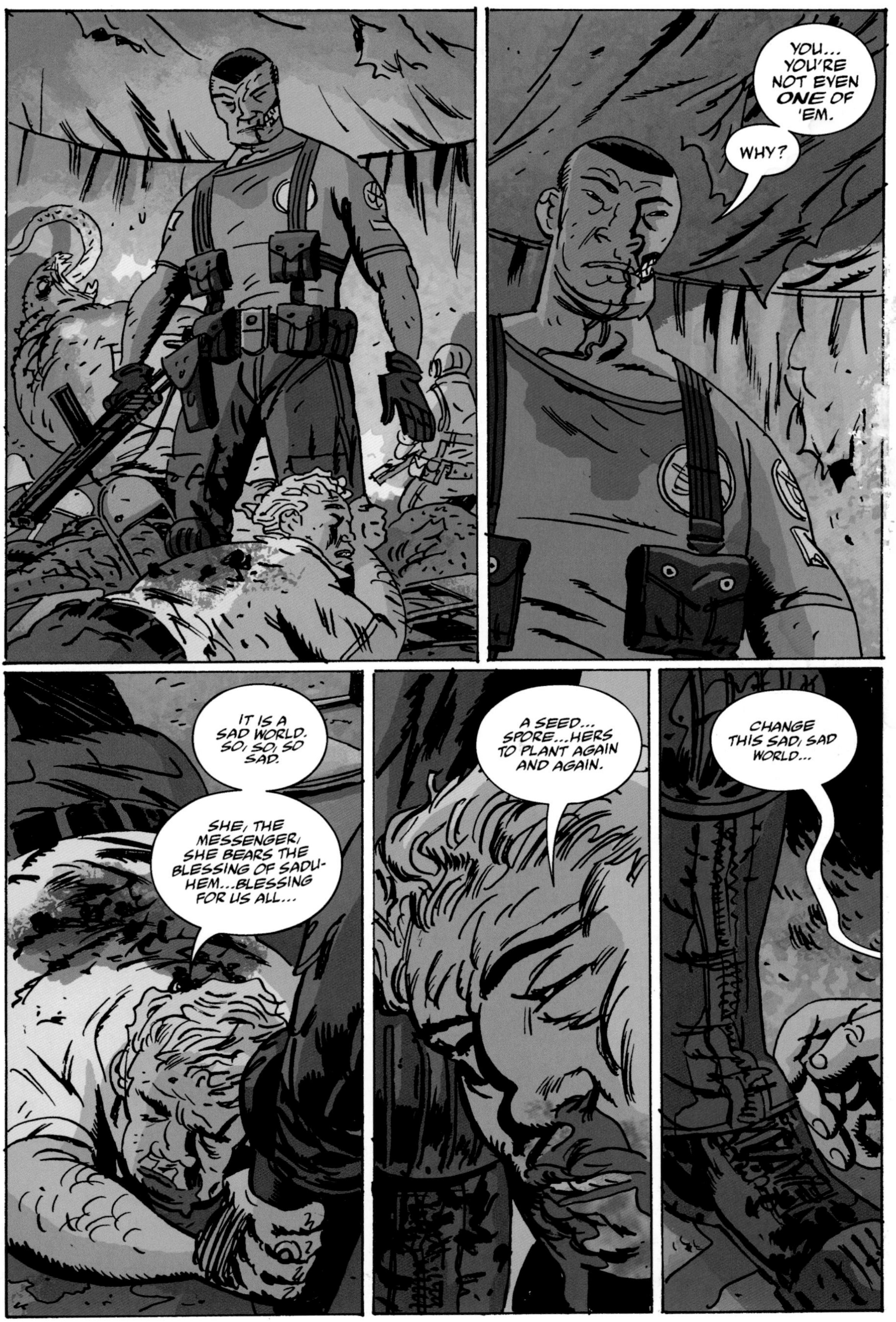
YOU... YOU'RE NOT EVEN ONE OF 'EM.
WHY?
IT IS A SAD WORLD. SO, SO, SO SAD.
SHE, THE MESSENGER, SHE BEARS THE BLESSING OF SADU-HEM...BLESSING FOR US ALL...
A SEED... SPORE...HERS TO PLANT AGAIN AND AGAIN.
CHANGE THIS SAD, SAD WORLD...

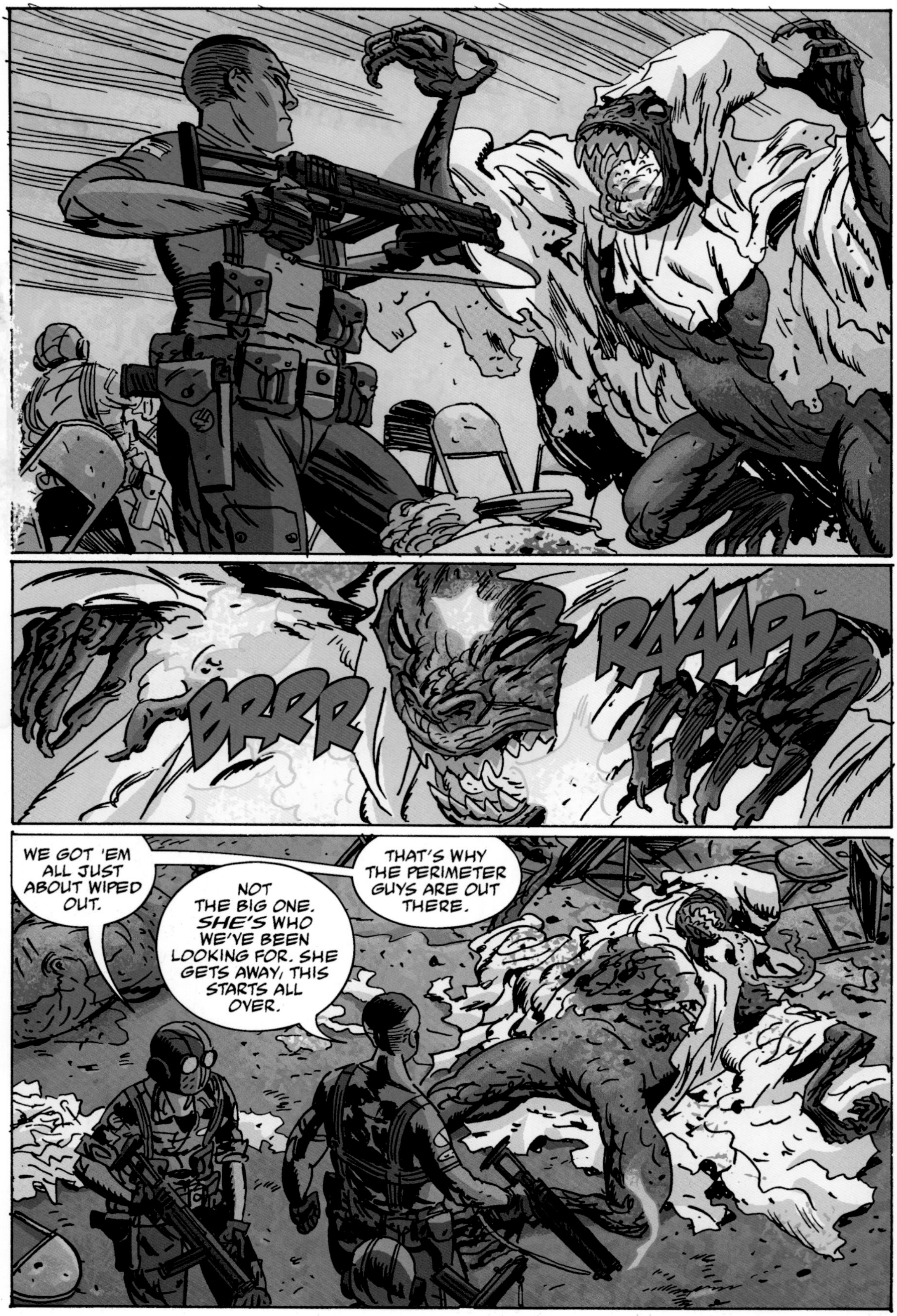
BRRR
RAAAPP
WE GOT 'EM ALL JUST ABOUT WIPED OUT.
NOT THE BIG ONE. SHE'S WHO WE'VE BEEN LOOKING FOR. SHE GETS AWAY, THIS STARTS ALL OVER.
THAT'S WHY THE PERIMETER GUYS ARE OUT THERE.

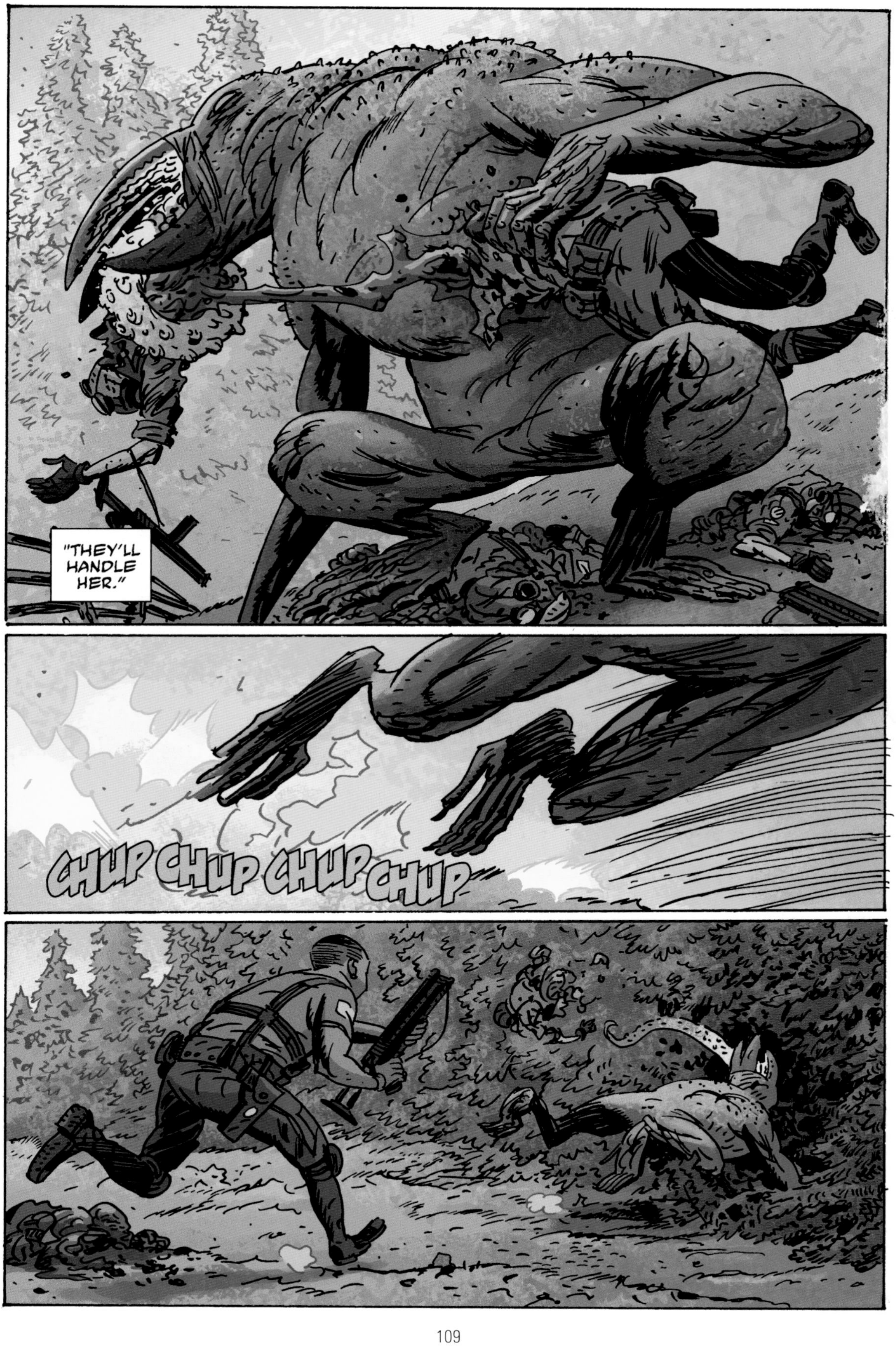
"THEY'LL HANDLE HER."
CHUP CHUP CHUP CHUP

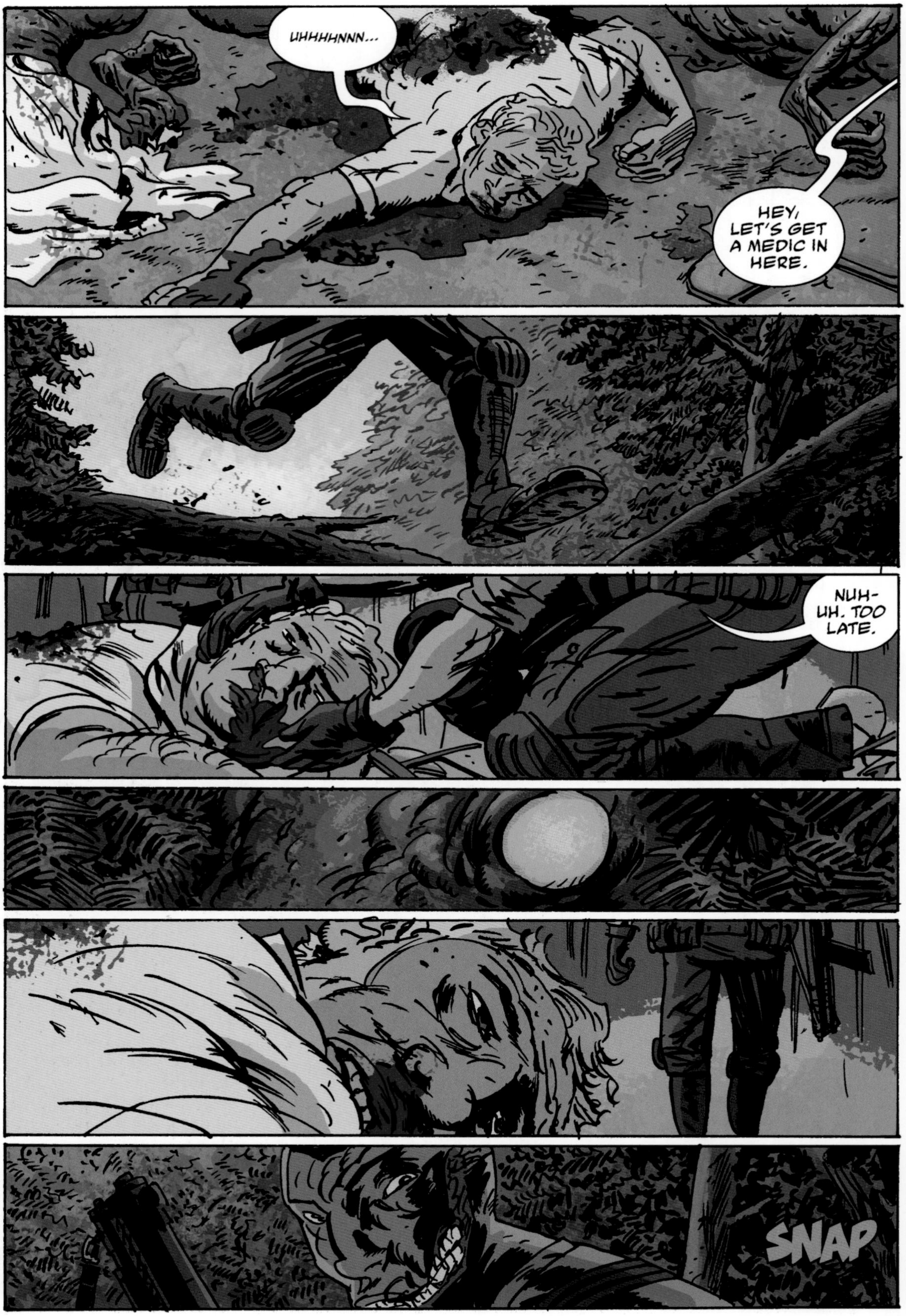
UHHHHNNN...
HEY, LET'S GET A MEDIC IN HERE.
NUH-UH. TOO LATE.
SNAP

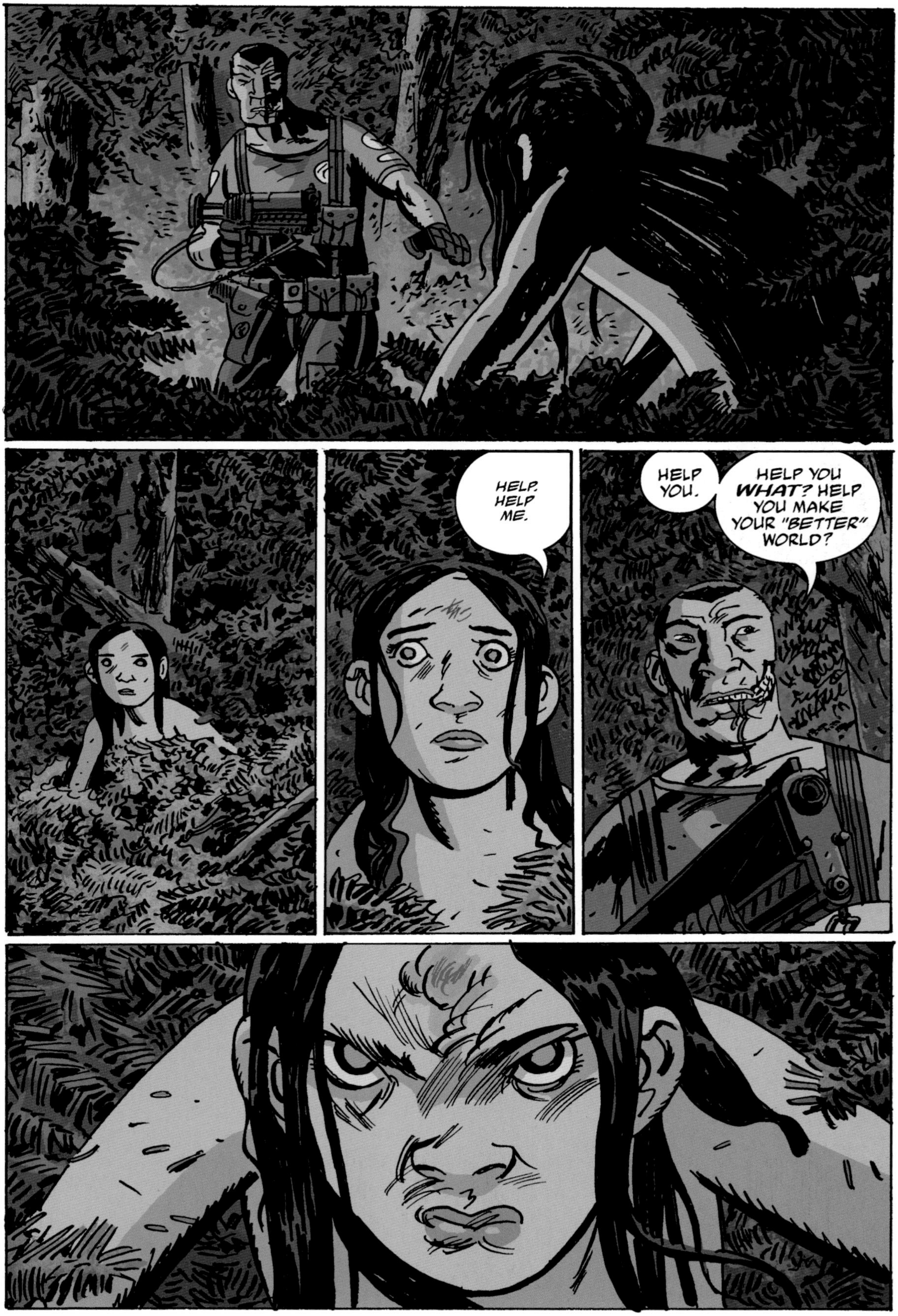
HELP. HELP ME.
HELP YOU.
HELP YOU WHAT? HELP YOU MAKE YOUR "BETTER" WORLD?

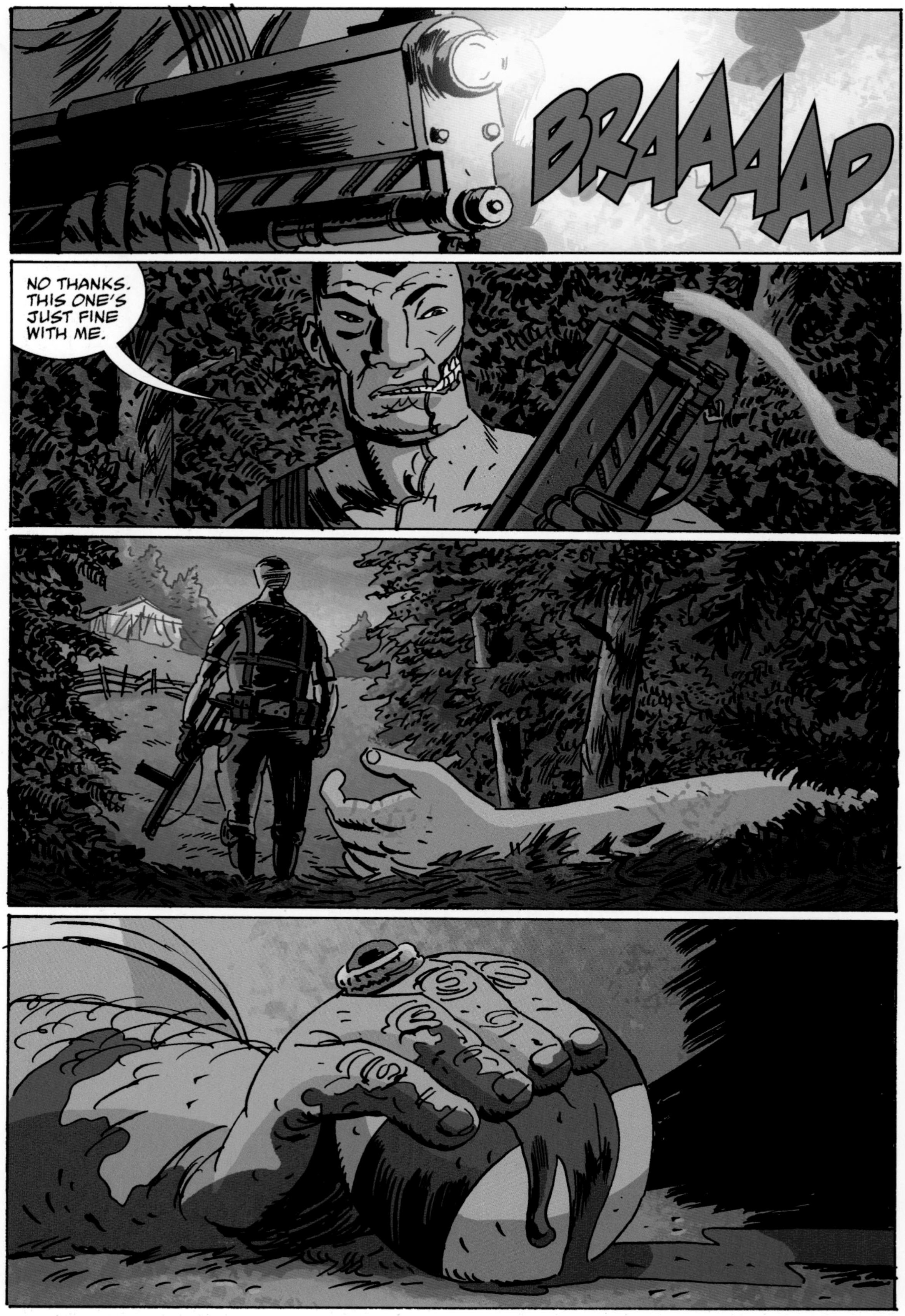
BRAAAAP
NO THANKS. THIS ONE'S JUST FINE WITH ME.
THE END

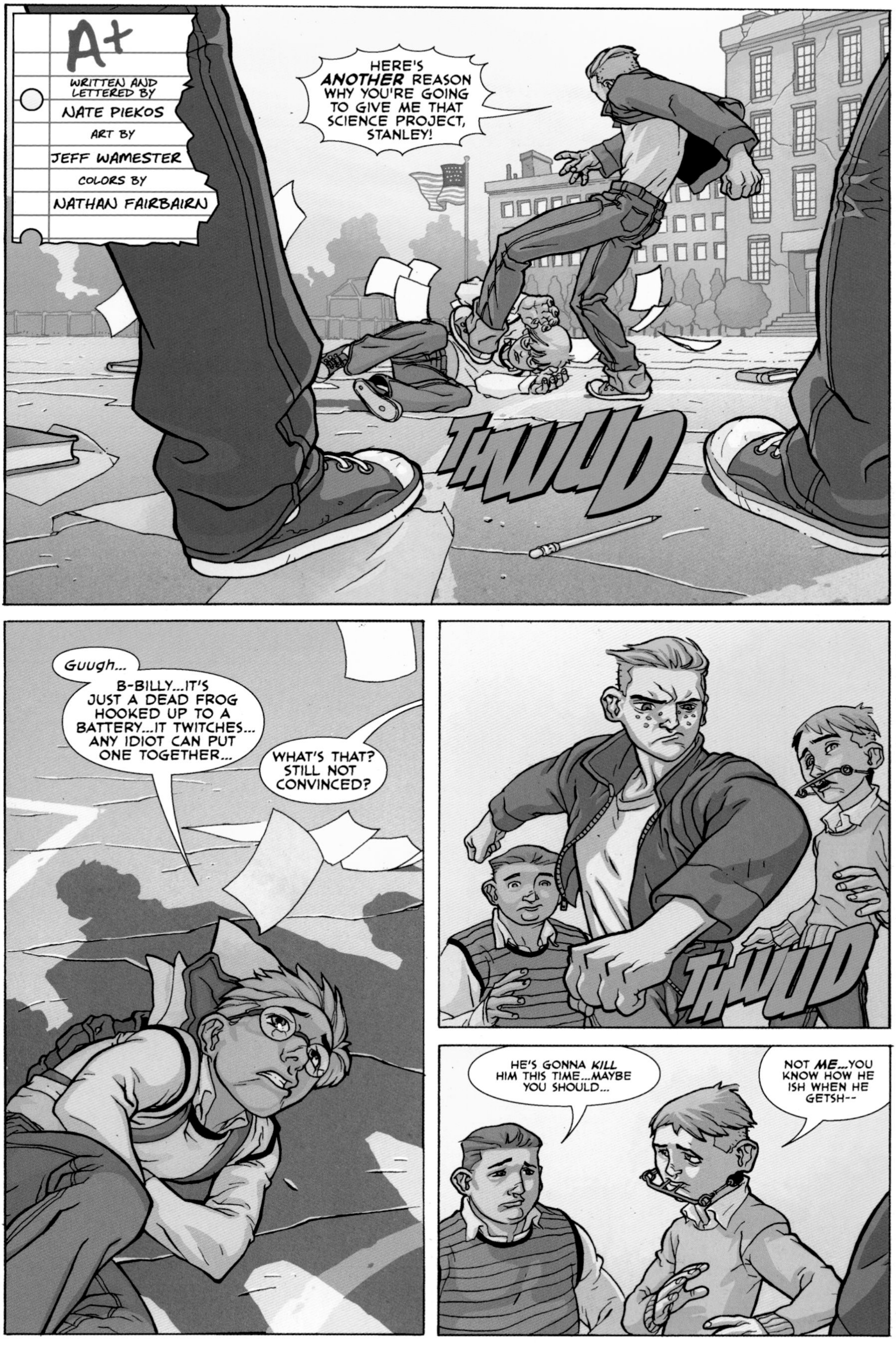
A+
WRITTEN AND LETTERED BY
NATE PIEKOS
ART BY
JEFF WAMESTER
COLORS BY
NATHAN FAIRBAIRN
HERE'S ANOTHER REASON WHY YOU'RE GOING TO GIVE ME THAT SCIENCE PROJECT, STANLEY!
THWUD
Guugh...
B-BILLY...IT'S JUST A DEAD FROG HOOKED UP TO A BATTERY...IT TWITCHES... ANY IDIOT CAN PUT ONE TOGETHER...
WHAT'S THAT? STILL NOT CONVINCED?
THWUD
HE'S GONNA KILL HIM THIS TIME...MAYBE YOU SHOULD...
NOT ME...YOU KNOW HOW HE ISH WHEN HE GETSH--

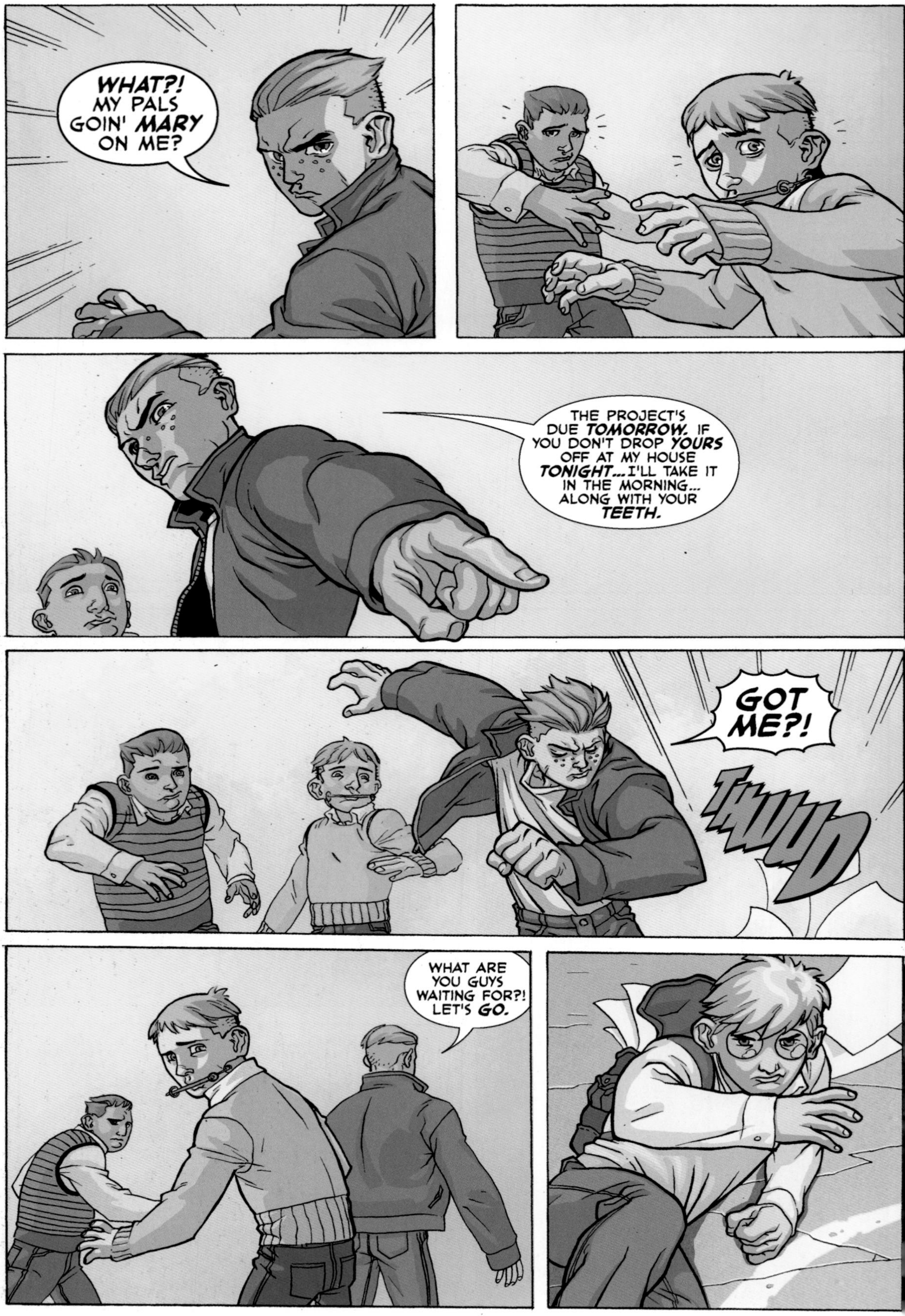
WHAT?! MY PALS GOIN' MARY ON ME?
THE PROJECT'S DUE TOMORROW. IF YOU DON'T DROP YOURS OFF AT MY HOUSE TONIGHT... I'LL TAKE IT IN THE MORNING... ALONG WITH YOUR TEETH.
GOT ME?!
THWUD
WHAT ARE YOU GUYS WAITING FOR?! LET'S GO.

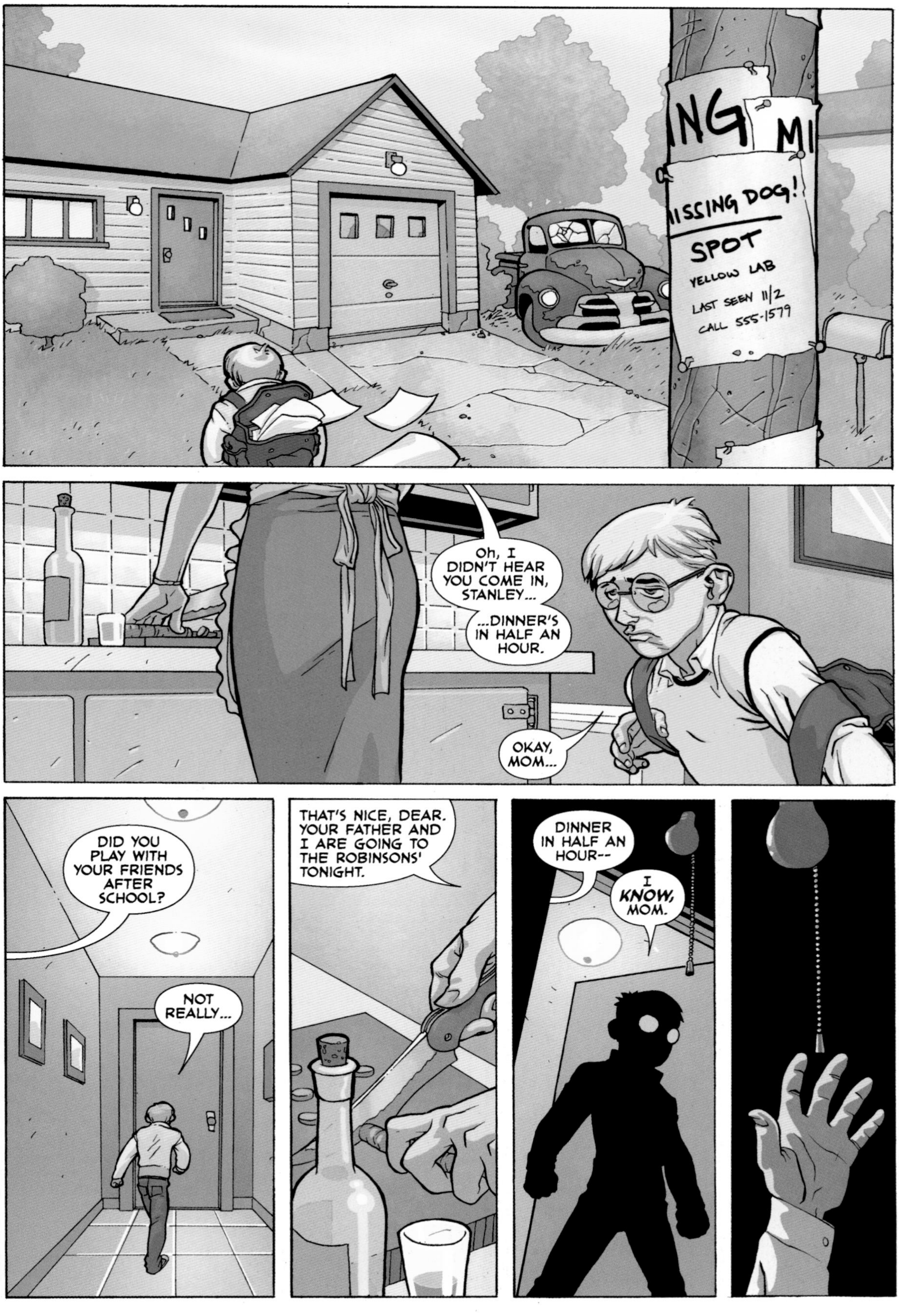
NG
MI
ISSING DOG!
SPOT
YELLOW LAB
LAST SEEN 11/2
CALL 555-1579
Oh, I DIDN'T HEAR YOU COME IN, STANLEY...
...DINNER'S IN HALF AN HOUR.
OKAY, MOM...
DID YOU PLAY WITH YOUR FRIENDS AFTER SCHOOL?
NOT REALLY...
THAT'S NICE, DEAR. YOUR FATHER AND I ARE GOING TO THE ROBINSONS' TONIGHT.
DINNER IN HALF AN HOUR--
I *KNOW,* MOM.

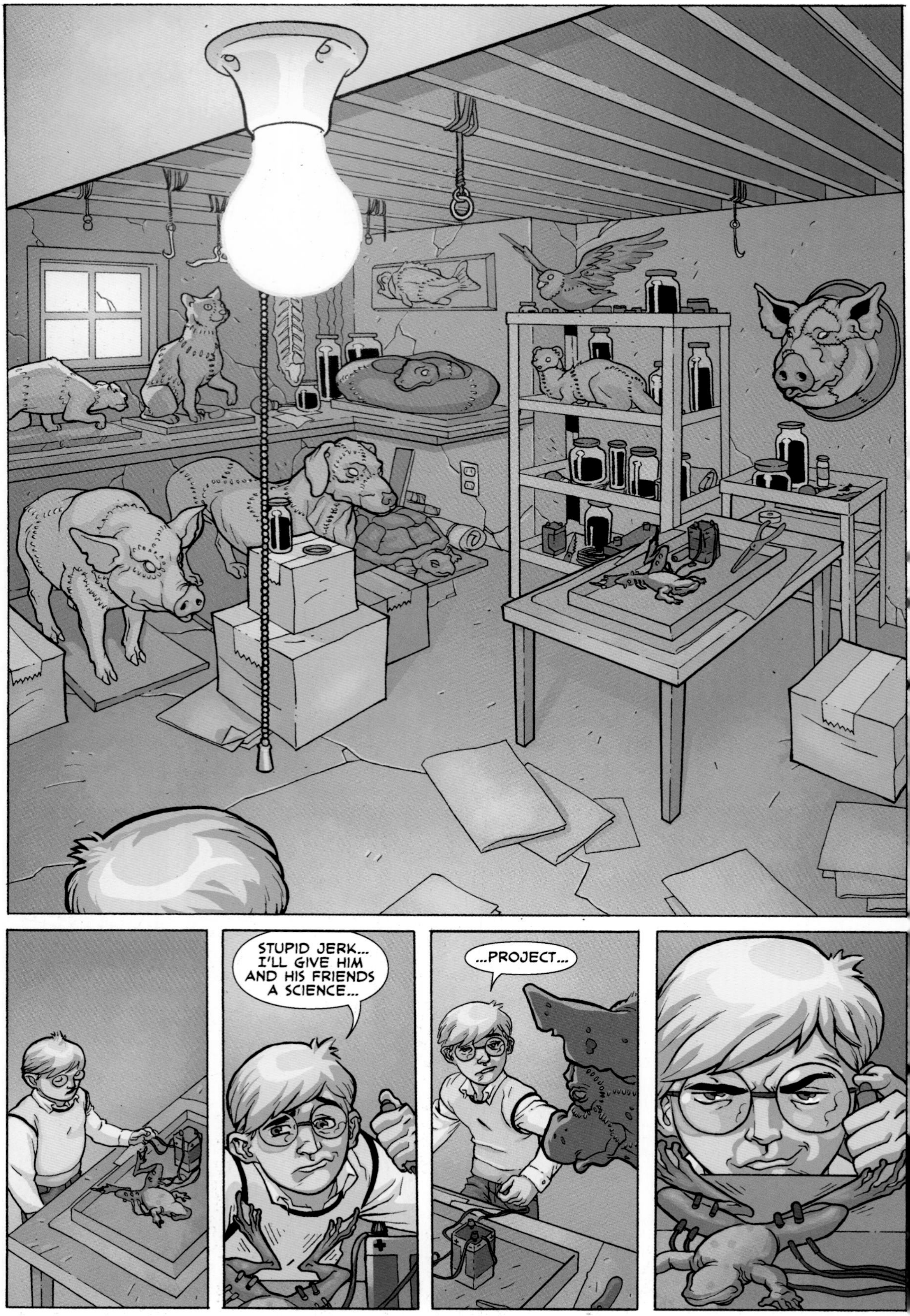
STUPID JERK... I'LL GIVE HIM AND HIS FRIENDS A SCIENCE...
...PROJECT...

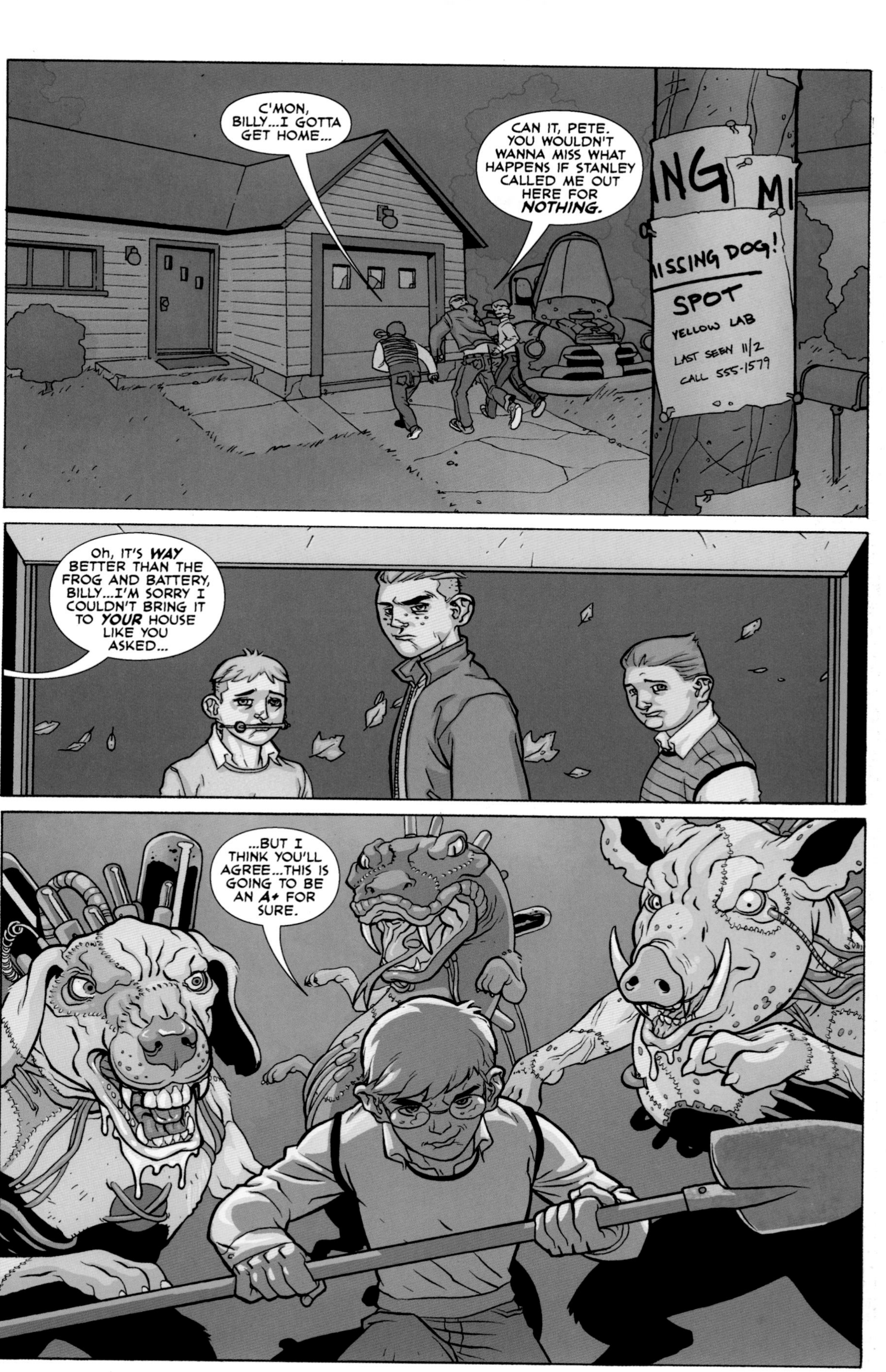
C'MON, BILLY...I GOTTA GET HOME...
CAN IT, PETE. YOU WOULDN'T WANNA MISS WHAT HAPPENS IF STANLEY CALLED ME OUT HERE FOR NOTHING.
NG
MI
MISSING DOG!
SPOT
YELLOW LAB
LAST SEEN 11/2
CALL 555-1579
Oh, IT'S WAY BETTER THAN THE FROG AND BATTERY, BILLY...I'M SORRY I COULDN'T BRING IT TO YOUR HOUSE LIKE YOU ASKED...
...BUT I THINK YOU'LL AGREE...THIS IS GOING TO BE AN A+ FOR SURE.

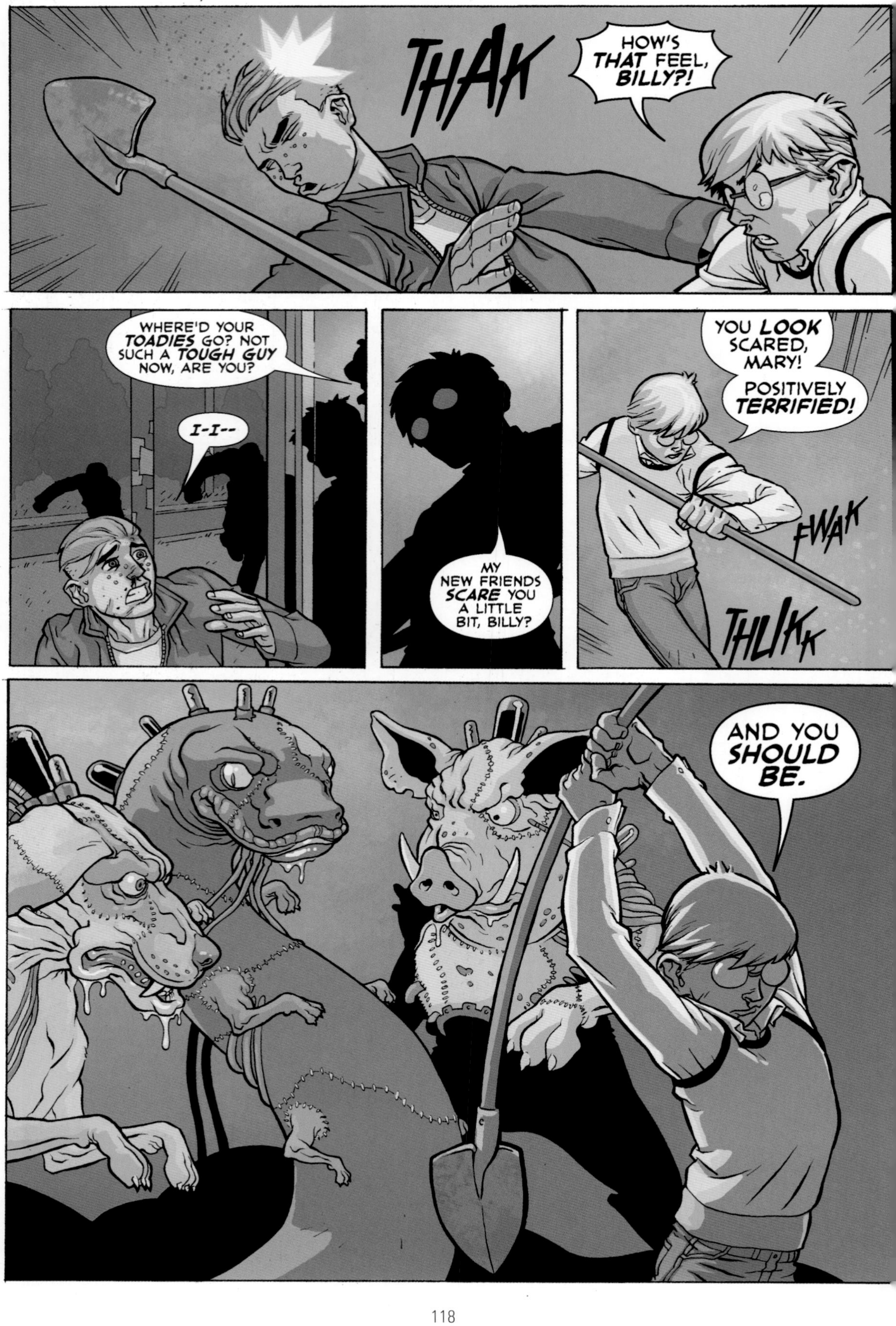
THAK
HOW'S THAT FEEL, BILLY?!
WHERE'D YOUR TOADIES GO? NOT SUCH A TOUGH GUY NOW, ARE YOU?
I-I--
MY NEW FRIENDS SCARE YOU A LITTLE BIT, BILLY?
YOU LOOK SCARED, MARY!
POSITIVELY TERRIFIED!
FWAK
THUKK
AND YOU SHOULD BE.

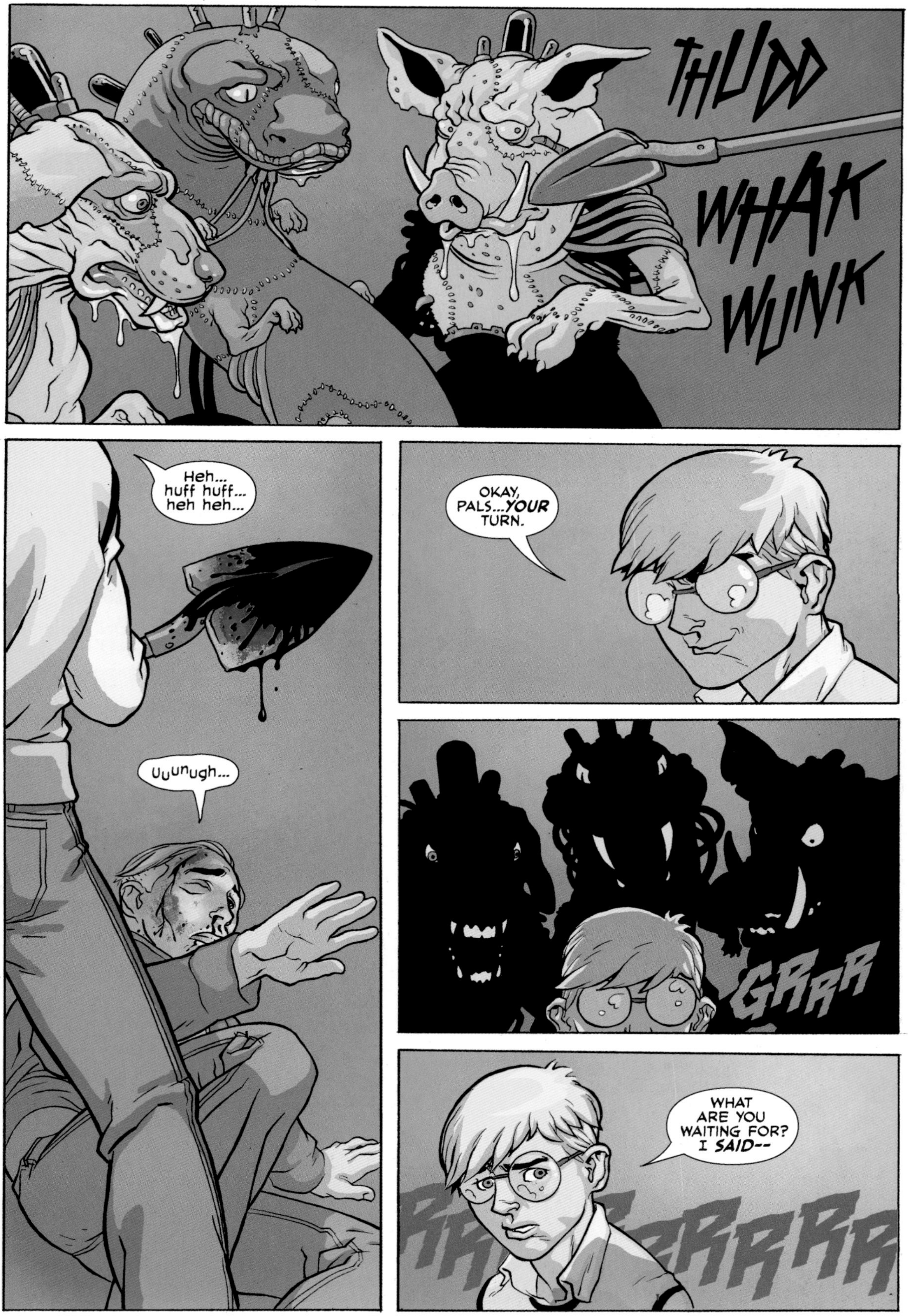
THUDD
WHAK
WUNK
Heh... huff huff... heh heh...
Uuunugh...
OKAY, PALS...YOUR TURN.
GRRR
WHAT ARE YOU WAITING FOR? I SAID--
RRRRRRRRRR

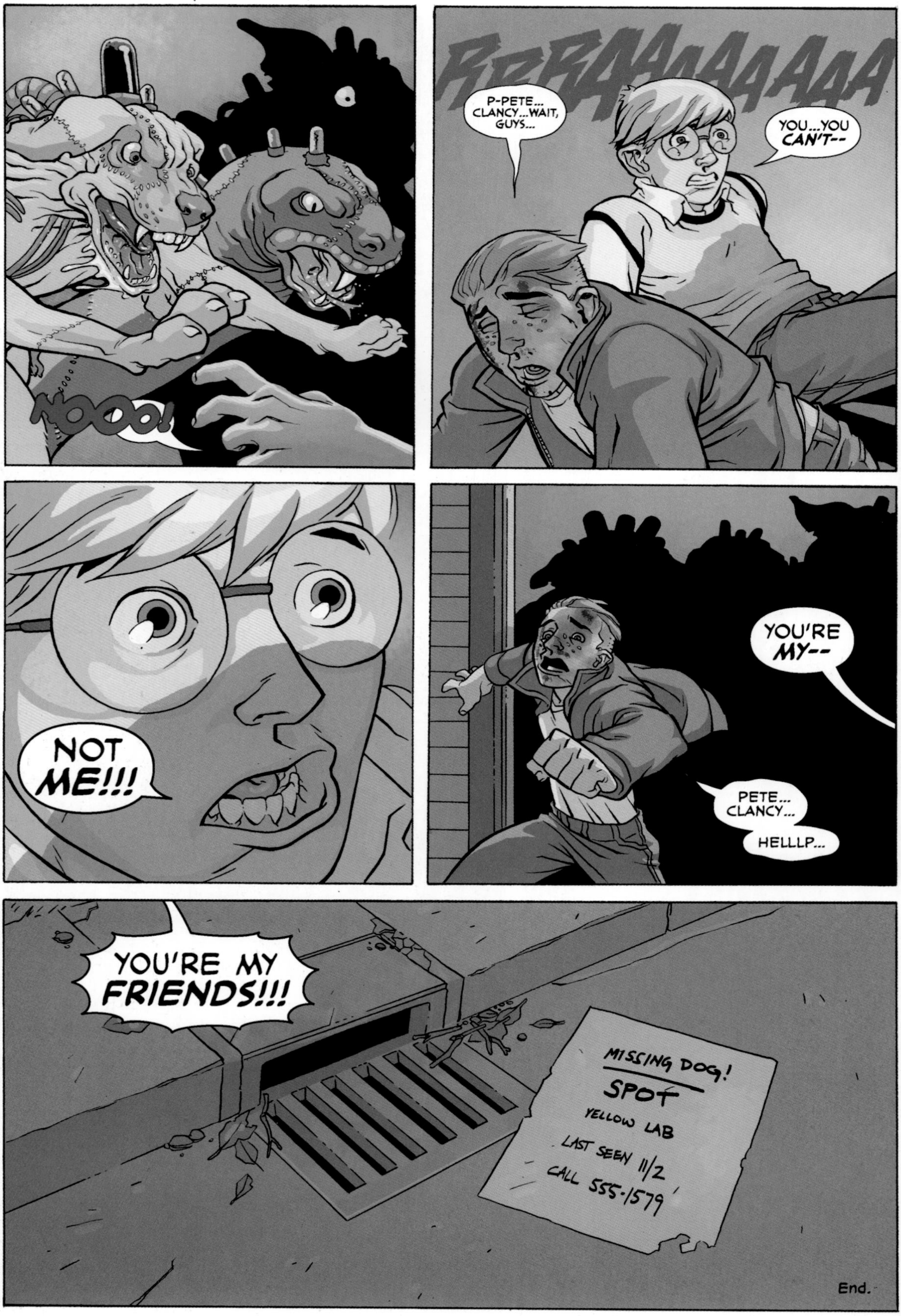
NOOO!
RRRAAAAAAAA
P-PETE... CLANCY...WAIT, GUYS...
YOU...YOU CAN'T--
NOT ME!!!
YOU'RE MY--
PETE... CLANCY...
HELLLP...
YOU'RE MY FRIENDS!!!
MISSING DOG!
SPOT
YELLOW LAB
LAST SEEN 11/2
CALL 555-1579
End.

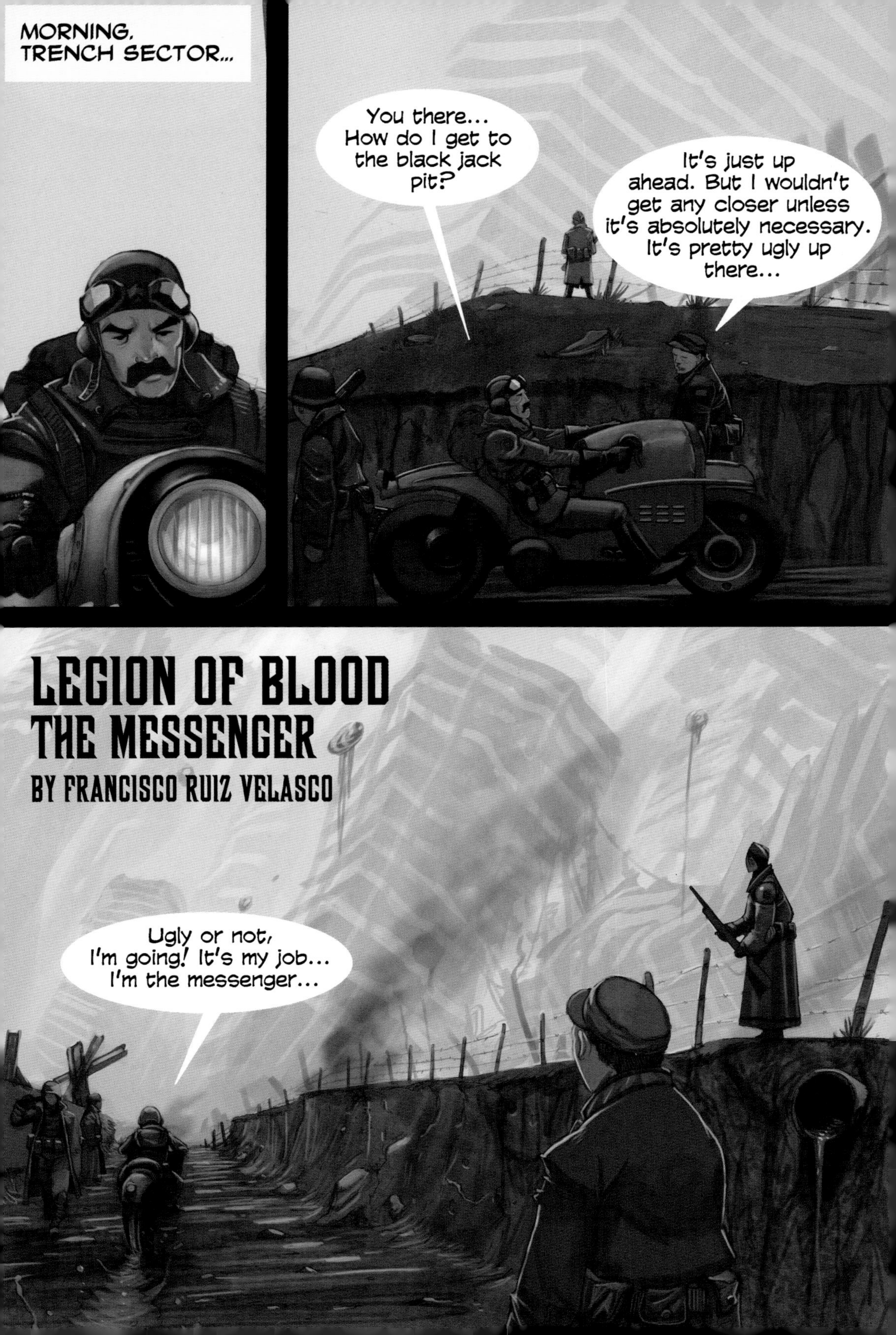
MORNING, TRENCH SECTOR...
You there... How do I get to the black jack pit?
It's just up ahead. But I wouldn't get any closer unless it's absolutely necessary. It's pretty ugly up there...
LEGION OF BLOOD
THE MESSENGER
BY FRANCISCO RUIZ VELASCO
Ugly or not, I'm going! It's my job... I'm the messenger...

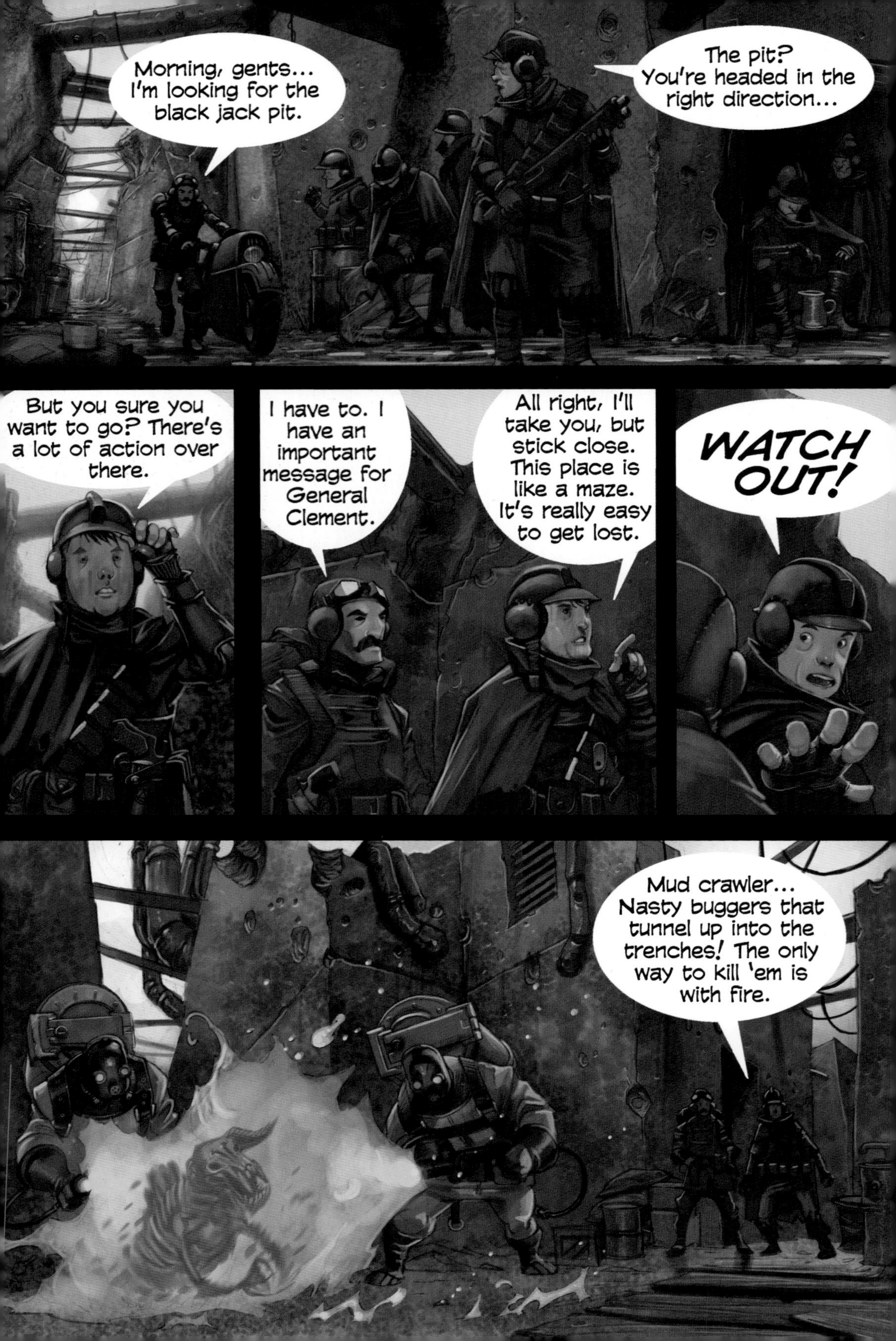
Morning, gents... I'm looking for the black jack pit.
The pit? You're headed in the right direction...
But you sure you want to go? There's a lot of action over there.
I have to. I have an important message for General Clement.
All right, I'll take you, but stick close. This place is like a maze. It's really easy to get lost.
WATCH OUT!
Mud crawler... Nasty buggers that tunnel up into the trenches! The only way to kill 'em is with fire.

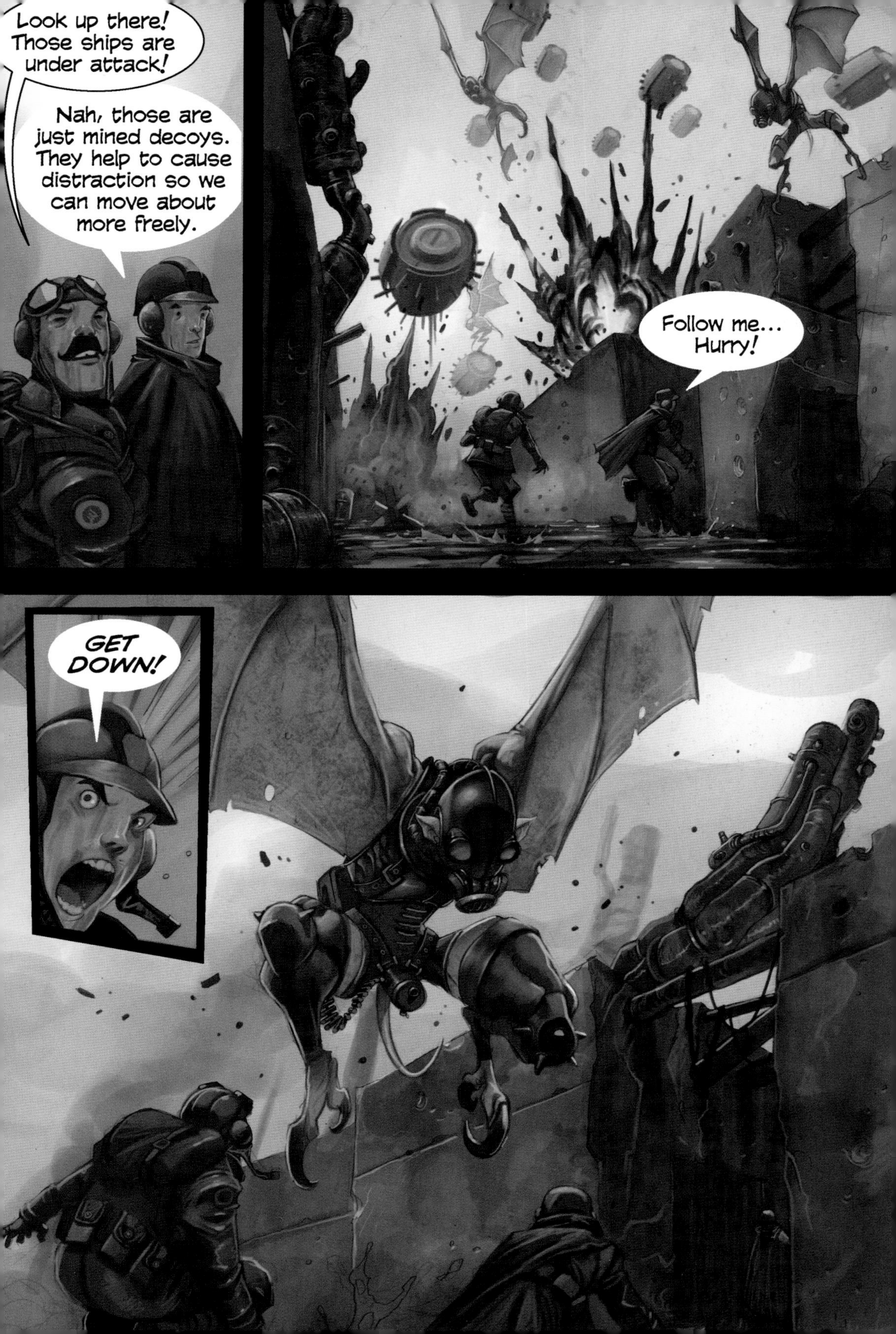
Look up there! Those ships are under attack!
Nah, those are just mined decoys. They help to cause distraction so we can move about more freely.
Follow me... Hurry!
GET DOWN!

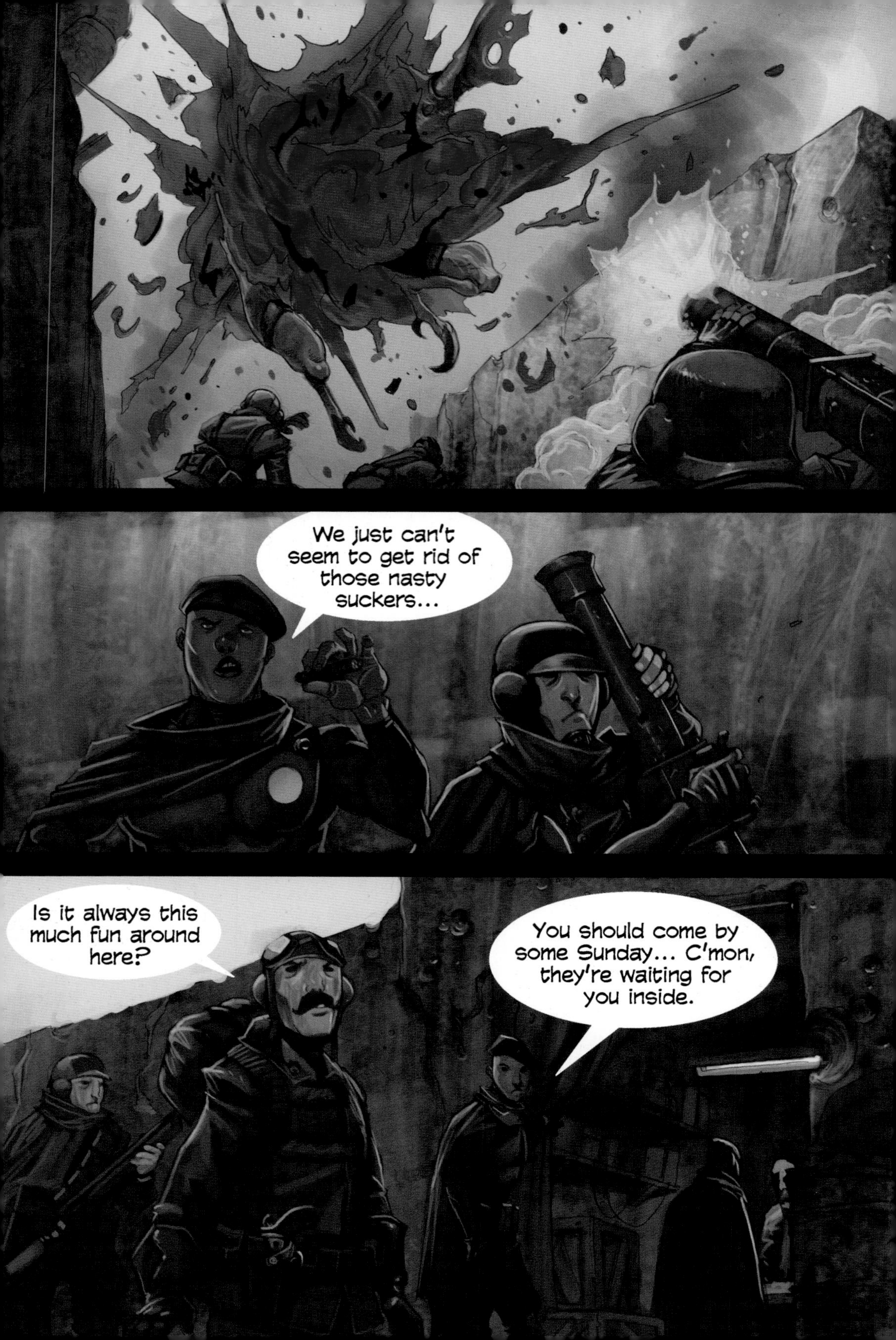
We just can't seem to get rid of those nasty suckers...
Is it always this much fun around here?
You should come by some Sunday... C'mon, they're waiting for you inside.

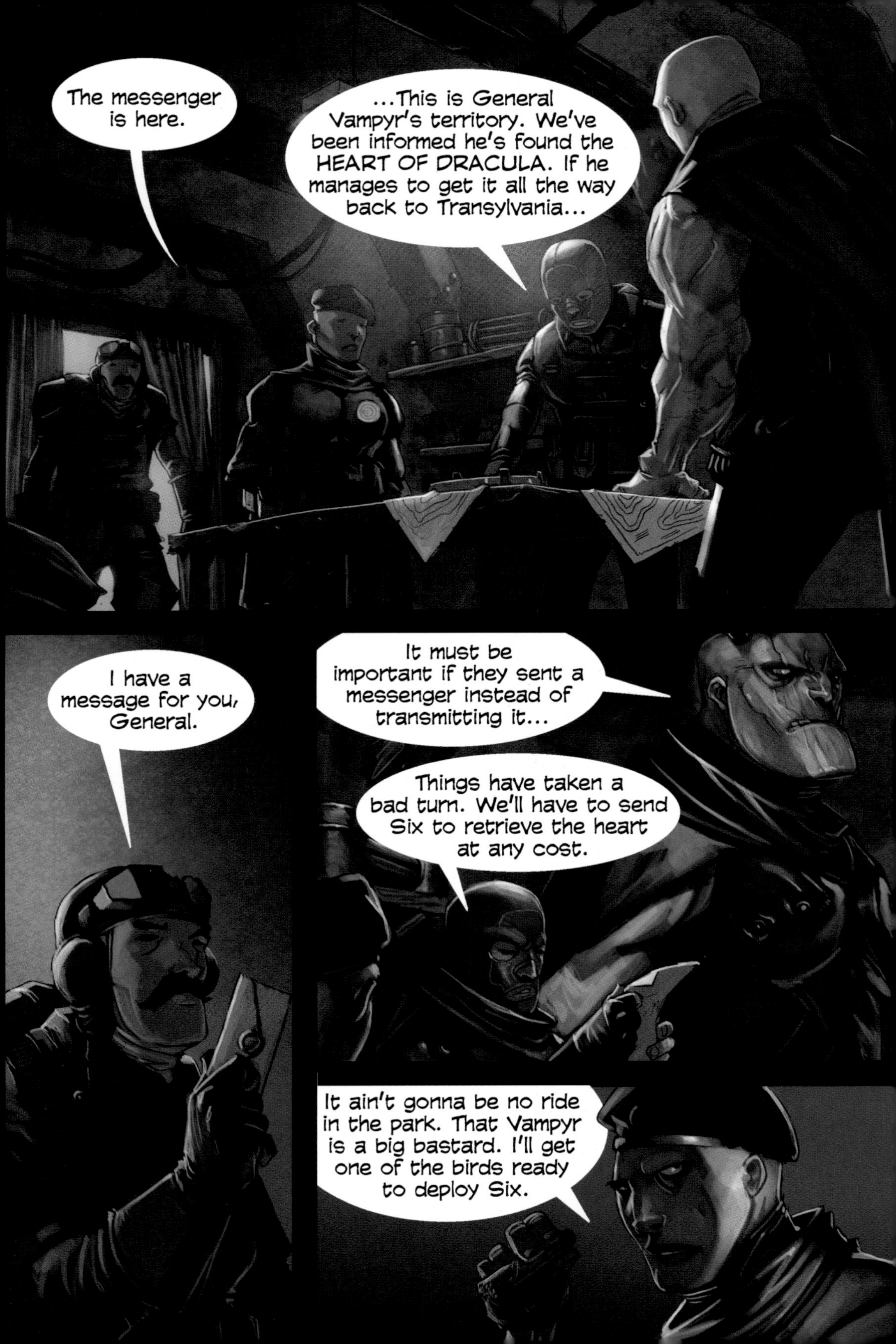
The messenger is here.
...This is General Vampyr's territory. We've been informed he's found the HEART OF DRACULA. If he manages to get it all the way back to Transylvania...
I have a message for you, General.
It must be important if they sent a messenger instead of transmitting it...
Things have taken a bad turn. We'll have to send Six to retrieve the heart at any cost.
It ain't gonna be no ride in the park. That Vampyr is a big bastard. I'll get one of the birds ready to deploy Six.

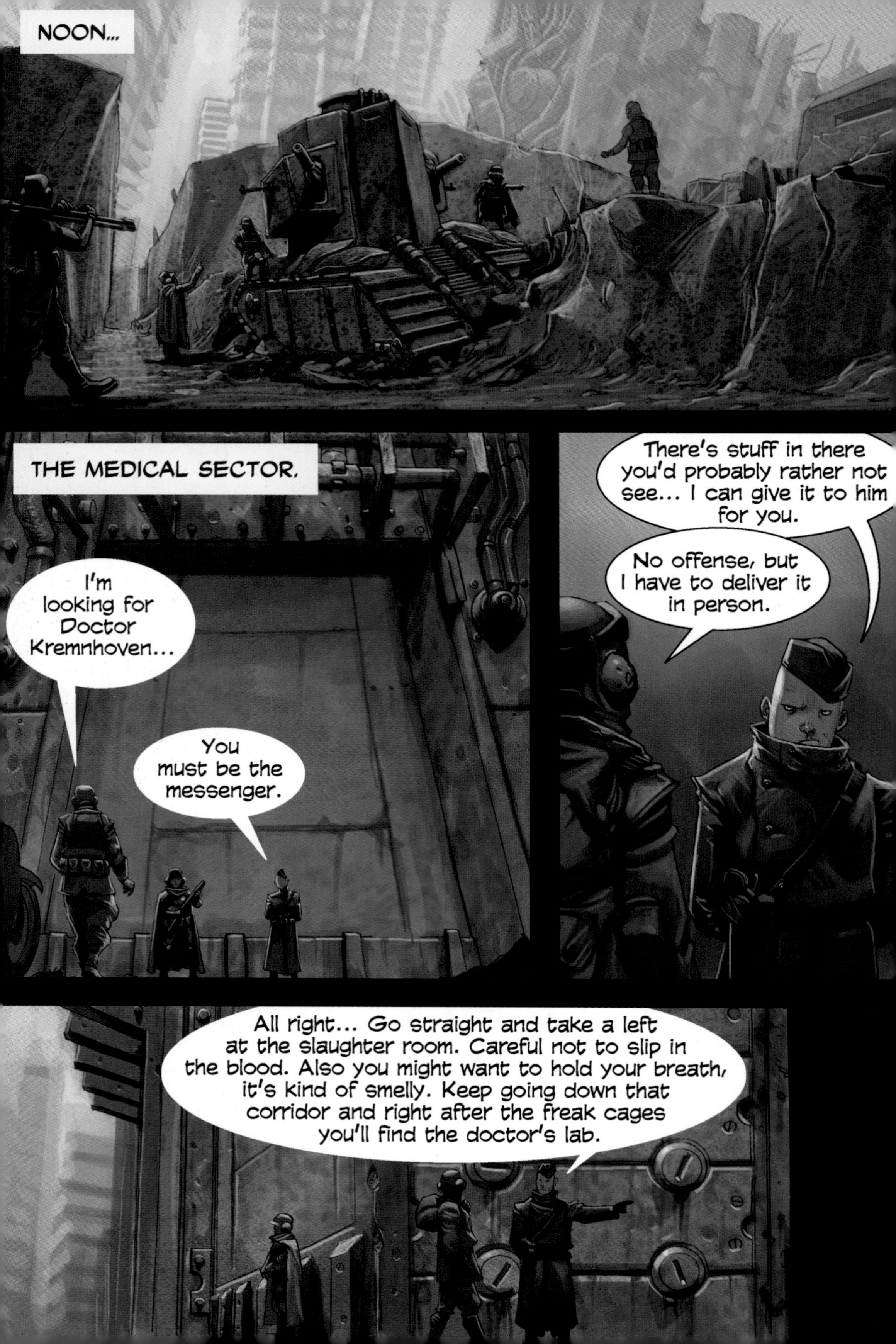
NOON...
THE MEDICAL SECTOR.
I'm looking for Doctor Kremnhoven...
You must be the messenger.
There's stuff in there you'd probably rather not see... I can give it to him for you.
No offense, but I have to deliver it in person.
All right... Go straight and take a left at the slaughter room. Careful not to slip in the blood. Also you might want to hold your breath, it's kind of smelly. Keep going down that corridor and right after the freak cages you'll find the doctor's lab.

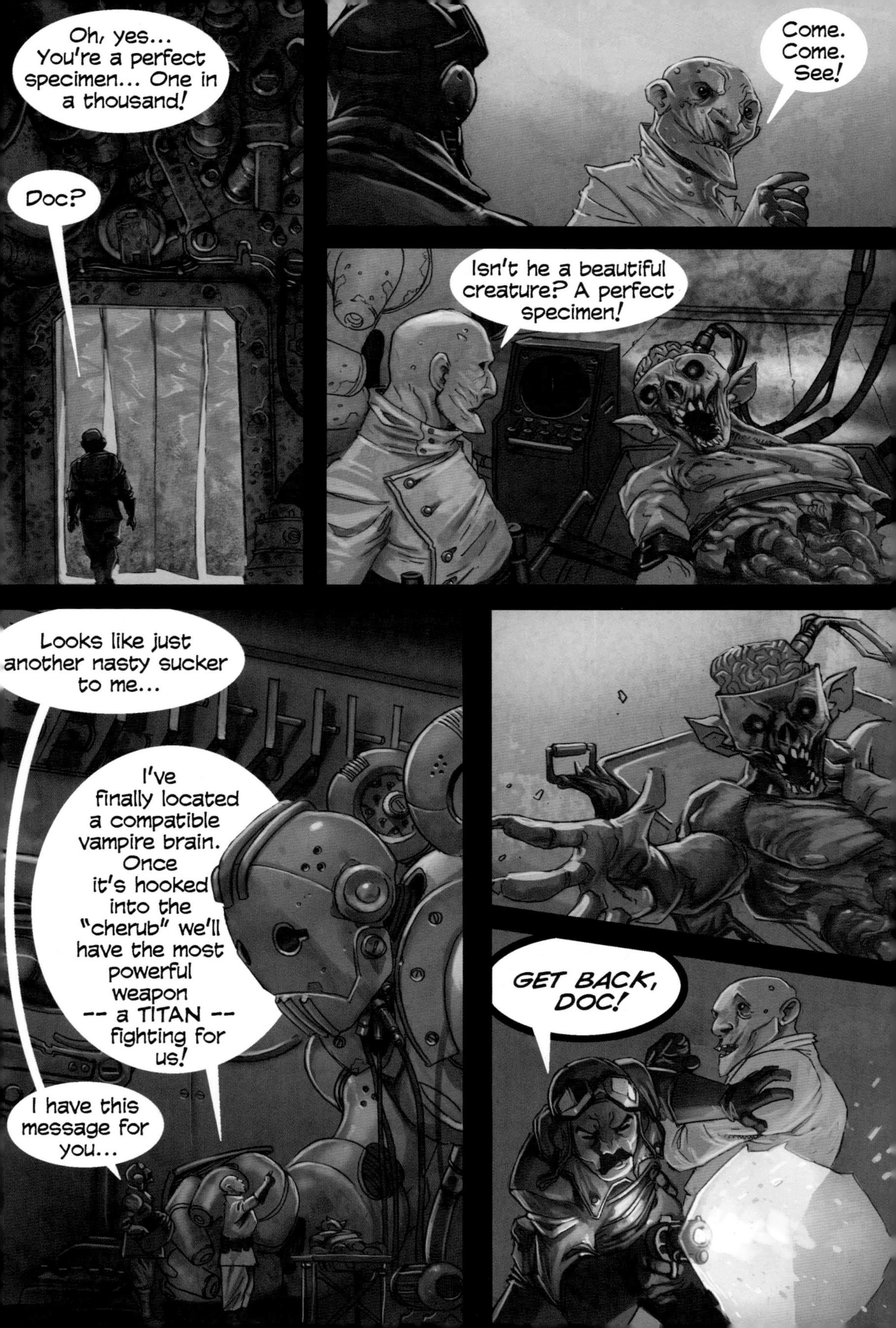
Oh, yes... You're a perfect specimen... One in a thousand!
Doc?
Come. Come. See!
Isn't he a beautiful creature? A perfect specimen!
Looks like just another nasty sucker to me...
I've finally located a compatible vampire brain. Once it's hooked into the "cherub" we'll have the most powerful weapon -- a TITAN -- fighting for us!
I have this message for you...
GET BACK, DOC!

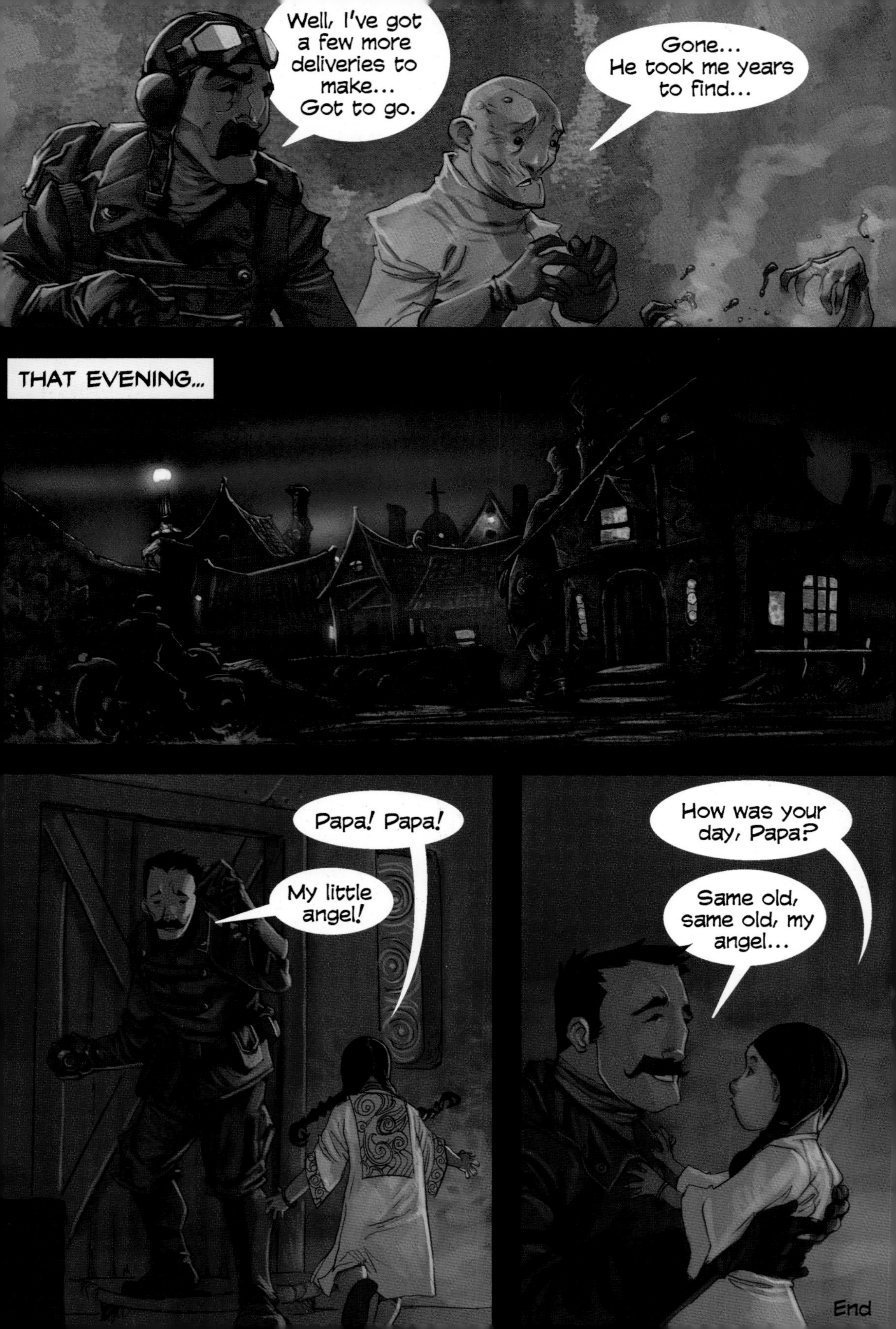
Well, I've got a few more deliveries to make... Got to go.
Gone... He took me years to find...
THAT EVENING...
Papa! Papa!
My little angel!
How was your day, Papa?
Same old, same old, my angel...
End

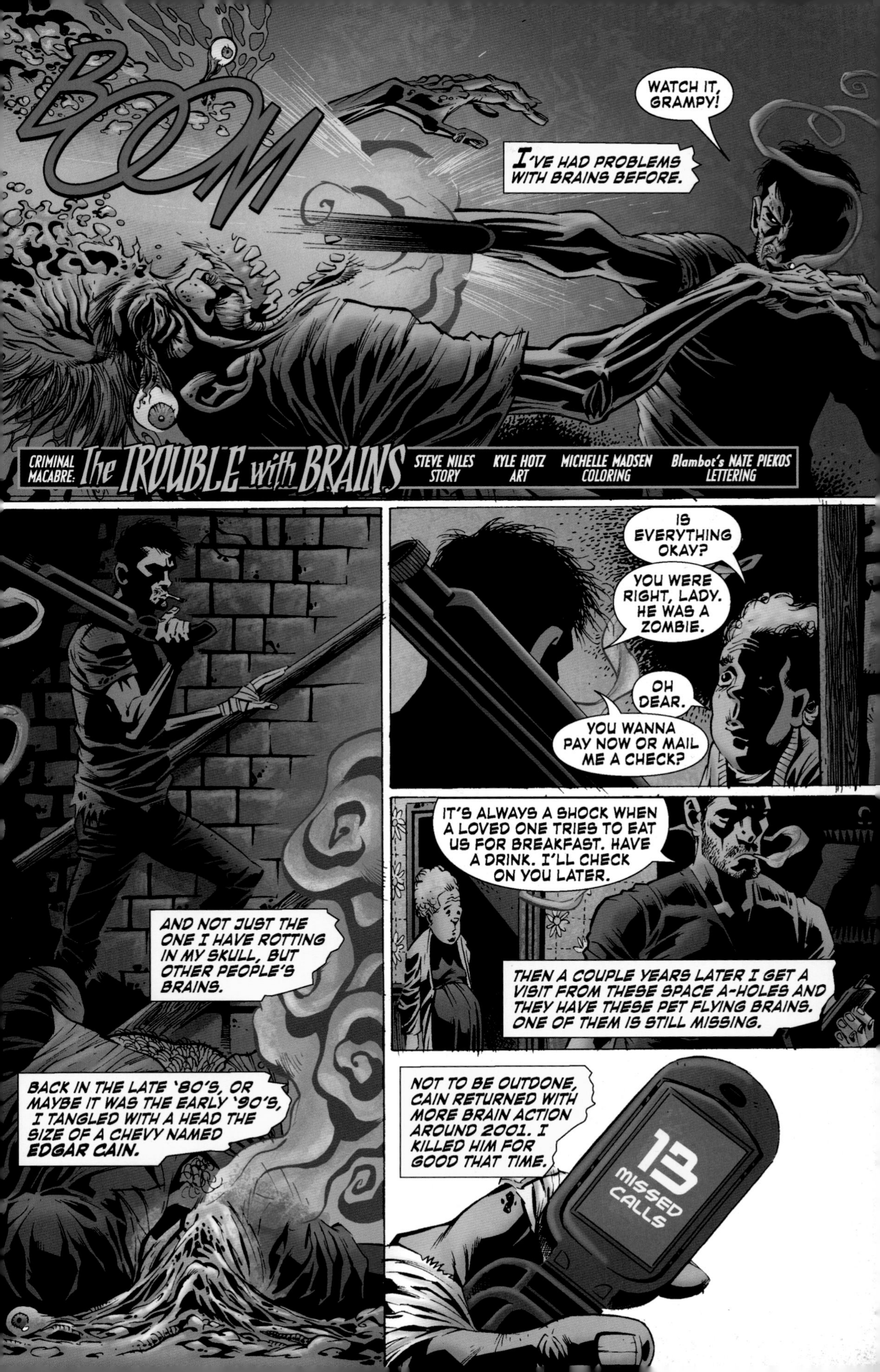
BOOM
WATCH IT, GRAMPY!
I'VE HAD PROBLEMS WITH BRAINS BEFORE.
CRIMINAL MACABRE: The TROUBLE with BRAINS
STEVE NILES STORY
KYLE HOTZ ART
MICHELLE MADSEN COLORING
Blambot's NATE PIEKOS LETTERING
AND NOT JUST THE ONE I HAVE ROTTING IN MY SKULL, BUT OTHER PEOPLE'S BRAINS.
BACK IN THE LATE '80'S, OR MAYBE IT WAS THE EARLY '90'S, I TANGLED WITH A HEAD THE SIZE OF A CHEVY NAMED EDGAR CAIN.
IS EVERYTHING OKAY?
YOU WERE RIGHT, LADY. HE WAS A ZOMBIE.
OH DEAR.
YOU WANNA PAY NOW OR MAIL ME A CHECK?
IT'S ALWAYS A SHOCK WHEN A LOVED ONE TRIES TO EAT US FOR BREAKFAST. HAVE A DRINK. I'LL CHECK ON YOU LATER.
THEN A COUPLE YEARS LATER I GET A VISIT FROM THESE SPACE A-HOLES AND THEY HAVE THESE PET FLYING BRAINS. ONE OF THEM IS STILL MISSING.
NOT TO BE OUTDONE, CAIN RETURNED WITH MORE BRAIN ACTION AROUND 2001. I KILLED HIM FOR GOOD THAT TIME.
13 MISSED CALLS

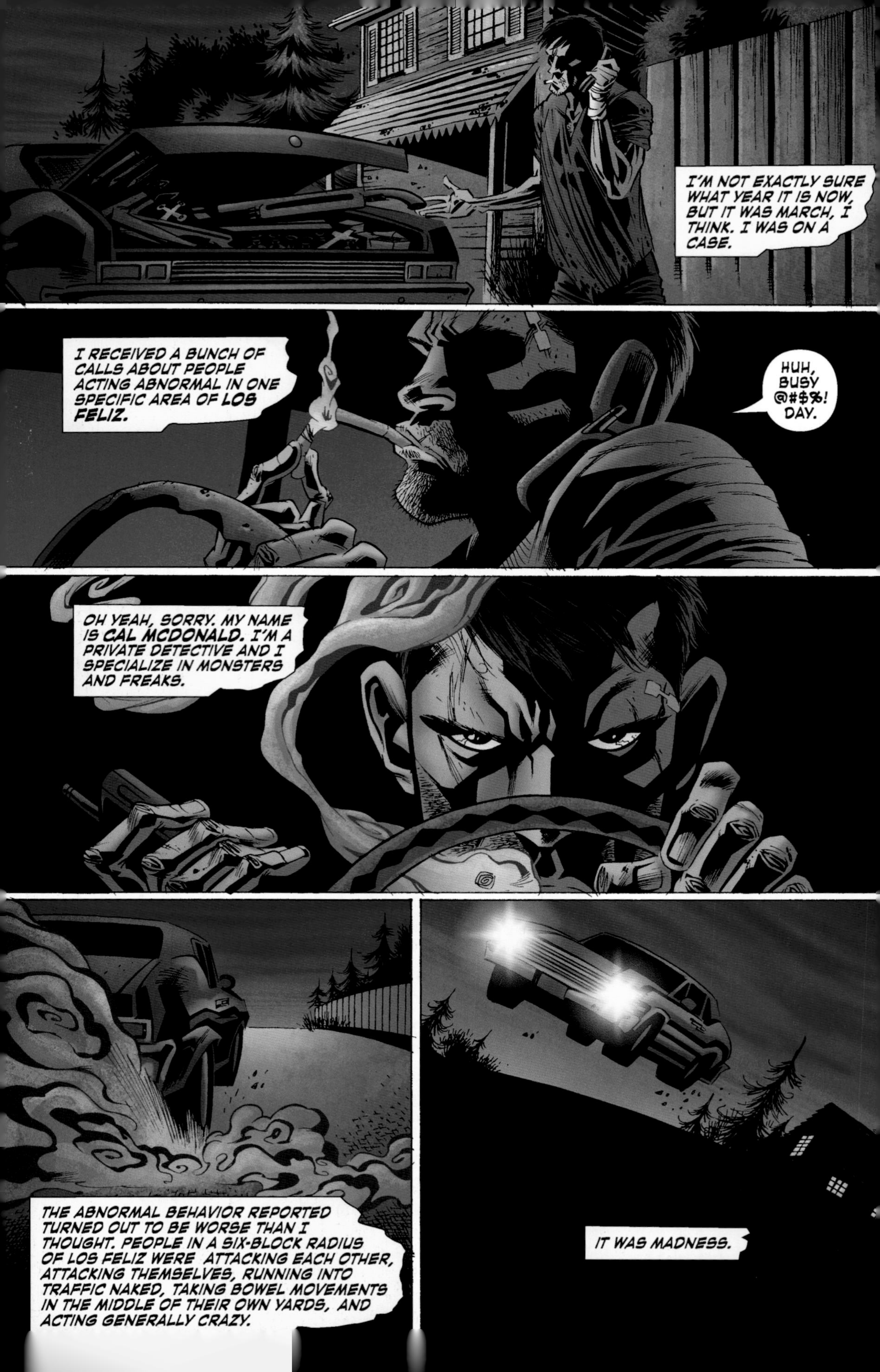

I'M NOT EXACTLY SURE WHAT YEAR IT IS NOW, BUT IT WAS MARCH, I THINK. I WAS ON A CASE.
I RECEIVED A BUNCH OF CALLS ABOUT PEOPLE ACTING ABNORMAL IN ONE SPECIFIC AREA OF LOS FELIZ.
HUH, BUSY @#$%! DAY.
OH YEAH, SORRY. MY NAME IS CAL MCDONALD. I'M A PRIVATE DETECTIVE AND I SPECIALIZE IN MONSTERS AND FREAKS.
THE ABNORMAL BEHAVIOR REPORTED TURNED OUT TO BE WORSE THAN I THOUGHT. PEOPLE IN A SIX-BLOCK RADIUS OF LOS FELIZ WERE ATTACKING EACH OTHER, ATTACKING THEMSELVES, RUNNING INTO TRAFFIC NAKED, TAKING BOWEL MOVEMENTS IN THE MIDDLE OF THEIR OWN YARDS, AND ACTING GENERALLY CRAZY.
IT WAS MADNESS.

AND EVEN WEIRDER WHEN AS SOON AS I HIT THE PROBLEM AREA MY RADIO WENT HAYWIRE, SCREECHING AND SQUAWKING ON BOTH AM AND FM. VERY ODD.

CAL.

GAH!

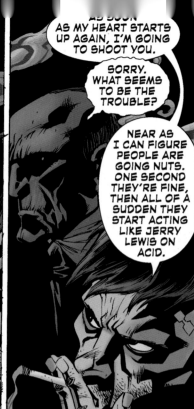

AS SOON AS MY HEART STARTS UP AGAIN, I'M GOING TO SHOOT YOU.

SORRY. WHAT SEEMS TO BE THE TROUBLE?

NEAR AS I CAN FIGURE PEOPLE ARE GOING NUTS. ONE SECOND THEY'RE FINE, THEN ALL OF A SUDDEN THEY START ACTING LIKE JERRY LEWIS ON ACID.

PERHAPS THEY ARE DRUGGED, OR IT'S MASS HYPNOSIS.

WE'LL FIND OUT SOON ENOUGH. THIS IS THE--

I'M NOT GONNA RULE OUT EITHER.

PUTTIN' OUT THE CALL! PUTTIN' OUT THE CALL!

HOW ODD.

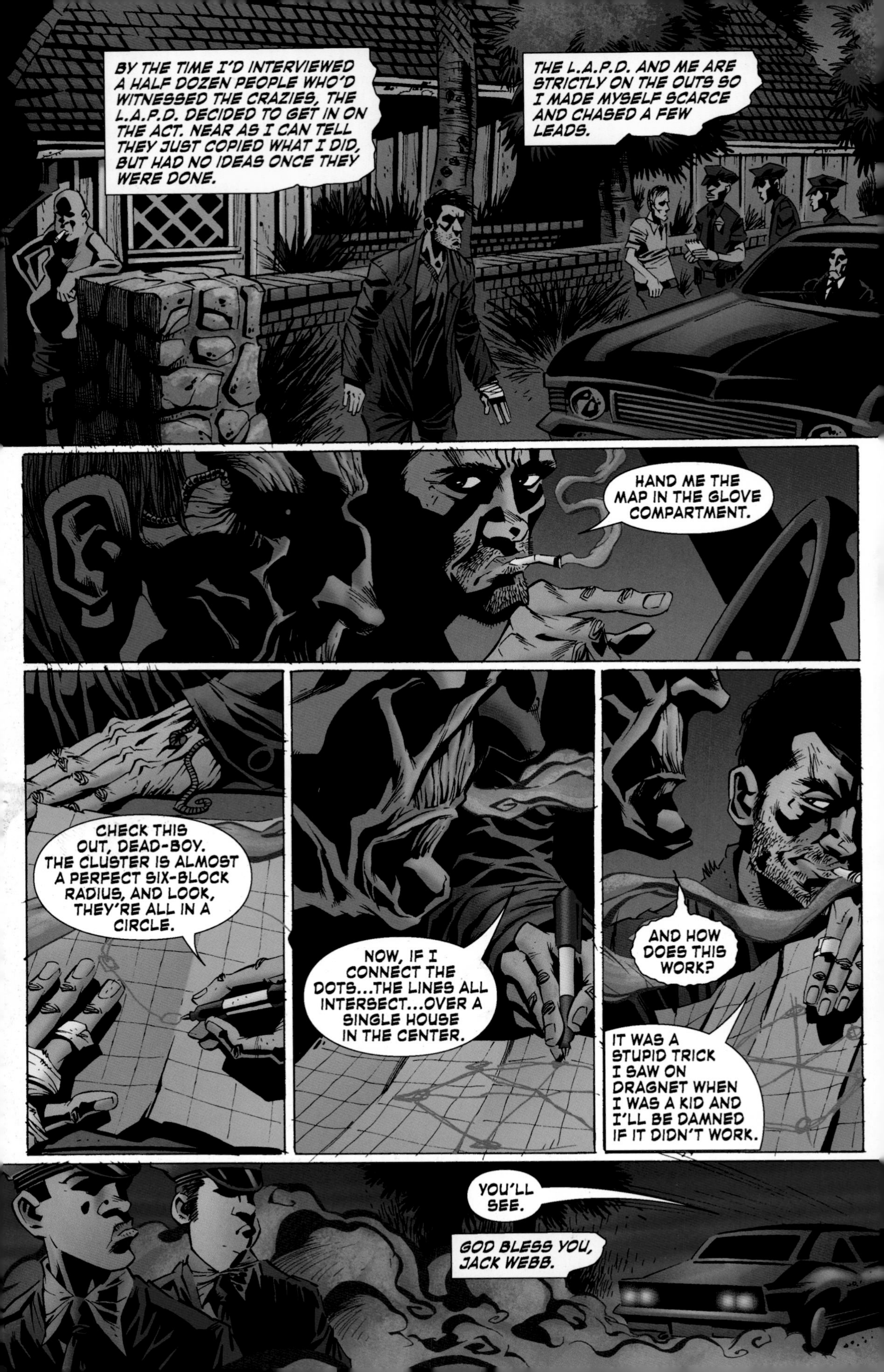
BY THE TIME I'D INTERVIEWED A HALF DOZEN PEOPLE WHO'D WITNESSED THE CRAZIES, THE L.A.P.D. DECIDED TO GET IN ON THE ACT. NEAR AS I CAN TELL THEY JUST COPIED WHAT I DID, BUT HAD NO IDEAS ONCE THEY WERE DONE.
THE L.A.P.D. AND ME ARE STRICTLY ON THE OUTS SO I MADE MYSELF SCARCE AND CHASED A FEW LEADS.
HAND ME THE MAP IN THE GLOVE COMPARTMENT.
CHECK THIS OUT, DEAD-BOY. THE CLUSTER IS ALMOST A PERFECT SIX-BLOCK RADIUS, AND LOOK, THEY'RE ALL IN A CIRCLE.
NOW, IF I CONNECT THE DOTS...THE LINES ALL INTERSECT...OVER A SINGLE HOUSE IN THE CENTER.
AND HOW DOES THIS WORK?
IT WAS A STUPID TRICK I SAW ON DRAGNET WHEN I WAS A KID AND I'LL BE DAMNED IF IT DIDN'T WORK.
YOU'LL SEE.
GOD BLESS YOU, JACK WEBB.

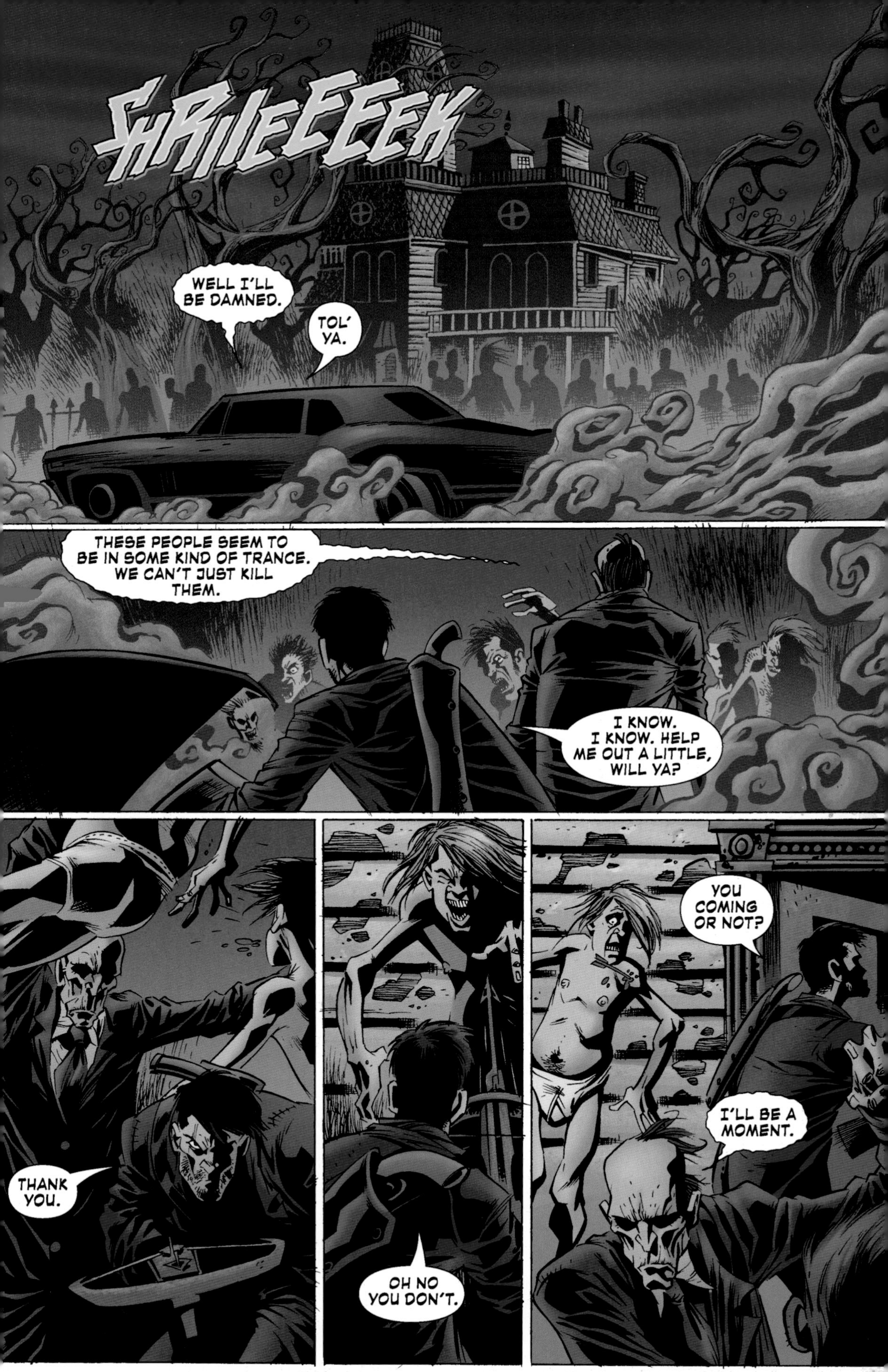
SHRIIEEEEK
WELL I'LL BE DAMNED.
TOL' YA.
THESE PEOPLE SEEM TO BE IN SOME KIND OF TRANCE. WE CAN'T JUST KILL THEM.
I KNOW. I KNOW. HELP ME OUT A LITTLE, WILL YA?
THANK YOU.
OH NO YOU DON'T.
YOU COMING OR NOT?
I'LL BE A MOMENT.

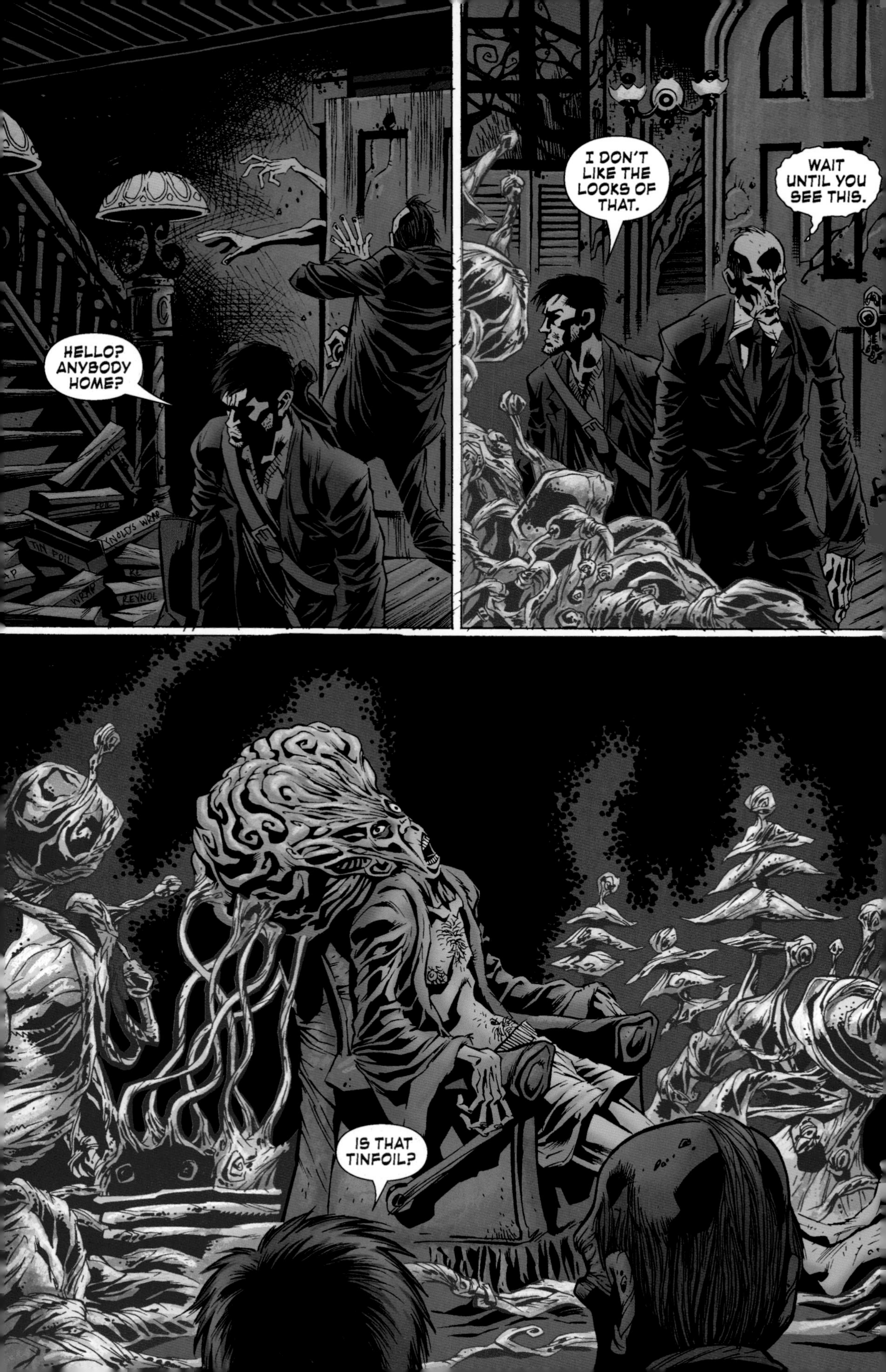
HELLO? ANYBODY HOME?
TIN FOIL
I DON'T LIKE THE LOOKS OF THAT.
WAIT UNTIL YOU SEE THIS.
IS THAT TINFOIL?

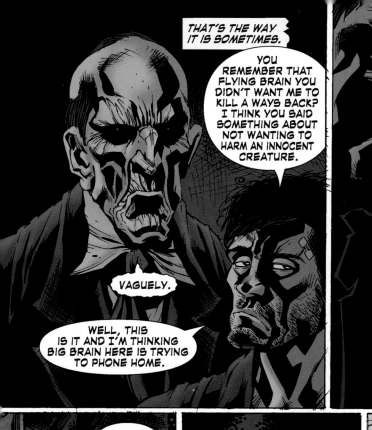

THAT'S THE WAY IT IS SOMETIMES.

YOU REMEMBER THAT FLYING BRAIN YOU DIDN'T WANT ME TO KILL A WAYS BACK? I THINK YOU SAID SOMETHING ABOUT NOT WANTING TO HARM AN INNOCENT CREATURE.

VAGUELY.

WELL, THIS IS IT AND I'M THINKING BIG BRAIN HERE IS TRYING TO PHONE HOME.

THIS TIME I'M KILLING IT AND YOU CAN'T STOP ME.

I WON'T.

UH-OH. LOOKS LIKE BUTTHEAD WANTS TO FIGHT.

SOMETIMES CASES COME BACK TO HAUNT YOU.

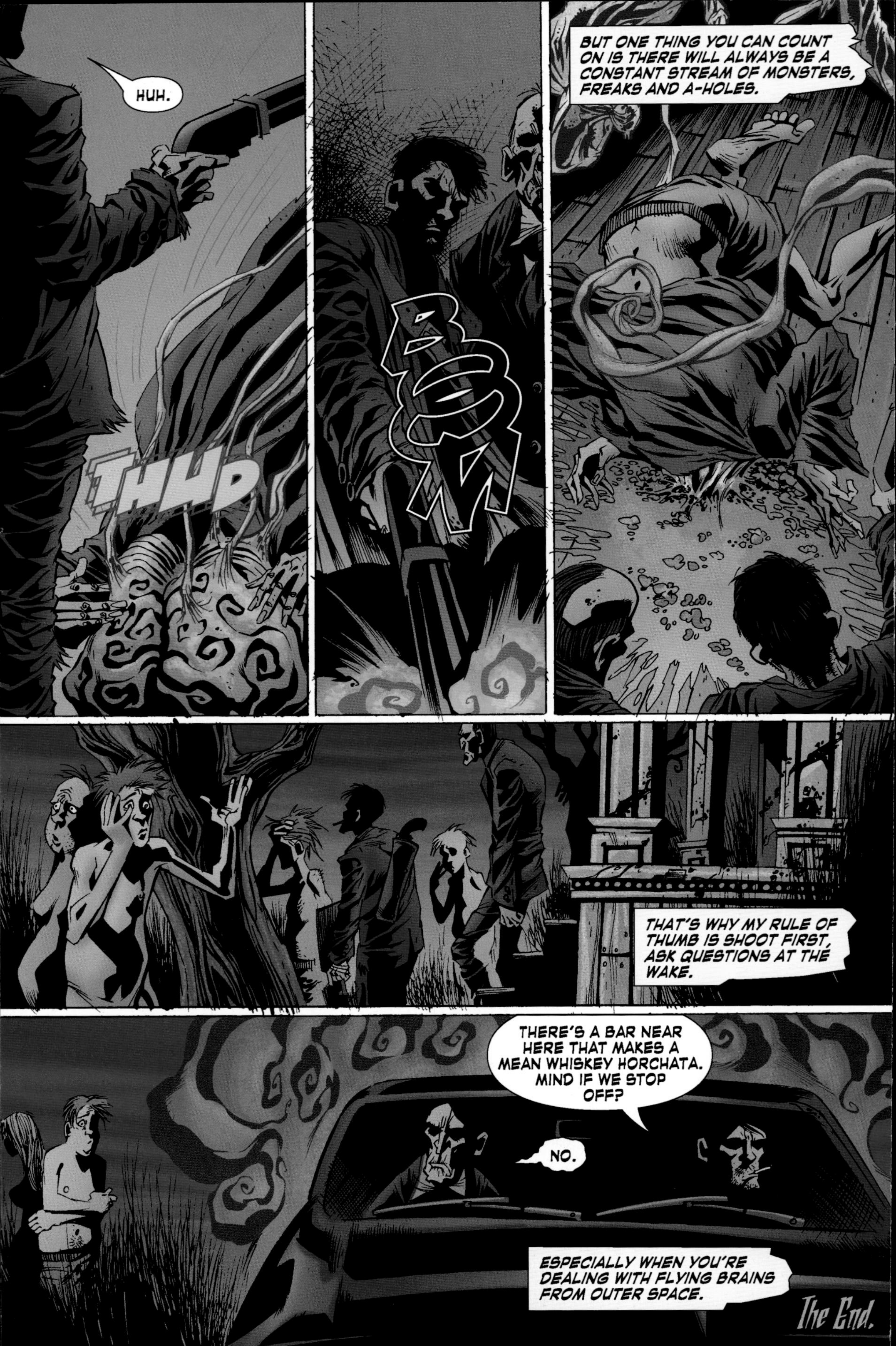
HUH.
THUD
BOOM
BUT ONE THING YOU CAN COUNT ON IS THERE WILL ALWAYS BE A CONSTANT STREAM OF MONSTERS, FREAKS AND A-HOLES.
THAT'S WHY MY RULE OF THUMB IS SHOOT FIRST, ASK QUESTIONS AT THE WAKE.
THERE'S A BAR NEAR HERE THAT MAKES A MEAN WHISKEY HORCHATA. MIND IF WE STOP OFF?
NO.
ESPECIALLY WHEN YOU'RE DEALING WITH FLYING BRAINS FROM OUTER SPACE.
The End.

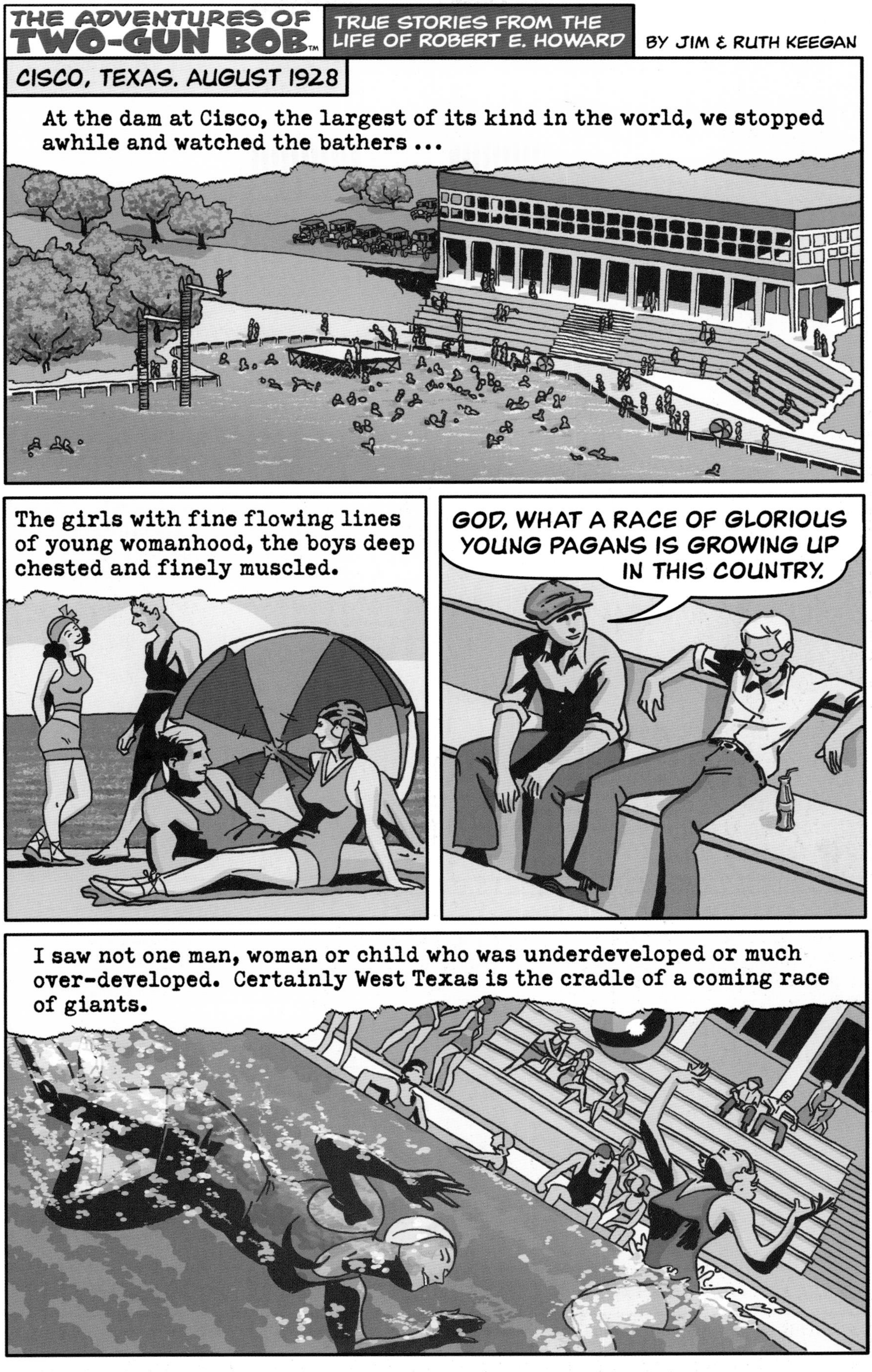
THE ADVENTURES OF TWO-GUN BOB™
TRUE STORIES FROM THE LIFE OF ROBERT E. HOWARD
BY JIM & RUTH KEEGAN
CISCO, TEXAS. AUGUST 1928
At the dam at Cisco, the largest of its kind in the world, we stopped awhile and watched the bathers ...
The girls with fine flowing lines of young womanhood, the boys deep chested and finely muscled.
GOD, WHAT A RACE OF GLORIOUS YOUNG PAGANS IS GROWING UP IN THIS COUNTRY.
I saw not one man, woman or child who was underdeveloped or much over-developed. Certainly West Texas is the cradle of a coming race of giants.

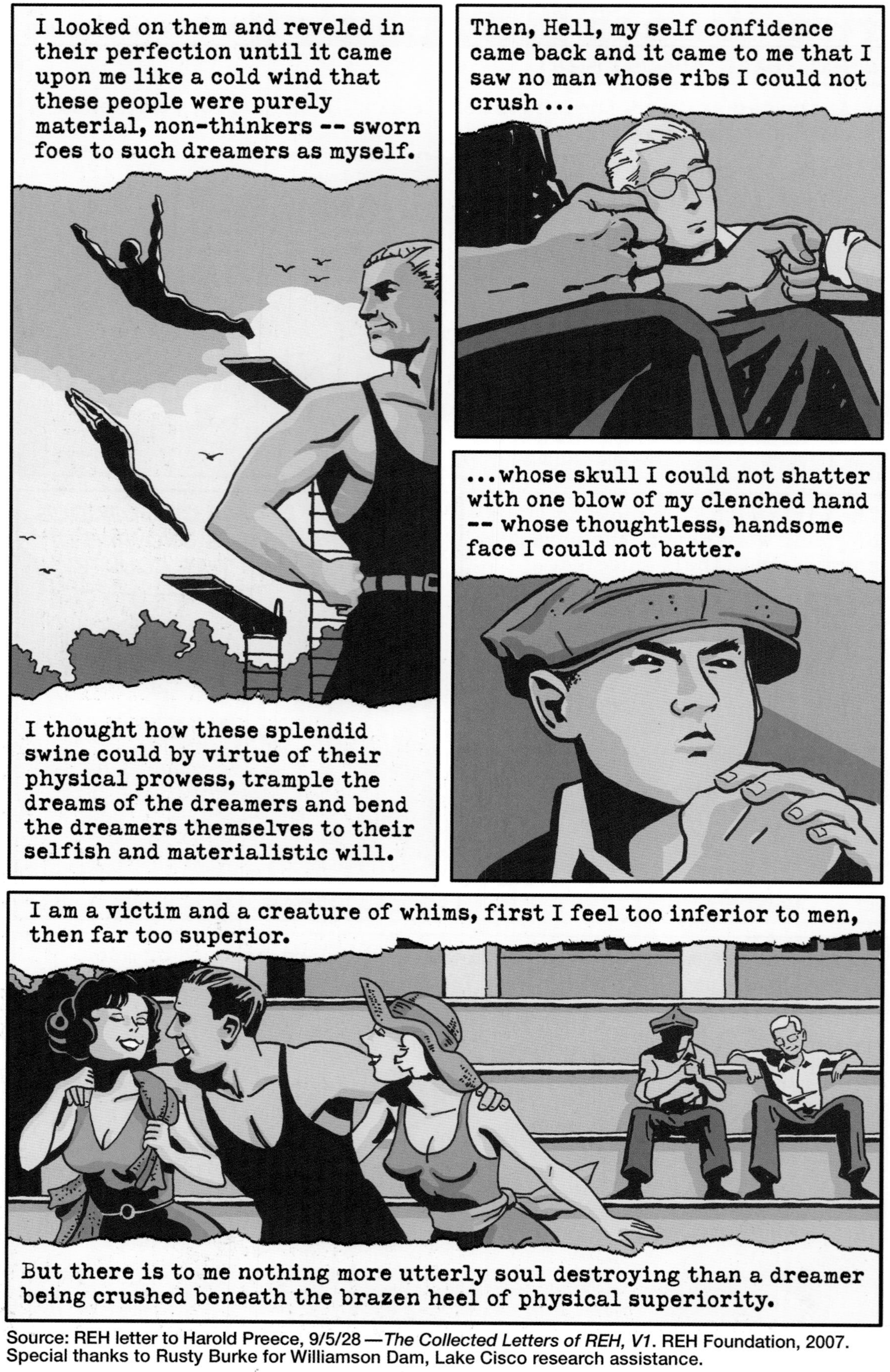
I looked on them and reveled in their perfection until it came upon me like a cold wind that these people were purely material, non-thinkers -- sworn foes to such dreamers as myself.
I thought how these splendid swine could by virtue of their physical prowess, trample the dreams of the dreamers and bend the dreamers themselves to their selfish and materialistic will.
Then, Hell, my self confidence came back and it came to me that I saw no man whose ribs I could not crush ...
...whose skull I could not shatter with one blow of my clenched hand -- whose thoughtless, handsome face I could not batter.
I am a victim and a creature of whims, first I feel too inferior to men, then far too superior.
But there is to me nothing more utterly soul destroying than a dreamer being crushed beneath the brazen heel of physical superiority.

Source: REH letter to Harold Preece, 9/5/28 —*The Collected Letters of REH, V1*. REH Foundation, 2007.
Special thanks to Rusty Burke for Williamson Dam, Lake Cisco research assistance.

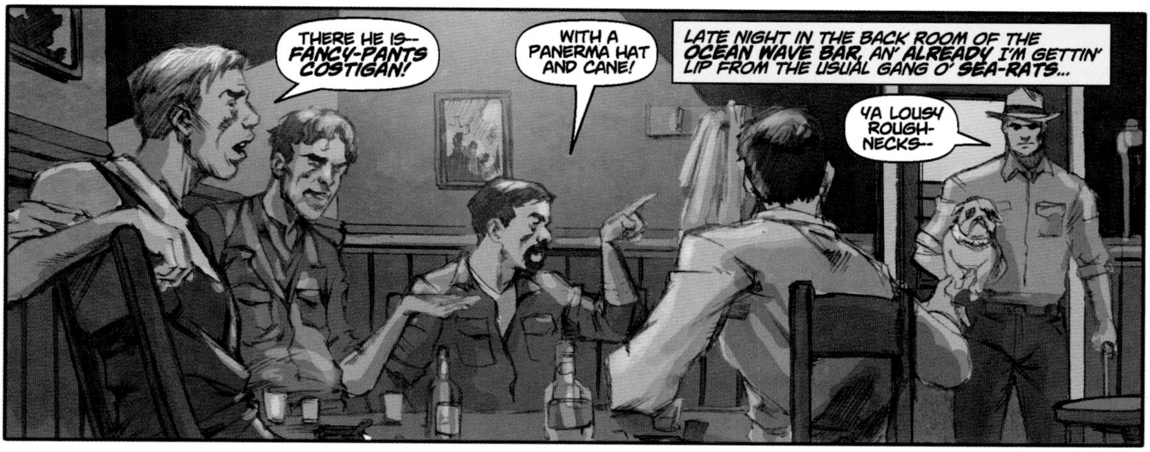
THERE HE IS-- FANCY-PANTS COSTIGAN!
WITH A PANERMA HAT AND CANE!
LATE NIGHT IN THE BACK ROOM OF THE OCEAN WAVE BAR, AN' ALREADY I'M GETTIN' LIP FROM THE USUAL GANG O' SEA-RATS...
YA LOUSY ROUGH-NECKS--

SAILOR STEVE COSTIGAN

by Casey, Mhan, Villarrubia, and Comicraft

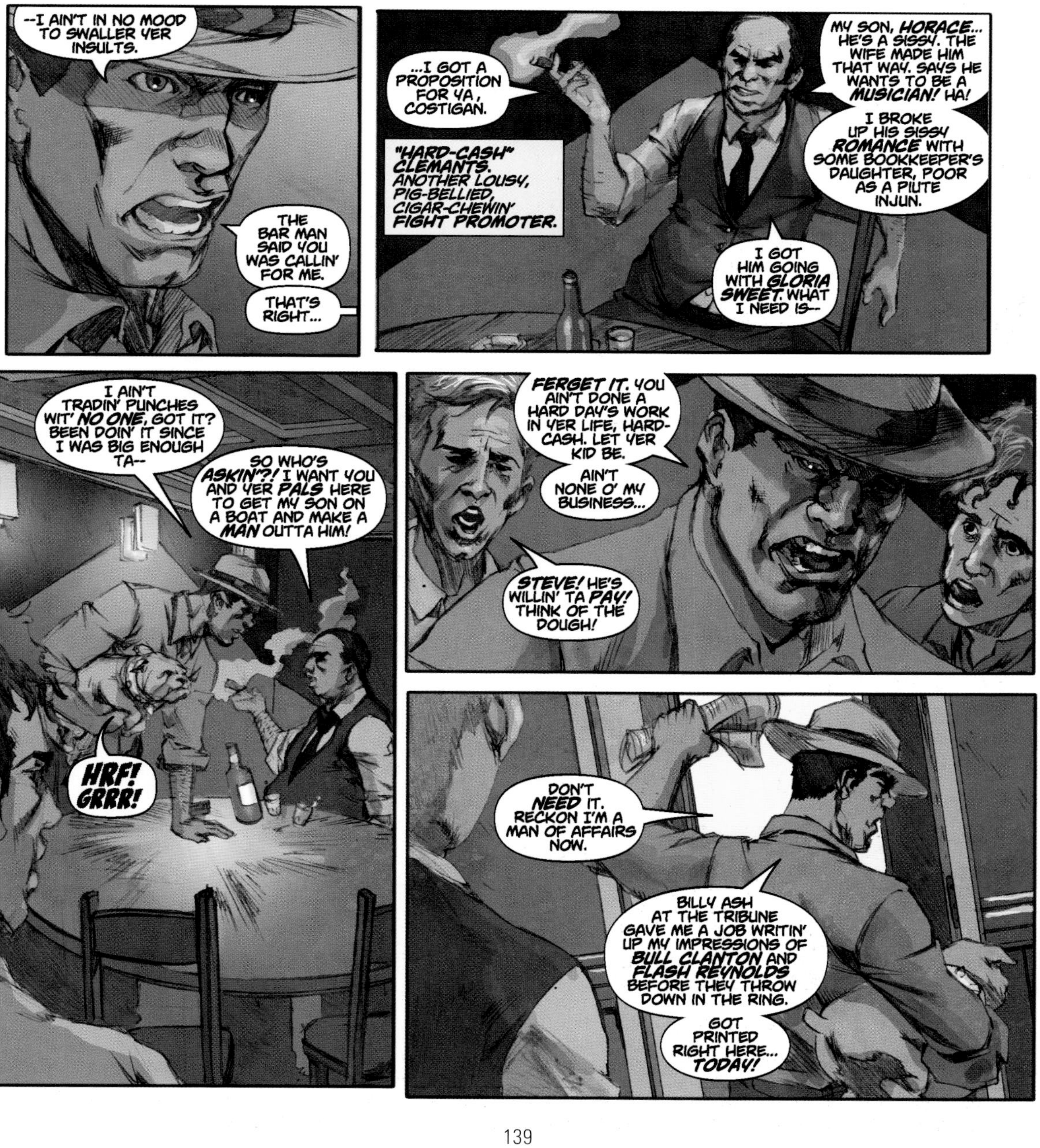
--I AIN'T IN NO MOOD TO SWALLER YER INSULTS.
THE BAR MAN SAID YOU WAS CALLIN' FOR ME.
THAT'S RIGHT...
...I GOT A PROPOSITION FOR YA, COSTIGAN.
"HARD-CASH" CLEMANTS. ANOTHER LOUSY, PIG-BELLIED, CIGAR-CHEWIN' FIGHT PROMOTER.
MY SON, HORACE... HE'S A SISSY. THE WIFE MADE HIM THAT WAY. SAYS HE WANTS TO BE A MUSICIAN! HA!
I BROKE UP HIS SISSY ROMANCE WITH SOME BOOKKEEPER'S DAUGHTER, POOR AS A PIUTE INJUN.
I GOT HIM GOING WITH GLORIA SWEET. WHAT I NEED IS--
I AIN'T TRADIN' PUNCHES WIT' NO ONE, GOT IT? BEEN DOIN' IT SINCE I WAS BIG ENOUGH TA--
SO WHO'S ASKIN'?! I WANT YOU AND YER PALS HERE TO GET MY SON ON A BOAT AND MAKE A MAN OUTTA HIM!
HRF! GRRR!
FERGET IT. YOU AIN'T DONE A HARD DAY'S WORK IN YER LIFE, HARD-CASH. LET YER KID BE.
AIN'T NONE O' MY BUSINESS...
STEVE! HE'S WILLIN' TA PAY! THINK OF THE DOUGH!
DON'T NEED IT. RECKON I'M A MAN OF AFFAIRS NOW.
BILLY ASH AT THE TRIBUNE GAVE ME A JOB WRITIN' UP MY IMPRESSIONS OF BULL CLANTON AND FLASH REYNOLDS BEFORE THEY THROW DOWN IN THE RING.
GOT PRINTED RIGHT HERE... TODAY!

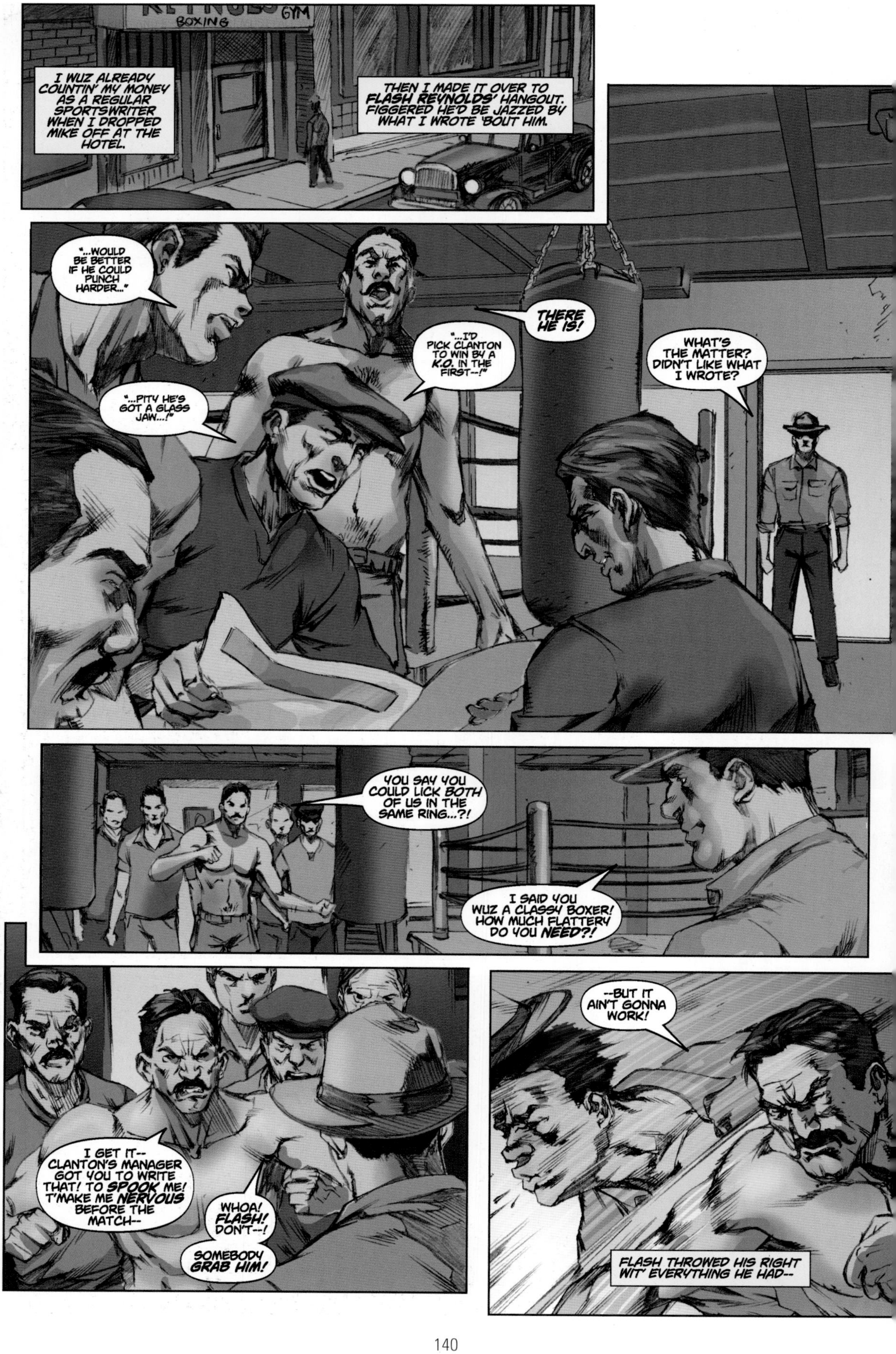
REYNOLDS GYM
BOXING
I WUZ ALREADY COUNTIN' MY MONEY AS A REGULAR SPORTSWRITER WHEN I DROPPED MIKE OFF AT THE HOTEL.
THEN I MADE IT OVER TO FLASH REYNOLDS' HANGOUT. FIGGERED HE'D BE JAZZED BY WHAT I WROTE 'BOUT HIM.
"...WOULD BE BETTER IF HE COULD PUNCH HARDER..."
"...PITY HE'S GOT A GLASS JAW...!"
"...I'D PICK CLANTON TO WIN BY A K.O. IN THE FIRST--!"
THERE HE IS!
WHAT'S THE MATTER? DIDN'T LIKE WHAT I WROTE?
YOU SAY YOU COULD LICK BOTH OF US IN THE SAME RING...?!
I SAID YOU WUZ A CLASSY BOXER! HOW MUCH FLATTERY DO YOU NEED?!
I GET IT-- CLANTON'S MANAGER GOT YOU TO WRITE THAT! TO SPOOK ME! T'MAKE ME NERVOUS BEFORE THE MATCH--
WHOA! FLASH! DON'T--!
SOMEBODY GRAB HIM!
--BUT IT AIN'T GONNA WORK!
FLASH THROWED HIS RIGHT WIT' EVERYTHING HE HAD--

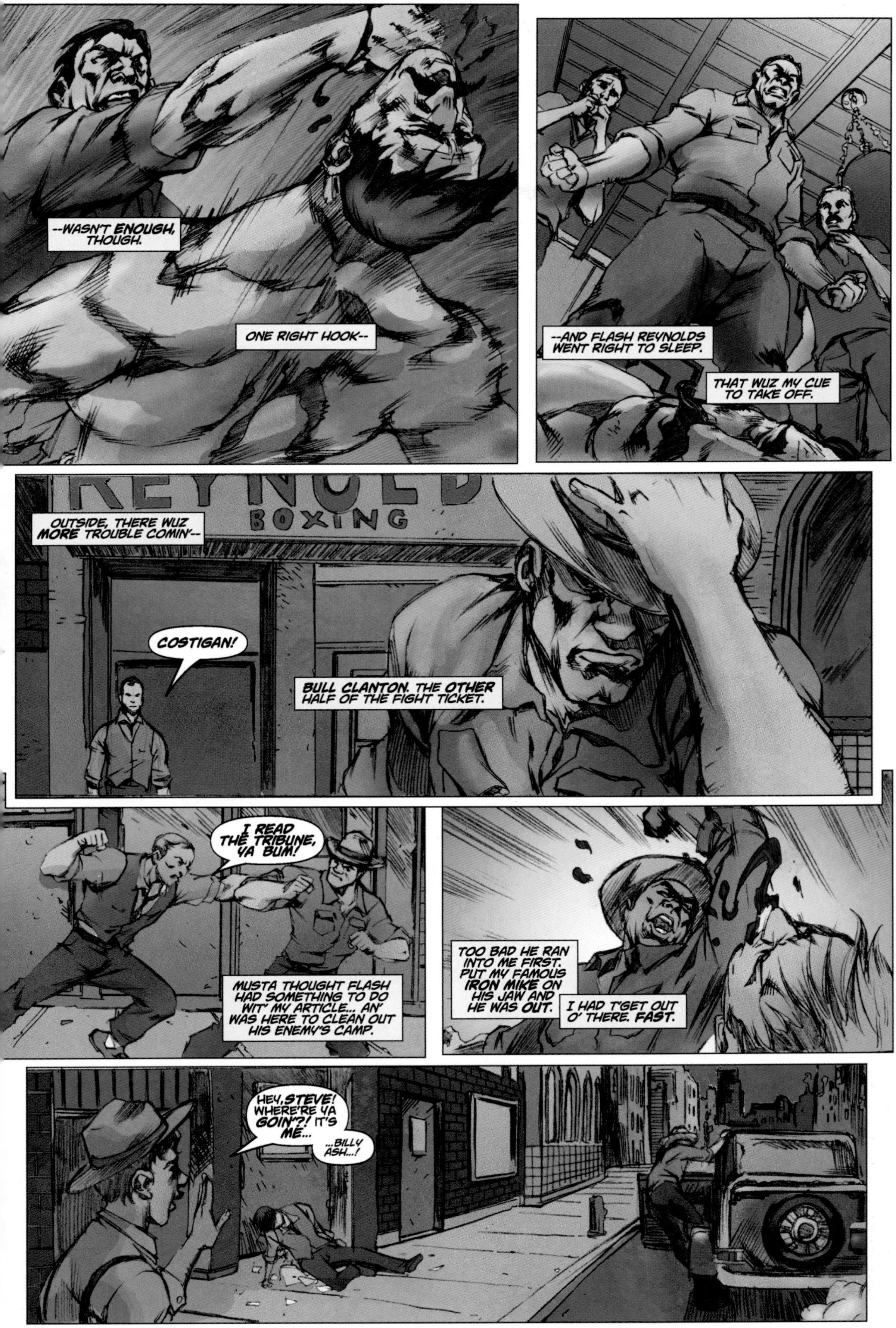
--WASN'T ENOUGH, THOUGH.
ONE RIGHT HOOK--
--AND FLASH REYNOLDS WENT RIGHT TO SLEEP.
THAT WUZ MY CUE TO TAKE OFF.
REYNOLD
BOXING
OUTSIDE, THERE WUZ MORE TROUBLE COMIN'--
COSTIGAN!
BULL CLANTON. THE OTHER HALF OF THE FIGHT TICKET.
I READ THE TRIBUNE, YA BUM!
MUSTA THOUGHT FLASH HAD SOMETHING TO DO WIT' MY ARTICLE... AN' WAS HERE TO CLEAN OUT HIS ENEMY'S CAMP.
TOO BAD HE RAN INTO ME FIRST. PUT MY FAMOUS IRON MIKE ON HIS JAW AND HE WAS OUT.
I HAD T'GET OUT O' THERE. FAST.
HEY, STEVE! WHERE'RE YA GOIN'?! IT'S ME...
...BILLY ASH...!

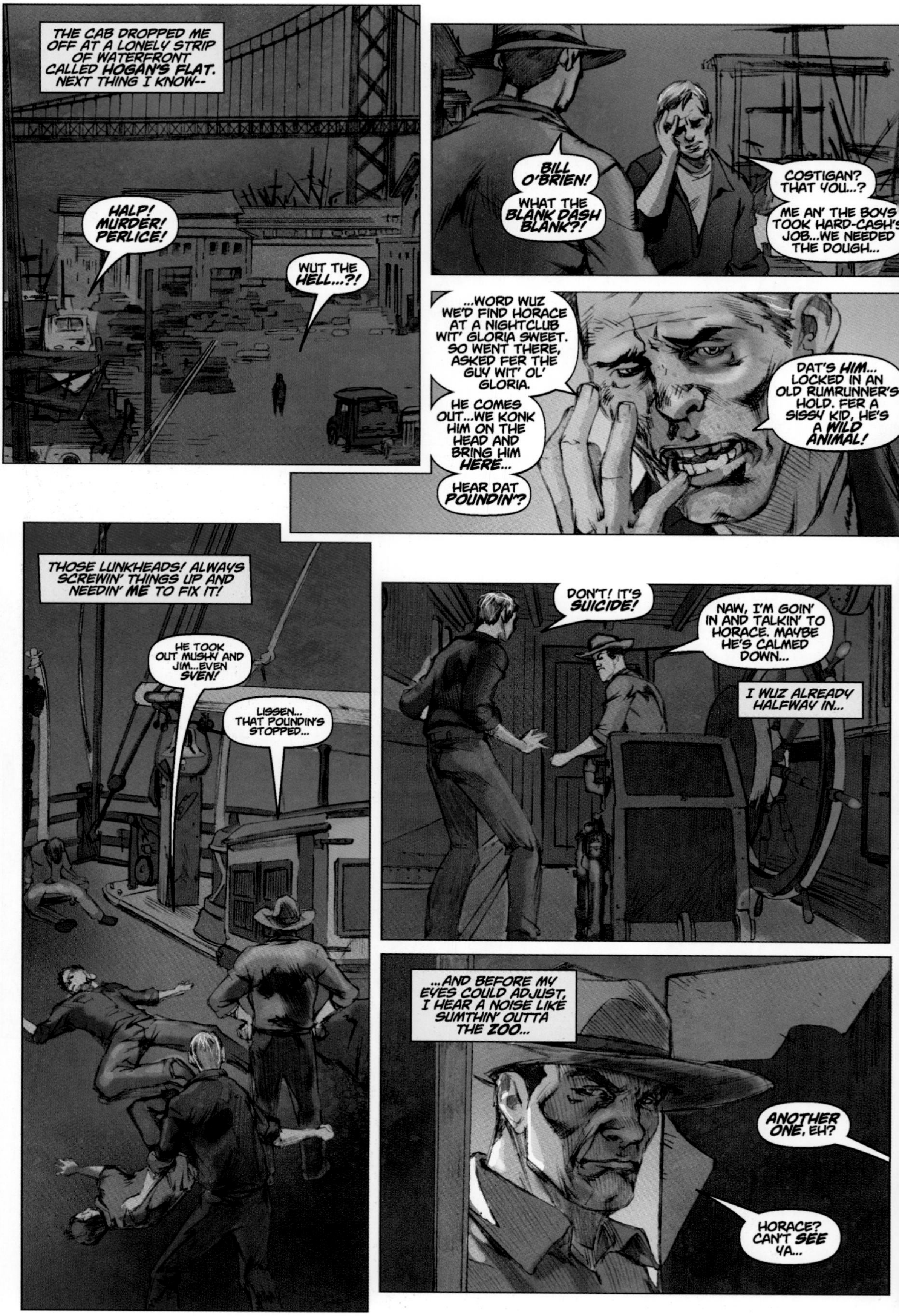
THE CAB DROPPED ME OFF AT A LONELY STRIP OF WATERFRONT CALLED HOGAN'S FLAT. NEXT THING I KNOW--
HALP! MURDER! PERLICE!
WUT THE HELL...?!
BILL O'BRIEN!
WHAT THE BLANK DASH BLANK?!
COSTIGAN? THAT YOU...?
ME AN' THE BOYS TOOK HARD-CASH'S JOB...WE NEEDED THE DOUGH...
...WORD WUZ WE'D FIND HORACE AT A NIGHTCLUB WIT' GLORIA SWEET. SO WENT THERE, ASKED FER THE GUY WIT' OL' GLORIA.
HE COMES OUT...WE KONK HIM ON THE HEAD AND BRING HIM HERE...
HEAR DAT POUNDIN'?
DAT'S HIM... LOCKED IN AN OLD RUMRUNNER'S HOLD. FER A SISSY KID, HE'S A WILD ANIMAL!
THOSE LUNKHEADS! ALWAYS SCREWIN' THINGS UP AND NEEDIN' ME TO FIX IT!
HE TOOK OUT MUSHY AND JIM...EVEN SVEN!
LISSEN... THAT POUNDIN'S STOPPED...
DON'T! IT'S SUICIDE!
NAW, I'M GOIN' IN AND TALKIN' TO HORACE. MAYBE HE'S CALMED DOWN...
I WUZ ALREADY HALFWAY IN...
...AND BEFORE MY EYES COULD ADJUST, I HEAR A NOISE LIKE SUMTHIN' OUTTA THE ZOO...
ANOTHER ONE, EH?
HORACE? CAN'T SEE YA...

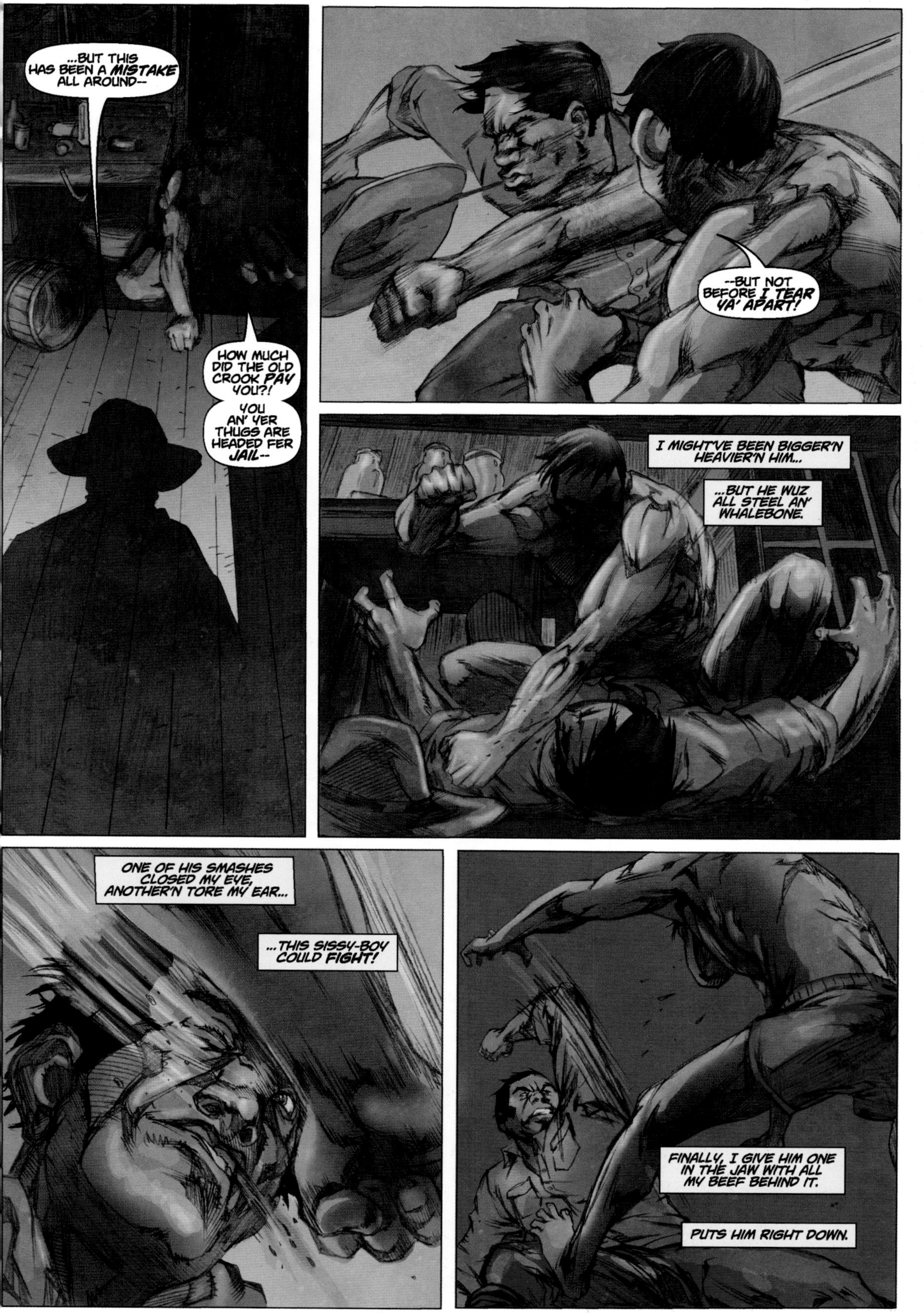
...BUT THIS HAS BEEN A MISTAKE ALL AROUND--
HOW MUCH DID THE OLD CROOK PAY YOU?!
YOU AN' YER THUGS ARE HEADED FER JAIL--
--BUT NOT BEFORE I TEAR YA' APART!
I MIGHT'VE BEEN BIGGER'N HEAVIER'N HIM...
...BUT HE WUZ ALL STEEL AN' WHALEBONE.
ONE OF HIS SMASHES CLOSED MY EYE, ANOTHER'N TORE MY EAR...
...THIS SISSY-BOY COULD FIGHT!
FINALLY, I GIVE HIM ONE IN THE JAW WITH ALL MY BEEF BEHIND IT.
PUTS HIM RIGHT DOWN.

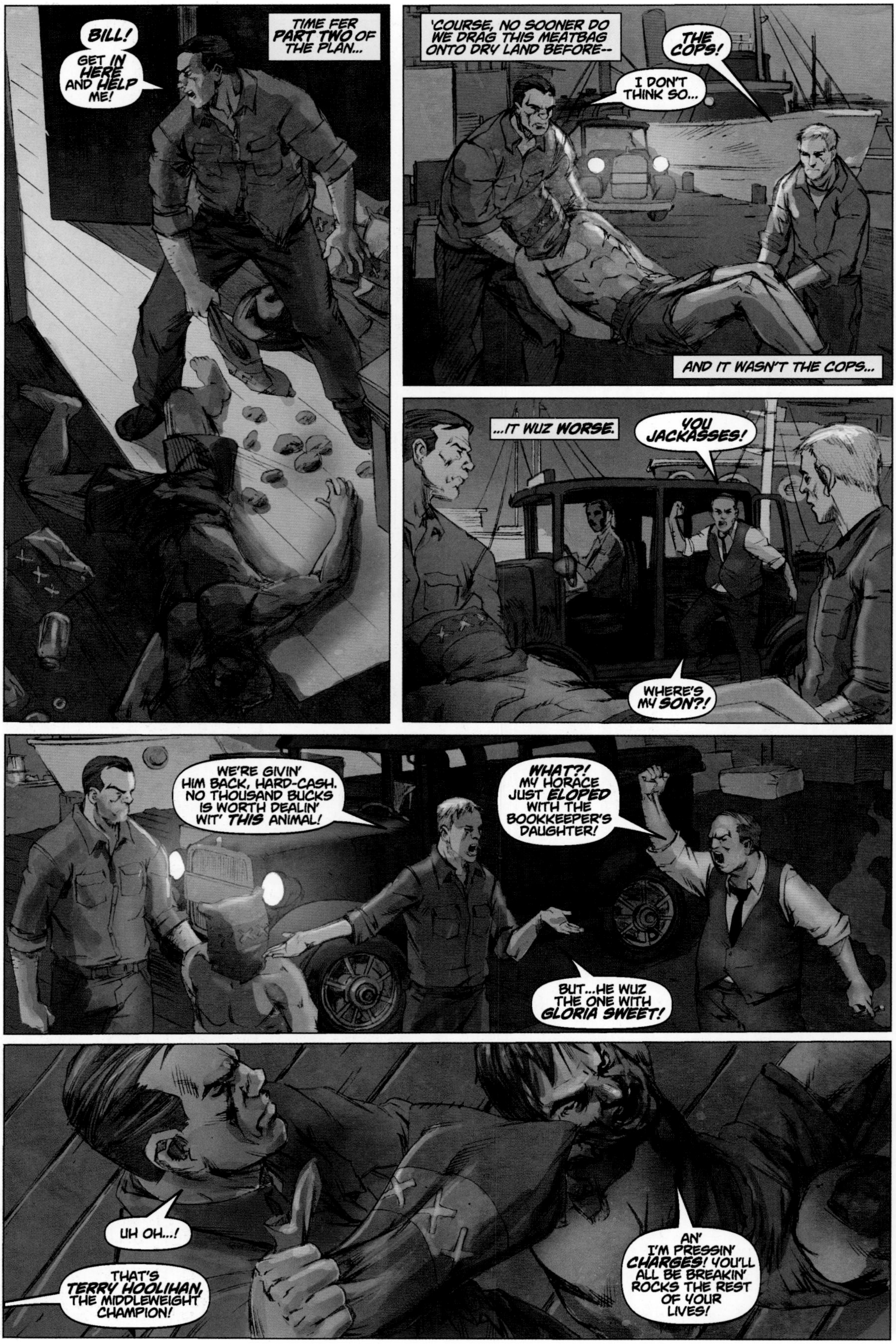
TIME FER PART TWO OF THE PLAN...
BILL!
GET IN HERE AND HELP ME!
'COURSE, NO SOONER DO WE DRAG THIS MEATBAG ONTO DRY LAND BEFORE--
THE COPS!
I DON'T THINK SO...
AND IT WASN'T THE COPS...
...IT WUZ WORSE.
YOU JACKASSES!
WHERE'S MY SON?!
WE'RE GIVIN' HIM BACK, HARD-CASH. NO THOUSAND BUCKS IS WORTH DEALIN' WIT' THIS ANIMAL!
WHAT?! MY HORACE JUST ELOPED WITH THE BOOKKEEPER'S DAUGHTER!
BUT...HE WUZ THE ONE WITH GLORIA SWEET!
UH OH...!
THAT'S TERRY HOOLIHAN, THE MIDDLEWEIGHT CHAMPION!
AN' I'M PRESSIN' CHARGES! YOU'LL ALL BE BREAKIN' ROCKS THE REST OF YOUR LIVES!

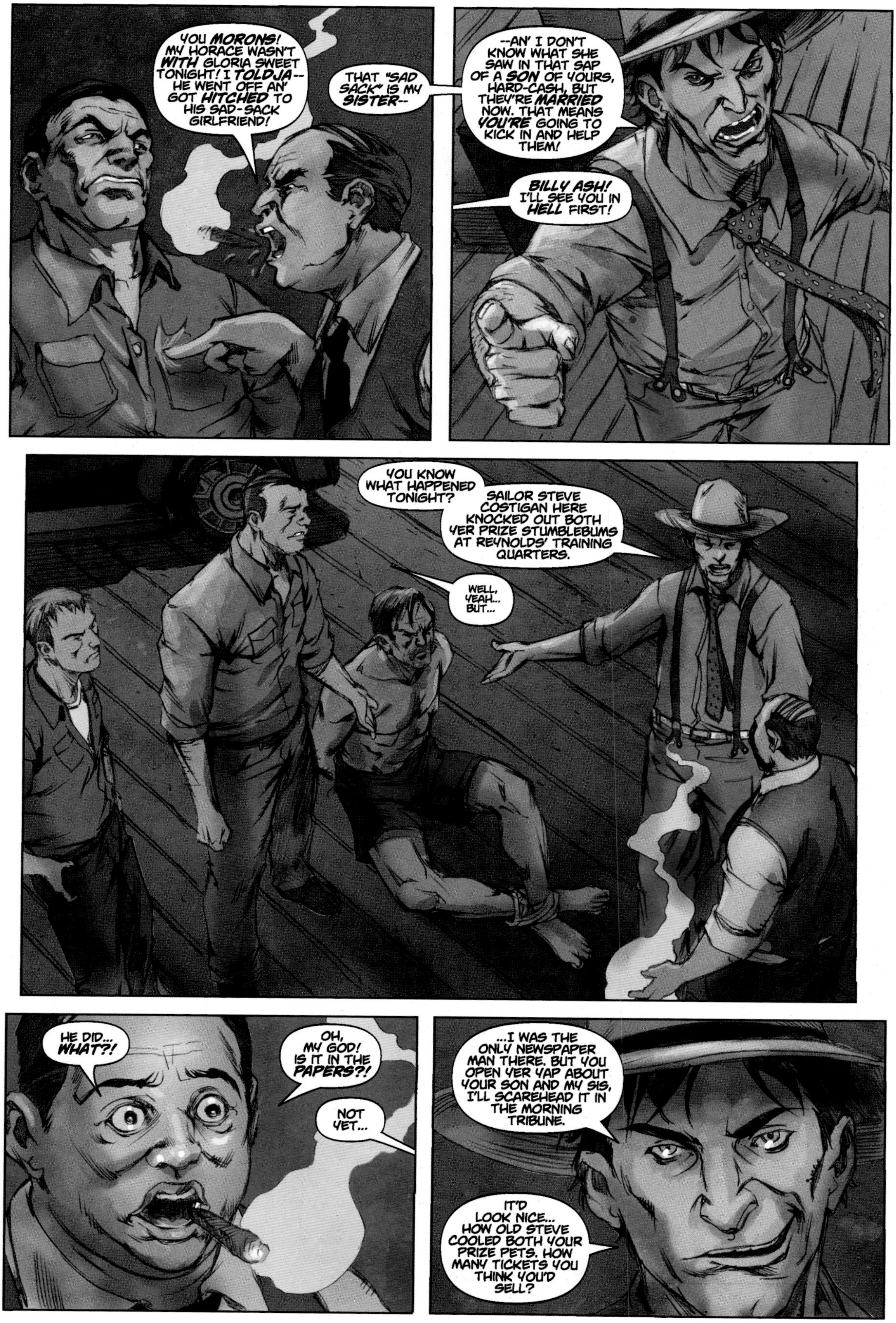
YOU MORONS! MY HORACE WASN'T WITH GLORIA SWEET TONIGHT! I TOLDJA-- HE WENT OFF AN' GOT HITCHED TO HIS SAD-SACK GIRLFRIEND!
THAT "SAD SACK" IS MY SISTER--
--AN' I DON'T KNOW WHAT SHE SAW IN THAT SAP OF A SON OF YOURS, HARD-CASH, BUT THEY'RE MARRIED NOW. THAT MEANS YOU'RE GOING TO KICK IN AND HELP THEM!
BILLY ASH! I'LL SEE YOU IN HELL FIRST!
YOU KNOW WHAT HAPPENED TONIGHT?
SAILOR STEVE COSTIGAN HERE KNOCKED OUT BOTH YER PRIZE STUMBLEBUMS AT REYNOLDS' TRAINING QUARTERS.
WELL, YEAH... BUT...
HE DID... WHAT?!
OH, MY GOD! IS IT IN THE PAPERS?!
NOT YET...
...I WAS THE ONLY NEWSPAPER MAN THERE. BUT YOU OPEN YER YAP ABOUT YOUR SON AND MY SIS, I'LL SCAREHEAD IT IN THE MORNING TRIBUNE.
IT'D LOOK NICE... HOW OLD STEVE COOLED BOTH YOUR PRIZE PETS. HOW MANY TICKETS YOU THINK YOU'D SELL?

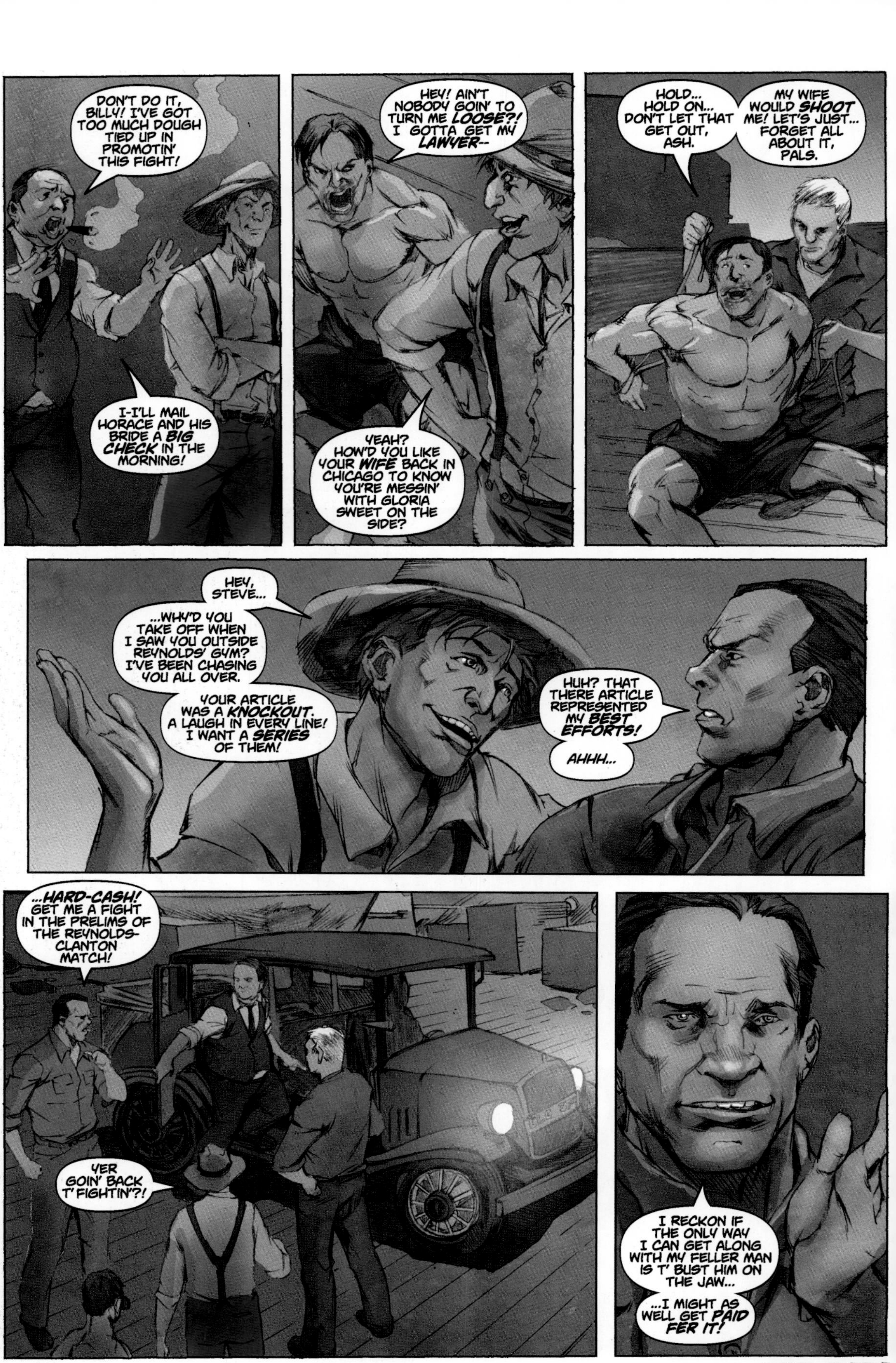
DON'T DO IT, BILLY! I'VE GOT TOO MUCH DOUGH TIED UP IN PROMOTIN' THIS FIGHT!
I-I'LL MAIL HORACE AND HIS BRIDE A BIG CHECK IN THE MORNING!
HEY! AIN'T NOBODY GOIN' TO TURN ME LOOSE?! I GOTTA GET MY LAWYER--
YEAH? HOW'D YOU LIKE YOUR WIFE BACK IN CHICAGO TO KNOW YOU'RE MESSIN' WITH GLORIA SWEET ON THE SIDE?
HOLD... HOLD ON... DON'T LET THAT GET OUT, ASH.
MY WIFE WOULD SHOOT ME! LET'S JUST... FORGET ALL ABOUT IT, PALS.
HEY, STEVE...
...WHY'D YOU TAKE OFF WHEN I SAW YOU OUTSIDE REYNOLDS' GYM? I'VE BEEN CHASING YOU ALL OVER.
YOUR ARTICLE WAS A KNOCKOUT. A LAUGH IN EVERY LINE! I WANT A SERIES OF THEM!
HUH? THAT THERE ARTICLE REPRESENTED MY BEST EFFORTS!
AHHH...
...HARD-CASH! GET ME A FIGHT IN THE PRELIMS OF THE REYNOLDS-CLANTON MATCH!
YER GOIN' BACK T' FIGHTIN'?!
I RECKON IF THE ONLY WAY I CAN GET ALONG WITH MY FELLER MAN IS T' BUST HIM ON THE JAW...
...I MIGHT AS WELL GET PAID FER IT!

THE END!

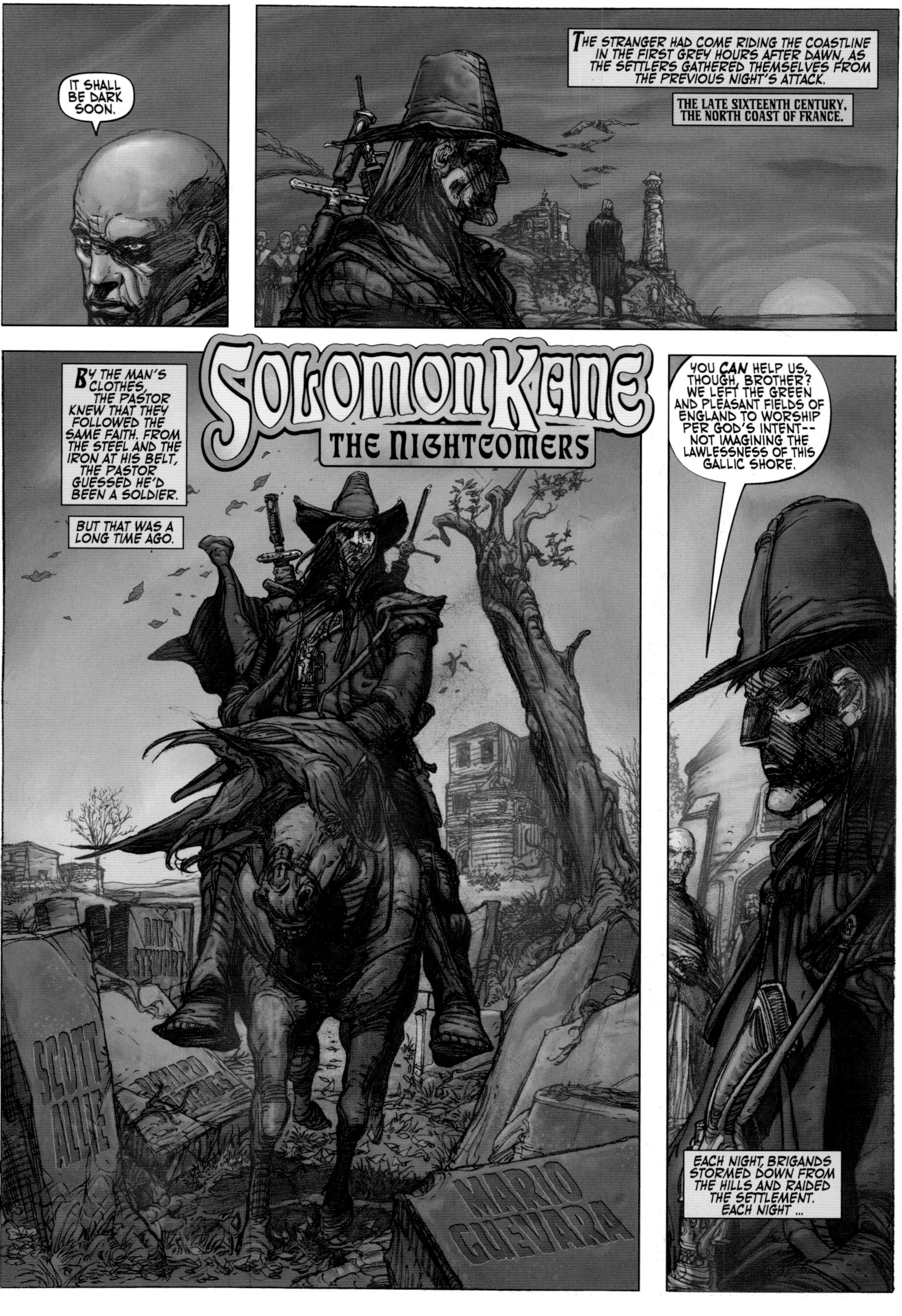
IT SHALL BE DARK SOON.
THE STRANGER HAD COME RIDING THE COASTLINE IN THE FIRST GREY HOURS AFTER DAWN, AS THE SETTLERS GATHERED THEMSELVES FROM THE PREVIOUS NIGHT'S ATTACK.
THE LATE SIXTEENTH CENTURY, THE NORTH COAST OF FRANCE.
SOLOMON KANE
THE NIGHTCOMERS
BY THE MAN'S CLOTHES, THE PASTOR KNEW THAT THEY FOLLOWED THE SAME FAITH. FROM THE STEEL AND THE IRON AT HIS BELT, THE PASTOR GUESSED HE'D BEEN A SOLDIER.
BUT THAT WAS A LONG TIME AGO.
DAVE STEWART
SCOTT ALLIE
MARIO GUEVARA
YOU CAN HELP US, THOUGH, BROTHER? WE LEFT THE GREEN AND PLEASANT FIELDS OF ENGLAND TO WORSHIP PER GOD'S INTENT-- NOT IMAGINING THE LAWLESSNESS OF THIS GALLIC SHORE.
EACH NIGHT, BRIGANDS STORMED DOWN FROM THE HILLS AND RAIDED THE SETTLEMENT. EACH NIGHT ...

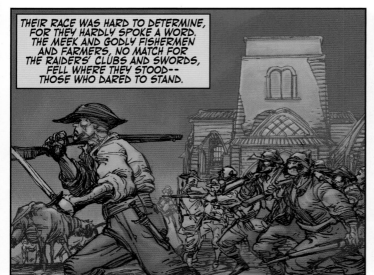

THEIR RACE WAS HARD TO DETERMINE, FOR THEY HARDLY SPOKE A WORD. THE MEEK AND GODLY FISHERMEN AND FARMERS, NO MATCH FOR THE RAIDERS' CLUBS AND SWORDS, FELL WHERE THEY STOOD-- THOSE WHO DARED TO STAND.

THEY COULD OFFER NO RESISTANCE AS THE BASTARDS WENT AFTER THEIR WOMEN.

EACH NIGHT ...

AND SO SOLOMON KANE VOWED TO DEFEND THE SETTLEMENT THIS ONE NIGHT, THEN LEAD THE ENGLISH THROUGH THE TREACHEROUS HILLS, TO LILLE, OR BRUXELLES.

WHAT'S THAT COLD HAND ON MY NECK?

I--I ONLY MEANT TO ... TO SHOW MY-- OUR GRATITUDE, M'LORD.

YOU THINK I TRADE IN THE SAME CURRENCY AS THESE ATTACKERS?

GUARD YOUR VIRTUE, WOMAN--

"--LEAVE ME TO GUARD THE TOWN."

WE LIVE IN GOD'S END TIMES, MY BOY.

THE CHURCH DIES BY DEGREE AT THE HANDS OF THOSE IDOLATROUS PAPISTS ...

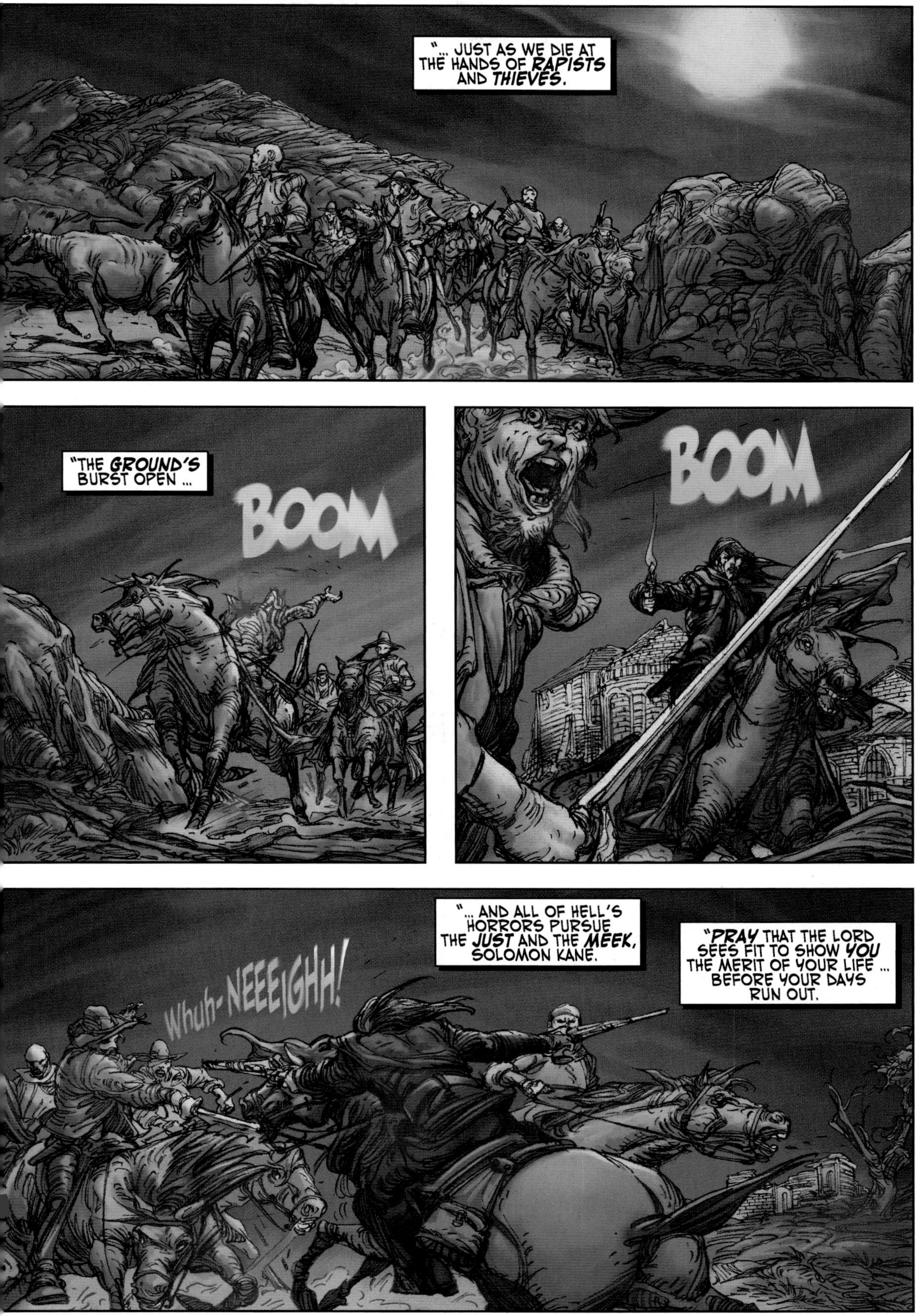
"... JUST AS WE DIE AT THE HANDS OF RAPISTS AND THIEVES.
"THE GROUND'S BURST OPEN ...
BOOM
BOOM
"... AND ALL OF HELL'S HORRORS PURSUE THE JUST AND THE MEEK, SOLOMON KANE.
"PRAY THAT THE LORD SEES FIT TO SHOW YOU THE MERIT OF YOUR LIFE ... BEFORE YOUR DAYS RUN OUT.
Whuh-NEEEIGHH!

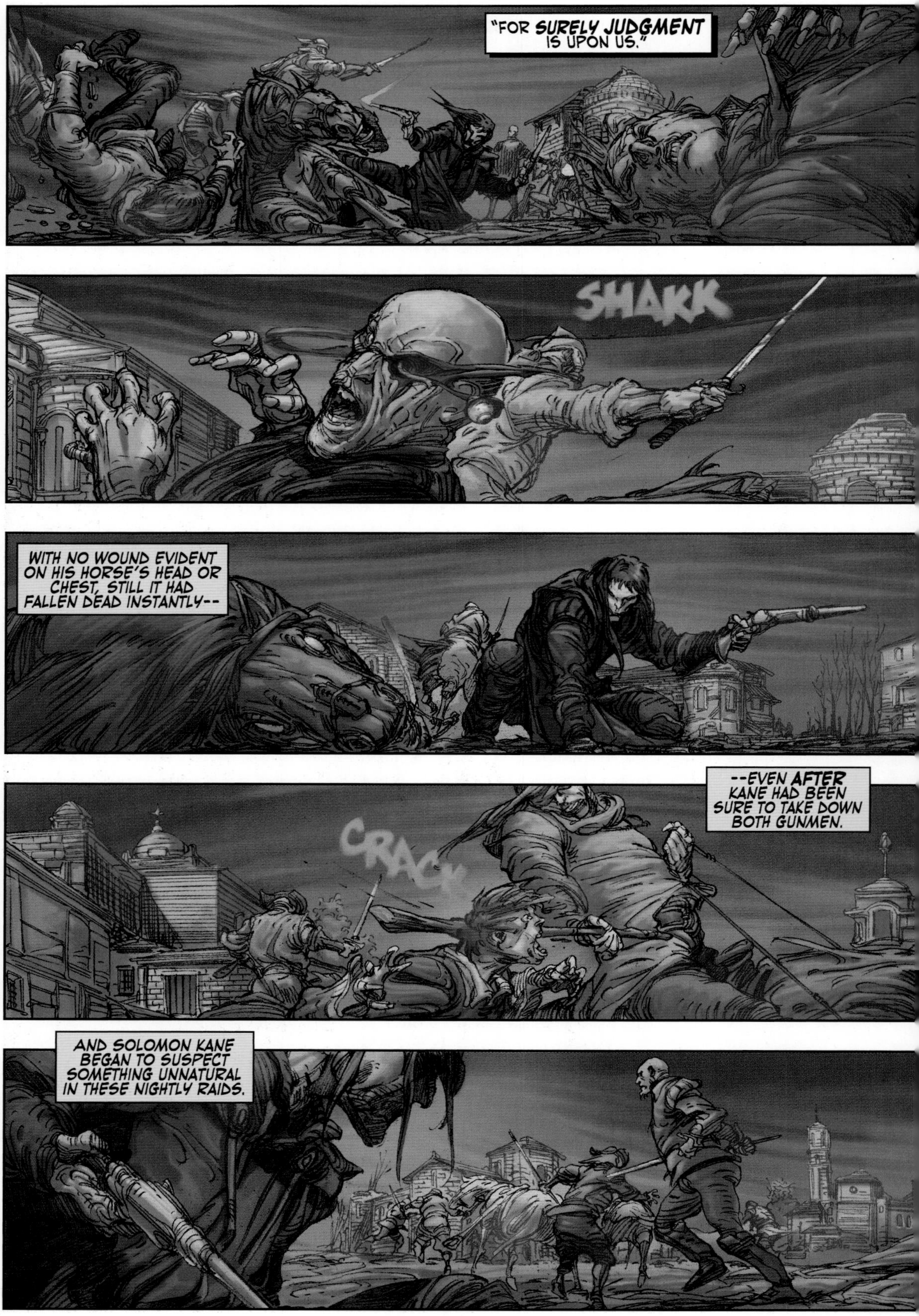
"FOR SURELY JUDGMENT IS UPON US."
SHAKK
WITH NO WOUND EVIDENT ON HIS HORSE'S HEAD OR CHEST, STILL IT HAD FALLEN DEAD INSTANTLY--
--EVEN AFTER KANE HAD BEEN SURE TO TAKE DOWN BOTH GUNMEN.
CRACK
AND SOLOMON KANE BEGAN TO SUSPECT SOMETHING UNNATURAL IN THESE NIGHTLY RAIDS.

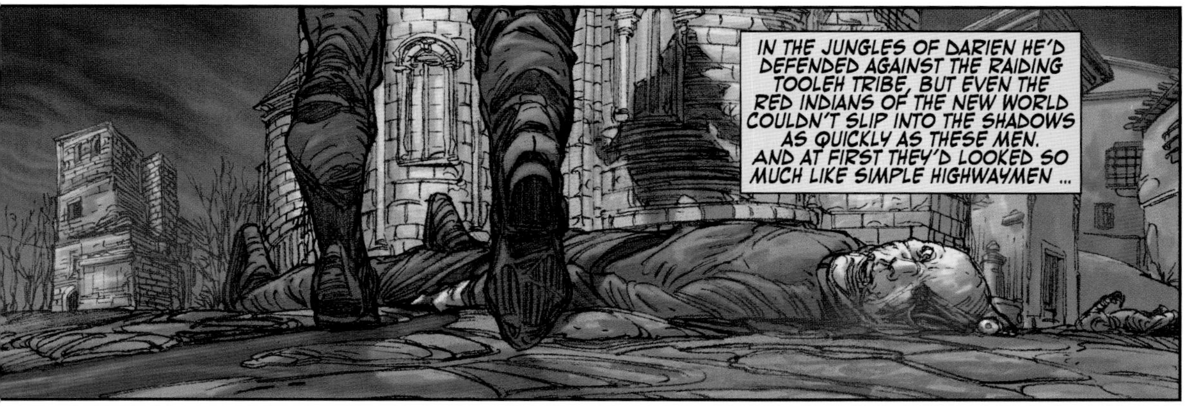
IN THE JUNGLES OF DARIEN HE'D DEFENDED AGAINST THE RAIDING TOOLEH TRIBE, BUT EVEN THE RED INDIANS OF THE NEW WORLD COULDN'T SLIP INTO THE SHADOWS AS QUICKLY AS THESE MEN. AND AT FIRST THEY'D LOOKED SO MUCH LIKE SIMPLE HIGHWAYMEN ...

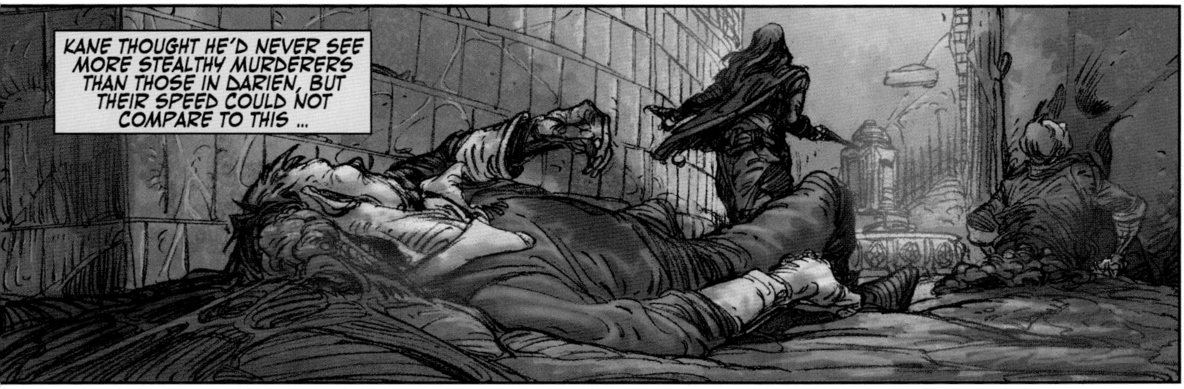
KANE THOUGHT HE'D NEVER SEE MORE STEALTHY MURDERERS THAN THOSE IN DARIEN, BUT THEIR SPEED COULD NOT COMPARE TO THIS ...

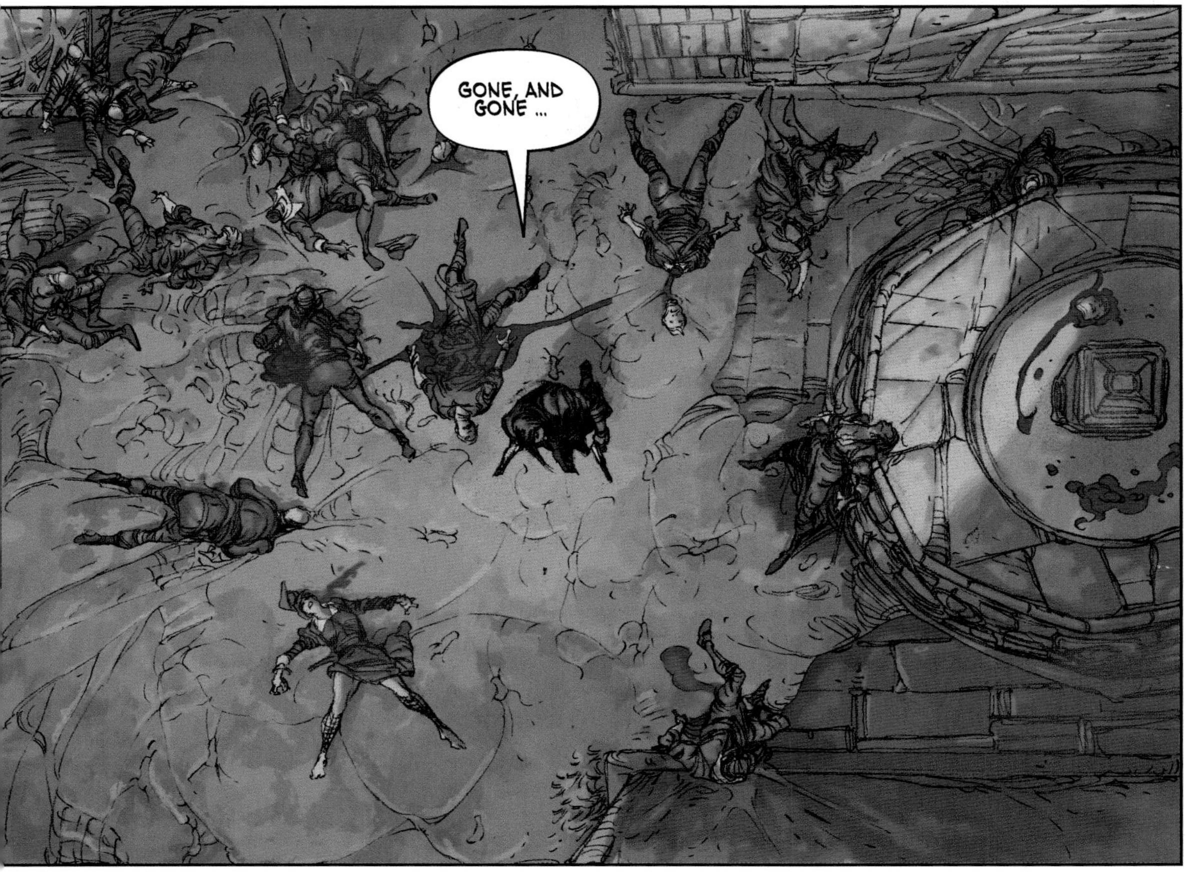
GONE, AND GONE ...

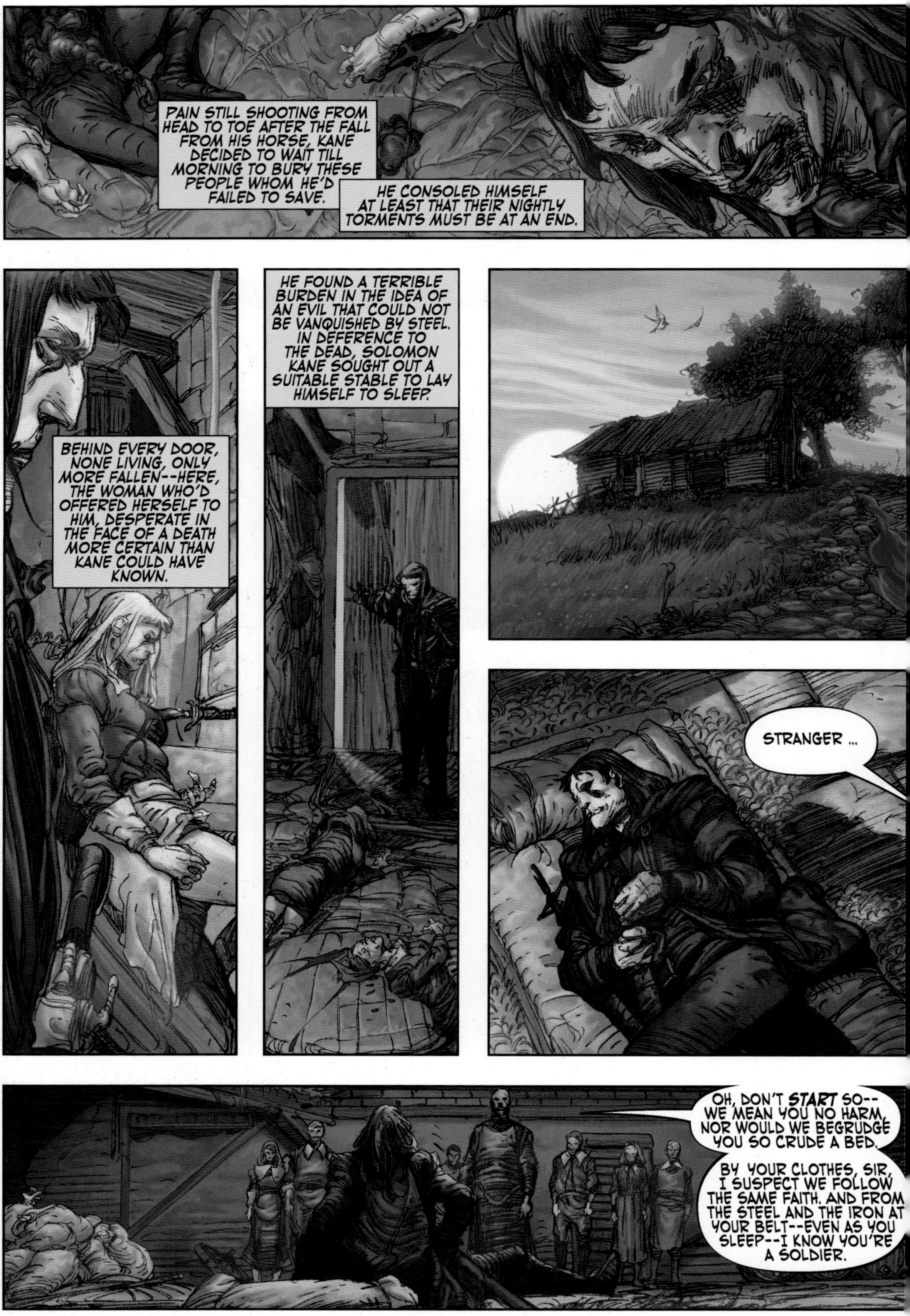
PAIN STILL SHOOTING FROM HEAD TO TOE AFTER THE FALL FROM HIS HORSE, KANE DECIDED TO WAIT TILL MORNING TO BURY THESE PEOPLE WHOM HE'D FAILED TO SAVE.
HE CONSOLED HIMSELF AT LEAST THAT THEIR NIGHTLY TORMENTS MUST BE AT AN END.
BEHIND EVERY DOOR, NONE LIVING, ONLY MORE FALLEN--HERE, THE WOMAN WHO'D OFFERED HERSELF TO HIM, DESPERATE IN THE FACE OF A DEATH MORE CERTAIN THAN KANE COULD HAVE KNOWN.
HE FOUND A TERRIBLE BURDEN IN THE IDEA OF AN EVIL THAT COULD NOT BE VANQUISHED BY STEEL. IN DEFERENCE TO THE DEAD, SOLOMON KANE SOUGHT OUT A SUITABLE STABLE TO LAY HIMSELF TO SLEEP.
STRANGER ...
OH, DON'T *START* SO-- WE MEAN YOU NO HARM, NOR WOULD WE BEGRUDGE YOU SO CRUDE A BED.
BY YOUR CLOTHES, SIR, I SUSPECT WE FOLLOW THE SAME FAITH. AND FROM THE STEEL AND THE IRON AT YOUR BELT--EVEN AS YOU SLEEP--I KNOW YOU'RE A SOLDIER.

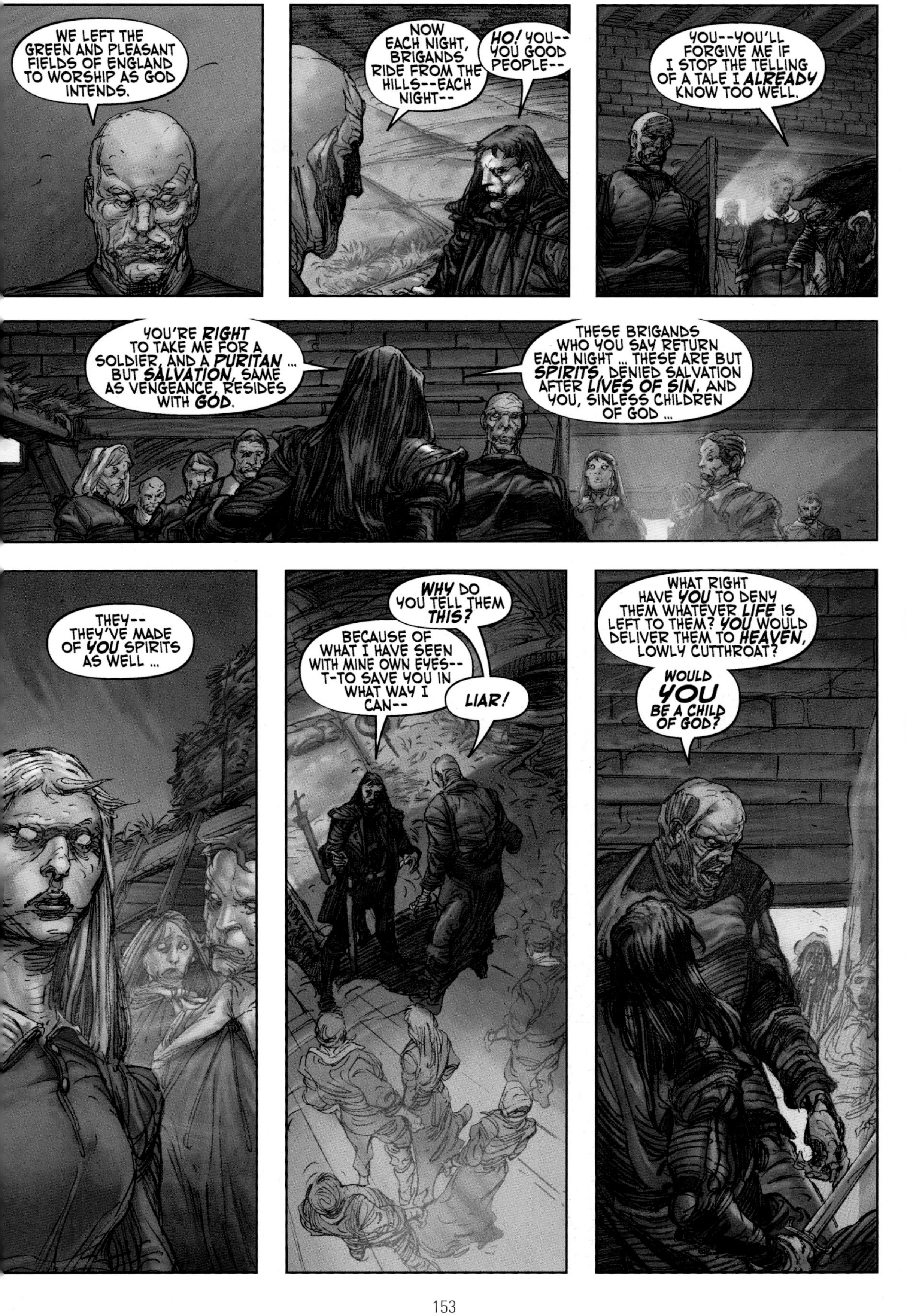
WE LEFT THE GREEN AND PLEASANT FIELDS OF ENGLAND TO WORSHIP AS GOD INTENDS.
NOW EACH NIGHT, BRIGANDS RIDE FROM THE HILLS--EACH NIGHT--
HO! YOU--YOU GOOD PEOPLE--
YOU--YOU'LL FORGIVE ME IF I STOP THE TELLING OF A TALE I ALREADY KNOW TOO WELL.
YOU'RE RIGHT TO TAKE ME FOR A SOLDIER, AND A PURITAN ... BUT SALVATION, SAME AS VENGEANCE, RESIDES WITH GOD.
THESE BRIGANDS WHO YOU SAY RETURN EACH NIGHT ... THESE ARE BUT SPIRITS, DENIED SALVATION AFTER LIVES OF SIN. AND YOU, SINLESS CHILDREN OF GOD ...
THEY--THEY'VE MADE OF YOU SPIRITS AS WELL ...
WHY DO YOU TELL THEM THIS?
BECAUSE OF WHAT I HAVE SEEN WITH MINE OWN EYES--T-TO SAVE YOU IN WHAT WAY I CAN--
LIAR!
WHAT RIGHT HAVE YOU TO DENY THEM WHATEVER LIFE IS LEFT TO THEM? YOU WOULD DELIVER THEM TO HEAVEN, LOWLY CUTTHROAT?
WOULD YOU BE A CHILD OF GOD?

HOW MANY MEN HAVE YOU *SEPARATED* FROM THEIR LIVES? AND LOOK WHAT YOU'VE *DONE,* KILLER, TO MY WEARY LAMBS--!

IN GOD'S NAME BACK!

AHH!

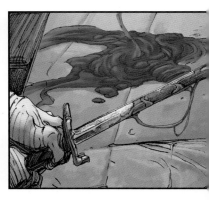

SOLOMON KANE TOOK A LAST TOUR THROUGH THE VILLAGE, AND SAW THAT DEATH HAD SETTLED HERE LONGER AGO THAN HE HAD IMAGINED. IT WAS NOT ONLY THE MARAUDERS WHO HAUNTED THE PLACE, BUT THE VILLAGERS THEMSELVES, NIGHT AND DAY.

PERHAPS THE BRIGANDS WERE ALIVE STILL, RAIDING OTHER SETTLEMENTS, HAVING LEFT BEHIND MERE SHADOWS TO NIGHTLY PLAY THEIR PART IN THE MORBID TRAGEDY, WHATEVER THEIR FATE ...

... SOLOMON KANE SPENT ALL OF THAT DAY BURYING VERY OLD BONES.

THE END

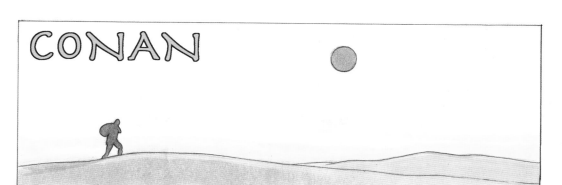

CONAN

Written By
Tim Truman
&
Ben Truman

Drawn By
Marian
Churchland

Lettered By
Brandon
Graham

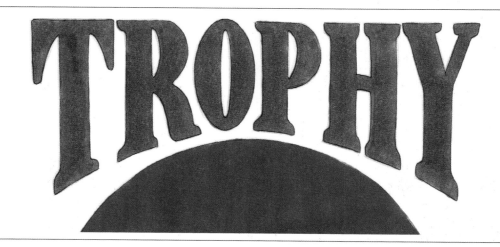

TROPHY

In the desert of Shem at a crossroads of the caravan routes, there was an oasis. At this oasis was a caravanseral, and at the caravanseral was an inn owned by a man named Fatuu.

Fatuu's inn was a place of grand reputation--eagerly sought by the rich caravans and courtly entourages that plied this ancient causeway.

Awash in the inn's notorious pleasures, the great merchants, emissaries, ambassadors, and royals of the south found respite from the desert's sun and the chill of its night.

At Fatuu's only those of certain wealth and prestige were served.

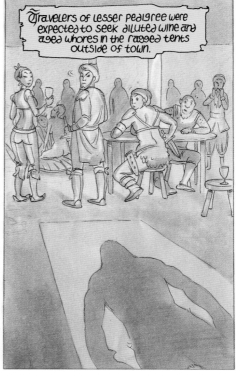

Travelers of lesser pedigree were expected to seek diluted wine and aged whores in the ragged tents outside of town.

156

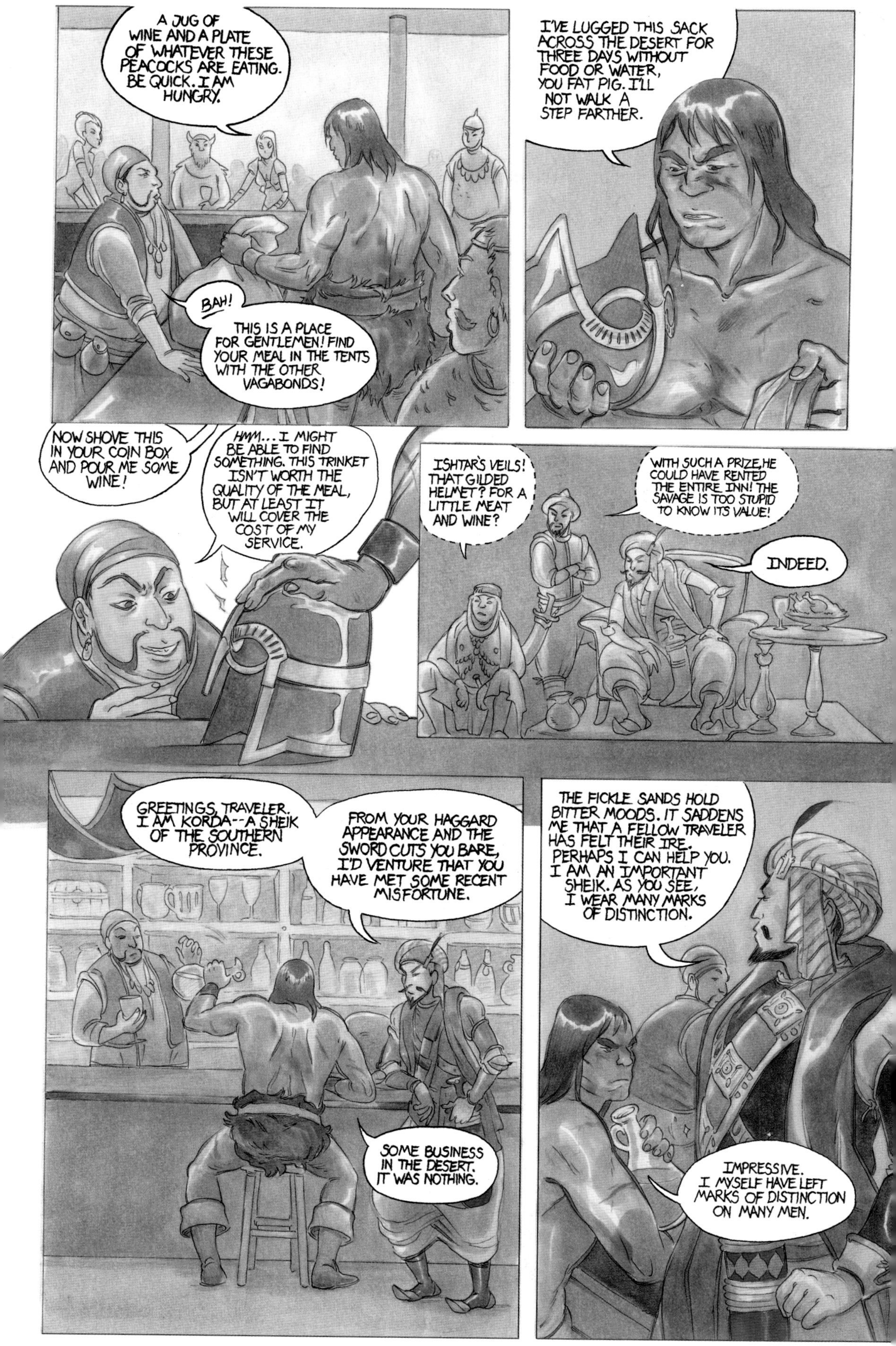
A JUG OF WINE AND A PLATE OF WHATEVER THESE PEACOCKS ARE EATING. BE QUICK. I AM HUNGRY.
BAH!
THIS IS A PLACE FOR GENTLEMEN! FIND YOUR MEAL IN THE TENTS WITH THE OTHER VAGABONDS!
I'VE LUGGED THIS SACK ACROSS THE DESERT FOR THREE DAYS WITHOUT FOOD OR WATER, YOU FAT PIG. I'LL NOT WALK A STEP FARTHER.
NOW SHOVE THIS IN YOUR COIN BOX AND POUR ME SOME WINE!
HMM... I MIGHT BE ABLE TO FIND SOMETHING. THIS TRINKET ISN'T WORTH THE QUALITY OF THE MEAL, BUT AT LEAST IT WILL COVER THE COST OF MY SERVICE.
ISHTAR'S VEILS! THAT GILDED HELMET? FOR A LITTLE MEAT AND WINE?
WITH SUCH A PRIZE, HE COULD HAVE RENTED THE ENTIRE INN! THE SAVAGE IS TOO STUPID TO KNOW ITS VALUE!
INDEED.
GREETINGS, TRAVELER. I AM KORDA--A SHEIK OF THE SOUTHERN PROVINCE.
FROM YOUR HAGGARD APPEARANCE AND THE SWORD CUTS YOU BARE, I'D VENTURE THAT YOU HAVE MET SOME RECENT MISFORTUNE.
SOME BUSINESS IN THE DESERT. IT WAS NOTHING.
THE FICKLE SANDS HOLD BITTER MOODS. IT SADDENS ME THAT A FELLOW TRAVELER HAS FELT THEIR IRE. PERHAPS I CAN HELP YOU. I AM AN IMPORTANT SHEIK. AS YOU SEE, I WEAR MANY MARKS OF DISTINCTION.
IMPRESSIVE. I MYSELF HAVE LEFT MARKS OF DISTINCTION ON MANY MEN.

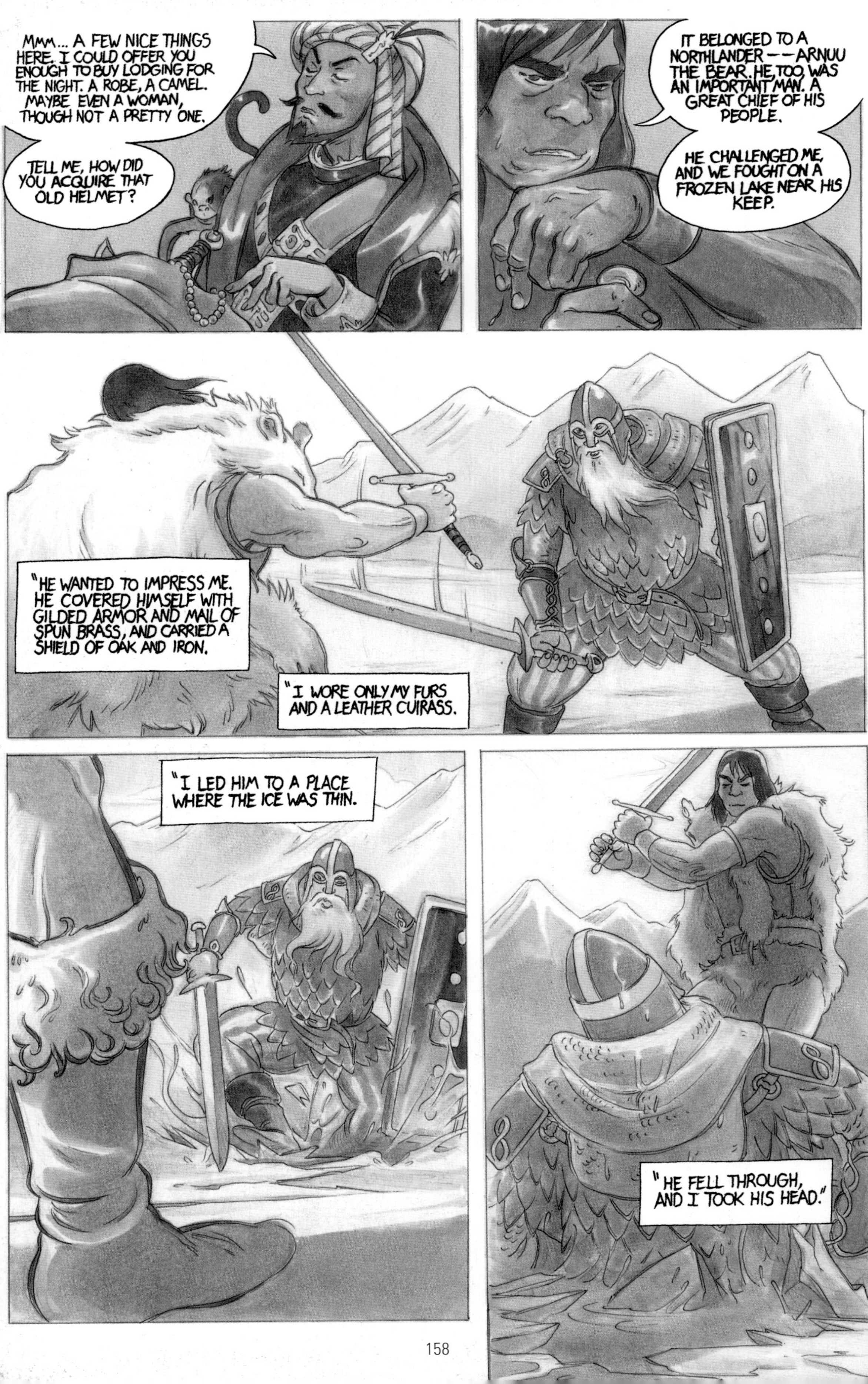
MMM... A FEW NICE THINGS HERE. I COULD OFFER YOU ENOUGH TO BUY LODGING FOR THE NIGHT. A ROBE, A CAMEL. MAYBE EVEN A WOMAN, THOUGH NOT A PRETTY ONE.
TELL ME, HOW DID YOU ACQUIRE THAT OLD HELMET?
IT BELONGED TO A NORTHLANDER --- ARNUU THE BEAR. HE, TOO, WAS AN IMPORTANT MAN. A GREAT CHIEF OF HIS PEOPLE.
HE CHALLENGED ME, AND WE FOUGHT ON A FROZEN LAKE NEAR HIS KEEP.
"HE WANTED TO IMPRESS ME. HE COVERED HIMSELF WITH GILDED ARMOR AND MAIL OF SPUN BRASS, AND CARRIED A SHIELD OF OAK AND IRON.
"I WORE ONLY MY FURS AND A LEATHER CUIRASS.
"I LED HIM TO A PLACE WHERE THE ICE WAS THIN.
"HE FELL THROUGH, AND I TOOK HIS HEAD."

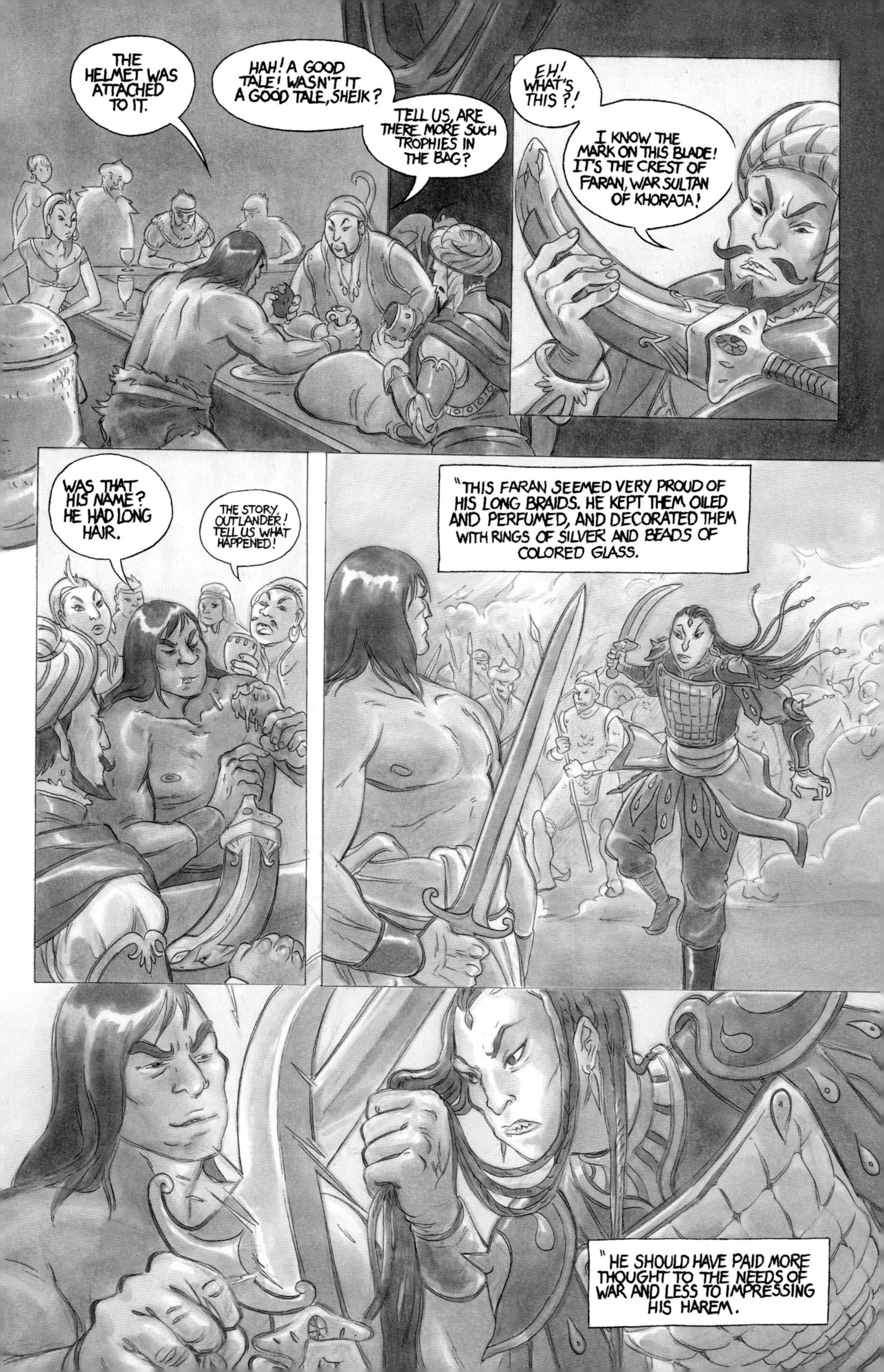
THE HELMET WAS ATTACHED TO IT.
HAH! A GOOD TALE! WASN'T IT A GOOD TALE, SHEIK?
TELL US, ARE THERE MORE SUCH TROPHIES IN THE BAG?
EH! WHAT'S THIS?!
I KNOW THE MARK ON THIS BLADE! IT'S THE CREST OF FARAN, WAR SULTAN OF KHORAJA!
WAS THAT HIS NAME? HE HAD LONG HAIR.
THE STORY, OUTLANDER! TELL US WHAT HAPPENED!
"THIS FARAN SEEMED VERY PROUD OF HIS LONG BRAIDS. HE KEPT THEM OILED AND PERFUMED, AND DECORATED THEM WITH RINGS OF SILVER AND BEADS OF COLORED GLASS.
"HE SHOULD HAVE PAID MORE THOUGHT TO THE NEEDS OF WAR AND LESS TO IMPRESSING HIS HAREM.

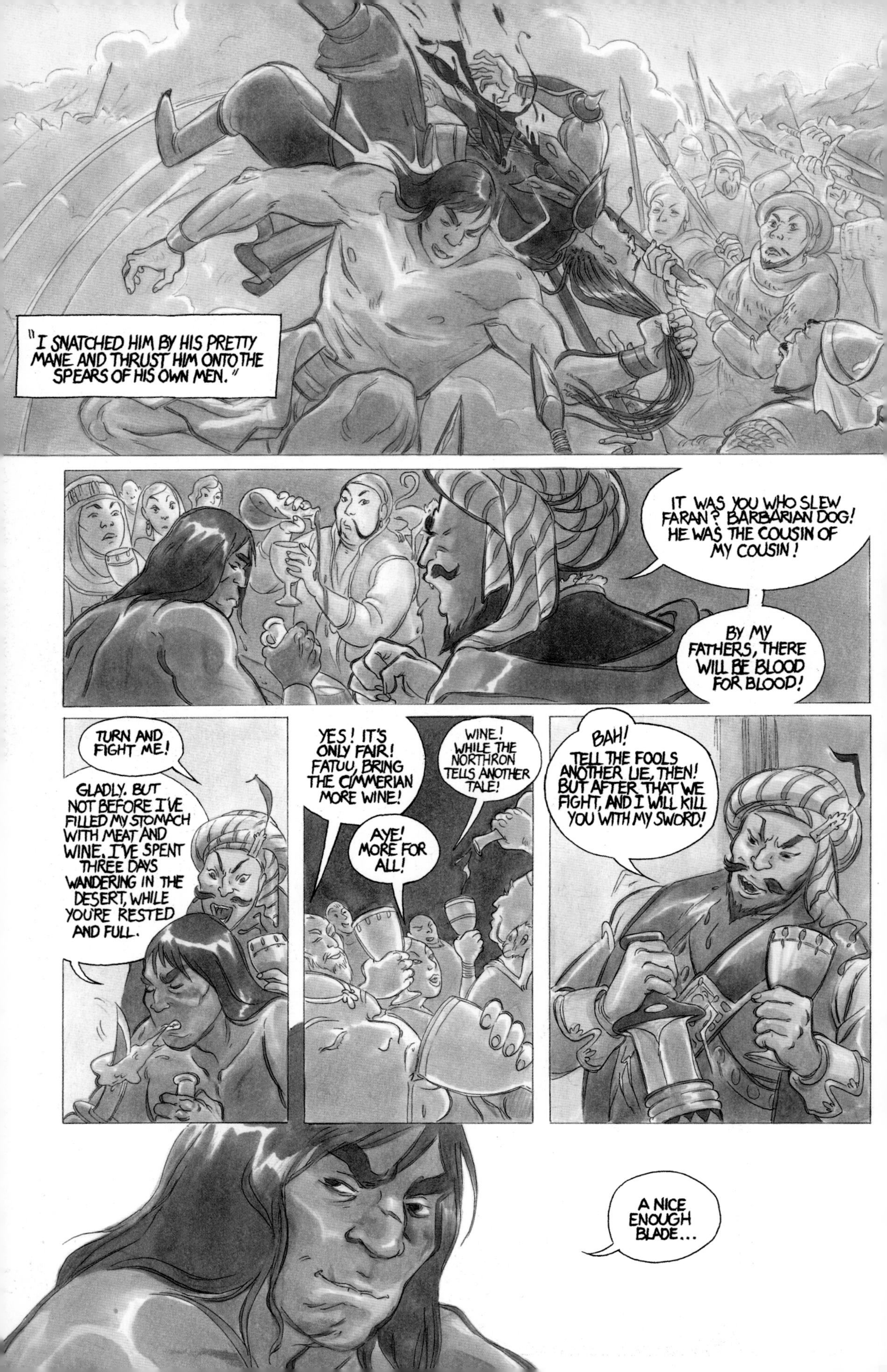
"I SNATCHED HIM BY HIS PRETTY MANE AND THRUST HIM ONTO THE SPEARS OF HIS OWN MEN."
IT WAS YOU WHO SLEW FARAN? BARBARIAN DOG! HE WAS THE COUSIN OF MY COUSIN!
BY MY FATHERS, THERE WILL BE BLOOD FOR BLOOD!
TURN AND FIGHT ME!
GLADLY. BUT NOT BEFORE I'VE FILLED MY STOMACH WITH MEAT AND WINE. I'VE SPENT THREE DAYS WANDERING IN THE DESERT, WHILE YOU'RE RESTED AND FULL.
YES! IT'S ONLY FAIR! FATUU, BRING THE CIMMERIAN MORE WINE!
WINE! WHILE THE NORTHRON TELLS ANOTHER TALE!
AYE! MORE FOR ALL!
BAH! TELL THE FOOLS ANOTHER LIE, THEN! BUT AFTER THAT WE FIGHT, AND I WILL KILL YOU WITH MY SWORD!
A NICE ENOUGH BLADE...

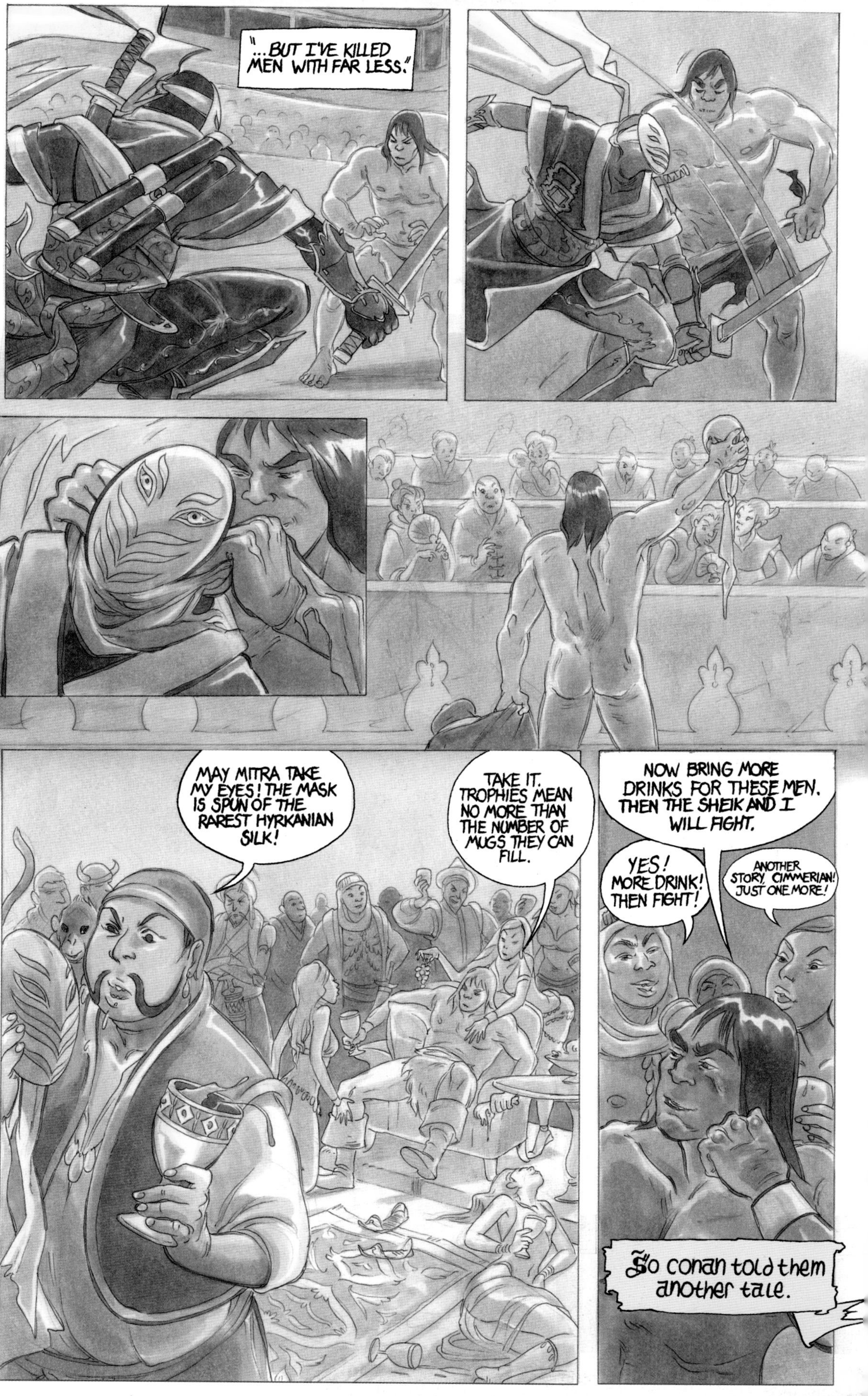
"...BUT I'VE KILLED MEN WITH FAR LESS."
MAY MITRA TAKE MY EYES! THE MASK IS SPUN OF THE RAREST HYRKANIAN SILK!
TAKE IT. TROPHIES MEAN NO MORE THAN THE NUMBER OF MUGS THEY CAN FILL.
NOW BRING MORE DRINKS FOR THESE MEN. THEN THE SHEIK AND I WILL FIGHT.
YES! MORE DRINK! THEN FIGHT!
ANOTHER STORY, CIMMERIAN! JUST ONE MORE!
So conan told them another tale.

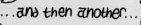
...and then another...

...until the dawn sun crawled from its sleep into the desert sky.

EASIER THAN I THOUGHT.

COME, MY FRIEND.

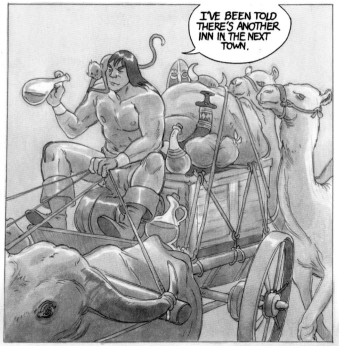

I'VE BEEN TOLD THERE'S ANOTHER INN IN THE NEXT TOWN.

THE END

ACTUAL DISCUSSION

MDHP *editors sat down with writers Evan Dorkin (*Milk & Cheese, Beasts*), Gerard Way (*The Umbrella Academy*), and Zack Whedon (*Dr. Horrible, Captain Hammer, Fringe*) and discussed their individual takes on heroes—likes, dislikes, and the overwhelming surge of "superheroes" in popular media. The discussion began there (well, it began before that, but we suffered some technical difficulties . . . my apologies), and then . . . well, you'll see . . .*

WHO READS SUPERHERO COMICS?

Evan Dorkin: I'm raising my hand.

Gerard Way: I read *All-Star Superman*.

ED: That's over.

GW: I read that. I think that counts, for sure. It's the purest one.

Zack Whedon: Nothing for me. Growing up, my comics tastes were very middle-of-the-road, like not interesting and cool . . . Like *Little Lotta*. I read whatever Joss handed me, and it was, y'know, Frank Miller *Batman* and stuff like that, but [I don't have] an extensive knowledge of regular superhero books.

ED: You had a life, it sounds like.

ZW: I had a *brilliant* life.

ED: You did things. You talked to women?

ZW: I talked to a few girls.

ED: There you go. See?

ZW: I don't own any Fredric March dolls.

ED: I don't know what you're talking about. We didn't record any of that, so you can't bring that up. Who's Fredric March? Did he have a lightsaber? I don't know who Fredric March is. What are you talking about?

ZW: Oh, man . . .

ED: Right, now when everything's recording you attack me.

GW: I started by reading *X-Men*. I worked in a comics shop. I think what makes [mainstream superheroes] less readable *now* is that they're basically casting the film right away, and they're drawing them how they're going to look in the film, so it's kind of like, why would you read the comic? Or why would you go see the film?

CAPTAIN HAMMER art by Eric Canete

I can't figure it out—you might wanna go see one of them or read one of them, but there's no differentiation between the two anymore.

ED: You get them every week; that's the difference. You want your drug every week—you gotta go to the comics. You can wait a couple of months for an *Iron Man* movie instead of buying fifteen comics. The industry's boiled it down to whoever's just willing to get smacked in the face with that $2.99, $3.50 superhero comic every week, whether it tells a story or not. I mean, I probably had more superhero comics than the two of you combined. I'm a total geek, worked in a comics shop, the whole deal. Lived in a comics shop for a few months once . . .

THE UMBRELLA ACADEMY art by Gabriel Bá

ON REALISM IN SUPERHERO COMICS

GW: For me, comics feel like ideas, in that really purest idea form, like Stan Lee and Jack Kirby sitting in an office chain-smoking and coming up with crazy stuff—that's the kind of superheroes that I like.

ED: Too many superhero comics have thirty-five to seventy years of narrative chains pulling them down because they feel that they have to solidify the whole seventy years. "Why did Batman carry a gun? Here's six issues explaining that." "Where did Peter Parker's glasses go between issue blah-blah-blah and blah-blah-blah? Hey, I got six issues of that." And it's crazy. Who *cares?* Is he doing cool stuff, does he make interesting decisions, and is the art and the writing enough to keep me going back to it? I find that it's not.

Verisimilitude is why Marvel kicked everyone's asses in the sixties and seventies. "My outfit got wet and I got sick." Not "My outfit got wet, I got sick, I got low blood sugar, oh and I forgot my glasses and here's an issue on that." You know what I mean? End of the month, something cool

happened, and nobody had to have their hands ripped off, or their heads ripped off, or get raped, or dumped into a refrigerator. That was just a shocking thing they'd pull out once in a blue moon. A character dying was an important thing . . . Today people . . . need bigger highs. Ten CCs of this wasn't enough, now I need thirty. They're dealers and users, and everybody in the industry is. I'm a dealer and a user. I've worked on superhero stuff. I've made fun of it for money, but I do like it. But I just don't understand needing to sit down and really work out how the kingpin runs his organization. Who cares?

GW: *Batman* the cartoon appealed to me more than *Batman* the comic, because I'd watch *Batman* the cartoon and it was the most direct storytelling I could watch. The continuity chains was one of the things in comics I always found to be a big problem and was one of the reasons why I stopped reading modern superhero books.

ED: [The cartoon] appealed to a lot more people than the comic.

GW: Yeah, so that's the thing—the continuity. So the point, when I finally decided to write a comic, was to say no to continuity and just assume that there was a whole bunch of stuff that happened that the reader doesn't care about. I've had people ask me about [the *Umbrella* character] Hargreeves—are we ever going to see where he's an alien from or what? I don't really care. I don't think anybody should care . . . A lot of the mantra that goes into making the comic is when someone asks a specific thing, it's "Who cares?" That's what I'm trying to train people with when reading it. You shouldn't care about someone's backstory. It's about what they do next.

ED: Look at *Hellboy*. Sometimes it's just "big dog monster." It's spooky over there, big dog monster, that makes sense. If you look at a lot of manga, these are generalizations we're all talking about, but a lot of times the alien comes down and they just go, "He's an alien." Ultraman, nobody cares, cut its head off, go, sell toys. Dazzle the kids, sell toys.

ZW: I don't understand the impulse, especially in movies, to ground these things in reality. To, when they're making the movie of a comic book, do the realistic version. While they can do it in a cool way and everything, I don't understand why that is the impulse, I don't understand why they don't just demand of the audience from the get-go the suspension of disbelief.

ED: You watch a Shaw Brothers kung fu flick and they give you just the exposition you need. Otherwise these people can walk across telephone wires.

GW: And I love that. That's like *Zu Warriors from the Magic Mountain*, where you just don't care, there's no explanation.

ED: Yeah, *Heroic Trio* does not tell you why these people have superpowers; they just do. I really enjoy that. I wanna see the spectacle. I don't go to superheroes for literary merit. It can be in there, but that's not where I go for it. I'd much rather see them do what they do well, which is to me spectacle, and I just wanna go, "Wow," and "Cool."

ON COMPELLING HEROES

ZW: In terms of making fun of Captain Hammer, I found a lot of joy in that. Just because it's fun to write stupid people, and he's in love with himself and oblivious to everything. That's a lot of fun. In terms of the heroes that I am drawn to, I like the everyman hero, the guy that I can relate to, that isn't that spectacular. I think of John McClane in *Die Hard* and people like that, people with real-world problems. Those are the people that I'm drawn to.

ED: I like *Die Hard* a lot, too. There's no hard, fast rules. I just find there's something wrong with the culture at the superhero companies right now in the last fifteen years that I just can't get into. If I ran DC or Marvel—and I probably would have run it into the ground; I'm not saying I know what I'm talking about—my gut reaction for [more realistic] characters would be to create other universes for that stuff. That's why you have *Planetary* or *The Authority* or *Watchmen* and *Marshal Law*. I have nothing wrong with people ripping each other's legs off and having sex with each other or whatever. Mayhem is fine. A lot of my books are not very clean for the kids, but I actually get a little squeamish seeing things like that happen to Superboy. I don't think that resonates for me. I just think that that's a really kind of cynical, last-ditch . . . There's

nothing left, I just think it's empty. I don't get off on it. I prefer commentary on the superheroes from something like *Marshal Law*, where they can really go over-the-top and you know who the corollary characters are; you know there's a Superman. I can't shake the feeling that these characters have been around for seventy years and to see them suddenly transform into these kind of monstrous characters . . .

Hulk Hogan doesn't need to curse and shoot people at WWA, you know what I mean? I realize that wrestling also has the tweeners and stuff, but they've kept it fairly . . . I don't know, it's a different time, different superheroes. If that's what folks want, that's fine, but I prefer the stuff to be kind of straightforward, adventurous, and have people that I can root for, and I'd rather see the obstacles be kind of narrative rather than these cheap, soul-searching, trying to write a play for superheroes kind of thing. I just think it's bogus.

HUMAN HEROES VS. SUPERHEROES

ZW: We've now pushed it so that the characters on [the television show] *Fringe*—while they are regular people, one of them does have all the information in the world. He is phenomenally brilliant, to an extent that no human being is. Then you look at characters like Iron Man and Batman in particular—there is such an emphasis in those movies about making them *real*. We're going to do the *real-world* version of Batman. Trying to ground superheroes in some way, which I think is just a choice and not necessary, but I think it's sort of leveled the playing field a bit. We don't have to compare those people, but we do end up creating these villains that have abilities that nobody else in the world has. We try and make it science-related, but it is ten steps beyond reality, for sure.

In Joss's work in particular, when you make a show about high school, it doesn't make sense that every week something terrible is going to happen, that someone's going to have cancer and then get addicted to crystal meth and then their mom's going to have cancer. That just doesn't happen in the real world. But if you're sitting on top of a Hellmouth, for instance, it makes their trials more realistic in a way, because there's some sort of logic behind it.

ED: I always thought it was fine to have that, and that's why I always argue verisimilitude versus realism, because realism just can't be achieved in superhero books. There's always going to be something that makes no sense. There's always going to be, "Why doesn't Tony Stark make a thousand suits of armor for his mega-army, or to help save the world?" And superhero comics people always have to ruin it, because they don't have ideas, and because they do something which I think is a very bad choice, like having 9/11 in their continuity, and that really strains credulity and realism, because if you're going to tell me that these people have super-science and can't stop something as horrible as what happened . . .

I don't want to talk like I'm complaining about 9/11, but I do think that having the Hulk crying over 9/11, or having Reed Richards not stop it from happening, it makes no sense. I did something for the 9/11 benefit book, and I decided not to draw superheroes, because it felt so trivial. I understand that some people felt it was fine to have the Hulk holding up a flag. I really don't want to condemn what they're doing, but I just think that once you go that route, once you start having real-life events in there, it's a can of worms. You can never put it back in. You can't say that the universe reboots every ten years, because we showed Kennedy and then we showed Nixon . . . The characters now never were in World War II, but we know they were. I mean, just let it go. Let the crazy stuff happen, but if it rains, people's costumes should get wet. I understand why characters all now get their costumes torn every issue. That was a big thing. And if Superman wants to cry, that's fine, but it makes no sense to have the real world come in.

GW: Being a New Yorker, too, I remember when I met Evan, and that was right after 9/11. I was also directly affected by it. What you're seeing now in comics is instead of Superman or Captain America punching Hitler, they're punching terrorists. You watch *Iron Man*, and I really enjoy the film, but he's beating up the terrorists and you're confused by it. It's straight up like the Fleischer *Superman* cartoon.

ED: "Japoteurs," yeah.

GW: That kind of thing, where you're like, is this now why they've instituted all this realworld stuff, so now we can fight evil and the reader feels better about it? I don't know.

ED: I find that kind of discomforting, but at the same time, I just don't like it from a pure narrative point of view. I just feel that superhero comics have always been riddled with short-term thinking, because they weren't supposed to have long-term thinking. It's not like [Everett] "Busy" Arnold and all these guys were sitting around saying, "Look, we gotta have a game plan for five years from now." They just pumped the stuff out.

I get a thrill when I'm reading *Hellboy* knowing crazy stuff's going to happen on the next page. I like this team of characters. I like their designs. That's another thing: the art of designing a costume seems to be dead. People seem to be embarrassed by the costumes these days. The X-Men got taken out of them and everybody wears leather jackets. Do they have costumes on *Heroes*? They're just in plain clothes, right? I mean, I guess actors look silly in costumes on the whole, but I'm personally a purist. I'm out of step and I know it. I like cool costumes, even if they don't make sense.

GW: The old sixties *Batman* show still looks amazing.

ED: To me, that's superhero comics in a lot of ways, but if you say that in the comics shop, people think you're old.

MILK AND CHEESE art by Evan Dorkin